O, MY ANCESTOR

O, MY ANCESTOR

*Recognition and Renewal for the Gabrielino-Tongva
People of the Los Angeles Area*

Claudia Jurmain and William McCawley

HEYDAY BOOKS, BERKELEY, CALIFORNIA
RANCHO LOS ALAMITOS FOUNDATION, LONG BEACH, CALIFORNIA

This book was made possible in part by a generous grant from the BayTree Foundation.

Library of Congress Cataloging-in-Publication Data

Jurmain, Claudia K.
  O, my ancestor : recognition and renewal for the Gabrielino-Tongva people of the Los Angeles area
  Claudia Jurmain and William McCawley.
      p. cm.
  Includes bibliographical references.
  ISBN 978-1-59714-115-4 (pbk.)
  1. Gabrielino Indians--California--Los Angeles Region--Social conditions. 2. Gabrielino Indians--California--Los Angeles Region--Ethnic identity. 3. Gabrielino Indians--Land tenure--California--Los Angeles Region. 4. Gabrielino Indians--California--Los Angeles Region--Interviews. 5. Indian leadership--California--Los Angeles Region. 6. Recognition (Philosophy) 7. Social change--California--Los Angeles Region. 8. Los Angeles Region (Calif.)--Ethnic relations. 9. Los Angeles Region (Calif.)--Biography. 10. Interviews--California--Los Angeles Region. I. McCawley, William, 1952- II. Title.
  E99.G15J87 2009
  979.4'94--dc22
                          2009009812

Cover illustration: "The Ascension of Chinigchinich into the Heaven of Stars" by Jean Goodwin, from *Chinigchinich* by Father Geronimo Boscana, Fine Arts Press, 1933. Reproduced by permission of Rancho Los Alamitos. Father Boscana's version of the Gabrielino-Tongva creation story was first published in 1846; this woodcut is from the 1933 edition, now a collector's item. Partially funded by Fred and Florence Bixby, previous owners of Rancho Los Alamitos, the 1933 edition includes the first publication of Smithsonian anthropologist John P. Harrington's detailed notes on the Tongva and the Indians of southern California. The artist has offered her own interpretation of Tongva body art; more commonly, the Tongva decorated themselves with fine lines of dark blue tattoos or dots and stripes of red, white, and black paint.

Book Design: Lorraine Rath

Printed in Korea by Tara TPS through Four Colour Print Group

Orders, inquiries, and correspondence should be addressed to:
Heyday Books
P. O. Box 9145, Berkeley, CA 94709
(510) 549-3564, Fax (510) 549-1889
www.heydaybooks.com

10   9   8   7   6   5   4   3   2   1

"O, my ancestor, O, my ancestor, listen to my heart
O, my ancestor, here is my heart."

—from the Tongva honor song

Contents

Note: *Conversations edited and annotated by Claudia Jurmain*

Acknowledgments

SINCE 1982, RANCHO LOS ALAMITOS FOUNDATION HAS PRESENTED EDUCATIONAL PROGRAMS in cooperation with the Tongva community. The book O, My Ancestor is the culmination of that shared process, and one which underscores the lasting connection between the nature of a place and a people's identity, for the enduring spirit of Rancho Los Alamitos comes from the heart of Povuu'ngna and its descendants.

O, My Ancestor was a collaborative process, made possible only through the participation of many within the Tongva community. In particular, and from the very beginning, Cindi Alvitre, Craig Torres, and Kimberly Morales Johnson were extraordinarily generous with their time and suggestions, and spread the word of our intent throughout their communities. And so our appreciation also extends to: Gloria Arellanes, Vivian Morales Barthelemy, Michael Barthelemy, Angie Dorame Behrns, David Campio and Bonnie Shapin, Earl and Loretta Campio, Virginia Carmelo, Linda Gonzales, Jacob Gutierrez, Al and Dolores Lassos, Desirée Martinez, Andrew Morales, Anthony Morales, Art Morales, Janice and Nicole Ramos, Patty Barthelemy Roess, and Stacy Thompson. As they shared their personal and family stories and considered the impact of the past on the contemporary Tongva community, their words gave new voice to history and a fresh perspective for today and tomorrow.

The purpose, process, and publication of this work were made possible through the support of Rancho Los Alamitos Foundation as well as the unceasing vision of its executive director, Pamela Seager, and the institutional support of the Foundation's board of trustees. Without hesitation, they encouraged and underwrote the project through its many years of development, research, and writing. In addition, the book received generous backing from: Employees Community Fund of Boeing California, Joan M. Hotchkis, The Hotchkis Foundation, Preston B. Hotchkis, The Elizabeth Bixby Janeway Foundation, Katharine A. Johnson, LEF Foundation, Long Beach Unified School District, and The Earl B. and Lorraine H. Miller Foundation.

The process of recording and editing the conversations and obtaining the graphics depended on the very particular talents of the following individuals: Cindi Adams and Alison R. Spack, who transcribed the conversations and brought professionalism and ease to a difficult process. The contemporary photography of Ty Milford, Cristina Salvador, and Frank Magallanes and Althea Edwards provides a stunning record of individuals within the contemporary community and their activities. Several individuals and families went out of their way to share their historical photos for inclusion in the book, while Margaret Monti, Rancho Los Alamitos archivist, undertook the difficult and often tedious task of scanning, organizing, and preparing the images for publication.

In addition to the willing contribution of so many within the Tongva community, O, My Ancestor rested on the scholarship and reputation of William McCawley, whose previous work The First Angelinos: The Gabrielino Indians of Los Angeles (1996) remains the seminal work on the precontact Gabrielino-Tongva to date. Much of the confidence given this project was a result of Bill's previous effort, which had already earned him a place of honor within the Tongva community and allowed us to explore the present and future with some measure of cautious confidence. My great respect and lasting appreciation go to Bill for undertaking this risky journey with me. He has delved into subject matter where other scholars have yet to go, and done so with accuracy and grace.

Certainly, this work also reflects the input of many notable historians, anthropologists, writers, and designers, but my resounding thanks must be reserved for James J. Rawls, L. Thomas Frye, the late James D. Houston, Gordon Ashby, and especially Kevin Starr, for agreeing to place O, My Ancestor within the larger context of southern California, ever an extraordinary, changing place and people with a story to tell.

In closing, Heyday Books and publisher Malcolm Margolin recognized the need for, and the worth of, the story we hoped to tell, and in doing so moved O, My Ancestor from a doubtful publication of wishful thinking into a book of note. Gayle Wattawa, our extraordinary editor at Heyday Books, made that transformation possible and real—my deepest thanks to both, as well as to Jeannine Gendar, our impeccable, insightful copy editor, and to Lorraine Rath for an inspired book design.

This book is the story of ancestors and family who mean so much today. It is only appropriate that I close by thanking my own.

Claudia K. Jurmain
October 2008

THE AUTHORS WISH TO THANK THE GABRIELINO-TONGVA WHO PARTICIPATED IN THIS project and shared so selflessly of their time and spirit. Their stories are the heart and soul of this book; without them this project would not have been possible. I would also like to thank those individuals who assisted me at various stages of the historical research: Kimberly Morales Johnson, archivist for the Gabrieleno/Tongva Tribal Council of San Gabriel; Craig Torres and Desirée Martinez, who shared historical documents from their own family collections; Michael Brooks, editor of the 1980 interview with Fred "Sparky" Morales and Bea Alva by the students of Suva Intermediate School, and the late Dorothy Pool, who many years ago sent me a copy of the interview; and my friend Keith Dixon, who helped me sort out the archaeology of Los Angeles and Orange Counties as well as providing moral support. In addition, I would like to thank the research staffs of the Seaver Center for Western History Research/Natural History Museum of Los Angeles County, the Huntington Library in San Marino, and the National Archives in Laguna Niguel for their assistance.

A very special thanks goes to my coauthor and editor, Claudia Jurmain, and to Pamela Seager and Rancho Los Alamitos Historic Ranch and Gardens for giving me the opportunity to participate in this project. Claudia was the inspiration and driving force behind this endeavor; I hope our work together has lived up to her vision. Finally, I would like to thank my family and loved ones who patiently endured the disruption of their personal lives so that I could, once again, indulge my passion for history and writing.

William McCawley
January 2009

Foreword

Kevin Starr

AS IS THE CASE WITH ALL NATIVE AMERICAN CULTURES, THE CULTURE
of the Gabrielino-Tongva people—however embattled, however fragmented and
elusive it might seem in its present circumstances—is an end in itself. To be a
Tongva is a time-tested way of being a human being: of becoming more human,
more aware, loyal, and spiritual through bloodlines, family ties, and cultural
memory. Only Tongva can fully participate in this identity. Only they have fully
internalized that particular sense of place, family, and memory, tested by time and
tragedy, that is at the core of the Tongva sensibility. Yet even as they remain themselves—remain, that is, in dialogue with and pursuit of their identity, which can
prove at once steady and sustaining, fugitive and elusive—contemporary Tongva
people are in the process of creating a paradigm for, and hence making a gift to,
the rest of us, who must, like the Tongva people, search for a usable past, assemble
a viable identity, feel within ourselves a sense of family, memory, biodiversity,
and place.

The Tongva experience represents not only a departure point for the interaction of people and place in the Los Angeles Basin, it also constitutes a continuing gloss on the human record through the pre-European, Spanish, Mexican,
frontier American, contemporary American, and recent global encounter
between people and place in southern California. Dispersed in their present
circumstances, deprived of land and language, mixed in bloodlines and cultures,
the Tongva people have nevertheless survived through the centuries, and in the
course of surviving felt the impact of each successive era of human history in
the Southland. How have they done this? How have the Tongva people survived
the devastations of time and the hostility of successive waves of conquerors?
The answer is at once simple and complex. The Tongva have endured through
bloodlines and the memory of who they are as a people, preserved through

family and through their profound and enduring attachment to place: the islands, seashore, coastal chaparral, and interior savannahs of the Los Angeles Basin. Across the centuries this place has remained for them a sacred terrain, at once natural and spiritualized, ever generative of sustaining myth.

The Tongva pilgrimage through time belongs, most obviously, to themselves as a people. Yet Native Americans and non-Native American southern Californians alike share in and have been shaped by the unfolding southern California experience, which is an epic of encounter between dramatically different kinds of peoples. Hence the Tongva experience constitutes not only the primal human experience in its region and is to be respected as such, it also functions as a kind of choral commentary on the subsequent and successive waves of social development in the Southland. An historian might be tempted, in fact, to discern in the losses and gains of the Tongva people, including their present struggle to reassemble their sense of place and identity, a prophetic paradigm and Baedeker's guide to the larger southern California experience.

Long before European contact, the Tongva people learned that the Los Angeles Basin could sustain and nurture human life in abundant and salubrious circumstances. Taking to the sea in plank canoes, settling the adjacent islands, gathering from the sea a nourishing harvest, feasting on shellfish from offshore shallows, hunting game or gathering acorns and seeds in the oak forests and grasslands of the interior, the Tongva lived well in simple circumstances. From this abundance was developed a biological vitality that sustained them in later times and has brought them into the present as a healthy and vigorous people.

From this natural goodness as well, this sustaining abundance, arose a sense of attachment, of gratitude even, to place that, like their biological vitality, would never be lost. And from this interaction of land and people there was nurtured as well a rich and sustaining interior culture expressed in collective myth and shared protocols for the profundities of birth, marriage, and death, and the ordinary requirements of daily living. Encountering their creation story, revolving around the figure of the prophet-god Chinigchinich, who had ascended into the heavens, the Franciscan missionary Gerónimo Boscana was astonished by its sophistication and parallels even to the Christian story.

The mission system, paradoxically, at once altered Tongva culture—negatively, most would argue—while bringing it into a new state of extension and awareness. Prior to the coming of the Spanish, the Tongva lived in a network of autonomous villages that included Yaanga at the bend of the Los Angeles River in what is now the epicenter of Los Angeles. Conscripted into Mission San Gabriel and Mission San Juan Capistrano, the Tongva people had their ancient way of life destroyed in an effort to transform them into Hispanicized Christians. But they were also given a new Tongva-wide identity, Mission Indians, that remains to this day a problematic point of reference, affirmed by some Tongva, rejected by others, regarded indifferently by an even smaller remnant.

The mission system was supposed to return the Tongva people to the land which had been theirs in the first place, and the magnanimous Mexican governor José Figueroa, himself of Indian descent, made every effort to do this in the mid-1830s. A few Tongva were confirmed in title to the land they had always owned, but by the end of the American frontier era—after the breakdown of Figueroa's plan, after the Land Act of 1851, with its crushing legal and financial burdens, and the outright deprivations and confiscations of the first American era—the Tongva people were left landless, with few exceptions. And so too, in the first decades of the twentieth century, did their language disappear as a living entity, recoverable only through the reconstructions of academic research.

What was left, then? Nothing, from one perspective—and from another perspective, everything; for the Tongva people refused to disappear. Just as the 1920s witnessed the influx of Anglo-Americans, the so-called Folks, into southern California, so too did the post–World War I era witness a kind of renewal among the Tongva families who had made it through the decades of deprivation that had taken their land and their language, forced them to veil their identity in a Mexican cloak, scattered them across the Southland, led them increasingly to intermarriage and family formation with other peoples, Native American and non-Native American alike, hence obscuring, for the time being, Tongva bloodlines. Family memories, so frequently coming from grandmothers, surviving today in scrapbooks and photographic albums, depict a story of recovery from the 1920s. In times past, the Tongva had migrated out into the dominant cultures: as near-slave labor in the 1850s, tragically, but also as respected vaqueros and cattlemen in the American ranch era and as farmers, orchardists, and artisans in the decades that followed. The 1920s and 1930s witnessed the further transformation of Tongva people into contemporary southern Californians, as defined by the dominant culture. Following World War II, this transformation intensified, gaining momentum in the 1960s. Today, the Tongva are by and large an urbanized people, represented in a variety of pursuits and professions, including the academy and the arts. They are also individuals with multiple identities, arising from the complexity of family and religious heritages history has bestowed—or enforced—on them across the decades.

Yet they have never forgotten who they were, who they are, and who they will continue to be. In certain times and among certain families, this knowledge came close to disappearing, but it survived, if only in stories told to children by grandmothers or the knowledge shared by a family, however obscurely, that they were, in various formulations, Tongva, Gabrielino, Gabrieleno/Tongva San Gabriel Band of Mission Indians, the Gabrielino/Tongva Nation, or, more colloquially, just plain Gabs. However assimilated they might be to the larger society, moreover, Tongva people never lost their affinity for the land: for the rolling brown hills of the interior, with its intermittent and fickle rivers, or the coastal chaparral overlooking the shoreline, sea, and islands in the distance. No matter who or what they had become in their modernity, they felt at peace beneath the oak trees of the region and experienced a special exaltation when they lifted their eyes to the distant hills. The land always seemed right to them—seemed home, as if they had always been there. The Tongva beheld and acknowledged the American civilization surrounding them—the cities and suburbs, freeways and shopping centers, the factories, high-rises, and university campuses, the mini-malls and fast food outlets—but they were also beholding, simultaneously, physically seeing from within, the unadjusted nature and the Tongva world that had once been theirs: the Kuruvangna sacred springs at Santa Monica; central to their creation myth, the ancestral village of Povuu'ngna on a hilltop overlooking the Rancho Los Alamitos Historic Ranch and Gardens at Long Beach—a village that for them, reconstructed in memory and imagination, survives as their city on a hill, their remembered polity, their Camelot. Amidst the freeways and high-rises of downtown Los Angeles, they remember and they see Yaanga, primal settlement of a world city.

Had they lost their land? They reclaimed it in memory and imagination. Had they lost their language and ritual dances? These could be reconstructed and re-assimilated through scholarship. Had they lost their families? No! Never! Family and bloodlines had never been surrendered. They remained families and hence a people, and were determined to reconstruct, re-understand, and reinvigorate that which had always been theirs.

In doing this, in reaching beyond the multiplicities and confusions of the present so as to forge a usable past that was also a present and future identity, the Tongva people represented in this book are doing something for themselves and for others. If they have lost much, so has southern California. If they are seeking a renewed sense of place in the sacred gift of the environment, so too are others seeking a reconnection with land and place. The Tongva people are seeking to remember their story and to have it told. So too are other southern Californians who desire to learn how to remember. In time, the Tongva people will reclaim what has been lost or taken from them. Their quest for renewal constitutes their gift to southern California, where they have always lived, always remembered.

Preface

Claudia Jurmain

RANCHO LOS ALAMITOS HISTORIC RANCH AND GARDENS IS A 7.5-acre historic site in Long Beach, California, twice listed on the National Register of Historic Places. One listing documents the site's origin as part of the ancestral village of Povuu'ngna, the place of emergence of the native Gabrielino-Tongva people. The other recognizes the cultural evolution of the 7.5-acre landscape, since the on-site historic structures, extensive gardens, and documented record of successive owners and workers evidence the eras and events of southern California from the time of Alta California through the early twentieth century. Though Rancho Los Alamitos' name clearly points to the rich Spanish Mexican heritage of the site, its roots go back much further, to a village called Povuu'ngna.

A sacred place then and now, Povuu'ngna is where the first people emerged, where Ouiot, the omnipotent first chief was born, and where Chinigchinich appeared to give the people their ways. Before the Spanish arrived in the late eighteenth century, and possibly as early as 500 A.D., Povuu'ngna drew people from the coastal, inland, and island villages for trade and seasonal and ritual ceremonies which may have taken place on the Alamitos hilltop where the historic Ranch House sits now. The core midden area found on-site today includes part of the front lawn and extends to the far east edge of the gardens, where it is still visible in the Jacaranda Walk.

Over the past thirty years, scholars and professionals have assessed ethnographic and archaeological evidence related to Rancho Los Alamitos and Povuu'ngna. The physical evidence is scant, and the ethnography subject to interpretation, but most believe that the village of Povuu'ngna was on and around the Alamitos hilltop, including the ranch land below the hill which now belongs to California State University at Long Beach.

Today's Rancho Los Alamitos is a small part of the original 300,000-acre Los Coyotes land grant awarded to José Manuel Perez Nieto in 1790 for his leather-jacket service on the Gaspar de Portolá expedition. Six years later Nieto's huge Spanish grant was reduced to 167,000 acres following his vigorous, protracted dispute with Mission San Gabriel over the "Indians who have no right to the land." After Nieto's death, Los Coyotes was divided into five great Mexican ranchos in 1833, including the 28,500-acre Rancho Los Alamitos, which contained Povuu'ngna within its boundaries. No one knows when the village disappeared, but in 1805, many years before Rancho Los Alamitos came to be, a San Gabriel Mission father recorded the last baptism of a Gabrielino-Tongva from Povuu'ngna.

Juan José Nieto, the son of Manual Nieto, was the first owner of Rancho Los Alamitos. He was followed by Governor José Figueroa, Yankee don Abel Stearns, and the Bixby family in the late nineteenth century—first John and Susan, and then Fred Bixby and his wife, Florence, through the mid-1900s. In 1968 the children of the Fred Bixby family deeded 7.5 remaining acres of Rancho Los Alamitos to the city of Long Beach. Since 1985, in a public-private joint venture with the city, Rancho Los Alamitos Foundation has assumed all responsibility for the administration, preservation, and restoration of the site for public use and education.

Today's award-winning historic landscape includes a classic California-style ranch house built around a Spanish adobe ca. 1806–33, five great working ranch barns from the early twentieth century, and four acres of renowned gardens designed in large part by the Olmsted Brothers Landscape Architects during the 1920s and 1930s. But underneath all remains the significance of Povuu'ngna for the Tongva people today.

The physical village of Povuu'ngna disappeared early on, but records indicate that Alamitos owners still interacted with the native community in coming years. Governor and owner José Figueroa was the one to secularize the missions, resulting in more displacement and urbanization of the Tongva people. Tongva and other California Indians continued to work at Alamitos through the mid-nineteenth century: in 1852, the Alamitos majordomo sought permission from owner Abel Stearns to buy Indian labor at the Los Angeles auctions to add to the Indians already on the payroll. Indians certainly worked on the ranch for many years, but twentieth-century owners Fred and Florence Bixby's interest was deeper: they donated almost two thousand dollars to the Presbyterian Indian Relief Fund and the Indian Board of Cooperation from 1928 to 1930, and supported an illustrated edition of Father Boscana's mission-era writings on the Tongva (Gabrielino) people. As Florence Bixby observed and wrote, "It was the feeling of the life that had been lived here before, a thousand human influences...as though a great river were flowing past, the continuity of life...that was the secret."

Rancho Los Alamitos continues to honor its relationship with the Tongva, past and present. *O, My Ancestor: Recognition and Renewal for the Gabrielino-Tongva of the Los Angeles Area* is a general publication in partnership with the Tongva people which considers how the past impacts their life today. The book will, for the first time, give voice to individuals, families, and groups within the Tongva communities today through a series of published conversations and essays, bringing the historical record up-to-date.

To begin, several lively, thought-provoking discussions with Craig Torres and Cindi Alvitre (both recognized cultural leaders and educators in the larger Tongva community and state), quickly moved from the historical implications of Povuu'ngna into the topical, often controversial issues of our times—land, federal recognition, and cultural continuity; discrimination, cultural confidence, and leadership. Their answers in our open-ended discussions shaped subsequent conversations with other Tongva, and suggested how their contemporary perspectives on historical events could be integrated into the essays to be written by William McCawley. Bill's well-received *The First Angelinos: The Gabrielino Indians of Los Angeles* had already documented the precontact era and early history of the Tongva people, giving us the sure footing needed to explore recent history and contemporary events with an all-encompassing view.

In October 2005 a series of more formal conversations began, starting with members of the Ti'at Society, a group of cultural educators who interpret Tongva culture through visual and performance arts. Open to all, the conversations naturally evolved with two criteria in mind: as possible, talk with different Tongva communities—formal and informal groups, and the families and individuals within, including leaders and elders; and include people across the traditional and contemporary Tongva land base from the coastal area and inland empire to people out-of-state.

From the beginning, the book project was a collaborative process which included Rancho Los Alamitos, Bill McCawley, and members of the Tongva community. Support and help from the Tongva who helped develop the project was crucial to the project's success. Tongva leaders helped spread the word through their own community networks. Cindi Alvitre and Craig Torres encouraged members of the Ti'at Society and suggested speaking to David Campio about his family's tradition of clay and pottery. Upon hearing of the project, Kimberly Morales Johnson, a member of the Gabrieleno/Tongva Tribal Council of San Gabriel, asked to learn more on behalf of her family and their group. Her efforts led to conversations with Anthony Morales (tribal chair of the Gabrieleno/Tongva Tribal Council of San Gabriel), Arthur Morales, Vivian Morales Barthelemy, Michael Barthelemy, Andy Morales, Al Lassos (a community elder now deceased), and Angie Behrns. Most conversations took place within the first year, except those with Virginia Carmelo (chair of the Gabrielino/Tongva Nation), and Desirée Martinez, who hadn't yet returned from Harvard.

After three years this project came to a close, but the larger effort will continue as many Tongva communities document their own stories. For the moment, however, there was agreement that the ten conversations completed represented a good sampling of shared and different perspectives within the larger Tongva community.

Although touching on the same themes and topics, the different vantages of the Tongva participants—the participants included community, political, and statewide leaders; cultural educators and teachers; writers and artists; and an attorney—shaped the discussion. Questions to the Ti'at Society explored cultural education, the old and new sacred significance of Povuu'ngna, and the mission legacy, as well as the growing confidence of the Tongva community. Because of their long-standing community and cultural continuity, the questions posed to members of the Gabrieleno Tongva Tribal Council of San Gabriel delved into the history of San Gabriel Mission and the associated Tongva community over time, as well as family, leadership and politics, federal recognition, land, and discrimination. The tradition of clay and pottery within the Campio family shaped their conversation. Questions to Cindi Alvitre reflected her academic credentials as well as her personal experience relating to cultural memory and the changing land; her insights on federal recognition and discrimination within the native community were also valuable to the project. Michael Barthelemy and Desirée Martinez also shared thoughts on all of these issues, offering the perspective of Tongva living outside their native region and home. Questions to Angie Behrns considered her efforts to establish the Gabrielino Tongva Springs Foundation in view of political activism. Finally, Virginia Carmelo was asked about how the contemporary creative dances of the Tongva are rooted in traditional forms, and to discuss the identity of her group, the Gabrielino Tongva Nation.

(And as an aside, it may be important to note that some conversations contain reference to a 2003 lawsuit concerning membership in the Gabrieleno Tongva Tribal Council of San Gabriel which has already been settled and therefore not gone into at length or in detail in this project. The event underscored the fact that the larger Tongva community includes many individuals and communities within, who may have different priorities and viewpoints.)

The candid, insightful conversations usually took place at Rancho Los Alamitos or in the homes of the Tongva participants. Professional transcribers recorded each two-to-three-hour discussion, making possible the edited versions for the book. To enhance the flow of the conversations, unnecessary interview questions were omitted or rephrased during the editing process. Each conversation was edited for the sake of content and length, but it is important to note that all retain their original sequence, context, and intent. Read together or apart, the conversations resound with the voices of many Tongva today. To ensure the intent and accuracy of their words, the participants have reviewed their own edited conversations. Further clarifications or corrections appear in brackets.

The full transcripts of the conversations are housed in the archives of Rancho Los Alamitos, along with the original photo portraits that appear in the book. Documenting a moment in time for the future, this new, significant archival material adds to the spoken, written, and visual record of the Tongva people, whose story began here at Povuu'ngna.

Introduction

William McCawley

I always had an identity that was Native American....[You] know, you're proud [but] sometimes you're ashamed. Are you Indian for the money? Where is our language? Are we too lazy to twist our tongues to the old-time manner anymore?...But that's the reality of being Native American—identity crises, dealing with the Bureau of Indian Affairs, not dealing,....having a roll number—what does it mean? Who's Indian and who's not? Our whole family—we all know we're Indian, but how are we going to self-identify and when is it appropriate?
—David Campio[1]

THE STORY OF A PEOPLE IS MORE THAN MERE HISTORY—THE CATALOGING of people and places, dates and events, causes and effects—it is a composite of the dreams and aspirations, the joys and suffering, the triumphs and tribulations, and even the failures, of those people. Like most stories, it is best told in the words of those who lived it, yet it can never be finished because it is retold with each new generation and renewed with every fresh life that draws breath in this world. It is a cloud pattern projected on a landscape that constantly changes with time and the turning of the seasons and the deeds of man. The story of a people looks ahead to the future and back to the past as it redefines itself in the present.

Winners may write history, but they do not own it. People may be conquered, subjugated, assimilated, or even marginalized, but still they have their own voices and their own stories, stories made more poignant by their existence in two worlds simultaneously, the world of their own traditions and the world of their rulers. Histories ancient and modern are replete with such tales. But this story is different and special, in part because of its setting—the greater Los Angeles region, one of the largest and most modern urban centers in the world—and in part because of its central characters, the Gabrielino-Tongva Indians who call this place their homeland. This is a story of revitalization and renewal, of a people who have continuously redefined themselves by blending their own cultural traditions with the cultures of newcomers—whether Spanish, Mexican, or American—to create a unique heritage that has been a central part of the story of Los Angeles for more than two centuries.

Land is an integral part of this tale. In fact, the landscape of Los Angeles and Orange Counties—the foothills and prairies, seacoasts and islands—underlies this story and is embedded in it. It links today's Tongva to their ancestors and their descendants yet to be born. Desirée Martinez recalls, "When I was back east for school I missed my mountains—[they] tell me who I am....I don't want to say the land is calling to me, but...this is where I am. This is where my heart is."[2] Many Tongva today would agree. They pursue their lives and careers in this place, the greater Los Angeles region. They are teachers and school administrators, youth counselors, graduate students, artists, actresses, engineers, attorneys, law enforcement professionals, and businesspeople. Although they are a small part of the cultural and ethnic mix that makes up Los Angeles, their numbers belie their signature role and unique contribution to this place and its history.

Historically speaking, the Tongva were not a single "tribe," but a collection of lineages (a lineage is a group of families with a common ancestor) that shared a language, culture, religion, and lifestyle that distinguished them from neighboring Indians like the Chumash or Cahuilla.[3] This sense of shared identity still unites them today, even though they may diverge in many other ways. "I think that we do have a collective identity," says Michael Barthelemy. "If you talk to any other people who know that they descend from the Gabrielino people, you'll find common themes. In that respect, I think we have a community of thought and belief, and a common racial inheritance. I think that the history shows that we have maintained that common identity."[4]

One of these themes is a connection to this land, the greater Los Angeles region. This is where their identity was forged, in the volatile and often violent crucible of California's history. Until the Spanish came here in the late eighteenth century, the Tongva were a sovereign people, a people of the land and sea, their identity molded by the environment and their relationship to it. But when the Spanish colonized them (Mission San Gabriel, the first mission in their territory, was founded in 1771), they imposed a new identity, one that served the needs of the provincial government in Mexico City. Later Mexican and American governments did the same.[5]

The Tongva adapted by assimilating with the newcomers and their cultures. Over a span of more than two centuries they evolved from a society of hunter-gatherers living in sovereign villages to a colonial citizenry laboring at the missions and ranchos under Spanish and Mexican rule, to a landless tribe living in an urbanized and industrialized American society. Their identity changed tremendously throughout this time, but it did not disappear and it did not lose its connection to the past. After more than two centuries it survives as a unique Tongva identity and with this comes a sense of confidence. Kimberly Morales Johnson observes, "You start to raise your kids, and then you're looking for what you're going to give them to pass on. [It's] that sense of family and having that common thread that started way back when....A sense of pride...[in] being the Gabrielinos from the Mission."[6] Her aunt Vivian Barthelemy echoes this sentiment: "I think there is pride that we originated here. Who can say that?"[7]

Historical Background and Sources

This is not a history of the Tongva. Rather, it is the story of the contemporary Tongva people and their world, of how they view themselves and their place in history: their hopes and dreams, successes and failures, as well as their unique vision—both individual and collective—for their future. As much as possible, this story will be told in their own voices and in their own words, remaining true to their spirit and intent.

While this is not a history book, history nonetheless provides much of the background and context for the story. The Tongva did not have their own written language—their laws, histories, genealogies, stories, and fables were all memorized and passed down by word of mouth from generation to generation—and the earliest written accounts of them were penned by Spanish explorers and missionaries beginning in the sixteenth century.[8] Perhaps the most complete account of their lifestyle and culture was written around 1822 by a Spanish Franciscan padre, Gerónimo Boscana, who was stationed at missions San Gabriel and San Juan Capistrano. It was during his residence at Capistrano Mission that Boscana wrote his book *Chinigchinich*, taking its title from the name of the Tongva's chief spiritual being and creator god.[9] Boscana drew upon information gleaned from personal observations as well as interviews with three elderly Indians—two local chiefs and a shaman—and despite his Catholic viewpoint, he was a careful and thoughtful observer of Indian culture. His account is a rich source of information on the lives of these California Indians before, and during, the early mission years.[10]

Thirty years later a Scottish immigrant named Hugo Reid published a second account of the Tongva in a series of "Letters" he wrote for the *Los Angeles Star* newspaper. Reid immigrated to Mexican California in 1832 and married an Indian woman, Victoria, the daughter of a local village chief; she and her family members undoubtedly provided Reid with much of his information. His letters were published in 1852, almost two decades after the missions ended, and provide an important glimpse of the Tongva after the American takeover of California. Reid died shortly after his stories were printed, but Victoria was a well-known member of the San Gabriel community until her death from smallpox in 1868.[11]

After Reid, historians paid little attention to the Tongva for the remainder of the nineteenth century.[12] although linguists like Henry Henshaw, Albert Gatschet and Oscar Loew visited California and collected vocabularies from them.[13] Antiquarians were also busy digging up Tongva villages and cemeteries and selling the artifacts to collectors, and to museums like the Smithsonian Institution, the Heye Foundation in Chicago, and the Peabody Museum at Harvard.[14] But after the turn of the century, interest in the Tongva and other California Indians increased. In 1903, anthropologist C. Hart Merriam interviewed Narcisa Higuera Rosemyre, a Tongva raised at Mission San Gabriel, and collected information from her about traditional funeral rites, puberty rituals, and other religious ceremonies.[15] Another anthropologist, J. P. Harrington of the Smithsonian Institution, interviewed members of the Tongva community extensively over several decades in the early 1900s; his notes have been published on microfilm by the National Anthropological Archives.[16] Anthropologist Alfred Kroeber of the University of California also worked with members of the tribe and included their information in his *Handbook of the Indians of California*.[17]

Merriam, Harrington, Kroeber, and other early researchers focused their attention on the Tongva's past; their goal was to collect as much information as possible about traditional, pre-mission language, religion, lifestyle, and culture. They worked tirelessly to preserve the precious stories of elderly Indians before they passed from this earth. These anthropologists had little inclination to study the contemporary Tongva community of the early 1900s and this has left an unfortunate gap in our knowledge, a void this work attempts to help fill.

Historical Periods

Oftentimes traditional history glosses over details in search of broader patterns and trends; people and their lives are reduced to stereotypes and neat chronological categories that bear only a limited resemblance to real world events. As Art Morales cautions, "In the American way, things always have to be identified, categorized, and...labeled."[18] But the Tongva story is a continuum spanning generation after generation, one that delights in defying historical patterns. Mindful of this caution, some basic time frames are nonetheless needed to give structure and continuity to the narrative.

The Tongva's period of sovereignty ended with the founding of Mission San Gabriel in 1771, although it took the Spanish several decades to consolidate their gains and achieve complete control of the territory. The Mission Period, which officially began with the establishment of Mission San Diego in 1769, ended at San Gabriel in 1834 when the mission was secularized (turned over to civilian administrators) and its lands sold to private ranchers.[19] The Mission Period straddles the era of Spain's empire in California (which ended with Mexico's independence in 1821) and the quarter-century of Mexican rule until the American conquest in 1847. The Rancho Period is sometimes loosely equated with the years of Mexican rule (1822–1847); however, the first private rancho in the Tongva's territory was actually granted much earlier, in 1784,[20] and cattle ranching remained the dominant economic force in the region until the late 1860s.[21]

The Tongva's cultural history during this tumultuous period is complicated. Some of the Indians (but by no means all of them) converted to Christianity and entered the missions at San Gabriel, San Fernando, and San Juan Capistrano. Others remained in their ancestral villages through the early 1800s, living as hunter-gatherers while also doing seasonal work at nearby ranchos or in the Pueblo of Los Angeles. By the time California came under American rule in 1847, the Tongva had been absorbed into the local economy. They spoke Spanish (as well as their own language) and worked as skilled tradesmen, or as farmworkers, ranch hands, and household servants.[22]

This economic pattern continued throughout the nineteenth century; however, the Tongva paid a steep price for their assimilation. Under American rule, California Indians faced political, legal, economic, and social discrimination. They could not vote or own land and they were denied equal protection under the law. Schools were closed to them; job opportunities were limited.[23] Survival was their primary concern. Under these circumstances, many submerged their Indian identities and blended into the greater Hispanic population to protect themselves and their children from violence and discrimination, as well as improve their opportunities for a better life. As Janice Ramos asks, "How many people's ancestors stayed pure, stayed in touch with their history and their background as a Tongva, and how many assimilated into the culture? My family certainly assimilated into the culture."[24]

During these difficult times many elders stopped passing their stories on to younger generations and much of the language and traditional knowledge was lost. Art Morales notes, "The stories...were not really spoken of because it had been drilled into...[our elders] that it wasn't the right thing to do."[25] Some Tongva became separated from their heritage and culture, although their family connections remained strong. As Stacy Thompson explains, "You have to remember there are people out there completely disconnected from any cultural knowledge...[who] don't have family stories passed down to them."[26] Craig Torres observes, "We grew up with a lot of family stories, you know....We didn't grow up with a lot of the traditional culture...because a lot of it...[had] disappeared by then."[27] Others were more aware of their Indian identities. Says Michael Barthelemy, "I knew all the time. I knew my grandpa was an Indian, and my grandma was an Indian, too. It was made known to us from the time we were very small."[28]

Conditions for most of California's Indians improved during the twentieth century, yet even today the Tongva remain a federally unrecognized tribe, one of many such tribes throughout the state.[29] The lack of recognition has prevented them from having access to federal health and education programs, reservation land, or gaming rights; it has also hampered their ability to protect sacred sites such as burial grounds. However, it has not prevented them from pursuing recognition from individual federal agencies, or from state and local governments. Nor has it prevented them from rediscovering their individual Tongva identities. For most of them this connection—this awareness—is an unfolding process, not an epiphany or life-altering experience. It continues throughout one's life. As David Campio explains, "My identity didn't come overnight. It's continuing to grow…it's definitely a continuum."[30]

The Essays

The three essays in this volume explore different aspects of the contemporary Tongva community and their world. The first essay discusses the Tongva's Indian identity and what it means to them. It explores how—and why—this identity has changed over the past two centuries, as well as the forces that brought about these changes, and it discusses how they have maintained their special link to the past. The second essay focuses on the Tongva's unique connection to Los Angeles and the central role this land still plays in their lives and culture. It examines how they lost their land during the nineteenth century and how this loss has affected their community. The third and final essay looks at the Tongva's vision for their future—both individually and as a community—and what it entails: federal acknowledgment, cultural recognition, and the economic development needed to move forward as a tribe, including the role Indian gaming could play in this process. An important theme throughout these essays is the way the Tongva have negotiated the competing social forces of their history to renew and redefine their identity. In ancient times the Tongva honored Eagle—the First Captain—who died and was reborn, and whose spirit they believed to be eternal. There is perhaps no more fitting allegory for this people.[31]

The quotations presented in the essays have been drawn primarily from interviews conducted over a three-year period, from 2005 to 2008, and are edited to flow with the narrative, while keeping to the spirit and intent of the originals. The individuals who participated in these interviews represent several generations of the Tongva community. Some belong to families that have resided in the San Gabriel area since mission times, while others are descended from ancestors who left San Gabriel to seek better opportunities for themselves and their families. Their life experiences differ markedly. Some always knew they were Tongva; others discovered their Indian heritage later in life. Their opinions differ as well, especially on sensitive issues such as federal recognition and Indian gaming, although most share a deep desire for federal recognition of their tribe. As their comments reveal, all are engaged in an ongoing process of exploring and understanding their Tongva identities. Quotations by Fred "Sparky" Morales[32] and Bea Alva are from a 1980 interview edited by Michael Brooks and published by the students of Suva Intermediate School in Bell Gardens, California. Citations are referenced in the endnotes and sources are listed in the bibliography; interview transcripts are on file at Rancho Los Alamitos in Long Beach. Readers interested in learning more about Tongva history and culture can refer to *The First Angelinos: The Gabrielino Indians of Los Angeles* (McCawley), or an earlier work, *California's Gabrielino Indians*, by Bernice Eastman Johnston.

The Tongva have been known by a variety of names over the past two centuries. Although they did not originally have a single tribal name for themselves, this has not prevented some scholars and writers from assigning one to them. They have at various times been referred to in the literature as Gabrielino, Gabrieleno, Gabrieleño, Tobikhars, Kij, Pipimaris, Tongva, and Mission Indians.[33] Today individual preferences on this subject vary; some call themselves Gabrielino or Gabrieleno,[34] while others prefer Gabrielino-Tongva or Tongva. Feelings on this subject can run hot and deep. "My family never said 'Tongva,'" says Desirée Martinez. "In fact, my grandmother refuses to use the name 'Tongva.' She's always identified herself as either Mission Indian or Gabrielino."[35] To respect these individual preferences, while avoiding the constant and cumbersome use of a hyphenated name, "Gabrielino-Tongva" will be used to introduce the essays and "Tongva" will be used thereafter, while direct quotations will follow the original wording.

THE FIRST ESSAY DEALS WITH IDENTITY AND ITS ROLE IN THE LIVES OF individuals and their society. Identity is an intrinsic part of the human experience, a psychological complement to the physical characteristics like body height and hair color that define us as humans. But identity also plays a significant social function in daily life by defining the roles people play in their families, their peer groups, and society at large. The Tongva's unique identity began forming centuries ago when their ancestors established themselves in their southern California homeland. The ancient Tongva held two different creation stories to explain their emergence. One described how their creator god Chinigchinich formed the first Indians out of clay scooped from a nearby lakebed; the other told how a wise captain led them down from the north into their new home, where he assigned each village its land.[36]

Today anthropologists believe the Tongva's ancestors (who spoke a language belonging to the Uto-Aztecan linguistic stock) migrated south from the Great

Basin[37] and spread into southern California many centuries, perhaps even millennia ago. But they entered a place already occupied by ancestors of the Hokan-speaking Chumash peoples.[38] Did the Uto-Aztecans and the Hokan speakers compete, or did they peacefully coexist, blending together their lifeways and identities over countless generations? Perhaps both creation stories are true; perhaps the two peoples intermarried and in this way planted the seed that would grow to become the Tongva people and their culture. To truly understand the Tongva and their story, one must first look to the past. For as Lakota Sioux writer Joseph Marshall notes, "We are all from the past."[39]

ONE

Continuity within Change: Identity and Culture

William McCawley

All Indian people are between two worlds....But if you're so attached to what was that you can't function in the present day...you're in trouble. You're giving up too much. —*Michael Barthelemy*[1]

WHAT DOES IT MEAN TO BE A GABRIELINO-TONGVA INDIAN IN TODAY'S world? Is being Tongva simply a measure of one's blood or a byproduct of one's genealogy? Or is it also based on a person's culture and beliefs? Who has the right to decide who is—and is not—Tongva? The government? The tribe? Or the individuals themselves? And how can a Native American people like the Tongva, a people who have lost their land and been assimilated into non-Indian societies and cultures for more than two centuries, preserve a separate and distinct identity, one that is uniquely theirs and not Spanish, Mexican, or American? These questions and others like them strike to the very heart of identity for today's Tongva.

Identity is a dynamic, shifting mosaic that evolves throughout our lives in response to the demands— and opportunities—of a changing world, as we strive all the while to remain connected to our personal and cultural past. As individuals and societies change, so do their identities. David Campio observes, "A culture, any indigenous group...is altering daily....The seasons change, everything changes."[2] For some, the knowledge of their Tongva heritage and identity has always been there. "I was very conscious of myself as an Indian person and see myself as that principally," says Michael Barthelemy.[3] The same was true for Desirée Martinez:

> I remember I was in junior high. They were trying to do a census of all the ethnic backgrounds of the students. The teacher would go one by one [asking], "What are you?" and it came to me.

Craig Torres, 2006. A member of the Ti'at Society, Craig is using clapper sticks, a traditional Tongva percussion instrument. Striking the clapper sticks against his palm, he marks the beat for Tongva songs and dance.

Desirée Martinez in the Jacaranda Walk, Rancho Los Alamitos, 2008. CRISTINA SALVADOR PHOTOGRAPHY

"Oh, I'm Native American, Gabrielino." [The teacher said]..."Well, your last name is Martinez." From the very earliest times I always had to fight against this idea that I was Mexican.[4]

But for others the realization came later in life. "I really didn't know about it until after I got a little bit older," Al Lassos recalled. "My mother used to tell us all the time that we were. [But] I just really went to school to play football, and eat my lunch. So it would go in this ear and come out this ear." [5]

Identity is complex and multi-layered, each level representing a different aspect of how we perceive ourselves and are perceived by others. At the broadest level there is cultural identity, the collective traits that bind together people who share (or once shared) a common homeland, history, and heritage: traits such as language, religion, social customs, and traditions. Cultural identity transcends geography and time, extending beyond national borders and over generations. A second level, political identity, comprises the sovereign identity of an independent people, or the foreign identity imposed upon colonial peoples (or expatriate communities) by a ruling power. Finally there is personal identity, which includes family and kinship, occupation, and self-image. All three layers of identity help define how the Tongva perceive themselves and are perceived by others.[6]

Cultural memory is an important aspect of identity, but what exactly is it? Is cultural memory a collection of images residing in the minds of those who share the same history? Is it a genetic memory carried in the DNA of people with the same bloodlines? Is it an instrument of social and political change, fashioned from deeply held ambitions and unfulfilled dreams? Or is cultural memory an academic fiction created by anthropologists, sociologists, and historians to classify and organize the people they study? Are cultural memory and identity the same or are they different? Does cultural memory change over time, and if so, what can this tell us about the people who share it?

Cultural memory is derived from the past, but it is not the same as history. Archaeologist Cornelius Holtorf writes:

Cultural memory is not about giving testimony of past events, as accurately and truthfully as possible, nor is it necessarily about ensuring cultural continuity: it is about making meaningful statements about the past in a given cultural context of the present....Individuals...retain the freedom to...offer alternative views of the past which may themselves later become part of the collective memory. As interpretations of the past constantly change, so do cultural memories. 7

Cindi Alvitre believes that "Cultural memory travels—something that is situated in the past and travels to the present—perhaps to create unknowingly, unconsciously, a future."8 Rooted in the past, yet redefined by the present, cultural memory is a living thing, constantly reshaped by the social, political, and cultural events of today.

What does it mean, then, to be a Tongva in today's world? The answer for each person is different, although there are common themes derived from their collective history and shared culture. It is a story multiplied thousands of times over the past centuries. Sadly, most of these stories are lost to us. But the life of one Indian whose experiences spanned more than a century of California's history gives us a rare glimpse into the complexities of being Tongva.

The traditional ti'at *of the Tongva people (in the foreground) is in the waters alongside a* tomol, *the traditional plank canoe of the neighboring Chumash people. Ti'at Festival, Catalina Island, September 1998.*
FRANK MAGALLANES AND ALTHEA EDWARDS PHOTOGRAPHY

THE STORY IN THE *LOS ANGELES TIMES* ON FEBRUARY 10, 1921, BOLDLY proclaimed the end of an era. "Race Vanishes as Juncio [sic] Dies," it stated. The accompanying article told how José de los Santos Juncos, an Indian living at Mission San Gabriel, died in his sleep at 106 years of age and how "with him died the last vestige of personal remembrance of the golden age of the California missions." A grainy black-and-white photograph accompanying the story showed Santos Juncos as an elderly man with close-cropped hair, a wide nose, and a drooping white moustache. The *Times* solemnly avowed that "the death of Santo Juncio at the San Gabriel Mission yesterday afternoon marked the passing of a vanished race."[9] What must the living Tongva have thought upon hearing the news that their "vanished race" was extinct? One can only wonder.

The extinction myth still shadows the Tongva to this day. Al Lassos encountered it while on vacation with his family:

> I went to Catalina one year and took one of my granddaughters. [The tour guide] said that at one time the island was inhabited by Gabrielinos. Since then, he said, "There's only about fifty of them and they all live in San Gabriel. There are no more here on the island. I've been on this tour for about ten years, and I've never ever met one." After the tour was over, I went over and shook his hand and said, "Now you met one." He said, "Oh, really?" I said, "Yes, and there's more than fifty of us...You're telling these stories and they're not really true."[10]

Americans created this myth during the nineteenth and early twentieth centuries by disparaging, and denying, the Indian identities of descendants of mixed Hispanic–California Indian marriages. [11] For example, the B. D. Wilson Report of 1852, which describes the conditions of the Indians living in southern California, stated that the Juaneño Indians of San Juan Capistrano "are now nearly extinct, from intermarriage with the Spaniards."[12] The Tongva still feel the effects of this double standard, as David Campio learned when he was a young schoolboy:

She said, "There are no Gabrielino Indians left. Sit down, be quiet." I got sent to the principal's office that day. —DAVID CAMPIO

> I remember when I was in the third grade or fourth grade, when the teacher started talking about the San Gabriel Mission, I stood up proudly and I said, "I'm Gabrielino Indian." She laughed at me. [She said,] "There are no Gabrielino Indians left. Sit down, be quiet." I got sent to the principal's office that day. Well, I went home devastated. I don't think I ever told my mom, but I did tell my grandfather. He said, "You're going to get that the rest of your life. If somebody asks you, just say we're businessmen. We'll keep our identity here in our backyard in the pottery shop." That's just how it was. [13]

José de los Santos Juncos's life is an important illustration of the complex (and often contradictory) ways that the Tongva's identity has been, and still is, defined by non-Indians. He was born at San Gabriel Mission and lived there until after the Mexican-American War, when he went to Los Angeles and resided for a time in the household of a local attorney, Colonel Kuhn, and later with the family of Indian sub-agent (and Los Angeles's first American mayor) Benjamin D. Wilson. Santos Juncos worked with Smithsonian anthropologist J. P. Harrington from 1910 to 1920 and provided him with much of his information on the Tongva. Yet according to Harrington, this remarkable Indian was actually of Juaneño descent, both of his parents having been born at Mission San Juan Capistrano.[14] Because Santos Juncos lived most of his early life at San Gabriel and was most familiar with the Tongva culture—because his *cultural memory* was primarily Tongva—the anthropologist defined him as such, rather than Juaneño, as his ancestry or blood indicated.

Harrington does not tell us what Santos Juncos thought.

THE FOLLOWING ESSAY EXPLORES THE COMPLEX WAYS THE TONGVA'S identity has redefined itself over more than two centuries. It examines the three different aspects of their identity—cultural, political, and personal—and how these evolved under Spanish, Mexican, and American societies and governments. It explores two recurrent themes in the Tongva's story: "continuity within change," that is, the way the Tongva have kept a connection with their past while assimilating with other peoples and cultures, and "diversity within a shared identity," how they have accommodated a variety of viewpoints within their collective identity. The essay is organized around the major transitions in the Tongva's culture, rather than the standard milestones of California history. Part I, "From Village to Mission," deals with the Tongva's period of sovereignty, which ended in 1771. Part II, "Identity Divided," covers the Mission Period, from 1771 until 1834. Part III, "Identity Redefined," covers the end of the Mission Period in 1834 to the present day.

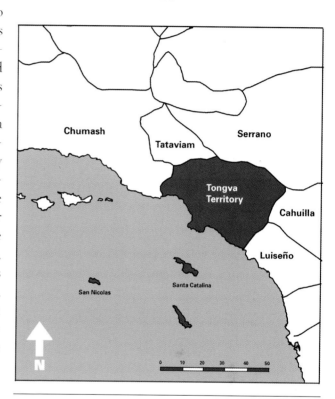

Gabrielino-Tongva territory and neighboring Indian groups. Gabrielino-Tongva territory covered 1,500 square miles, most of Los Angeles and Orange Counties today, in addition to Santa Catalina, San Clemente, San Nicolas, and Santa Barbara Islands. MAP BY WILLIAM McCAWLEY, DRAWING BY WILLIAM S. WELLS

I. From Village to Mission: A Shared Identity, Prehistory to 1771

Before the Spanish came to California, the Tongva recognized a common bond in language, religion, and lifestyle, a shared culture—a shared identity—that distinguished them from neighboring Indians like the Chumash and Cahuilla. Their society was based on kinship and land. Every family belonged to a lineage (a group of families sharing a common ancestor) and these lineages formed the primary landholding bodies, with one or more lineages residing in each village.[15] The Tongva still feel this shared identity today, an identity tied to their history and to their land. As Cindi Alvitre explains, "It's not a racial identity...It's not a biological identity. It's absolutely a cultural [and] socially constructed way of perceiving yourself in relationship to [a] certain space geographically, and to a particular lineage of history in California."[16]

The Tongva were a people of the land and sea. They supported themselves as hunter-gatherers, rather than farmers, although they realized that agricultural Indians living to the east of them along the Colorado River grew corn and other crops in river-flooded lowlands.[17] Why? Tradition may have played a part in their choice, but there were practical reasons as well, since farming without benefit of irrigation is perilous in southern California's arid, rainless summers. Instead, the Tongva relied upon the acorn, a reliable, seasonal staple they harvested each fall.

They also hunted a wide variety of game animals and sea mammals, fished, and gathered nuts, berries, roots, cresses, seeds, and other wild plant foods that ripened at different seasons throughout the year.[18] They followed a pattern called "central-based wandering," hunting and gathering throughout their lineage-controlled territory but seasonally returning to their home village.[19] "Our people had it easier than most," says Michael Barthelemy, "because they had the most...plentiful land to live [on] and [the] sea close by. They had the land-based animals and the sea to feed them."[20]

Although the Tongva shared a common language and culture, the land shaped and molded their villages in different ways. The character of the Los Angeles region—one of the most geographically diverse places in the world, with high mountains and foothills, broad valleys and prairies, seacoast and offshore islands—impressed itself upon them, engendering differences in lifestyle and wealth, especially between the Indians living on the seacoast

A contemporary vision by Jacob Gutierrez of a Tongva basket, with a ti'at in the center. COURTESY OF JACOB GUTIERREZ

and those further inland. The coastal Indians benefited most from this diversity of resources. They had many of the same foods as their inland neighbors—game such as deer, antelope, rabbits, and squirrels as well as plant foods like acorns, seeds, and bulbs—but they also had fish, seals, sea lions, seabirds, and shellfish. By comparison, the Indians living in the valleys had a more restricted diet and were more likely to suffer from droughts and famines.[21] In 1773, Father Francisco Palou wrote that the inland villages were "very poor, on account of the small crops of wild seeds they receive from the plains and...the poor results of the chase. [And because] they lack also...the fisheries, since the beach is about eight leagues distant."[22]

The coastal Indians also carried on a rich trade with the island Tongva in roots, plant foods, otter skins, shell beads, and luxury goods like soapstone, a mineral

In 1992 members of the Ti'at Society of the Tongva people helped build the first traditional ti'at (plank canoe) in almost two centuries. The Moomat Ahiko *(Breath of the Ocean) was first launched on September 9, 1995, on a fourteen-mile voyage from Two Harbors to Avalon, on Catalina Island. Since then, the* Moomat Ahiko *has returned to the ocean many times. Ti'at Festival, (Avalon Casino in background), Catalina Island, September 1997.* FRANK MAGALLANES AND ALTHEA EDWARDS PHOTOGRAPHY

quarried on Santa Catalina that was easily carved into fireproof cooking pots.[23] This trade brought prosperity to the villages on Catalina as well as the mainland coast. When the Spanish visited Santa Catalina in 1602, they discovered a large village (which they called a "pueblo," or town) at the isthmus near the west end of the island. Father Antonio de la Ascención described the large houses made of a willow framework covered with "a mat of rushes very closely woven" so that "neither rain nor the sun penetrates them." These houses were "so spacious that each will hold fifty people." He also praised their "well-made canoes of boards fastened together," some of which were large enough "that they would hold more than twenty people."[24]

These regional differences went beyond material goods and economic wealth; there were cultural and even philosophical differences as well. The Tongva spoke at least three distinct dialects of their language, one on the Channel Islands and mainland coast, another in the San Gabriel Valley, and a third in the San Fernando Valley (a fourth dialect spoken on distant San Nicolas Island may have been related to the language of the Luiseño Indians to the south).[25] They traded, and even intermarried, with different neighboring tribes like the Chumash, Serrano, and Cahuilla.[26] And they had different religious beliefs about how the world was created and how Indians came into being. The coastal Indians believed that Nocuma, or "Sky," an invisible and all-powerful being, created the earth and its oceans as well as all the trees, plants, animals, fishes, and man. The Indians living in the interior valleys, on the other hand, honored Earth as the giver of all life and held that their creator god Chinigchinich formed man and woman out of clay from a nearby lakebed.[27]

ORIGINALLY THE TONGVA DID NOT HAVE A SINGLE TRIBAL NAME OR government; instead they lived in approximately fifty major villages, each holding its own territory, that were scattered across their fifteen hundred square miles of homeland. While they shared a cultural identity and lifestyle, they drew their political identities from their villages. People typically identified themselves by adding the suffix "vit," "bit" or "pet" to their village name—for example, Yaangavit, "I am from Yaanga." Villages generally held fifty to one hundred and fifty people, although coastal and island villages could be larger; each village controlled its own territory and had its own chief, known as the *tomyaar*.[28]

Sharing has always been an important aspect of Tongva life. A tradition of sharing intellectual and cultural property such as songs, stories, ceremonies, and religious practices goes back to a time before the missions, when the Tongva traded and intermarried with the Chumash, Luiseño, Cahuilla, and other tribes. Sharing was also practiced within their own villages; the Tongva abhorred stinginess and food hoarding and required everyone to contribute to a communal food reserve for emergencies.[29]

Rituals and ceremonies also helped bond together members of the same community and strengthen their shared identity. To validate its ownership of land, each lineage had special migration stories and "songs of travel" that recounted how their people came to reside in a particular place. These stories and songs were recognized as proof of their right to occupy that land. One such song recorded by musicologist Helen Roberts in the early 1900s told how a lineage moved from Catalina Island to the mainland near Oceanside. The lineage owned a magical stalk of cane; when the cane stalk was planted in the soil of their new home everything flourished, thereby giving proof of their right to settle in that place. Other rituals confirmed the privileges and authority held by chiefs and secular and religious officials.[30]

While a shared cultural and political identity drew community members together, the demands of daily life often placed them at odds with one another. Small disagreements between individuals and families were resolved through consultation with the lineage leaders or the village chief, but more serious disputes between lineages could split a village and cause one group to leave and found a new settlement.[31] Feuding or warfare occurred when the members of one village trespassed or poached in a neighboring village's territory. Father Palou complained in 1773 that the Indians "wage continual wars among themselves that makes it impossible [for the Indians in the interior] to go to the beach to fish...at the shore. This shore is the...[harbor] of San Pedro."[32]

THE FAMILY HAS ALWAYS BEEN THE HEART OF TONGVA SOCIETY. In modern times, social events—formal occasions like weddings and funerals, as well as informal gatherings on weekends and holidays—provide welcome opportunities for the members of extended families to visit and keep in touch. Virginia Carmelo recalls how her family "used to gather in Santa Ana every Sunday....We would get the food and we'd go down to the river, the Santa Ana River."[33] Angie Behrns remembers similar family gatherings when she was a child:

> In the forties, we'd also go to Rancho de los Marquez, in Santa Monica Canyon, where the old families would gather....The old oak trees that are no longer there—I remember climbing them....And all the old families knew each other. Like in San Gabriel, when they gathered.[34]

"Everybody used to visit," says Cindi Alvitre. "Back then on the weekends, you were visiting. You were going all the way up Foothill Boulevard to Tujunga to go visit my Aunt Ruby up there, or out to Pala, or out to Rincon. It was traveling on the weekends, lots of traveling."[35] Craig Torres says, "I remember my aunt talking about...when they used to live on the Chapman Ranch, she remembers Sparky [Fred] Morales's family coming...they used to come on one of the horse and buggies."[36]

Traditional village life also centered on the family. Maintaining strong kinship ties was vital since wealth, property, social position, political power, and even ritual knowledge were all inherited.[37] While most Tongva men had only one wife, wealthy men might have more. These wealthy families sometimes lived in large homes that could comfortably hold several generations of relatives. Women resided in their husbands' villages once they were married. They could return to their own villages if they divorced; however, divorce was usually allowed only if a wife was unfaithful or barren, or if a husband was abusive or failed to support his family.[38]

Men and women normally married within their own social class, of which there were three. At the top of society was an elite class of chiefs and shamans, who governed the lineages and who controlled the best lands, including the richest hunting and fishing grounds and the most productive acorn groves. Next came a second group, made up of village officials, bureaucrats, and skilled craftsmen. Third were the commoners. Slaves, vagabonds, and outcasts filled out the remainder of the population. This class system was hereditary, although an ambitious person

Painting of Mission San Gabriel by Ferdinand Deppe, 1832. In the lower right corner is a traditional Gabrielino-Tongva home; the rows of adobe buildings to the left of the mission were occupied by neophytes (Mission Christian Indians). COURTESY OF SANTA BARBARA MISSION ARCHIVE-LIBRARY

could still advance himself—in effect, renegotiate his personal identity—if he was intelligent, resourceful, and determined to succeed. For example, while shamans normally came from elite families, supernatural power was theoretically available to anyone disciplined and determined enough to acquire it; therefore, a shaman could emerge from any social class. In other cases, a gifted craftsman could be adopted into one of the professional guilds and thereby advance his position in society.[39]

THE TONGVA'S SHARED IDENTITY STAMPED THEM AS ONE PEOPLE WITH a common culture that extended across their territory, varying in the finer details, yet broadly woven of the same cloth. By the late 1700s, however, this world was drawing to a close. There had been earlier warnings of changes to come; Spanish ships had sailed these coastal waters from the mid-sixteenth century, and several expeditions made landfall on Santa Catalina Island. But the appearance of Spanish soldiers on the mainland in 1769 presaged a changed world order. Two years later another Spanish expedition founded Mission San Gabriel and introduced a new level of cultural diversity and complexity to the Tongva's world.

The founding of Mission San Gabriel was the watershed moment in Tongva history. Nothing before or after it has had such a profound and far-reaching impact upon them as a people and culture. The establishment of the mission brought the Tongva's period of sovereignty to an end (although it took the Spanish several decades to consolidate their power). A short while later, when the first Tongva convert joined the mission community, their identity became divided. From that day forward they were either Christians or pagans, neophytes or gentiles, Mission Indians or wild Indians. The founding of Mission San Gabriel created new points of divergence for the Tongva and, ultimately, a new identity.

II. Identity Divided: Spanish Rule and the Missions, 1771–1834

The missionaries' primary goal was to replace the Tongva's Indian identity with a new one: Catholic subjects of the Spanish crown. Politically, this was motivated by Spain's desire for a buffer state to protect its Mexican colonies from encroachment by the Russian and English settlements to the north; spiritually, it was driven by the missionaries' religious zeal and fervor to save souls for Christ.[40] The Franciscans' strategies included: baptizing the Indians and drawing them into a central mission community, where they could be trained as farmers and craftsmen; persuading (and even coercing) them to adopt the Spanish Catholic religion, lifestyle, and culture; and replacing their native tongue with the Spanish language. In theory, each mission was to be converted into a parish church after ten years.[41] The pact between Indian converts and missionaries was straightforward: the Indians would become Christians and labor to build the mission into a prosperous community; the missionaries would protect them and hold the mission lands in trust for them until the Indians were ready to manage these properties on their own.[42] Of course, this pact was not wholly voluntary, since once an Indian accepted baptism he or she was no longer free to renounce Catholicism or abandon the mission.[43]

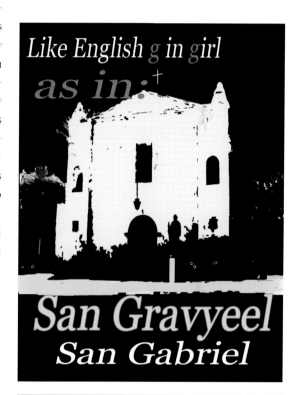

This contemporary illustration of Mission San Gabriel by Jacob Gutierrez pictures a sound in the Tongva language. COURTESY OF JACOB GUTIERREZ

At first the missionaries used food, small gifts, and personal kindnesses to attract the Indians. The availability of food at the mission must have been a powerful incentive to the Indians. Rafael Verger, father guardian of the College of San Fernando, remarked wryly, "Faith enters through the mouth."[44] However, the dynamics of the situation changed when the Indian population declined due to European diseases, and when ranching and farming altered the countryside to the point the Indians could no longer live as hunter-gatherers. As their ancestral villages slowly drained into the earth, many surviving Tongva joined the missions at San Gabriel, San Fernando, and San Juan Capistrano.[45]

But others disdained mission life and its drawbacks: overcrowding, authoritarian structure, regimented work schedules, lack of personal freedom, and high disease and death rates. These Indians sought work in the Pueblo of Los Angeles or on the enormous private ranchos spreading across the countryside. They, too, learned Spanish and many became Catholics. Some learned skilled trades, while others made up the labor force that built early Los Angeles. Tongva also intermarried with Spanish and Mexican settlers.[46] Speaking of his own family, Fred Morales noted proudly, "Here's the Lugos. They were related to us. Anna María Lugo was married to one of my ancestors. All of these people were related. We have the Duartes here....María and Soledad are in our family tree."[47]

PERHAPS THE GREATEST CULTURAL IMPACT THE MISSIONS HAD UPON THE Tongva was in the area of religion. Today many Tongva belong to one of the major faiths and attend an organized church. More than two centuries ago their ancestors threaded organized religion's moral code into the fabric of their own traditional religious beliefs. But the transition was not an easy one. Cultural conflict was implicit in the missionaries' goal of transforming Tongva society. Their low opinion of the Indians' culture and intellect—they considered them "adult children," fully human yet too immature to care for themselves or manage their own affairs[48]—rationalized the methods they used to remold them. Traditional Catholic beliefs and practices conflicted with Tongva religion at almost every turn. Catholic doctrine disdained the earthly world and focused on death, the afterlife, and the need to seek redemption from sin. Catholic dogma guided believers to lead moral lives and prepare for admittance into heaven. The Franciscans were the central authorities in this religious system and they allowed only limited participation by Christian Indians, whom they referred to as "neophytes," or "new converts," that is, baptized Indians.[49] Their religious code demanded submission to authority and rigid self-control of human appetites; it sought to regulate every aspect of an individual's personal life, including his or her sexual desires. Thus in the missionaries' view marriage and sex were intended for procreation, while premarital sex, extramarital sex, homosexuality, birth control, abortion, and infanticide were sinful and forbidden.[50]

The contrast with traditional Tongva beliefs could not have been more profound. Tongva religion focused on living a proper life on earth. Rather than preparing them for death and the afterlife, the Tongva's moral code defined their social and ritual obligations to the community and its members. Tongva ceremonies were tuned to the natural world, the seasons, and the major passages in human life such as birth, marriage, and death. These ceremonies were held, in part, to create opportunities for lineages to share food and prevent local famines, thereby lowering the chance of conflict.[51] Some of these ceremonies were still being performed in the late 1800s. Craig Torres recalls a family story about a ceremony in San Gabriel:

> My aunt used to talk about her grandmother...and she relates the story about...when she was a very young girl...she remembers them having a ceremony right at San Gabriel, and there was this huge fire and a lot of the Indians that lived in the mountains came down to participate, and she remembers that all of them were dancing around the fire and then throwing different things into the fire and there were so many people that she got lost in the crowd and she became really scared.... And the way she describes it...sounds like...a mourning ceremony....[My] great-grandmother was born, I believe, in the 1860s, so this was around the 1870s, maybe early 1880s when this was going on.[52]

Vivian Morales Barthelemy at Mission San Gabriel, 2006. The mother of Michael Barthelemy, she was married at Mission San Gabriel and is active in the San Gabriel community.
Ty Milford Photography

The Tongva pantheon included a supreme spiritual being, Chinigchinich, who created the Indians and anointed the chiefs and shamans to rule over them.[53] The Tongva spiritual universe comprised three parallel worlds arranged one above the other: the upper world (sky or heaven) was the abode of gods and supernatural beings; the middle world was the home of humans; and the lower world was the dwelling place of evil and dangerous creatures.[54] The shaman was the most important person in this system, for only he had the power to travel between the three worlds and intercede with the gods. Shamans made these supernatural journeys by consuming a beverage brewed from a hallucinogenic plant, *Datura wrightii*, commonly known as Jimson weed. *Datura* produces trance-like visions and sensations of flying and has been used in religious rituals by peoples throughout the world.[55]

Over time these two currents of faith—organized religion with its emphasis on moral order, and traditional Tongva religion with its emphasis on sacredness, the land, and the natural world—blended to become a new set of religious beliefs and values. As Cindi Alvitre notes, "We have a very unique identity, a very unique history, and a way of seeing the land around us. That in itself is very important."[56] Today many Tongva feel a profound sense of nature's majesty but also acknowledge the moral guidance of organized religion. Michael Barthelemy has known both in his life:

> I was away from the church from fourteen to the age of thirty-one. During that time you could say I was searching for my Indian roots or wanting

to be with other Indian people....I was wanting to take the step beyond hand's reach and see the supernatural aspect [of the world]....But...I found out two things. First, nature is cruel....We can't be too romantic about nature....I realized that, and that I do believe there's a moral order to the universe....That's why I returned to faith in the Church and its founder. So now I'm a Catholic.[57]

A TONGVA'S POLITICAL IDENTITY CHANGED DRAMATICALLY ONCE HE or she was baptized into the mission community. Although a neophyte retained his or her lineage and family ties (indeed, the missionaries relied upon these connections to attract more converts), once baptized they could not renounce their conversion or return to their villages except with the priests' permission. If they tried to escape, the mission guard hunted them, and anyone who helped or harbored fugitives was arrested and punished as a criminal. The soldiers also enforced mission discipline and regulations, and the penalties for breaking rules included corporal punishments such as lashing, flogging, and confinement in the mission stocks.[58]

> *We can't be too romantic about nature....I realized that, and that I do believe there's a moral order to the universe....That's why I returned to faith in the Church and its founder.* —MICHAEL BARTHELEMY

The priests held all political power within the mission, while a *mayordomo*, or manager, ran day-to-day operations, assisted by a number of Indian *alcaldes* (magistrates) and *regidores* (councilmen). Although Spanish Governor Felipe de Neve ordered in 1778 that the Indians at each mission elect *alcaldes* and *regidores* from among their own numbers, the Franciscans carefully managed this process by selecting the candidates for office.[59] Hugo Reid disparaged the *alcaldes* at San Gabriel, claiming that they were "appointed annually by the Padre, and chosen from among the very laziest of the community."[60] But studies of records from other missions suggest that whenever possible, the missionaries chose candidates from those Christianized Indians who also held traditional leadership positions.[61] The priests at San Fernando may have alluded to this practice when they wrote in 1813 that the Indians "respect only those who were the chiefs of their rancherias [villages] in paganism."[62]

Not all Tongva accepted the political and cultural changes the mission introduced into their world. There was violent opposition from both non-converted Indians living outside the mission walls and neophytes living inside them. Revolts were staged against San Gabriel in 1771, 1773, 1779, 1785, and 1810; however, these attacks failed due to the superior military training and weaponry of the Spanish, weaponry that included horses, steel-bladed lances, firearms, and arrow-proof body armor made from quilted buckskin.[63]

A Tongva's personal identity within the mission—the way he defined himself and his place in the community—was a far cry from village life. Unlike the small, lineage-based villages, the mission was an enormous community housing up to seventeen hundred Indians, including not only Tongva, but also members of other tribes like the Serrano, Kitanemuk, and Cahuilla.[64] The Indians' lives within the mission were rigidly managed; their work was assigned to them and their personal freedom was restricted. The mission was essentially a rudimentary factory system where Indians were assigned tedious, repetitious jobs like plowing, planting, or cloth weaving in place of traditional tasks like hunting, fishing, or gathering plants. They were required to work six to eight hours per day, six days a week, as well as attend church services several times a day. Their personal time was limited to one day per week, on Sundays.[65]

Family life changed as well. Christian Indians were allowed only one wife, regardless of their social status, and divorce was forbidden. Their sexual lives were subject to Catholic rules that forbade birth control, abortion, infanticide, extramarital sex, and homosexuality. To prevent premarital sex, unmarried girls eight years and older were taken from their parents' homes and locked in a dormitory at night under the supervision of a female guard. This dormitory, known as the *monjerío*, was a complex of workshops, patios, and cramped sleeping rooms that housed fifty to one hundred young women. [66]

Not all converts accepted this new life, and many Indians fled the mission, despite the severe punishment they faced if captured. By 1817, more than 8 percent of the Tongva baptized at San Gabriel had run off. Others who stayed behind found different ways to reject Spanish customs and culture, especially the Catholic faith.[67] Father Boscana described one Indian at Capistrano who

> *When [my grandfather] was on his deathbed, they called the priest in to give him the last rites. He woke up enough to say, "Get the hell out of here, I'll tell my sins to the God."* —Cindi Alvitre

renounced Catholicism on his deathbed. Neither his friends nor the priests could persuade him to confess his sins and partake of Holy Communion before he died. When asked why he refused, the Indian snapped, "If I have been deceived whilst living, I do not wish to die in the delusion!"[68] Cindi Alvitre tells a similar story from her own family:

> My grandfather...was one who was not Catholic at all. The priest came to him and told him, "Juanito, you should come to church, or you're going to go to hell." He told the priest, "You need to leave here, or I'm going to make sure you go to hell after I kill you," and he pulled a shotgun out at the priest. When he was on his deathbed, they called the priest in to give him the last rites. He woke up enough to say, "Get the hell out of here, I'll tell my sins to the God."[69]

ANTHROPOLOGIST RANDALL MILLIKEN ARGUES THAT THE MISSIONARIES used psychological violence against the Indians to destroy their self-confidence and leave them feeling that they "deserved to be powerless, to be ordered about, and to be punished." He writes that "to accept a foreign culture as inherently superior to one's own is, in a sense, to deprecate one's self," thereby denying one's self-worth.[70] Michael Barthelemy observes:

> I've heard that [this happened] among other tribal groups, like the Navajos...during the boarding school period, for example, when they were given the impression and came to believe that they were lower or lesser because they were Indians. I suppose that could occur where you have a dominant group of non-Indians who are telling you all the time that you're worthless.[71]

More than a century and a half earlier, Hugo Reid described the symptoms of culture shock the Tongva displayed at Mission San Gabriel: "At first, surprise and astonishment filled their minds; a strange lethargy and inaction predominated afterwards."[72]

Many factors undoubtedly contributed to this reaction: the loss of their traditional lineage-based community and hunter-gatherer lifestyle, overcrowding, the demeaning and demoralizing effect of corporal punishment, rigid time management and the lack of personal freedom, enforced Catholic rules of marriage and family life, conflicting sexual mores, and the high rate of disease and death. Statistics tell just how serious the disease problem was inside the mission: from 1781 to 1831 the mean birthrate at San Gabriel was forty-four per thousand, well below the mean death rate of ninety-five per thousand.[73]

For the Tongva, the mission legacy remains complex and often contradictory. For some, it is a painful reminder of the loss of their traditional culture and sovereignty as a people. "We always hated any...[mention of Mission] San Gabriel," says Linda Gonzales. "We have a revulsion. Usually if it's mentioned, or any of the missions, it would be with a sneer from my parents."[74] But for others the mission is a powerful symbol, a point of origin for their people as a community and tribe, and a connection to their past in a world where almost everything else has been taken from them. "My mother would always tell me that this is where we come from," says Craig Torres. "'We didn't come from Mexico...that's your dad's side'....She was referring to the San Gabriel Mission because that's where our people were taken....She knew San Gabriel Mission, being Gabrielino."[75] Angie Behrns visited the mission with her family as a child. "My dad would take us....[I can] remember the little skull as you entered the cemetery, and he would just go stand by his grandmother's grave."[76] Art Morales offers his own personal connection to the mission: "I believe...my great-great-great-grandmother is interred there, and her headstone [is still] there."[77]

Historically speaking, Mission San Gabriel can be seen as the genesis of the Tongva people as a single tribe, rather than a multitude of smaller tribelets. It was the point in time when the many independent, village-based lineages came together in one large community. As Desirée Martinez explains, "My grandmother has an attachment to San Gabriel Mission, and sees that as a point of origin, if you want to think about it technically, because...[the tribe] didn't exist until the mission was created. I mean in terms of that [common] identity."[78] This consolidation, as well as the creation of new secular forms of leadership, laid the foundation stones of a unified political identity. Tragically, the high mission death rate and subsequent realignment of the surviving lineages probably contributed to this process. But the mission also provided the Tongva with the skills they needed to survive in the new economy that was emerging in California. As Janice Ramos notes:

> *As negative as the missions were in so many ways, they allowed my great-great-grandmother to survive. They gave her the skills to survive in the world.* —JANICE RAMOS

> As negative as the missions were in so many ways, they allowed my great-great-great-grandmother to survive. They gave her the skills to survive in the world....They gave her...the ability to speak the language...so she could tell you some of the stories, and translate....That's what the mission gave her....As negative as it was, it was still a meeting place where we were together." [79]

In the end, only the Tongva can judge the true consequences of the mission. As David Campio notes:

> We were taught the missions were good. Now, study the subject. Pick up two different books and you've got two different stories. What's the correct one? You have to find a balance in there somewhere, and I think I've found the balance. Some of my cousins are very strong Catholics, [but they also] identify with being Indians and Gabrielino.[80]

III. Identity Redefined: The Tongva after the Mission, 1834–Present

The mission was one of three institutions the Spanish created to consolidate control of their territory in California; pueblos and private ranchos formed the other two-thirds of the triad. Within the Tongva's own territory, the Pueblo of Los Angeles was founded in 1781, while the first private rancho, Rancho San Pedro, was granted three years later, in 1784.[81] For the next fifty years, mission and rancho were the pivot points of Spanish colonial society and an antagonism quickly developed between these two powers.

This struggle goes back to the earliest land grants. For example, in 1790 Manuel Nieto, one of the "leatherjacket" soldiers who accompanied Gaspar de Portolá and Father Junípero Serra to California in 1769, received the three-hundred-thousand-acre grant of Los Coyotes. But part of this grant included lands also claimed by Mission San Gabriel. In a letter to Spanish Governor Borica, Nieto complained that the missionaries were trying to take his land. Governor Borica eventually settled the dispute by dividing the property between Nieto and the mission, allowing Nieto to retain the land that he had already placed under cultivation.[82]

The feud between the missionaries and rancheros was driven by competition for land and for Indians to work it. The ranchos kept large numbers of unconverted Indians out of the missions' orbit by hiring them as workers; this gave the Indians a way to get Spanish goods without converting to Christianity or giving up their personal freedom. The missionaries despised this. In 1795, Father Vicente de Santa María saw that "the whole pagandom...along the beach, along the camino real, and along the border of the north, is fond of the Pueblo of Los Angeles, of the rancho of Mariano Verdugo, of the Rancho of Reyes." These unconverted "pagan Indians care neither for the Mission nor for the missionaries," he complained bitterly.[83] Twenty years later, two other priests echoed Father Vicente's lament about the influence the ranchos had on the Indians: "The [Indian] adults delay in having themselves baptized. In the service of their masters they live according to their pagan notions and practices. The freedom which they lose by adopting Christianity, inspires them with great disaffection."[84] The rancheros, in turn, coveted the enormous land holdings of the missions. Although the legal ownership of this land was vested in the Spanish Crown, much of it was held in trust for the Indians, and Indian rights of occupancy were acknowledged and protected.[85]

When Mexico achieved independence from Spain in 1821, the new government developed plans to secularize the missions and turn their lands over to non-Indian settlers.[86] Legally, this amounted to a renunciation of the Spanish government's pledge to hold the mission lands in trust for the Indians. When the Mexican government finally secularized Mission San Gabriel in 1834, it marked the close of the long-running battle between the missionaries and the rancheros.[87] It also marked an enormous political and economic setback for the Tongva, who had long hoped the mission would be converted into a pueblo and its lands—their lands—returned to them. But that was not to be. In the following decades the rancho became the unrivaled social and economic institution in California. It remained so through the American conquest in 1847, until a new wave of change swept across the state in the late 1860s, a wave that gradually overwhelmed the ranchos and swept away the old social order, shaking the Tongva's world yet again.

EUROPEANS AND AMERICANS WHO IMMIGRATED TO MEXICAN-controlled California in the 1820s, 1830s, and 1840s accepted Indians as members of their society (although usually at a lower social class). Some also intermarried with them. However, many Americans who came to California after 1847 had a different view. They regarded the California Indians as somehow less than human and referred to them as "Diggers," a dehumanizing term based on a false belief that they lived primarily on roots dug out of the ground.[88] Under American law, Tongva and other California Indians became noncitizens; they received little or no legal protection for their lives or their property and were subject to indentured servitude for the most minor infractions.[89] These dangers convinced many Indians to try to renegotiate their identity to a higher, non-Indian status, where they would face less discrimination, have greater legal protection from crimes against their persons, and perhaps even get the chance to own land. This renegotiation was possible because of the complex and paradoxical way that the definitions of race and social status were interwoven in California during the Mexican and American periods.

Sociologist Tomás Almaguer observes that white Americans living in California after the takeover by the United States drew racial distinctions among different classes of Mexicans based on perceived class and physical characteristics. The identification of a person as "white" was not simply a matter of skin color or ancestry, but of "the way European Americans came to define what they meant by race." Dark skin color mattered most for persons of the "uncivilized" Indian race.[90] Renegotiating one's identity, a carefully choreographed dance of race, property ownership, and legal rights that allowed some families to improve their standard of living and provide better opportunities for their children, also had the unintended consequence of creating an identity paradox for those Indians. The story of one Tongva woman, Victoria Reid, the wife of Scottish immigrant Hugo Reid and a landowner in her own right, illustrates the curious dilemma that this system sometimes created.

Race versus Perception: The Story of Victoria Reid

Although the United States officially commenced its first federal survey of California in 1850, census agent John R. Evertson did not actually begin work until January of the following year. On February 12, 1851, he arrived at Rancho Santa Anita, the home of Hugo and Victoria Reid.[91] During his brief visit to the rancho, Evertson recorded ten people living in the Reid household. Along with husband Hugo and wife Victoria were Felipe and Carlos, Victoria's Indian sons by her first marriage (two of Victoria's children, José Dolores and María Ygnacia, had died of smallpox the previous year); her daughter-in-law María (Felipe's wife); and five others, two of whom were likely Victoria's grandchildren (Felipe and María's children). The other three were probably servants.[92]

Surprisingly, when Evertson filled out his census register for the Reid family he did not list Victoria or any of her children as California Indians, despite the fact that they were full-blooded Tongva (Hugo and Victoria Reid did not have any children of their own). This was not an oversight, for Evertson clearly placed an "I" in the column of the census form to identify the Reids' three servants as Indians (shown in the record as "Refugio, Carota and Manuel").[93] And there is no reason to think

Vivian Morales Barthelemy and her brother Art Morales at Mission San Gabriel,
2006. TY MILFORD PHOTOGRAPHY

that Victoria Reid denied her Indian heritage. She was well known in the Los Angeles and San Gabriel communities and her family undoubtedly provided much of the information Reid included in his Tongva stories in the *Los Angeles Star* newspaper.[94] Only one conclusion remains: Evertson did not regard Victoria or her children as Indians. But how can that be?

The answer lies in the curious way that race was perceived in California during the Spanish, Mexican, and early American periods. Historian Lisbeth Haas notes that throughout the Spanish Americas, "a person's or family's racial status could be negotiated over the course of a person's lifetime, and the regional meaning of race identity...was far from constant." Census takers generally recorded their information based on an individual's word and physical appearance. Civilized people were considered *gente de razón* (literally "people of reason"), while uncivilized people were regarded as *indios* or *gente sin razón* ("people without reason"). "Whiteness was... not a singular or static category, but included a range of color," writes Haas.[95] Thus, *gente de razón* could include people of mixed blood, an important point since Spaniards had been intermarrying with Tongva since 1784, when Pueblo settler José Carlos Rosas took an Indian wife named María Dolores.[96]

Returning to Victoria Reid's story then, she was raised at the mission, spoke fluent Spanish, and held land in her own name, having received two grants of mission land from the Mexican government: the Rancho Huerta de Cuati ("Pear Orchard") and Rancho Santa Anita, both originally belonging to Mission San Gabriel. Prior to her 1837 marriage to Reid, she was married to a Tongva named Pablo María and bore him four children: Felipe, José Dolores, María Ygnacia de Jesús, and Carlos. She married Reid after Pablo María died from smallpox.[97] Had Victoria's Indian husband survived, and had he and Victoria been living with their children at the mission in 1851, census agent Evertson would probably have listed them as Indians. But because of Victoria's background, status, and marriage to Reid, Evertson perceived her as white, even though her blood and heritage were Tongva.

Stories passed down in Craig Torres's family show the pain this identity conflict could bring into some Indians' lives. One of Torres's ancestors is Prospero Elias Dominguez, a Tongva who held one of the few Indian-owned land grants near Mission San Gabriel.[98] "I had heard," says Torres, "that Prospero went out of his way to raise his children as white, that he didn't want them to identify with being Indian, because of...the stigma."[99] However, Prospero's youngest daughter, Candelaria, who was born shortly after her father died, must have participated in a traditional girl's puberty ceremony, because her face was tattooed with two lines of markings on her cheeks. "Just from what I know...she must have gone through some type of initiation ceremony, because that's when the girls would usually...get those markings," says Torres. Caught between two identities, Candelaria "would just never want to talk about who she was, or her heritage....They would ask about these markings that she had on her cheeks [and]...she would say that she was born like that."[100]

These complex and often contradictory attitudes toward race and social class continued into the twentieth century. "When we first moved into Arcadia, we had racial problems," says Vivian Barthelemy:

> People really looked down on us until they realized that maybe we were financially on an even keel with them. But now I find...somehow I'm getting the respect I never had because I am Gabrielino and from San Gabriel. All of a sudden I am from the land, I'm here, [now] they...[are] the immigrants.[101]

Prejudice and discrimination as well as housing segregation were once common. "People could only buy a house in certain areas," recalls Virginia Carmelo, "and in the area that I lived, there was only one elementary school. Everybody was brown. There were a few blacks, a couple Asians, and here and there, one or two whites."[102] Al Lassos remembered how "people would call me 'half-breed, you damn Indian.' I used to get a lot of fights over that. It was common knowledge, because [the] guys I grew up with were more Spanish."[103]

Art Morales had similar incidents during his childhood in San Gabriel. "I remember this kid telling me, 'My dad told me about how filthy you guys were. You would rub yourself with animal fat, and you stunk'....I had bouts all the way through high school because either I was a dirty Mexican, or a dirty Indian":

Morales family at Grandma Modesta's home at 501 E. El Monte, San Gabriel, ca. 1910. Presentación, the great-grandmother of Art, Vivian, and Anthony Morales, is seated in the center of the photo. Grandma Olgeria (Modesta) is seated at far right. The young boy in a white shirt is Arthur Morales, the father of Vivian Morales Barthelemy and Art Morales. COURTESY OF ART MORALES

There were white rich areas around us, and we were right here in our own little town. You couldn't move out. It wasn't going to happen. You weren't going to move into San Marino. Next to San Gabriel was the San Gabriel Village, and it was all white....[When] I grew up...you couldn't speak Spanish. The sisters would hit you with a ruler across the hand. Showing any ethnicity...was a big no-no....My first day in the fourth grade, I got in a fight before I even went into the classroom because a guy called me a dirty Indian, and I'll never forget that.[104]

"I went to school at Our Lady of Mount Carmel in Santa Ana," says Cindi Alvitre:

> *My first day in the fourth grade, I got in a fight before I even went into the classroom because a guy called me a dirty Indian.* — ART MORALES

Actually there's two Mexican Catholic schools...Our Lady of Guadalupe in Santa Ana, and Our Lady of Mount Carmel....The discipline was excessive...very abusive....They considered us Indians. There was my brother and another family, the Melendez family. We would get taunted and teased....We were called "Indios" at the school....That wasn't a time you acknowledged something like that [being an Indian], especially in the Mexican community. If you looked at the social caste and the whole social hierarchy, to be Indians...[was to be] at the lowest level.[105]

Nor is such prejudice confined to interactions with the white world. "I was very conscious of myself as an Indian person and see myself as that principally," says Michael Barthelemy. "[But] my dad didn't perceive...himself as an Indian, although he recognized his mother was an Indian":

I was at a meeting of the Native American Law Students Association...and I talked to this Pueblo fellow who is a member of their council—very dark features, black hair—could be full-blood, although a lot of the Lagunas are married in with Spanish. He asked me if I'm a native person. I've sort of got to the point where I'm over feeling slighted by that, because I recognize, looking at myself in the mirror, I don't look like a full-blood. I can see the Spanish inheritance, I can see the European inheritance. So it doesn't disturb me.[106]

For a young Tongva student, even a school field trip could raise questions about identity, questions hard for a child to answer. "In the fourth grade we went to the Southwest Museum and they said the Gabrielinos were extinct," Desirée Martinez recalls:

A lot of my friends didn't believe I was Gabrielino, because they would look at the dioramas and see that they were living in traditional housing and half naked....[They'd say,] "Well, you're one of us. You live in a house, you wear clothes, so you can't be Indian."[107]

The Tongva Community after the Mission

The Tongva's cultural identity has always been rooted in their community, though the nature and character of that community have changed profoundly. When the Mexican government dissolved the missions and distributed their vast land holdings, most of the land went to non-Indians. However, some was granted to neophytes who had connections to local Mexican officials, or who had a strong record of service to the missions. [108] In discussing the land grant allotted to his own family, Anthony Morales explains, "When the missions were told by the Mexican government they had to allot some of the land back to the local Indian people, not everybody got land. We were pretty fortunate—I'm thinking [it was] because of our involvement [in the mission]."[109]

Despite the legal, economic, and social discrimination they faced under American law, the Tongva remained a small but active community centered on San Gabriel. The federal census of 1850 lists 116 California Indians living in or near the mission, and although it does not give their tribal affiliations, it is likely that most were of Tongva descent. Extended families seem to have occupied the old Indian quarters at the mission, since the census shows most of them residing in only two buildings. Thirty-three of these Indians were children under fifteen years of age, while fifty were between the ages of fifteen and forty-nine, and another thirty-three were fifty years or older. Thirty-eight of the men (representing approximately one-third of the population) were laborers, including twelve of the men over age fifty.[110]

Morales family, ca. 1890s. Modesta Morales (grandmother of Vivian Barthelemy Morales and Art and Anthony Morales) and her sister are seated on the left. Modesta's grandfather is seated second to the right. COURTESY OF ART MORALES

Joaquín Romero was the overseer of the mission community. He himself may have been Tongva, for although the 1850 census does not list him as a California Indian, he is so identified in the 1860 census.[111] Some of the Indians shown in the 1850 census were property owners of substance. Romero owned real estate valued at $300, while Samuel, a laborer with $250 of real estate, may be the Tongva that historian W. W. Robinson identified as the owner of a tract of land near Mission San Fernando that "he planted with oranges, pears, and pomegrantes." Another Indian, named Roman, a farmer who owned $1,000 of real estate, may be one of the three grantees of the four-thousand-acre Rancho El Encino. Urbano Chari, a farmer with $500 of real estate, may be one of the three grantees of Rancho El Escorpión in the San Fernando Valley.[112]

By the time the 1860 census was taken there were fewer Indians living at San Gabriel and their households were more dispersed. There were also more non-Indians and Mexican Indians mixed into the community. The census recorded seventy-nine California Indians living in twenty-nine different households at San Gabriel. Twenty-two of them are under fifteen years of age, while another forty-two are between the ages of fifteen and forty-nine, and fifteen are fifty years of age or older. Some familiar names from the 1850 census reappear, such as Joaquín Romero and Urbano Chari (misspelled in the 1860 census as "Jorbon Charis"). By 1860, Chari's personal estate has grown to $1,000. Other California Indians with substantial amounts of personal property include Juan Mavis with $1,000 of real estate and $900 of personal property, Jacinto with $300 of personal property, and Baltazar with $1,000 of personal property.[113]

Changes in how the census was recorded in 1870 and the following decades make the records more difficult to interpret.[114] But family histories tell of a strong, continuing Tongva community in San Gabriel. Fred "Sparky" Morales recalls how his family and others lived on the small farms and ranchos scattered around the town in the early twentieth century, a lifestyle rooted in the post-mission community:

> They used to hunt rabbits, cottontails. They used to make a living skinning rabbits....My uncle used to go out into the prairie land and the rabbits would come out after a rain. My uncle used to use greyhounds to catch rabbits....
>
> A lot of corn was planted by the Indians and they used to grind the corn and make corn tortillas. They had a lot of oranges then and they had grapes. A lot of vineyards were here. They used to grow other vegetables. They had ranches around the mission also....
>
> This was cattle country but a lot of it changed into agricultural land. We grew everything on the outskirts of San Gabriel. Corn, potatoes, watermelons were grown here and we picked a lot of watermelons about a mile from the mission. My dad had a little ranch on Rosemead. We used to plant a lot of different crops. We used to grow corn, chiles, tomatoes. We grew our own food and my dad used to sell what we had left over in the old L.A. produce market. We used to have a horse and buggy and used to haul our crops to market via horse and buggy....The people that owned the land around the mission leased it for hardly anything just to keep the land clean. There was nothing but prairie land just a mile from here. So a lot of Indians got this land.[115]

As a child, Bea Alva's mother knew a San Gabriel that was dotted with small Indian settlements. As Alva recalls:

> She used to say that they had little villages throughout the town called rancherías. When they would go to their little fiestas, or get-togethers... they'd have firecrackers. There were so many Chinese people here at the time. But the men would get on top of the roofs and throw down pieces of yardage. Not clothing, but just pieces. They were in all colors and it was real pretty. They were thrown down like you throw the balloons or like confetti. But these were big pieces that you could sew on....
>
> We have a wash between Alhambra and San Gabriel....The Indians seemed to live up on the little knolls and these knolls would slope down into the wash. This was after the missionaries because they talked of oranges and other fruits. These oranges would fall when the flood season came and flow into this wash. And they would get buried in the sand and debris that came with the floods. The waters would roll away or subside and the Indians would walk down the wash bed and get all of this fruit that was embedded in the sand. And so you had a kind of refrigeration deal going there. And they would pick up fruits like that.[116]

My aunt was an Indian and she used to use a lot of herbs and other plants....All of the herbs and plants that she used grew wild.

—FRED "SPARKY" MORALES

Herbalists still practiced their craft well into the twentieth century. Fred Morales remembers:

> My aunt was an Indian and she used to use a lot of herbs and other plants. They used to make a lot of medicines from plants. They would pick them or dig them and dry them and store them in bags that they hang from the ceilings. All of the herbs and plants that she used grew wild.[117]

Cindi Alvitre's grandfather "would take off into the Santa Ana Mountains for days at a time, sometimes a week, sometimes longer, usually with my great-uncle Vidal, his brother," she says. "He would go gather herbs, medicine, bring them back, and dry them out." [118]

TONGVA WHO DID NOT RECEIVE LAND AFTER SAN GABRIEL MISSION WAS secularized in 1834 either sought work at the Pueblo of Los Angeles or on the ranchos, or left the area. Hugo Reid wrote in 1852 that almost all the Tongva went north to Monterey, although "a few are still to be found at San Fernando, San Gabriel and the Angeles."[119] One factor that contributed to this exodus was the limited availability of land around San Gabriel. Historian Father Zephyrin Engelhardt reported that 1320 neophytes lived at the mission in 1832, just two years before it was secularized and turned over to civilian administrators.[120] It may have been impossible to provide suitable grants to such a large number of neophytes when non-Indian settlers were also vying for the same land.

The migration out of San Gabriel continued throughout the late 1800s. Craig Torres recalls that his family moved to the Chapman Ranch after they lost their land grant in San Gabriel during the 1860s. "It was a ranch that was established by Alfred B. Chapman...in the late 1800s, in East Pasadena, and it was right next to the Sunnyslope Ranch," says Torres. "They became attached to that ranch for a long time, up until the 1920s, when I believe that it kind of broke up."[121] Says Virginia Carmelo, "When my great-grandparents left the mission....they headed out towards what was the Riverside area....That would have been 1880 or so, 1887.... They went out there to live and just stayed."[122] Cindi Alvitre explains, "My father was born [in] 1926. My grandmother was born—I don't remember the exact year, 1880, my grandfather was 1870....There was still a lot of open land":[123]

> My father was born in a little house [at] Euclid [Avenue] and Westminster [Boulevard]. There is what they call...[a] "colonia" there, a little community. My father was born in a little adobe house, and my grandfather had a little...shack in the back. I don't know what my grandfather did for a living....He spent a lot of time with herbs. He used to go out for weeks at a time up into the mountains with his burlap sack, and all his stuff to collect. He would come back and people would come see him....He just had a particular knowledge of herbs, and he lived very much off the land....[My] father was raised off the land, the Santa Ana River. During winter when the geese would come over, they would shoot the geese.[124]

Tongva traveled wherever their work took them. "My grandfather used to work on cattle ranches," says Fred Morales. "They worked out in the hills. A lot of vaqueros went to Bakersfield and used to ride the range up there. They used to pay them but they got low wages. Forty dollars a month or something like that."[125] Women played an even stronger role in families where men's work took them away from home for long stretches of time. "My aunts, my grandmothers—I remember them being very quiet," says Art Morales. "They always had words of wisdom. But as the years have gone on, I've seen that they were actually very strong women. It's just that the role that they took...[it] was not one of being outspoken."[126]

Changing Realities, Changing Identities

The Tongva's political identity after the missions was determined largely by their legal status and economic opportunities. On the ranchos, all authority lay in the hands of the owner, the ranchero, and his mayordomo (overseer). Wealth and social position were based on land ownership, and under this system the Indians were accepted as laborers at the lowest level of Mexican society. They received most (though not necessarily all) the benefits of Mexican citizenship; they had protection under the law (including some protection of their land and property rights) and they could intermarry with other Mexicans. However, since most Indians did not own land, they were vulnerable to economic exploitation.[127] The rancheros used persuasion, economic pressure, and even physical violence and abuse to control them. The French traveler Duflot de Mofras observed this in the Pueblo of Los Angeles during the 1840s. He wrote, "All labor in El Pueblo is done by Indians recruited from a small ranchería on the banks of the river....These poor wretches are often mistreated, and do not always receive in full their daily pay."[128]

Political realities shifted again after the United States took over California. The Treaty of Guadalupe Hidalgo that concluded America's war with Mexico stipulated that the United States would honor Mexican land rights (with certain restrictions) and extend American citizenship to Mexican citizens living in California at the time the treaty was signed. However, the new government did not acknowledge the Indians' legal ownership of land, nor did it extend American citizenship to them, even to those Indians who had enjoyed citizen status under Mexican law. And although California was admitted to the Union as a free state, it quickly legalized indentured servitude for Indians as a way to ensure a cheap labor supply.[129]

In 1850 the state legislature passed "An Act for the Government and Protection of the Indians" that made it illegal for able-bodied Indians to "be found loitering and strolling about, or frequenting public places where liquors are sold, begging, or leading an immoral or profligate course of life." Under this new legal system, any person could arrest an offending Indian and take him before a justice of the peace and have him convicted (conversely, the law *prohibited* Indians from testifying in a court of law against white persons). That person could then post bail and have the Indian bound over to him for a period of work service not to exceed four months. When the Los Angeles town council passed a similar ordinance in August 1850 it became common practice to arrest Indians for drunkenness on Sunday nights and auction them to local landowners the following morning.[130] The writer and historian Horace Bell described the scene in Los Angeles in 1852:

> About sundown the pompous marshall, with his Indian special deputies... would drive and drag...[the Indians] to a big corral in the rear of Downey Block...and in the morning they would be exposed for sale, as slaves for the week. Los Angeles had its slave mart, as well as New Orleans and Constantinople—only the slave at Los Angeles was sold fifty-two times a year as long as he lived, which did not generally exceed one, two or three years....They would be sold for a week, and bought up by the vineyard men.[131]

Army Captain Edward O. C. Ord, who was in California in 1856, offered his own assessment of the situation:

> Indians out here...are by state laws held in bondage by the owners of large

estates, as the slaves are in the south—excepting that the slave, being a sale-able chattel [chattel], always producing something, it is to the interest of the owner to keep him in good health and working order....But the Indian here...is only saleable...for debts due, which he must work out, and when the purchaser or owner has no more work for him, he ceases to credit him, drives him off, & he may die.[132]

Under American law Indians were also denied the right to vote or own real estate (except for a few whose grants were confirmed to them by a federal land commission). As a result, Indians could easily be dispossessed of their land. Crimes by whites against Indians increased—crimes like rape, kidnapping, and murder—since these offenses could only be prosecuted if a white person testified in court against the criminals.[133] According to one estimate, one hundred thousand California Indians perished in the decade from 1845 to 1855, the period when the United States took control of California; they were victims of starvation, disease, and physical violence. The state made little effort to stem this ethnic cleansing; in fact, it abetted the killing by reimbursing some paramilitary groups that carried out attacks on Indians.[134] "This is why we Native Americans here in California had to keep a low profile, had to assimilate with other ethnic groups," says Anthony Morales, "because of the injustices imposed upon us. We were wanted people—they wanted to exterminate us. They wanted us gone."[135] The physical danger Indians faced at this time is illustrated by a news story reported in the *San Diego Herald* in December 1856. According to the *Herald*, an Indian was stoned to death by a group of "thrill-seeking" and intoxicated Mexican Americans "till he quietly laid down and died." The *Herald* warned that if "our magistrates don't trouble themselves about such little matters, the play will be repeated."[136]

After the missions, Tongva leadership rested once more with the heads of families and lineages. A few of these were religious leaders; Hugo Reid wrote in 1852 that there were only four Tongva chiefs in San Gabriel, all of them young, and they were primarily responsible for scheduling religious ceremonies.[137] There were also secular leaders who played the role of middlemen or labor bosses, negotiating with white landowners on behalf of their own Indian communities. Some of these leaders may have been landowners themselves; others probably had long associations with local ranchers. Captain Edward Ord saw an example of this firsthand when he visited Rancho del Chino in 1856. The American ranch owner, Isaac Williams, gave Ord:

> an interesting exhibition of how the Indians of this county are managed, he having the principal chief of the nearest band as his head cattle driver, some dozen or two as work hands or vaqueros. This Indian chief waited at the door after sunset with his hat in his hand to report the state of the cattle drive to a distance, for, from little rain, the grazing this year is very thin on the estate.[138]

These secular leaders enabled the Tongva community to survive in a society that regarded Indians as little more than a source of cheap labor. But as the ranchos declined in the 1860s (due to drought and falling cattle prices) the economy of southern California shifted to farming, citrus production, and sheep ranching.[139] These and other changes continued throughout the end of the nineteenth century and into the twentieth as Los Angeles grew into a modern industrial center, and the Tongva faced new challenges as a landless urban tribe.

U.S. Citizenship and the Mission Indian Federation

During the early 1900s the Tongva became more politically active as they carved out their own place in American society. Vivian Barthelemy's grandfather David Morales acted as a representative of the San Gabriel Indian community in its dealings with the town government. "I can't remember anyone ever trying to improve things for the Indians as my grandfather did. I don't remember anyone that strong, to come out and speak for them," she says. Her father, Arthur Theodore Morales, also worked with the local government:

Morales family, ca. 1915. David Morales (grandfather of Vivian Morales Barthelemy and Art Morales) is holding Fred "Sparky" Morales (Anthony Morales's father). On the left are Arthur Morales (Art and Vivian's father) and David Morales (uncle to Vivian, Art, and Anthony). COURTESY OF ART MORALES

> He did go to [San Gabriel town] council meetings, [and] they [the residents in San Gabriel] always looked to him [to tell them] "Who do we vote for that would help us, help the old town of San Gabriel, who would put in streets and help with the water system?"...[That was in] the thirties.[140]

In 1924 the United States government granted citizenship to all American Indians, in part out of recognition and gratitude for their service in the First World War, and in part to further the government's goal of assimilating them into the general population.[141] As a landless urban tribe, the Tongva well understood the importance of citizenship. Vivian Barthelemy recalls how her grandfather David worked to get Indians the vote. "Oh, he couldn't get to vote, and he fought for

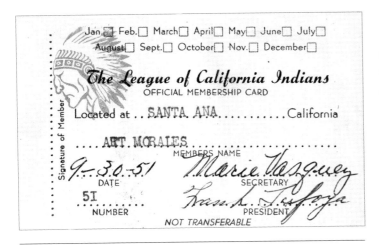

Jan.☒ Feb.☐ March☐ April☐ May☐ June☐ July☐
August☐ Sept.☐ October☐ Nov.☐ December☐

The League of California Indians
OFFICIAL MEMBERSHIP CARD

Located at .. SANTA ANA .... California

.... ART. MORALES ....
MEMBERS NAME

Signature of Member

9—30-51
DATE

51
NUMBER

Marie Vasquez
SECRETARY

PRESIDENT

NOT TRANSFERABLE

Arthur Morales's membership card for the League of California Indians, a pan-Indian organization, Sept. 30, 1951. Courtesy of Art Morales

it," she says. "That's how come my dad went into doing city work...he'd go to the council meeting...because my grandfather really fought for the vote."[142] Art Morales, David's grandson, says, "I get after my kids if they won't vote. I say, 'After all, your grandfather fought for the vote.'"[143]

It was around this period that other California Indians also began organizing politically. Since the early 1890s, Indians living on reservations in southern California had been unhappy with the Bureau of Indian Affairs and its land management policies. They particularly objected to BIA reservation boundary surveys that gave Indian land to white settlers, as well as the BIA's policy of allotting reservation lands to Indians without first considering which families were actually using those lands, or taking into account any improvements they had made on them. By 1919 this opposition led to the formation of the Mission Indian Federation.[144]

Although the Tongva were an urban tribe without a reservation of their own, they followed these political developments closely. Cindi Alvitre notes there were "interactions between all these people from San Gabriel, like with the Sandoval family, Chris Sandoval and his mom. She's the one that I think was holding the meetings in Santa Ana...[for] the Mission Indian Federation."[145] Some Tongva became members of the federation. "My dad was part of that," Art Morales says proudly. "In fact, I have his membership card at home."[146] Art's cousin Anthony Morales learned from one of his elders, Ruby Jimenez, that family members attended meetings of the Mission Indian Federation:

> She and Grandma Modesta used to go to the meetings in Santa Ana. That was back during [the] Indian Federation...she gave me a date, the 1920s, and said she was just a little girl. She was about five, six years old, and the grandmother, who was a full-blood Gabrielino from San Gabriel, would travel to Santa Ana for quarterly meetings.[147]

The Mission Indian Federation made its political clout felt in 1927 when the California State Legislature passed the California Indians Jurisdictional Act. That act authorized the state's attorney general to sue the United States government on behalf of the Mission Indians over the eighteen treaties negotiated by federal commissioners in 1851 and 1852 but never ratified by the United States Senate. Claims were filed in 1928, and sixteen years later, in December 1944, the U.S. Court of Claims awarded the Indians of California $17.5 million in compensation for the lands surrendered in the unratified treaties. (Congress subsequently reduced this award to recover money the government had spent on the Indians during the intervening years.) In 1950, a sum of $150 each was awarded to thirty-six thousand qualified Indians. Additional claims were filed in 1946 to cover lands not included in the initial award and an out-of-court settlement (known as Docket 80) was reached in 1964. Eight years later, in 1972, the government distributed the awards to seventy thousand California Indians.[148] Angie Behrns remembers, "We got $664, our share for the California Judgment Fund."[149]

The Mission Indian Federation and the California Indians Jurisdictional Act marked important milestones for the Tongva and other California Indians. The Indians Jurisdictional Act acknowledged individual Tongva as part of the Mission Indians. However, neither the Tongva nor the neighboring Juaneño were recognized as separate tribes,[150] despite the fact that Indians were required to enroll on the California Indian Rolls and state a tribal affiliation to participate in the settlement. This led many Tongva to delve more deeply into their family backgrounds and cultural heritage. Bea Alva recalled in 1980 that:

> Somewhere in the background we used to say that we knew that there was some Indian blood but it was never really brought out until around the early 1930s. Someone came out from Los Angeles and was looking up all the people that had Indian ancestors here because the government was going to give us some money because of the Indian rolls.[151]

Virginia Carmelo remembers that her great-grandmother "identified both her parents being born at San Gabriel Mission....There's a question on...[the enrollment form] that says, 'What lands do you claim as your traditional land?' [and she answered] all the city of Los Angeles."[152] Some families also had their genealogies prepared using information from public records and the mission registers of San Gabriel and San Fernando. San Gabriel City Historian Thomas W. Temple compiled many of these family trees. Stacy Thompson recalls, "As long as I can remember, about once a month my grandfather would get out all of the letters, and genealogy, and paperwork that had been done by Tommy Temple, read it all to me, and interpret it."[153] Cindi Alvitre says that Temple prepared her family genealogy as well. "He did the lineages," she says, "with the Alvitres too, we have those. If you look at everybody's genealogy, it's the same handwriting, it's

In his certifications, Thomas Workman Temple II states that Charles T. Thompson (Stacy Thompson's ancestor) is a direct lineal descendant of María Antonia Perez, a Gabrielino Mission Indian, based on the Mission records, the 1850 census of the City and County of Los Angeles, and the 1860 census of El Monte Township. April 16, 1951.
COURTESY OF STACY THOMPSON

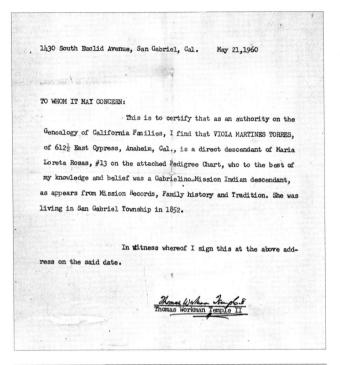

1430 South Euclid Avenue, San Gabriel, Cal.   May 21, 1960

TO WHOM IT MAY CONCERN:

This is to certify that as an authority on the Genealogy of California Families, I find that VIOLA MARTINES TORRES, of 612½ East Cypress, Anaheim, Cal., is a direct descendant of Maria Loreta Rosas, #13 on the attached Pedigree Chart, who to the best of my knowledge and belief was a Gabrielino Mission Indian descendant, as appears from Mission Records, Family history and Tradition. She was living in San Gabriel Township in 1852.

In witness whereof I sign this at the above address on the said date.

Thomas Workman Temple II

Prepared by Thomas Workman Temple II of San Gabriel, who researched the genealogies of many Tongva families, this document certifies the Gabrielino-Tongva ancestry of Viola Martinez Torres (mother of Craig Torres). She is a direct descendant of Loreta Rosas, a Gabrielino Mission Indian descendant appearing in the Mission records. May 21, 1960. COURTESY OF CRAIG TORRES

Viola Torres (mother of Craig Torres) is standing with members of her family at "Brownie Beach" in Newport. n.d. COURTESY OF CRAIG TORRES

the same ink, everything is the same. Everybody's is."[154] Craig Torres explains:

> There were a lot of Indian families that were having their genealogies done by Tommy Temple from San Gabriel. And the one line that he established for us was through the Rosas' side...the original settlers of Los Angeles....[This] particular soldier or settler had actually married a woman from [the village of] Yaanga.[155]

But not all Tongva were enrolled. Some, like members of Desirée Martinez's family, were left out due to bureaucratic errors. All of her family was enrolled "except my grandmother's oldest brother because they sent it to the wrong address."[156] Others, wary of past dealings with the government, resisted enrollment. Speaking of her own family, Cindi Alvitre says, "They wanted nothing to do with the money....My father said, 'We don't want any damn money. We want land, the land is what's valuable, not the money.'"[157] Earl Campio faced similar resistance in his family. "I traced our family history by going to the mission," says Earl Campio:

[I] finally decided, "Okay, Dad, we're Indians, you're telling me the real truth. I'm getting on that roll."...And he [his father] said, "I don't want nothing from the government. They already took the land that we had there [at Prado]. If you're going to do it, you have to do it yourself." He said, "This is what I can tell you—what's been handed to me. Your [great-] grandmother was Mission Santa Barbara and your [great-] grandfather was from San Bernardino Indians. They were married in San Gabriel initially, and there you can probably find the records."...He wouldn't go with me. My mom went and we talked to a priest. He said, "What background—what can we look for?"....We started looking page after page, and boom, there it was....My great-grandmother and father were married Indian tradition, with the thumbprint and X.[158]

Sherman Indian School

Indian children were barred from attending the public school system in California for most of the years between 1860 and 1921; only in 1935 were all restrictions on Indians attending public schools finally removed. By 1909, however, the Bureau of Indian Affairs was operating four boarding schools and eighteen day schools in California. It also ran a vocational training school, the Sherman Institute, to give Indians the skills to seek employment. The Sherman Institute opened in Riverside in 1902 and was the successor to the Perris Indian School, a manual arts training school established largely through the efforts of Horatio Rust, the Indian agent from 1889 to 1893 for the Mission–Tule River Consolidated Agency.[159] Four Tongva were listed on the Perris Indian School roster for 1892-93: Lucretia Johnson, Albert Bildurain, Andreas Bildurain, and Arthur Romero.[160]

Desirée Martinez's grandmother and four of her grandmother's siblings attended the Sherman Institute. They were admitted to the school with the aid of a family friend, a woman who helped run the dormitory there. "They went in 1926 to Sherman," says Desirée:

[Because] it was really difficult to feed the family, there were seven kids....The boys learned carpentry. The girls learned home domestics—my aunt's a good cook....She always says she learned to do all that at Sherman....They had the "outing system," where she would go and work for a white family as a domestic, the maid, and things like that....When I talked to her, it was all positive—"I got a good education, three square meals. While I was sick they took me to the infirmary."...But her children and grandchildren remember her talking about how she got beat. She had a little doll and they stole it from her. They told her, "You can't be a baby."[161]

Manuel Antonio Perez (Stacy Thompson's ancestor) with two unidentified women, ca. 1860s. A genealogy report prepared by Thomas Workman Temple II in 1951 and filed with the Bureau of Indian Affairs certifies that Manuel Antonio Perez was a Gabrielino Mission Indian, based on the Mission records, the 1850 census of the City and County of Los Angeles, and the 1860 census of El Monte Township.
COURTESY OF STACY THOMPSON

On the left: María Giacomini Thompson Flores (descendant of Manuel Antonio Perez) with her husband, Harry Thompson, n.d. COURTESY OF STACY THOMPSON

Maria Giacomini Thompson Flores (ancestor of Stacy Thompson and descendant of Manuel Antonio Perez, a San Gabriel Mission Indian) is sitting "In the Patio at 'Ramona's Marriage Place,' San Diego," May 23, 1913.

Identity Redefined

In the early 1900s, San Gabriel and other towns with ties to the missions began drawing upon their Spanish heritage to attract tourists, increase land sales, and build up their local economies. Author and social critic Carey McWilliams wrote that "Southern California has created its own past." It was a past brought to life by "innumerable pageants, fiestas, and outdoor enactments of one kind or another; by the restoration of the Missions; and by the establishment of such curious spectacles as Olvera Street in the Old Plaza section of Los Angeles."[162]

One of those pageants was the Mission Play, a three-act performance that gave a fictitious and romanticized rendition of the California missions from the time of their founding by Father Junípero Serra until 1847. The Mission Play was first performed in San Gabriel around 1918 and was held in the Mission Playhouse, described by Henry Van Dyke in *The Century Magazine*:

> The first thing was an ambulatory surrounding the playhouse, containing models of all the missions in the order of their founding, set in a mimic landscape of green hill and dale....The next thing was the playhouse itself....It was not like a theater at all. It seemed as if some old monastic refectory, with its dark beams and high rafters, had been enlarged and fitted with benches for a thousand or fifteen hundred people.[163]

Despite its historical shortcomings, the Mission Play and other popular presentations contributed to the Tongva's growing awareness of their culture and history. Bea Alva had a role in the play:

> I played the part of an Indian girl....I just tried out for the play and I got the part of Juanita. The Mission Play was done here, right here in town. Many townspeople that lived here all of their lives were in it. It was something like the Hemet play. It stopped in 1932 and then they tried to revive it but it didn't work.[164]

Photo on Left: Joseph Morales (left) and his brother Arthur (father of Vivian Morales Barthelemy and Art Morales) in their dance costumes at the Santa Barbara Mission Festival, ca. 1935. Early on, they began to relearn their lost dances and traditions from neighboring tribes, including the Chumash. Photo on Right: Vivian Morales Barthelemy posing in her dance costume at the San Gabriel Mission Fiesta, ca. 1935. COURTESY OF VIVIAN MORALES BARTHELEMY

It was during this period that the Tongva organized their first dance group in modern times. Art Morales recalled how they turned to other tribes for help in learning the dances. "My uncle Joe said they learned [to dance] from other tribes," says Art. "That was back in the thirties....They were actually the first [modern] dancers of our tribe."[165]

For some, like Vivian Barthelemy, San Gabriel in the early decades of the twentieth century seemed to be a place free of most racial and ethnic tensions. She performed in the Mission Play and as a Spanish dancer in the fiestas and remembers that "people treated me differently, like I was privileged. I wasn't really, but they treated me like I was." For her, San Gabriel was "like a little village," the population "all a mix. We had as many Anglo as we did Indian, Mexican, or Spanish, [or] Japanese....An Arab had a little grocery store, a Jewish man had a grocery store, and a Greek. A couple of men had Mexican grocery stores."[166]

But racial tension and prejudice increased after World War II with a new wave of American immigration to southern California, much as it had eighty years earlier, following the close of the Civil War. "You had all these people come in after the war, and then all the tracts of homes went up, like North San Gabriel, and...the

Santa Barbara Pageant, ca. 1935. Arthur Morales (father of Vivian Morales Barthelemy and Art Morales) is back row center. Joseph Morales (Arthur's brother) is front row right. COURTESY OF VIVIAN MORALES BARTHELEMY

Mission Players at Mission San Gabriel, ca. 1936. On the left is Petra Morales. Her children Art and Vivian are standing next to her. COURTESY OF ART MORALES

Village and it really changed because a whole group of people from other states came," Vivian says:

> It reversed the whole thing....There was more prejudice, and more separa-
> tion. They didn't understand that we were a community of Indian, Spanish,
> [and] Mexican people, [with] a few Anglo. It was a community of all these
> different people, [who] really got along a lot better than...after the war.[167]

Ironically, this prejudice seemed to heighten the Tongva's awareness of their own unique culture and history, helping weave the many strands of their identity into whole cloth once again. Bea Alva:

> One day I was at our local parade; we had a parade every year on Labor Day.
> And I heard this master of ceremonies say that the Indians were extinct
> here. The Gabrielino Indians were extinct. When I heard him say that, I
> thought that we would have to do something about it. So we decided that
> year to put in children and adults of Indian ancestry that wanted to take
> part in the parade. We wanted to show ourselves in the parade to say that
> we were here. So we made a float.[168]

Using San Gabriel as a base, Bea Alva, Fred "Sparky" Morales, and others began organizing and reaching out to other groups. Fred Morales "started to communicate with...other tribes [who lived] outside of the San Gabriel area. That started with Santa Monica, I think," says Vivian Barthelemy, Fred's niece.[169] His great-nephew Michael Barthelemy recalls that Sparky "had that classic Gabrielino look....He really took the Indian affairs to heart, and because of that, he was recognized."[170] Art Morales says:

> That was...in the early seventies, might have started in the late sixties. He communicated with tribes from all over. Besides being a leader, he was a great ambassador. Tribes and elders from all the surrounding tribes knew of him, or knew him, recognized him, and they respected him...quite a bit.[171]

This renewed confidence led to the legal formation of the Gabrieleno/Tongva Tribal Council.[172] Other political organizations have followed in subsequent years as political differences emerged among members over difficult issues such as federal recognition, rules of membership, and Indian casinos (these topics are discussed further in the third essay in this volume). A variety of cultural and education groups have also been formed. These organizations, and others like them, will continue shaping the political and cultural future of the Tongva tribe, all the while keeping it connected to its unique history and culture.

Cindi Alvitre singing and dancing in the Jacaranda Walk. Rancho Los Alamitos, 2006. TY MILFORD PHOTOGRAPHY

Continuity within change; diversity within a shared identity. These principles have guided the Tongva throughout their long and often difficult history. "I see the culture developing more and being shared," says Virginia Carmelo, "and...young people...taking back their roots and their identity."[173] Even as they honor their traditions, and the ancestors who came before them, the Tongva look ahead to a future filled with new opportunities and possibilities.

They will never turn back.

A CONVERSATION with Vivian Morales Barthelemy, Arthur Morales, Kimberly Morales Johnson (daughter of Art Morales), and Patty Barthelemy Roess (daughter of Vivian Morales Barthelemy)

January 31, 2006
Arcadia, California

The Participants

VIVIAN MORALES BARTHELEMY IS NOW A RESPECTED ELDER IN THE Gabrieleno-Tongva Tribal Council of San Gabriel, but at the tender age of four, she was already known for her dancing at the San Gabriel Mission Fiesta and other fiestas in the region. In the early twentieth century, cities and towns associated with the Spanish missions celebrated their heritage by presenting mission festivals, parades, and pageants. Vivian continued to dance until she was twenty, and thereafter remained an active supporter of the festivals. (For information about the mission festivals refer to the essay "Continuity within Change: Identity and Culture.") Over the years, she has organized reunions of the San Gabriel Mission community and worked with the San Gabriel Historical Society, and she helps communicate news and information throughout the San Gabriel community.

Art Morales, brother of Vivian, has followed in the footsteps of the generations of leaders found in the Morales family. From the early 1950s on, he was a member of the League of California Indians, a California Indian advocacy group, and he was elected tribal chair of the Gabrieleno-Tongva San Gabriel Band of Mission Indians by the elders in the late 1970s. During his tenure, the tribe began to monitor and oversee the process for native reburials in the area. Along with others in his community, he has worked toward federal recognition, and he continues as an advisor. Most recently, Art and his daughter Kimberly Morales Johnson represented the Gabrieleno Tongva Tribal Council of San Gabriel at the 2004 opening of the National Museum of the American Indian at the Smithsonian Institution, in Washington, DC.

The Discussion

Members of the Gabrieleno Tongva Tribe of Mission Indians of Mission San Gabriel, Vivian Morales Barthelemy and Art Morales speak to their family's long-standing leadership on behalf of the native and civic community of San Gabriel and the mission. The conversation explores native voting rights, the Mission Indian Federation, and the family's efforts to preserve traditional dancing in the early twentieth century, including Vivian's acclaimed role as a child dancer at the mission festivals. Related comments reflect the changing San Gabriel Mission community, native identity, the sense of "Indianness," and discrimination in the mid-twentieth century, as well as views on achieving federal recognition.

Vivian Morales Barthelemy standing outside Mission San Gabriel, 2006.
Ty Milford Photography

Claudia Jurmain: Would you please state your name?

Vivian Morales Barthelemy: Vivian Morales Barthelemy.

CJ: In your family did you call yourself Gabrielino—or do you call yourself Tongva?

VMB: We never knew that word until just recently.

Bill McCawley: Did your parents talk about being Gabrielino?

VMB: Oh, yes. Oh, yes.

BMc: So it was always known to you—

VMB: Yes, because they're all buried at the San Gabriel Mission. They're still there. The monuments are still there and some of our records.

Art Morales: I believe my great-great-great-grand-mother, or our great-great-great-grandmother is interred there, and her headstone [is still] there. My father had been the caretaker at the mission when I was probably six, seven years old. She had a metal wrought iron gating around her burial site. The fathers at the church had removed it, and then placed it on the burial of a priest in the inner courtyard.

CJ: Had stories of your family traveled through time? Did you hear stories about your family?

VMB: Oh, yes, my father was into it. He always talked about it, but nobody ever wrote anything.

CJ: Has your family always lived right around the mission?

VMB: Yes. Actually, when they [father/mother] were first married, they lived at the end of San Gabriel Boulevard and Rosemead. That was all oil land. They could hear the noises coming up. Somehow the story got around they had ghosts, or whatever, so my grandparents sold the land [to a woman who knew that there was oil on the property, but didn't say anything. They moved into the San Gabriel area now closer to the mission.] Later they found out the oil was making the noise, so my parents somehow missed the boat.

Art Morales at Mission San Gabriel, 2006. Art is Vivian Morales Barthelemy's brother. Ty Milford Photography

AM: My uncle Joe, who was the youngest, passed away recently. He had stories my grandmother shared with him about guys on horses, with the hoods, [who] would come down and try to chase them out. They were trying to scare them off the property. They were probably defrauded from the property, different types of harassment—trying to chase them out. It had to be in the 1800s, late 1800s. I'm sixty-two.

VMB: I am seventy-six.

CJ: Did your father live at the mission when he was a caretaker there?

VMB: I don't think so. It seemed to me they always had the house they lived in. I don't ever remember them living there.

The young Mission Fiesta dancer on the right is Vivian Morales Barthelemy, ca. 1935.
COURTESY OF VIVIAN MORALES BARTHELEMY

AM: It was within walking distance of the mission. When I was a young boy, one of the things that always stood out in my mind, all the ladies [were] going to church early in the morning [with] their heads covered. They all went to church every day, every morning.

VMB: Once they opened the school, the kids all went there. I can remember my mother saying that even non-Catholics went because they only had Washington School in San Gabriel, and they had the mission. So if you lived within the area, it didn't matter if you were Catholic or not, you went to the school.

CJ: Your family practiced Catholicism. Did you also retain any memories, or any practices reflecting traditional practices of the Gabrielino people?

VMB: No, actually it [the memories, practices] combined with the Mexican people that lived there. You always have tamales at Christmas. Even my Indian grandmother made tamales, and my aunt always made tamales. They made them the old-fashioned way, grinding the chili. I can remember her fixing rabbit a lot, and it was very, very good. I've never had rabbit like hers before. It was an old, old recipe. The Mexican, the Spanish, and the Indian all combined in that small area.

Kimberly Morales Johnson: The Mission Fiesta was always something. Do you remember the first one? Because I know you danced.

VMB: Yes, I got pictures of my family at the fiesta. It was really a great fiesta—horses and Monte Montana and Leo Carrillo coming right through San Gabriel.* I was three.

---

* Both Monte Montana and Leo Carrillo were grand marshals in the Mission Fiesta parade, and Vivian recalls having her picture taken with them. Monte Montana (1910–1998) was an actor who appeared in several John Wayne movies, and a well-known rodeo circuit rider and entertainer. Descended from a distinguished Californio family, Leo Carrillo was an actor, preservationist, and conservationist who served on the California Beach and Parks Commission for eighteen years. But for many still, he is perhaps best known for playing the role of Pancho in *The Cisco Kid.*

CJ: Was there anything about those fiestas that stands out as being Gabrielino as opposed to Mexican?

VMB: Well, everybody knew each other, but it was a combined effort.

AM: In the days of the fiesta you would travel to Santa Barbara.

VMB: Oh, yes. San Fernando—they all had fiestas and everybody went to each other's fiestas. We were very close with the Santa Barbara people involved in the fiestas. They were also a combination of Spanish and Indian. They did talk about being related, but no one ever wrote anything about it. There were always cousins or aunts or whatever—the Santa Monica people. My grandmother had a sister in the Santa Monica area.

AM: Our grandmother—my mother said she spoke fluent Gabrielino.

VMB: I remember them there, but it's a blur as to them talking. I was way too young.

BMc: Do you know when your grandmother was born?

AM: She was born on March 6, 1878, in San Gabriel. The great-great-grandmother—her name was Maria Rita Bermudez. We have her listed as being born on June 25, 1824, at the mission. Then she had a daughter named Maria Manuela Quintero. She was born October 1, 1857. She was my grandmother's mother. So they're all direct descendants. There may be some relatives that go back even further, but [we] haven't been able to find them.

CJ: Both of you know you're direct descendants, and that you're Gabrielino, but can you tell me if that "knowing" takes any other form? Did people tell you stories? Or was it just a fact?

VMB: It was just a fact—the records were at the mission, and they were buried there.

CJ: Was there any feeling that your background shouldn't be talked about in public?

VMB: No. There was some tension like there is when you have other nationalities living within an area. I can remember my mother, especially my dad, never talked about those things. He got along with everybody, and he was always in city council, and all of that. But on my mother's side you could hear they didn't get along always. You had people that came from Mexico, and the few Spanish

Arthur Morales, his wife, Petra, and their daughter Vivian Morales Barthelemy at the San Gabriel Mission Fiesta, ca.1935. COURTESY OF VIVIAN MORALES BARTHELEMY

they called "Poches." "Poches" were early Californians of any combination [of backgrounds], Spanish who came into the country and married Anglo, or married Mexican, or Indian. But in all I can say they got along.

BMc: Were there any special clubs, special gatherings, or traditions which were special just to the Gabrielino Indian people?

VMB: I can't remember them being separated from the others.

CJ: Your father knew Tom Temple because he was involved in politics and city business.

VMB: Yeah, and they called themselves *parientes*, which means a relative.

AM: At that time it was an extremely small community. People who had a history from Mexico versus those who were Native American from here—there has always been that distinction. There is still. If I go [somewhere] and there are people who I went to school with, they all clearly understand who I am, where I'm from, and where they were [from]. At times it's unspoken, but yet recognized. My grandfather on my mother's side came over around 1900, and I think that was about the time that the Mexican Spanish influence came into San Gabriel. Prior to that, it was basically Gabrielino people who lived there. But there was always that initial "them and us." Then you did have the intermarriages, and it went on from there. But I think from the time the mission was founded—in what, 1771?—for the next hundred years, it was nothing but removing all ethnicity out of the Native Americans. People always ask [about our] traditions or stories. By the time we came around, they had pretty much been killed or they weren't spoken about.

CJ: Today there's a core of people who were part of the San Gabriel community. Did your families interact with other people throughout the larger Gabrielino community in other areas because you knew they were Gabrielino?

AM: Driving long distances was very family oriented. My great-great-grandfather had moved up north and would make the trip every six months down to see the family. He would come into Monrovia. The family would come from San Gabriel, or other areas they had moved, on that Sunday, just to meet with him, to see him. I think that was Native American–related because we were all related [in] one form or another.

CJ: Do you ever hear any stories about your family receiving land from the mission, or people who lived there receiving land?

VMB: I think they did, but I don't know if they had it on paper. They lived right at the edge between the railroad and the mission. There were a little group of houses in there. There was a street that ran from the signal in front of the mission right through downtown where the school is, and they closed that. There was a strip of homes in there, just little tiny houses. I'm sure that land had been given, but they weren't really people we knew. We knew of them, through school and the mission, but I don't really have any paperwork, or anything that would say they bought, were given that land, but I'm sure they did.

CJ: How do you feel about the historical mission era?

VMB: Well, written things [say] that they were not treated well. But as far as I can think, I know my dad never talked about anything like that. He talked about his grandfather. I believe my grandmother's father was the bell ringer at one time, at the mission. They were just those kinds of stories—weren't bad stories really. There always was some prejudice, especially with the Mexican and the Spanish.

AM: When I was growing up, I recall stories of relatives who tried to move out of the San Gabriel area and weren't able to live in certain other areas. There were white rich areas around us, and we were right here in our own little town. You couldn't move out. It wasn't going to happen. You weren't going to move into San Marino. Next to San Gabriel was the San Gabriel Village, and it was all white. You knew your place—San Gabriel—within this certain area. But there was [a] certain amount of prejudice. I think that if you look at over one hundred years of treatment, a lot of our families just became part of it. You give in. You survive. A lot of things were taken away. I grew up after my sister. You couldn't speak Spanish. The sisters would hit you with a ruler across the hand. Showing any ethnicity [or] culture was a big no-no.

CJ: So you lost your identity twice.

AM: Oh, absolutely, absolutely. My first day in the fourth grade I got in a fight before I even went into the classroom because a guy called me a dirty Indian, and I'll never forget that. There were only two of us that were brown-skinned, and that's what it was.

KMJ: How about you, Auntie Vivian, did you ever experience anything like that?

VMB: Not really, because I went to Roosevelt School, which was outside of the area, near where my grandfather farmed. My dad used to get me a permit to go there. I had cousins who went there who lived in that area, too. I guess it [discrimination] was there. I never paid attention—I get it now. When I grew up, we were all a mix. We had as many Anglo as we did Indian, Mexican, or Spanish, Japanese in my era. To me it was like a little village. An Arab had a little grocery, a Jewish man had a grocery store, and a Greek. A couple of men had Mexican grocery stores. To think of it like Art, I don't really. Then I was always a dancer, and I was always at the fiestas. People treated me differently, like I was privileged because I had danced so much in different areas—Santa Barbara, San Fernando, all over, country clubs.

AM: You had a story you had mentioned before about Grandpa David. There was a vote that he was trying to get for our people. What was that?

VMB: Oh, they couldn't vote, and he fought for that right. That's how come my dad went into city work. He'd go to the council meetings and everything. My grandfather really fought for the vote, and he did get it, but it took him several years for Native Americans to vote.

AM: It had to be the twenties. I get after my kids if they won't vote. I say, "After all, your grandfather fought for the vote." They should go out and vote anyway.

BMc: Did you ever hear anyone speaking, perhaps your grandfather especially, about the Mission Indian Federation?

AM: My dad was part of that. In fact, I have his membership card at home.

CJ: What was the federation's purpose?

KMJ: I thought it was all the Mission Indians together. They [the Mission Indian Federation] were a political organization. My dad used to go to the meetings, our relatives used to go, and were a part of those meetings. We've hit dead ends every time we tried to do the research on the people that were actually the head of those organizations trying to get things done. But my dad was part of it, and probably my grandfather, 1930s, '40s.[*]

AM: I think it was the forties.

CJ: How do you feel about not being a federally recognized tribe?

---

[*] Groups across the country began to advance the cause of American Indians in the early twentieth century. As southern California Indian tribes objected to the land management policies of the Bureau of Indian Affairs, they too began to organize, assert their identity, and advocate their cause by joining the Mission Indian Federation established in 1919. The organization included non-native people and people from federally recognized tribes and reservations, as well as non-recognized southern California Indians. The Tongva fell into the latter status, but some followed political developments and joined the federation, which was also a social organization, and some also joined the California Indian League, which included both Tongva and Juaneño people in pursuit of recognition.

Passage of the California Indians Jurisdictional Act by the state legislature in 1927 testified to the power of the Mission Indian Federation, for it authorized a suit against the U.S. government on behalf of Indians over the eighteen nonratified federal treaties negotiated between 1851 and 1852. No treaties had been negotiated with either the Tongva or Juaneño people.

As part of the claims process, the Jurisdictional Act created a roll of California Indians which was based on individual ancestry, since the lawsuit represented individuals (not tribes) who descended from California Indians living in the state at the time of the 1851–1852 treaties. To enroll, individuals had to document their ancestors and list their tribe. Although the new government rolls approved individual ancestries and tribal affiliations, the Jurisdictional Act did not extend new formal federal recognition to the tribes who were not federally recognized at the time—but many enrollees were members of those unrecognized tribes.

Indians filing claims were required to submit an "Application for Enrollment with the Indians of the State of California under the Act of May 18, 1928." In 1933 the Secretary of the Interior approved the enrollment (1933 census list) based on the applications. In 1940, 1948, and 1950 Congress amended the 1928 Claims Act to add new eligible names and remove enrollees since dead. The new rolls were completed in 1955 and 1972. Claims filed in 1928 were awarded in 1944, and in 1950 a payment of $150 was distributed to each enrollee. Additional claims for land not previously included were filed in 1946 and an out-of-court settlement was reached in 1972. Each enrolled California Indian received $668.51. Refer to the essay "Continuity within Change: Identity and Culture" for more information.

AM: That runs deep because it goes back to that federation, and that there were two tribes that weren't recognized. Conveniently, they happen to be the tribes that would have been in Los Angeles and Orange County. That speaks for itself. I think like anything else it was done for political reasons, for gain. Once they have taken over the tribe in that specific area, they do whatever they want with the land. You see that going on nowadays. I know history books still say we're extinct. Kim is working hard, and has with different people in different parts of the community who are trying to show that we still exist, and we're still around. When all the Native American nations went for the presentation of the new Smithsonian [American Indian Museum], we went. We made sure we were photographed. We made sure that we were recorded as representatives of our tribe—alive and there. With any group, you're going to have different points of view, and people are going to belong to different parties. But with our core group it's more about culture. The point of being recognized—it's just important to us.

CJ: How do you make people aware that you exist, particularly when you don't remember your traditions? Are you just trying to make people aware you're alive, or are you trying to reclaim your heritage through traditions which someone may know?

AM: I think that there's a phrase you [may] know—when somebody finds their Indianness. You have people who have never felt that, most of their life. Then at some point they find it and want more. We really don't have a lot of written records. A lot of the history, I believe, is jaded because it's written through the eyes of a white man who doesn't have the deep understanding of why certain things were done, or maybe misunderstands. It's all interpretation. It's hard to describe. You know it. The phrase "you know it when you see it"—we know it when we feel it. It's when you have that sense you're Native American. Everyone pursues it a little bit differently. I've always felt it, even as a child I just had it.

Most conversations were [that] we needed to [be] recognized, not [to] lose the fact that we were Native American, the first people here. Remember that. Sadly, that's where a lot starts and ends, unless you go out and start doing your own research. In what I have read and been able to gather out of the books, we were the strongest tribe all around at one time. We aren't any longer, but the surrounding tribes have been affected by our culture and a lot would have been passed on. If we need to find our culture and our history, parts of it, we need to go out to surrounding tribes that have reservations, and have been able to preserve maybe some of the dances, some of the language. There were points in our history where people from our tribe were offered the opportunity to move to Pechanga.* They moved, live in Pechanga, and they're part of that reservation. Then there was a core that decided to stay in San Gabriel.

---

* The 5,500-acre Pechanga reservation is located near Temecula, California, and belongs to the Pechanga Band of Luiseño Indians, a federally recognized tribe. The original reservation was established by the executive order of President Chester A. Arthur and increased in size thereafter.

CJ: Have those people retained their Gabrielino identity?

KMJ: I've heard of some who live [on] Pechanga, Morongo, and Fort Tejon, and they still identify as being Gabrielino.* Members of the tribe, the predominant tribe, know Gabrielinos that live there, but they don't bother them and just coexist, I think.

VMB: We had a family that lived in San Gabriel and they've moved up to Pala, in that area, but you knew they were of the old Indian people from San Gabriel.** I think they were given land, that's why they moved to Pala. When it was starting to grow, they moved. I went to school with one of the younger ones, and I remember he and his wife moved after my husband and I were married, to Pala.

KMJ: As we try to reclaim federal recognition, we say "reclaim it or restore it" because [our people] went to Sherman Institute, because they were given land, because there was always a relationship with the government.† To me that's a relationship with the federal government. We are, to me, federally recognized, just not officially, politically.

BMc: What would it mean to you if it was official or political?

AM: It would mean a lot. It's hard to describe—just the fact that we would be federally recognized. There doesn't have to be anything else to go with it.

VMB: As a group of people itself. Yet we were given money. Way back, my dad received the first amount of money. He and his sister, and brothers, and then I received that at my time, and my children received [it in] later years. How can we receive the money if we're not recognized? Even my children's children have numbers.‡

---

* In March 1853 Congress authorized funding to establish five military reservations for California Indians on land to be owned by the U.S. government. Located at the southern end of the San Joaquin Valley, some sixty miles north of Los Angeles by Tejon Pass, the Sebastian Military Reserve (also known as the Tejon Reservation) closed in 1864. Established in 1865 through executive order by President Ulysses S. Grant, the Morongo Band of Mission Indians (Cahuilla) reservation is located in northern Riverside County and includes more than 32,000 acres.

** Located in northern San Diego County, the 12,273-acre reservation for the Pala Band of Mission Indians is home to both Cupeño and Luiseño Indians. In 1903, President Rutherford Hayes enforced a Supreme Court ruling ordering the Cupeño to move to a reservation which had already been established for the Luiseño people. Their descendants today consider themselves one people.

† Opened in 1902, Sherman Institute was a vocational training school run by the Bureau of Indian Affairs in Riverside, California. For more information, refer to the essay "Continuity within Change: Identity and Culture."
The BAR (Branch of Acknowledgment and Research) within the Bureau of Indian Affairs established seven mandatory criteria for federal recognition which for some California Indians, including the urban-based Tongva people, are extremely difficult to meet considering history. Petitioning tribes must meet all seven criteria. However, if a tribe can prove "previous acknowledgment" by the federal government at some point back in history, the seven criteria are mitigated to some degree. Petitioners need only prove they have been identified as an Indian group since the last federal acknowledgment in time. Indian groups must prove that they are a distinct group, and still exert political influence or authority over their members, but not that they exist separately. (Refer to the essay "The Enduring Vision: Recognition and Renewal" for more information on the subject of federal recognition.)

‡ To be eligible for an award under the California Indians Jurisdictional Act of 1927, people had to document their Indian ancestry dating back to the time of the negotiated (nonratified) treaties of 1851–1852, and submit enrollment papers to the federal government. Finally, in 1950 every eligible and enrolled Native Californian received $150. By that time, however, additional claims had already been filed in 1946 over lands not covered in the earlier award. An out-of-court settlement for these claims was reached in 1972. Each enrolled California Indian received $668. Not all eligible Tongva have opted to enroll; some do not believe they should have to prove their identity to the federal government. Other enrollment papers have been lost in the process. Unfortunately, for descendants of those families who chose not to enroll, the burden of proof required by the federal government and tribal councils makes required documentation more difficult.

KMJ: I think that whole roll number thing, when it happened, varied from place to place because so many scouts came out here. The way they did it in San Gabriel was different than the way they did it in the desert. What people said they were, and who could vouch for each other, I don't think there was a standard way of doing that.*

AM: [Our experience] hasn't been what people expect—a traditional tribe [from] the reservation. They would carry on traditions we don't. We [assimilated]. You're put into a different environment, and then everything else is taken from you. You're told that's not what you're doing anymore. You're not doing Indian things anymore. You're not doing Mexican things anymore. When you get raised that way, if you look at from 1771 to the late 1800s, when my grandmother was born—those things were killed, they were taken away. The hardest part for me is that [the loss inspires] anxiety—we don't have [our traditions anymore]. But it wasn't our fault. People continue to ask us for more information about it, and we say it was taken from us. We don't have it.

VMB: If it had been a reservation or something like that, it would have all been contained, but since we lived with so many varied people, the mission was our only hold.

AM: A lot of things were not defined. In the American way, things always have to be identified, categorized, and they're labeled. I think that [in] the gatherings, our families continued over time. It was an unspoken thing. We know who we were. This is what we do to keep that flowing. The stories and things were not really spoken of because it had been drilled into them that it wasn't the right thing to do.

BMc: Who was the earliest leader of the Gabrielino people that you remember in any sense of a leader? I know Sparky was considered a leader.

AM: Sparky was my father's brother. He was Fred Morales. I would say my grandfather David Morales and my dad were active.

VMB: I think my dad [Arthur Morales], but not just Indian [affairs]. He wanted to be recognized as part of San Gabriel, to be included in civic things. The Spanish American League really pushed for recognition for people originally from San Gabriel. They had a singing group and a group that put on fiestas, but it was a combined effort. It was never just Indian, but he [Arthur Morales] never lost that. He knew he was Indian.

BMc: Did he choose to do that because he wanted to or because the community looked to him as a leader because of family?

---

* As part of the enrollment process each claimant was required to submit the official "Application for Enrollment with the Indians of the State of California under the Act of May 18, 1928." Many contacted Tommy Temple, the city historian of San Gabriel, who was well known throughout the community for documenting the genealogies of Tongva families. For more information on Temple refer to the essay "Continuity within Change: Identity and Culture."

VMB: Since he did go to council meetings, they always looked to him. "Who do we vote for that would help us, help the old town of San Gabriel, who would put in streets and help with the water system?" He was more political—not so much to prove he was Indian. He figured they already knew he was. It was mostly for city things he wanted to.

AM: But people came to him for advice.

VMB: Yes, who to vote for.

AM: [He was an] air raid warden. He was the oldest of the family, and the type of person able to communicate with the city council and different people. The people in San Gabriel did rely on him for a lot of advice.

VMB: It was all a combined effort.

CJ: Would Sparky be a leader for the larger group of Gabrielino people throughout the region, including this area?

VMB: Fred [Sparky] took over that part of it.

BMc: When we're talking about your father, are we talking about late 1930s, 1940s?

VMB: The thirties. Arthur Theodore Morales.

CJ: It's unusual that he rose to a level of civic involvement considering the levels of discrimination that were going on in many communities at that time.

VMB: I think it was the fiestas and the mission. They all worked together. That's how they got to know the Temples, the Vigares, and the Carols. They were all old families of San Gabriel, so it became a combined effort.

CJ: What was Sparky's role, his beginning as a leader?

VMB: He started to communicate with the San Gabriel people and other tribes [who lived] outside of the San Gabriel area. That started with Santa Monica, I think.

AM: Right. That was in the early seventies, might have started in the late sixties. He communicated with tribes from all over. Besides being a leader, he was a great ambassador. Tribes and elders from all the surrounding tribes knew of him, or knew him, recognized him, and they respected him quite a bit.

VMB: Yes. His was strictly the Indian thing. That's what he was doing.

AM: My sister mentioned to me at one point—when you look at the different cultures and people that have lived in the San Gabriel area, it changed right after World War II because you had the influx of soldiers from different parts of the country. Then I think there was a little bit more prejudice. She recalled prior to that, even though you had a mixture of different people who lived in the San Gabriel area, they pretty much got along.

BMc: Your grandfather David was active in helping get the Indians the vote. That was probably in the 1920s era when he was very active?

VMB: I imagine the late twenties, early thirties.

BMc: Then your father, Art, became active, but more of a civic local level.

VMB: Yes.

BMc: Did David rekindle the interest in tribal matters, or in pursuing things that would benefit the people in this area?

VMB: It would have to be my grandfather [David], because I can't remember anyone ever trying to improve things for the Indians as my grandfather did. I don't remember anyone that strong, to come out and speak for them. Then somehow my dad, once he got married, took over too. He liked civic things, he liked city government. He knew so many of the older people.

AM: You've hit on something which has caused our tribe problems in the recent past. As far as we know, our tribe is the only band or group [of Gabrielinos] within the Los Angeles/Orange County area that has a continuity [continuous history] of involvement and unity with our Native American culture, our history, trying to keep things going.* Yes, there are people that are Gabrielino, who either their families have moved out, or maybe live in outlying areas—Santa Ana, other areas—but the core starts with the San Gabriel Mission. Those people have gone out on their own, and again, they maybe have found their Indianness and then made it whatever it's been, but it's been more as an individual—where with us, whatever we have, we have been able to hang on to it, and it's been continuing from one generation to the other.

CJ: You've a genetic sense of family starting with your history at Mission San Gabriel. For you that's a sacred place in many ways, rather than Povuu'ngna, which traditionally is seen as the place of emergence.

AM: Right, exactly. Povuu'ngna came to light when we had the reburial, pretty much. In all honesty, as far as knowing the names of the other villages, I think it emerged in the mid-seventies probably.

---

* Refer to the essay "The Enduring Vision: Recognition and Renewal" and the conversation with Anthony Morales for more on the San Gabriel community over time.

Left to right: Kimberly Morales Johnson, her father, Art Morales, and his sister, Vivian Morales Barthelemy, at Mission San Gabriel, 2006.
TY MILFORD PHOTOGRAPHY

CJ: Do you see it, as many do, as a new beginning because it's become a political reemergence?

VMB: The sad part is that there are so many leaders and they're all fighting each other. They're all trying [to work on behalf of the Tongva community] and they don't really work together.

CJ: Patty, what are the stories you remember? Did your mother, Vivian, pass on her sense of Indianness to you?

Patty Roess: Other than just knowing who we were, that we were different, when we lived in San Gabriel [the early fifties] there was a different sense. There were so many people. Even the grammar school I went to, there were just so many people, all different. I don't remember feeling any tension going to school, but moving here [to Arcadia] was a whole other ball game. All of a sudden, we were discriminated against because, like Art said, our color of skin was different. We happened to have a pool. Mom tried the hardest to keep us out of the water, but the tan happened. So going back to school every year was always, "Oh, we've got to go through this again." But then the questions started coming up, "Why is it different here?" Why was it different from San Gabriel? There was this strong sense of family. You always knew they were over there and family was a definite bond. Going into San Gabriel [to visit] later was always this magnet. Everybody would come around because we had moved out. We were probably one of the first of that period to move out. I remember it being a big deal, and we only lived 20 minutes from San Gabriel. You [Vivian] probably were told bad things because you moved out.

VMB: Even my friends today. It's hard for them to put the things together. I actually was here [in California and San Gabriel] before they were. It's really hard for them to understand it. They respect it to a certain point because now they're older. So anyway, they're really very respectful that we actually were here so many more years before anyone.

CJ: Kim, what was your "passing on?" Why are you sitting here at this table?

AM: I started thinking about it other the day. She really got involved over the last years, but she actually started with me—she was real young when we started. She went with me to the reburial along with my other daughter.

KMJ: It was the sense of family and togetherness. There was nothing shameful about it. It was always a good thing. Maybe it was just a sense of identity. You start to raise your kids, and then you're looking for what you're going to give them to pass on—that sense of family and having that common thread started way back when. You look forward to going to the fiestas, and I remember my parents would be happy, or to the Grapevine Room, or looking at pictures.* I always knew that Aunty Vivian was a dancer, and there was a sense of pride of being the Gabrielinos from the mission. So I went back, it just ignited.

CJ: What do you want to pass on to the next generation about what being Gabrielino means?

AM: What keeps resonating in my mind is what we have is just unspoken. Like my grandson, Tommy, I know he has interest. He comes to me with questions. He'll find himself at some point and carry that on. My sister's grandchildren, two daughters—even though I know they have never been actively involved, they have taken to it. We were seeking federal recognition three, fours years ago or longer. I went through and put a packet together for everyone [in the family], and made sure everybody was registered [with the Gabrieleno/Tongva Tribal Council of San Gabriel]. I think it had some effect—passing something that they have taken on. Even though they don't have regalia, or specifics, they know who they are. At this time that's the best we can do. We just don't have the resources, the time, or the money to be able to get more than that.

BMc: How does knowing that you're Gabrielino make your life better—because I assume it does in some way?

VMB: I think there is pride that we originated here. Who can say that?

AM: There's pride. I think the fact of knowing that—well, it's just an inner feeling. It's like we said earlier, "You know it when you see it. You know it when you feel it." When you meet someone else who says they're Native American, there is always that "Let's wait and see." You will get a bond, and know that person actually does feel that they are Native American, or that they don't. You just know. It's not something you can really describe.

KMJ: Nine times out of ten, it's unspoken. They don't have to say anything for you to know who they are inside, you just know. Nine times out of ten, they're not who they say they are. I think the old term is "an apple." It's just not there. They have no regard; they don't know. They don't know our ways. They don't know. And that's it.

---

* Planted near the Mission Playhouse in San Gabriel, the old grapevine was a cutting from the "mother vine" at San Gabriel Mission, perhaps the oldest vine in the San Gabriel Valley. It grew to ten thousand feet, creating an enormous trellis and covered patio, and a popular place for gatherings under the vine. The "Grapevine Room" was built on the site of the Grapevine Inn, where Helen Hunt Jackson began writing *Ramona* (1888), a very popular book which helped shaped the stereotype view of the region and California Indians.

CJ: Would you live anywhere else except the Los Angeles Basin, or is your sense of identity too directly tied to Mission San Gabriel and your lineage? Or is there a larger sense of just "Indianness" which would carry you anywhere?

AM: I stay here. It goes back to what we're talking about before—family. I'd like to live in Hawaii or San Diego, but it's all about family. I think that's what kept me here. The later generations are moving out further. But at the core, look how long our people lived in San Gabriel—we still have family members that still live in San Gabriel and will. Their kids are probably going to live in San Gabriel.

VMB: You can see it when you go to a funeral. Then you really see all the people come out, just many, many people.

CJ: Who were and are the elders within the community now?

AM: Bea Alva was a leader in the fifties, when I was a teenager, and would go to the meetings. She was a leader for a long time. My dad and my uncles were all, for lack of a better word, leaders, because they were the treasurer, vice president—if they used those terms—but they were always actively involved. They weren't just members.

CJ: Did leadership always have to do with federal recognition and the process of trying to obtain it?

KMJ: I think federal recognition was more of a backdrop. That's the ultimate goal, but they needed to take care of that day, week to week. People needed things. So I think that federal recognition was the larger goal.

AM: My experience growing up was much different than my sister's and other people I've spoken with.

VMB: Well, again, after the war it really changed. For me it was very different because my dad was so involved in city politics and I went to a different school. I only went to Mission one year, at the San Gabriel Mission. So my experience was way different. But when you had all these people come in after the war, all the tracts of homes went up—North San Gabriel and the [San Gabriel] Village—it really changed because people from other states came. They were service people or just people that moved here. It reversed the whole thing. There was more prejudice, and more separation. They didn't understand that we were a community of Indian, Spanish, Mexican people, a few Anglo. It was a community of all these different people, [who] really got along a lot better than they did after the war.

AM: When I was growing up, I remember the books were derogatory toward our tribe. We were "Diggers." We dug for roots. I remember this kid telling me, "My dad told me about how filthy you guys were. You would rub yourself with animal fat, and you stunk." It was all derogatory terms in the history books that any people around here knew. Part of federal recognition would give us good standing, and in a certain sense, wash away some of all that anger and misinformation about our people. I had bouts all the way through high school because either I was a dirty Mexican, or a dirty Indian. It was just that way. That was my schooling.

CJ: Do you think people still believe there are no longer any Gabrielino people?

VMB: Yes.

AM: When we were trying to get petitions to be federally recognized, several things emerged. One was that people had a great thirst and interest in [knowing] who the original people were here. There was no information, no accurate information out there. It was, "Oh, my goodness!"—total shock—and, "It's amazing!"

CJ: Do people often say, "You're Mexican," "You're something else"?

VMB: Yes, sure.

KMJ: No, "We killed all the Indians." I hear that a lot. Did you hear that growing up?

VMB: No.

KMJ: "There are no more native people in California." Even Indian people—they say you're something else.

VMB: You're told you're Mexican people.

AM: You're from the mission. If you're from the mission, then you're not recognized as an Indian.

CJ: Because there are many Gabrielino-Tongva communities, there are also different stories and pieces of information throughout. How does that knowledge get reconciled, or does it?

AM: That's a hot one. I think they all have a different goal and concept of what is needed. Some could be distant relatives. Some profess to be really experienced and really knowledgeable. My question to them would be, "How are you going to be that knowledgeable and that experienced when none of that core information was passed on?" We have the texts that were written by white people, and even if they were well intended, [it] doesn't mean that everything is correct. Other than that, we don't have a lot that was passed down. So how do these people profess to be all that knowledgeable and that experienced? They found their Indianness. This is what they're doing, and this is their personal point of view. It's their own truth.

KMJ: They created their own truth. When I was more active, I always had a sense of obligation to my family first because I had my aunt, I had Michael [cousin], and I had my dad if I wasn't in check, or had my own agenda. I was representing my whole family. I'm not just representing myself. I think it's easier [than] when you are representing yourself and your agenda, and your own truth. I think it gives you your ultimate goal—what is really lighting your passion from the inside.

AM: I think some of them have made stuff up, to tell you the truth, and that's just not right. It hurts me deeply to say we don't have stories to pass on, or things of that nature. It hurts because we don't have it, on one hand, to pass on to our children, yet if you look at the environment, and history, you can understand why it wasn't the thing to be.

BMc: Your grandmother Presentación—

AM: That was Grandpa David's mother. She was my great-grandmother.

BMc: She spoke Gabrielino?

AM: Yes. She was 100 percent, my mother said. My mother was the only one who knew her and had been around her when she spoke Gabrielino.

BMc: Was she part of the reason your grandfather David was so interested in the tribal affairs, because his mother was a speaker?

AM: Well, the mother and father both were.

BMc: Do you know what Presentación's husband's name was?

AM: It was José Morales. José Morales and Presentación were married, they had David Morales, and that was my grandfather.

BMc: So Presentación's maiden name was López?

AM: Yes. He [David] was my grandfather, and his father [and mother] were José and Maria Presentación. She is the one that spoke [Gabrielino]. The old records would just have the first name, [then] "Cristo [Christ] Indian." That's all. The "neophyte" was another word they would refer to [them as].

CJ: Do you have a place that you would consider sacred today, other than Mission San Gabriel, a new sense of sacredness? Povuu'ngna is becoming one for many.

AM: I would say the mission, and any site we've had a reburial, or where we found ancestors that had been buried. There is just a different sense of that area, who they were, and what the history may have been, whenever we've had reburial.

The Encino site was the first site we were able to perform as monitors.* It was an extremely large site, but it's just a certain sense there. There have been remains found throughout L.A. County we would respond to. There have been occasions where we've had to move the remains to another site.

At Povuu'ngna I thought that we had done the right thing—we reburied the remains. I think it was at least ten feet down, to make sure that if somebody took away the historical status it had, maybe they wouldn't disturb them.** Still not sure how that turned out. It's always trying to preserve the remains so they don't get disturbed again. Then you have the Native American view. Then you have to understand a bit of the current politics—can they do it on this specific property? Trying to negotiate, having to negotiate first of all, is not a good feeling—but you make the best decision you can with the remains as a priority, what you can do under the current environment. It becomes very difficult at times.

CJ: Someone commented that she felt that she was "being used" by other interests, environmental groups. "You are an Indian. They call you up that day because someone needs you that day. It's their agenda, not yours." Do you feel the same way?

AM: That happens all the time. They're very difficult. We start making phone calls to other members, other elders, people that are actively involved. That's what we do to check it out because we continue to be used. Then once someone receives, gets their agenda made, they forget about us, and basically we're still being used.

BMc: We've talked about all these different groups, Gabrielino, Tongva, different ideas, maybe different agencies—do you foresee a point in the future where they come together, where they find common ground?

---

* Under the California Environmental Quality Act (CEQA), developers and public agencies must assess the environmental impact of a project, including their impact on "historical and cultural resources." The state Native American Heritage Commission protects Native American burial and cultural resources in California. It identifies and designates the "most likely descendant" (a direct lineal descendant) to be contacted in the event Native American human remains are unearthed during the course of a project, to ensure their "appropriate treatment and disposition." Since 2007 state law requires owners to protect burials and associated grave material found on their property, and allow access to the designated "most likely descendants." In addition, the Native American Heritage Commission has established guidelines for Native American monitors/consultants who may be present during ground-disturbing work or onsite during the construction of projects which are known to be in culturally sensitive areas. (For more information on the new cemetery law refer to the conversation with Anthony Morales and the essay "The Enduring Vision: Recognition and Renewal.")

In 1984 and 1985, archaeological excavations in the city of Encino, California, near the intersection of Ventura and Balboa Boulevards, revealed evidence of a Gabrielino community that included a cemetery with human and animal burials. This may have been the ancestral village of Siutcanga. Radiocarbon dating revealed that a succession of Indian people had occupied the site since as early as 5000 B.C. Much of the site was destroyed by redevelopment, and only a small portion preserved under landfill.

** Together, Rancho Los Alamitos and California State University, Long Beach, comprise the "Povuu'ngna District," which has been listed on the National Register of Historic Places since 1974. Administered by the National Park Service (U.S. Department of the Interior), the official register records properties worth preserving for their significance to American history, architecture, archaeology, engineering, and culture, whether on a local, state, or national level. The impact on listed properties must be considered in the planning and development of federal or federally assisted projects. They are eligible for federal tax benefits and qualify for any federal historic preservation funds available. The area of Povuu'ngna now known as Rancho Los Alamitos is a protected historic site under the terms of the public/private agreement between the City of Long Beach and Rancho Los Alamitos Foundation. In the 1990s, following many legal disputes, CSULB stopped commercial development of the disputed Povuu'ngna site at the university. At the time, the university declared an administrative moratorium on any further development of the site and designated it protected open space. However, this moratorium does not legally bind future administrations to the same promise. For more information refer to the essay "A Connection to Place: Land and History."

Young Vivian Morales (Barthelemy) in dance costume, waving to the crowd as she rides in the Santa Barbara Mission Festival parade, ca. 1935. COURTESY OF
VIVIAN MORALES BARTHELEMY

AM: No.

KMJ: Not as long as there's a casino, not as long as that's an issue in California. It
will never happen, because money makes everything ugly. You see it in tribes that
have been federally recognized. They end up kicking members out. Money brings
out the ugliness of everybody. So there's even dissension in tribes where they have
federal recognition, and have been through things like we have. There is still dissension versus someone who's already scattered, and then put it back together. It's
just going to fall back apart again.

AM: Pretty much. You'd end up with people coming out of the woodwork saying
they were Gabrielino, and they wanted to be part of it. Then once the casino
was taken off the table, they'd leave, and you have your core people that have
always been involved. Others just come and go. If people found out tomorrow
that he [Anthony Morales, chair of the Gabrieleno Tongva Tribal Council of
San Gabriel] was seeking federal recognition again, the floodgates would be
open again, and people would just be coming in from all over for a hope of
something. It's just not going to happen, I don't think. We don't have enough

money. Even though we have had qualified people, attorneys, people in the Indian community have said that we're one of very few tribes that can legally and honestly qualify to be federally recognized, we're not, because we don't have enough money. We don't have the lobbyists. It's all about money. The casino people come in, or whoever it is. What they don't realize is that the Indian tribes maybe get 10 percent of all the taking. Everybody else [outside investors, managers, etc.] get the rest of the money. Eventually they're going to be losing control and then they keep getting a smaller portion of whateverit is.

CJ: The San Gabriel community was an informal group for years. How long has there been a tribal chair and formal structure, something which would be required for federal recognition?

AM: Well, I think that there has been a chair since the fifties and maybe the late forties.

BMc: Do you know who the first chair was?

AM: Probably, was it Bea Alva, or was there somebody before Bea Alva?

VMB: Vickie Duarte.

AM: So it goes back at least to the forties that we know, probably even to the thirties because that's when they were part of the Mission Indian Federation.

CJ: Were there elections?

KMJ: Now, after they got bylaws, but Anthony inherited it from his father [Sparky]. There is sketchy information from books and other tribes that some California tribes did have [an] inherited chiefdom.* Then they had bylaws, I think in the nineties.

AM: But we started—Bea was voted in, in the fifties, and so was I. There weren't bylaws, but votes were taken and they had some structure. It wasn't the formal structure that we have now, with all of the specific bylaws required by the government to be legal.**

BMc: Do you think you had a tribal chair as far back as the 1930s?

---

* In the late 1980s, Sparky Morales designated Cindi Alvitre the first appointed chair of the formal San Gabriel community. In 1991 Anthony Morales became the acting chair of the Gabrieleno Tongva Tribal Council of San Gabriel, and in turn has served as their elected chair since 1995. Anthony is the son of Sparky Morales, an early twentieth-century leader of the San Gabriel community. Anthony Morales, in his later conversation, indicates that he believes his family was descended from an ancestral village chief, or *capitán*.
  In ancestral Tongva villages, family lineages were brought together under the rule of a *tomyaar*, a chief who was most likely the head of the oldest or largest lineage. Usually a hereditary position, the *tomyaar* oversaw the religious and secular life of the village. It may be that some *tomyaars* oversaw several villages. On the other hand, *capitanes* were appointed by the missionaries as people of authority to keep order and protect the mission property in the area. Although given new authority, *capitanes* were chosen from the well-known headmen of prominent family lineages, maybe the *tomyaar*.

** To qualify for federal recognition, tribes must submit their papers indicating their governing procedures. The bylaws of the Gabrieleno Tongva Tribal Council of San Gabriel were rewritten as part of an ANA (Aid to Native Americans) grant with UCLA. For more information see the essay "The Enduring Vision: Recognition and Renewal" and the conversation with Anthony Morales.

AM: For sure in the fifties, I think it probably goes back to the forties. Before that it may have been informal in the respect that it was like my grandfather taking charge, leading certain events and things going on. My dad was involved when they had the California mission groups [the Mission Indian Federation]. We had our leaders then, so it had to have gone back to the thirties.

Stage setting for the Santa Barbara Mission Festival Pageant, ca. 1930s. Courtesy of Vivian Morales Barthelemy

BMc: Was your father a tribal chair?

AM: I don't know.

VMB: I don't know if they ever established that, or if he just did it. I have a feeling he just did it. No one else stepped up, and he just took over.

AM: It was one of those things just informally recognized. People understood.

VMB: He didn't mind speaking, going to meetings. He just took over, but that's the first time they ever had anything about recognition, when he got money. I don't know why—I think some of them did not get money [from the settlements previously described in this conversation], but I did. I don't know why they skipped a generation at that time, but they didn't get recognition either.

BMc: In your personal opinions, what should the priority be for the Gabrielino people in terms of what you do as group, not so much as individuals? Is it education, is it public awareness, is it recovering traditions?

VMB: Well, I think kids would really love it if they got education. I think in our group, it's been more about culture. They [Gabrieleno-Tongva Tribal Council of San Gabriel] have dancers. Right now they're burned out with all the events and requests. It would be nice to have some grants and money come in, but it's been more about the culture and passing it on to the younger kids. The dancers went to the Southwest Museum.* I believe that's where they

Unidentified Gabrielino-Tongva participants in the Santa Barbara Mission Festival, ca. 1935. As part of the historical pageantry, Tongva people and festival players would descend from the hills above. COURTESY OF VIVIAN MORALES BARTHELEMY

started. They learned some dances. They've gone on from there. I don't know where the pictures are, but my dad and my uncle danced at some of the fiestas and they would dress in regalia.

AM: My uncle Joe said they learned from other tribes. Then those were dances that they danced. But that was back in the thirties, maybe, when they started, so they were searching. They wanted to dance, so you go to another tribe. That's what they did. They were actually the first dancers of our tribe.

VMB: It was for the Santa Barbara fiestas. That's because I started dancing there when I was five. They found out that there were Indians from the San Gabriel area. Then they were approached as to whether they wanted to go dance. The Santa Barbara pageant was beautiful. They started with Indians, and then they had the Spanish coming down on horseback down the mountain.*

PR: But you notice she [Vivian] did Spanish dances, she did not do Indian dances.

---

* The Santa Barbara Bowl was a New Deal WPA project built in 1936 for the Santa Barbara Fiesta. During the pageant spectacle, first the California Indians, then Spanish missionaries and over one hundred horses carrying costumed riders holding torches descended from the hills into the amphitheater below.

A grown-up Vivian Morales Barthelemy in her Mission Fiesta dance costume sits on the steps of the Santa Barbara Courthouse. COURTESY OF VIVIAN MORALES BARTHELEMY

VMB: Yes. It was just the thing that you did. I was in the Mission Play [at San Gabriel].* My mother was in the Mission Play, and she played an Indian, and she was Mexican. The festival queens are all different. Some of them are Mexican and some of them are Spanish.

PR: This is really interesting, because I only got snippets as a child. It always seemed everything was present-day. You just lived today. What I'm realizing, listening to this, is that it was squashed a long, long time ago. They did a good job of it, whoever "they" are, if it was the mission environment that squashed it. Even if it sounds like you had a perfectly good experience at the mission, they didn't teach you anything about Indian, being an Indian [at school].

VMB: Only about the missions, when you were in fourth grade.**

PR: But that's all the Anglo end of it [what is taught is the Anglo version of events]. [What is taught] wasn't the historical value [of] being a Mission Indian.

VMB: Or about the people who lived there or participated in it.

PR: I just realized I'm kind of blown away as to how lost it really is.

---

* The Mission Play, a three-act, storybook version of the founding of the California missions by Father Serra through 1847, was first performed at Mission San Gabriel around 1918. For more information about the mission festivals, refer to the essay "Continuity within Change: Identity and Culture."

** Current History–Social Science Content Standards in the State of California require that all third grade students learn about the California Indians native to their community, past and present. General California history, including the mission era, is taught as part of the fourth grade Content Standards. U.S. Native American history is a core component of the fifth grade Content Standards.

A Conversation with Al Lassos, Dolores Lassos (wife of Al Lassos), and Art Morales (cousin of Al Lassos)

April 11, 2006
La Puente, California

The Participants

AL LASSOS WAS A RESPECTED MEMBER AND ELDER WITHIN THE Gabrieleno/Tongva Tribal Council of San Gabriel until his recent passing. He was also an alumnus of University High School in West Los Angeles, which in his time was known far and wide for the beauty of its campus and the Hollywood star quality of its student population. Over many years, Al Lassos and his wife, Dolores, worked with Angie Behrns and the Gabrielino/Tongva Springs Foundation, in their role as Tongva cultural educators, to help reclaim and protect the sacred springs. Once located near the ancestral village of Kuruvangna, the sacred springs mark the place where Gaspar de Portolá and Father Serra (the founder of the California mission system) passed by on their expedition north. For more information on the Gabrielino/Tongva Springs Foundation and the village of Kuruvangna, refer to the essay "The Enduring Vision: Recognition and Renewal," as well as the conversation with Angie Behrns.

The Discussion

In his comments, Al Lassos, an elder in the San Gabrielino community now deceased, shares memories of his strong-willed Gabrielino mother and growing up in the extended San Gabriel community family. He observes how his mother influenced his sense of native identity, his childhood and marriage, and his hopes for his children and the ongoing native community.

Al Lassos: My name is Al Lassos.

Claudia Jurmain: Where did you grow up?

AL: In West Los Angeles. Sawtelle.

CJ: Could you tell what year you were born?

AL: In '28. My mother was born in San Gabriel, and my father was born in Los Angeles. He came to a dance in San Gabriel, where he met my mother. They started going out and eventually got married. Once they got married, my father moved her to Santa Monica, but my father died when I was two; my mother raised ten of us by herself. We were living in West Los Angeles most of the time. When we lived on Granville just off Santa Monica Boulevard, the Sons of the Pioneers used to live right next door to us. We used to hear them playing guitars all the time. My brother Richard and I used to go over there and listen. But we lived all over West Los Angeles, and ended up in what they called lower Brentwood at that time—just one block the other side of Wilshire. We lived there since I was six or seven until I joined the Navy, got out, and got married.

Al Lassos, center, looking at family photos with his cousin Art Morales and his wife, Dolores, 2006.

CJ: The dance where your father met your mother in San Gabriel—was it at the mission?

AL: They used to have a dance right in front of the church at one time. I have their wedding certificate.

CJ: Both your parents were Gabrielino?

AL: No. My mother was full-blooded. My dad was supposedly Spanish, Indian, and French. My mother's name was Rose Valenzuela Lassos, and my father's name was Richard Lassos.

CJ: Your mother was full Gabrielino. Was that heritage part of your traditional family life, or were you simply trying to make a living and survive in Los Angeles during those years?

AL: I think that's put right, because my mother looked Mexican or Indian. People would come to the door and knock. She'd go to the door, and they would say, "Oh, Señora..." She'd say, "What are you trying to say?" They said, "Oh, you speak English." "Why of course. I was born and raised here. Why wouldn't I?" My mother was real sparky.

CJ: How did she raise and support ten children?

AL: To tell you the truth, most of us, when we got out of school and went to work, we used to come home and give her our check. She gave us an allowance. I wanted to buy a Navy flight jacket, one of the leather jackets with a fur collar. In those days it only cost about sixty bucks. And she said, "No, no, no—too much money." That's right. Most of it went for food.

CJ: Did she speak any of the Gabrielino language? Do you remember her using any words?

"Tía" Pastora, the aunt of Al Lassos, was a highly respected member of the San Gabriel community and storyteller. Al's cousin Art Morales recalls that there were always stories about Tía Pastora and her family in Santa Monica.
COURTESY OF ART MORALES

AL: Just a few words here and there. She was always trying to keep us straight and wanted us to get an education. I went to a public school. She just wanted me to grow up to be a real man, to have a family, and to do the best I could do for myself and my family.

CJ: Do you remember where her parents lived when you were growing up?

AL: No, I really don't know, because I never met my grandparents at all.

CJ: How about aunts, uncles, other cousins?

AL: Oh, yes. We had beautiful family reunions on weekends. They would roast a goat at my aunt Modesta's house in San Gabriel. They'd dig a pit and everything.

CJ: What years would that have been?

AL: In the forties someplace. Home was in Los Angeles, but we used to go to San Gabriel maybe two, three times a year to visit our relatives.

Bill McCawley: Was there a time when you first realized you were Gabrielino?

AL: To tell you the truth, I really didn't know about it until I got a little bit older. My mother used to tell us all the time that we were. It would go in this ear and come out this ear. I'm really sorry I didn't listen to her stories, because my kids used to get in a big circle and listen to her all day long. When I was about fourteen, fifteen years old it started to make a difference. I just got more interested. She used to tell us that we were from San Gabriel—from an Indian part of San Gabriel. Then she would say my grandfather, or my father, and my grandmother, were this and that. So consequently, we put it together that we were partly Indian.

According to [my niece], my mother was half, and we were one-quarter; but I put in for a scholarship for one of my daughters, and we got a slip from the Indian Affairs that said I was half and my daughter was a quarter.

CJ: Was she proud of the fact that she was Gabrielino?

AL: Yes, she sure was. She was real proud and would tell everybody. People would call me "half-breed, you damn Indian." I used to get a lot of fights over that. It was common knowledge, because the guys I grew up with were more Spanish. They used to tell me, "What are you doing here? Why don't you go back to your own country?" I said, "I am in my own country."

I went to Catalina one year and took one of my granddaughters. [The tour guide] said that at one time the island was inhabited by Gabrielinos. Since then, he said, "There's only about fifty of them and they all live in San Gabriel. There are no more here on the island. I've been on this tour for about ten years, and I've never ever met one." After the tour was over, I went over and shook his hand and said, "Now you met one." He said, "Oh, really?" I said, "Yes, and there's more than fifty of us. In my family in the south there are about five hundred of us." "Really? I didn't know that." I said, "Well, you're telling these stories and they're not really true." So he says, "Thank you very much. I appreciate you letting me know."

CJ: Did all your mother's sisters live in the San Gabriel community? Did you know other families from other areas?

AL: No. Most of all my relatives were here in San Gabriel, my aunts and uncles

CJ: Did you go to the mission festivals?*

AL: Yes, every once in a while, but you can't even get a place to park there now. My mother and father used to drive from Santa Monica in the buckboard all the way to San Gabriel down Wilshire Boulevard, which was nothing but a dirt road then.

BMc: I understand that for you, family and being Gabrielino are almost the same. When you grew up, was there anything beyond the family connection which meant "Gabrielino" to you?

AL: No. That's the only way I thought about being Gabrielino—and trying to be as best a citizen as I could. My mother always stressed, "Never get in trouble, and try to help each other."

BMc: Did your mother ever mention whether any relatives or friends of hers, or people that she knew, were living on any of the reservations?

AL: No, she never mentioned any to us.

CJ: Art, do you remember Al's mother, were you old enough?

Art Morales: No, I wasn't, but my mother did. My mother had countless stories about her, and she was really well respected. We always knew we had cousins in Santa Monica. We called her [Al Lassos' aunt] "Tía Pastora." There were always stories of her and her family in Santa Monica.

CJ: Was she the storyteller? Was she passing on the heritage to others? Did people go to her with that purpose in mind?

AM: That's the impression I got from my mother, yes.

CJ: Al, what year did your mother die?

AL: 1983.

CJ: When did you become aware that people were working on behalf of a larger Gabrielino community? As a kid, did you go and see Sparky [Morales] and listen to the stories?

AL: Always, yes. He was one of the elders, so consequently he knew more about it. He used to hang around with one of my older brothers, too.

CJ: Do you remember your mother having any opinions about the politics during those years?

---

* Mission festivals, pageants, and parades began in the early 1900s as San Gabriel and other towns associated with the history of the missions revived their Spanish heritage, architecture, and regional identity to attract tourists, increase land sales, and boost the local economy by promoting the romantic past.

AL: On everything—the way Indians were treated. I more or less got involved when I graduated, when I was older, when we started the Sacred Springs Foundation.* But I used to come to the meetings in San Gabriel.

CJ: When you joined the military, were you identified as a Gabrielino, or an Indian?

AL: No. I told them I was, but they didn't mention it. I guess I was considered one of the Mexicans because I had a lot of friends from Laredo, Texas, El Paso, and they all spoke Spanish. I didn't speak Spanish until one guy in the Navy taught me. Then when I got married to my wife, she taught me, so I picked it up.

CJ: What would you like to pass on to your grandchildren about being Gabrielino?

AL: To be proud of what they are. That's all I can really express. Everybody I know was proud to be what they are. The most important thing to me is to raise my family, which I have. They're all married now—and for them to be proud of me, like I am of them. You want them to lead a good life. So that's what we all strive for.

CJ: Does it matter if you have federal recognition?

AL: Not to me, because I'm an Indian through and through. Our school's—University High School—mascot was an Indian. They used to call it "The Warrior." One day they asked me—because they're Bobcats now—"How do you feel about being a Bobcat or a Warrior?" I said, "I was a Warrior when I played here, and I'm going to stay a Warrior, through and through." Life's been real good to me.

BMc: Are there other kinds of recognition besides federal recognition that would be important to you as a Gabrielino?

AL: Well, we have state recognition now, but we don't have federal.** It doesn't really make any difference to me because [for me there will be nothing because of my age]. The only reason I wanted to be federally recognized is maybe some of our elders need medicines, or for our kids' schooling, but I'm not interested in casinos. I'd like to see the Gabrielino get some kind of assistance as far as medicine goes.

CJ: What brought you to the sacred springs in West Los Angeles, and what does it mean to you?

---

* The Gabrielino Tongva Springs Foundation was established in the early 1990s to preserve the springs that were near the ancestral village of Kuruvangna. Today the springs are part of the University High School campus in Los Angeles. The foundation leases the springs and surrounding land from Los Angeles Unified School District, working to protect the springs, as well as to present educational programs to students and outside groups. For more information, refer to the conversation with Angie Behrns.

** In 1994, the state of California formally recognized the Tongva people in Assembly Joint Resolution 96, chaptered by the California Secretary of State as Resolution Chapter 146, Statues of 1994. It states, "Resolved by the Assembly and Senate of the State of California, jointly, That the State of California recognizes the Gabrielinos as the aboriginal tribe of the Los Angeles Basin and takes great pride in recognizing the Indian inhabitance of the Los Angeles Basin and the continued existence of the Indian community within our state."

AL: I went back to the springs because I took horticulture when I was at school, and everything started around the ponds. That was the most beautiful school in the whole unified school district. Everybody really enjoyed it. Our main interest was to try to keep it as beautiful as it was.

BMc: It's important to you in your life, and because of where you've lived. Do you think the springs are important beyond that? Do you think that the springs are a sacred place?

AL: I think so because Portolá stayed there at one time at an Indian village [Kuruvangna] as they went up through San Francisco.* For that fact only, I think it would be important to keep it more or less like it is. It would be something for us to hang on to because everything else has been taken away from us.

BMc: How do you feel about Indian burials, when they're discovered?

AL: I think that is sacred and should be left alone. I know there's progress, but couldn't they leave a space or something where our ancestors were buried, instead of being dug up and placed here and there forever? That's my only complaint. Other people complain about their relatives being moved. They raise a lot of Cain about it, but whenever they move an Indian burial, nobody ever says anything. If we say anything, they just overlook it anyway. "We're going to rebury them here, rebury them there," which I don't think is fair, really.

CJ: Mrs. Lassos, how has being married to a Tongva affected you? Do you know your own family history?

Dolores Lassos: My mother came to the United States when she was six years old. She met my father in New Mexico and they were married. After I finished grammar school, I went to Emerson Junior High, where Al also went, and to University High. [We didn't date] until the eleventh grade. My family was a strict Catholic family, and we were raised strict, period. He had to ask if he could date me. We married through the same procedure. His mother and brother had to come and ask my mom for my hand in marriage.

CJ: Were they concerned that you weren't marrying someone who was Mexican?

DL: No. My mom didn't know what he was. She just knew he couldn't speak Spanish. [Al's mother] had a little spiritual thing that she used to tell me when I got pregnant. "Don't go out in the full moon, wear something around your waist." It was a superstition. "Wrap it around in the full moon, and the child will be born in good health." They say if you don't wear it during the full moon, your child will be born either retarded or disfigured. She scared me, because she said they would

---

* A state landmark plaque records that the California expedition of Gaspar de Portolá and Father Serra passed by the springs on their way north in 1769.

grow up to be monsters, so I took that as very, very special information. I just stayed indoors.

She and I used to walk—when my son was of kindergarten age—to the school every morning, every afternoon. On Wilshire Boulevard there was a strip of land that went straight up past San Sandy, and there was a stream coming down. Where we walked, there was nothing but a lot of trees and wood branches, greenery. She would tell me, "Oh, the Indians came down from Santa Monica Mountains, and they would do the wash there."

BMc: When you were pregnant, and she was taking care of you, did she share other stories about her children?

DL: No, she just told me what to eat and what not to eat. She was very careful about certain things. She didn't give me very much information. She used to give us tea made of mint or made of rue [an herbal plant from the Mediterranean region used in traditional healing].

AL: She put potatoes on her head for headaches, and cucumbers in her eyes.

BMc: Did your mom have other stories about the mission? You know, the mission brings up so very strong emotions.

AL: She brought a lot of those stories up, but I didn't hear too many of them because I was out playing. Most of her feelings were good. She helped dust the pews at San Gabriel Mission when she was young.

CJ: Why is being Gabrielino important to you now, and has that changed during different times in your life?

AL: As far as my life goes, it's never changed. Since I have found out that I was Gabrielino, I stick to that. That's what I tell everybody, and I want my kids to do the same.

AM: When we were going for federal recognition, Kim [Art Morales's daughter] and I would go to the powwows, as Al and Lolly did, and we'd set up counters to get petitions to be federally recognized. Didn't take us anywhere, but we at least made the effort. It's difficult, especially when you're raising families. It somehow continues through at one point or the other. It's like a river, it just keeps flowing. No one is going to stop it.

CJ: Al, was your mother the oldest in the family?

AL: No, she was the youngest. My mother had brothers. Then there were my aunts. I think my mother took their word for what was going on until she became the eldest.

You know where the Baldwin Hills are? All the oil wells there used to belong to my family. My family owned land from San Fernando Valley all the way to Baldwin Hills. Tidewater wanted to get a clear deed to that land, but they couldn't because it belonged to the Indians. So they said, "We'll pay you off." They asked my mother and my aunts and uncles, "How much would you take, for a clear deed to this?" They said, "Well, you're making all the money. There are five of us left, we'll take five million dollars, a million dollars apiece." They said, "Oh, no, no. That's way over our heads." They said, "We'll just wait until you all die. You're going to be dead anyway, pretty soon."

That's exactly what happened. My mother, aunts, and uncles didn't get nothing. They specified right there that there were no other relatives besides the five—just my three uncles and two aunts. It was a deal just for them. We weren't included at all.

A CONVERSATION with Michael Barthelemy, Vivian Barthelemy (Michael's mother), and Patty Roess (Michael's sister)

April 9, 2006
Rancho Los Alamitos, Long Beach, California

The Participant

MICHAEL J. BARTHELEMY IS AN ATTORNEY LICENSED IN NEW MEXICO, Arizona, California, and on the Navajo Nation who primarily practices in the areas of personal injury, federal Indian law, and civil rights in employment. He heads the Indian Alumni Council of the University of New Mexico School of Law, is on the Navajo Nation Board of Bar Commissioners, and has long served as a catechist at the Immaculate Conception Church in downtown Albuquerque. Michael Barthelemy is married with three children.

The Discussion

Filled with poetic revelation and practical observations, the conversation with Michael Barthelemy reads much like a journal of personal exploration as he describes native culture and people. He considers the identity and cultural memory of the Gabrielino-Tongva people within the larger continuum of other native tribes today, exploring such matters as racial identity and the cultural memory of the people, as well as the differences and similarities between his San Gabriel family and community and those of his Mandan and Hidatsa wife. His ongoing work as a practicing attorney underscores his comments on native politics, law, and federal recognition while the evolution of his personal beliefs and contemporary commitments reflects his underlying native perspective as well as the Roman Catholic faith of his California Mission heritage.

Claudia Jurmain: For the record, please tell us your name.

Michael Barthelemy: Michael Joseph Barthelemy.

CJ: What made you want to become an attorney?

MB: Well, I visited a friend in Albuquerque, a fellow I had known up in North Dakota when I worked there. He was a Devil's Lake Sioux attending law school at UNM, and he informed me there was an area of federal Indian law. I never knew there was such a thing.

   My dad always wanted me to go to law school, but I never had an interest until I realized there was an area of law that I might want to work. I visited Kirk in Albuquerque, loved the blue sky and the billowy white clouds, and came right back home to California, grabbed my things, and went back right away. Even though it was a year until I would be enrolled, I went and worked at the Albuquerque Indian School for a year, and then enrolled at UNM.

CJ: What were you doing in North Dakota?

MB: I was a VISTA volunteer, and then they hired me as an adult education instructor at the United Tribes Employment Training Center in Bismarck, North Dakota. That's where I met my current wife, about 1978. She's half Mandan and half Hidatsa.

CJ: Tell me when you first became aware that you were Native American.

MB: Well, I knew all the time. I knew my grandpa was an Indian, and my grandma was an Indian, too. It was made known to us from the time we were very small.

CJ: When we asked Patty Roess [Michael's sister] that same question, her memories are more of moving to suburbia and having a sense that she was different, but not necessarily that her life was different. Celebrations weren't different, stories were not being told. Is that your recollection?

MB: I think I was more sensitive to it because I was always the darkest skinned among all of us and always experienced some amount of prejudice where we went to school. I think that made me aware earlier. Maybe the reason is I had inherited that quality. Some of the Indian blood came through and I showed it. We moved from San Gabriel to Arcadia when I was five and a half years old. I was halfway through my kindergarten year of school, and we moved to what was then a lily-white community. I was one of very few students who had darker skin.

   Our family is mixed-blood, so we had different cultural inheritances. My dad's father was a Frenchman and spoke French, English, spoke Spanish. His name

Left to right: Michael Barthelemy with his mother, Vivian Morales Barthelemy, and his sister, Patty Barthelemy Roess, in the Jacaranda Walk, Rancho Los Alamitos, 2006.

was Andre, and my son's name is Andre. Then my grandma is from Arizona, an Indian from Arizona. We had a pretty close relationship with my uncle Joe, a veteran of World War II, and I remember hearing stories about his being treated differently. I questioned him about being in the Army. In his war experience he was treated differently for the fact he was Native American. For example, he was interned in a prisoner-of-war camp exclusively Native American. He told me that when he returned from the war, they shipped in to an area in Seattle. The proprietor at the bar all the soldiers went to refused to serve him because at that time it was prohibited to serve Indians any alcohol in the state of Washington. These stories I heard along the way distinguished us as Indians.

My grandpa Arthur died when I was in utero, I think, but we saw pictures of him, and there's no mistaking that he was a Gabrielino. It was unmistakable. My uncle Sparky and my uncle Joe—all of them were quite distinctive. It's quite evident they were American Indians. Then my little Nana, my grandma's mother, she was a Pima Indian from Sacaton, Arizona, and she spoke Pima, I remember. It's a very clear recollection, hearing her speak Pima. So, I guess those were the accumulated experiences that gave me the distinct impression we were different.

BMc: Is your personal identity or feeling of connection to the Gabrielinos different than your feeling about being Indian? You have had a lot of influences in your life. Did you view yourself, and do you view yourself now, as Gabrielino?

Vivian Barthelemy: Yes, I do, I always have.

CJ: What does that mean? How is that different?

MB: For example, I started to tell you that my dad—his father was a Frenchman, his mother was an Arizona Indian—but my dad was fundamentally a European in his worldview and his temperament, and in his physical features. He had wavy hair, and he could grow a full beard. I can hardly grow a beard at all. I have dark skin; he had fair skin. I don't look too much like my dad at all. I know I inherited a lot of [traits], but he was a very handsome man, essentially European in his outlook.

He'd travel, take long drives on Saturday and Sunday and on the weekends, and he liked to pull off to the side of the road and buy a loaf of bread, a block of cheese, and wine. That for him was a great outing. In a respect he resisted, didn't understand, and didn't fully appreciate that I didn't really see myself that way. If I would share thoughts about being an Indian, it would just go right over his head. He had no real sense of himself as an Indian. He seemed to not have the genetic inheritance, and didn't really understand his own mother in a respect—why she would do certain things.

I was very conscious of myself as an Indian person and see myself as that principally. My dad didn't perceive, didn't view himself as an Indian, although he recognized his mother was an Indian. That's why I say there's some cultural splits within the family. It seems to me that the degree to which we view ourselves as Indian or as European is a function of how we look, and what kind of temperament we've inherited genetically. That's sort of a controversial idea, but in my experience, that's the case.

I've come to believe that to the degree that you inherit the physical features, you also inherit some of the inner workings—the personality, the temperament, and the worldview. I've related to a lot of Indian people from different areas, and I'm not always fully accepted as an Indian person either, which is real curious to me.

CJ: What identifies you as Gabrielino today, other than your DNA?

MB: I lived with Lakota people, and I came to recognize their physiognomy, their particular physical features. I could tell a Sioux from a Navajo any day of the week, whereas a lot of people who have never been around Indians, don't know anything about Indians, would never know the difference. I could tell a Northeastern Woodland Indian from a Pima from a Navajo to a Sioux. I can tell at a glance who's mixed-blood and who's not. You can see the inheritances. My wife is only three-quarters; her father was one-quarter English and her mother was one-quarter English, so she's three-quarters, really. If you look at her, she's got very distinctive Indian features, but you know she's not a full-blood Indian.

CJ: What does that mean for a community today, an urban community, where some Gabrielino are down to very small percentages? They would view it as racist to perceive them in terms of blood quantum.

MB: There is a degree of racism there—the very fact that the United States government would draw these lines of demarcation where you have to prove not only that you're one-quarter blood quantum but a member of a federally recognized tribe, in order to be qualified to receive government benefits.* That's a racist idea, but there's a lot of racism among Indian people [as well].

I'm not fully accepted as an Indian person. I was at a meeting of the Native American Law Students Association on Friday in Albuquerque and I talked to this Pueblo fellow who is a member of their council—very dark features, black hair—could be full-blood, although a lot of the Lagunas are married in with Spanish. He asked me if I'm a native person. I've sort of got to the point where I'm over feeling slighted by that, because I recognize, looking at myself in the mirror, I don't look like a full-blood. I can see the Spanish inheritance, I can see the European inheritance. So it doesn't disturb me. I always had an interest in being around Indians, particularly right after I graduated from college. That was my goal in going to North Dakota. I was forced to recognize early on that those people were not going to recognize me as Indian, because I don't have the full-featured, four-quarters Indian blood quantum. They are going to recognize other genetic inheritances, but they don't recognize Indian people look differently [in] other areas because they have a distinctive feature of their own. If they see an Indian person from another place, they might mistake them for a Hispanic, or a Mexican, or something.

I was sensitive about that at first. I guess it still gives me a twinge I've got to explain. This fellow from Laguna asked, and I said, "I'm a California Mission Indian, I'm from southern California." I don't really care to get into it too much deeper than that, because I'm past the point where I feel like I have to explain myself to people.

CJ: How do you explain yourself to your child, to your son? When you say "California Mission Indian," those are "controversial words" for many people. Is that because you're describing yourself to an outsider, or is that how you see yourself?

---

* Tribal enrollment criteria are determined by individual tribes, not the federal government; however, the government also establishes legal standards for Indian identity relating to federal legislation (benefits programs), usually 25 percent, sometimes even 50 percent. However, each tribe has the right to set its own standards for enrollment. "Blood quantum," or degree of ancestry, is the most used criterion, according to one expert. About two-thirds of all federally recognized tribes require a minimum (often 25 percent) blood quantum for tribal enrollment. But other federally recognized tribes require no minimum blood quantum; instead, new enrollees must be direct descendants of another tribal member. Because of their unique history and early urban culture, the ancestry of the Gabrielino-Tongva people is based on the latter criterion and adheres to standards for federal recognition for documentation of ancestry.

MB: That's how I see myself. But my kids, they all have their own problems to deal with because their parents are Indian, they grew up in the city, and they don't look that Indian. They are more fair than me and my wife. But I can see they have inherited the Indian features. For example, my daughter, she's sort of a light olive complexion, has long brown hair, whereas my wife has very dark black hair with salt and pepper like my sister. But if she dresses in the buckskins, and has the beaded yoke and the braids, there's no mistaking it.

My son, he's tall, got real skinny legs, a real big barrel chest—sort of the cartoon image of Northern Plains–type people. Because all his uncles are like that, he inherited that. When he was younger he looked very much like me, but now that he's older, fifteen years old, he's got very sharp, angular features like his cousin [whose] father is Hidatsa/Mandan, his mother is of German inheritance from North Dakota.

BMc: For so many years the common wisdom was that the Gabrielino were extinct, physically extinct. Then around the 1960s, in particular, archaeologists realized that that wasn't true, so they coined the term "culturally extinct." We know they are out there, but we don't know anything about them.

Because you have seen so many different Indian peoples in the United States, what today would you consider the essence of being Gabrielino, different than simply being a Native American? We know that cultures move through time. The Gabrielino are not living like they lived two hundred years ago, one hundred years ago, even fifty years ago, and yet there still is a continuity of culture because they are still here with us.

MB: We don't have many cultural practices. If we wanted to, if I had more time perhaps. My primary interest is not in reviving old cultural ways. I'm interested in how our people once lived, not in dressing up in buckskin and headdress, and dancing. A certain part of me wants to do that, but it's not what I do, who I am. I think that is the essence for me. I can't speak for others, but I see certain things in common with others who perceive themselves as Gabrielino, and that is an affinity for the landscape. I always felt an affinity for the dry chaparral terrain.

When I went to college, I would seek out areas that were pretty well undisturbed. Just south of Claremont College, I'd go up to Padua Hills and sit up in those canyons because I felt at home there, listen. There was an area immediately south of my dorm that was undeveloped, on campus. I don't know if it remains undeveloped today, but it was toyon and tuna, and ceanothus and manzanita, all growing wild, original, right there—then, of course, scrub oak, big oak trees. I'd go down there by myself. I didn't do it to prove anything to anybody. I came to realize that I had inherited a particular view of the cosmos that was animistic—you invest physical things with spiritual qualities. At that time in my life, I was looking to see the world in a particular way—wanting to see not only the physical, but its other-worldly aspect. And where does this come from?

CJ: We've asked different people what they consider sacred. The answer is always the land. You're describing that relationship. You became involved in protecting Povuu'ngna at Cal State University at Long Beach.* Where does that fit in with your sense of "I'm standing ground here, this is who I am, and this place is important"?

MB: In the late seventies, '78, '79, and then again after 1983, my uncle Sparky and I were identified by the California Indian Commission as the most likely descendants of any ancient burials unearthed in this area. We were the first to be contacted.**

On that occasion, a burial was unearthed somewhere on [the Cal State Long Beach] campus when a pipeline was being installed and excavated, and so we answered the call. We did a little research and realized that there was a nearby village [Povuu'ngna], that this was a very important place in which Chinigchinich, a law-giver god, had emerged. I got the idea that we would see to the reburial and commemorate the spot by recalling that this was the place of Chinigchinich, law-giver and god. I don't know if you've ever seen photos of that reburial, but that wood sign made to commemorate the spot—I don't know where it is, whether it's still preserved—I made that sign. That's what it was—an attempt to give some respect and honor to these people who lived here.

CJ: Had you heard of Povuu'ngna before that event?

MB: No, I hadn't.

CJ: Did you identify with the Mission San Gabriel community and consider it home?

MB: Yes. But the reason I went to Albuquerque is I love the crystal blue sky and the billowy white clouds. Like today, when the air is clear, the [San Gabriel] Valley as it once was—it was always, I think, a hazy place. It was known as the Valley of the Smoke. So people called it that. With forest fires and the beach fog, early-morning low clouds clearing to hazy afternoon sunshine has always been L.A. and San Gabriel Valley. But I was always wanting to see that blue sky. That's why I moved to Albuquerque, also because it's tri-cultural. You've got Anglos—recently [arrived] Anglos—Hispanics, and Indians.

---

* During the 1990s the Native American Heritage Commission and plaintiffs from the Tongva community filed suit against California State University at Long Beach to prevent commercial development of an archaeological and burial site of Povuu'ngna on university property. The university administration declared a moratorium on developing the site and protected the open space. The moratorium was not binding on future administrations. For more on Povuu'ngna refer to the essay "A Connection to Place: Land and History" and the conversation with the Ti'at Society.

** Under the California Environmental Quality Act (CEQA), developers and public agencies must assess the environmental impact of a project, including the impact on "historical and cultural resources." The state's Native American Heritage Commission protects Native American burial and cultural resources in California. It identifies and designates the "most likely descendant" (a direct lineal descendant) to be contacted in the event Native American human remains are unearthed during the course of a project, to ensure their "appropriate treatment and disposition." Since 2007, state law also requires owners to protect burials and associated grave material found on their property, and allow access to the designated "most likely descendants." Before this time, property owners were not legally required to permit access to the designated "most likely descendants." In addition, the Native American Heritage Commission has established guidelines for Native American monitors/consultants who may be present during ground-disturbing work or onsite during the construction of projects which are known to be in culturally sensitive areas. (For more information on the new cemetery law refer to the conversation with Anthony Morales and the essay "The Enduring Vision: Recognition and Renewal.")

Indian people have a really high status in Albuquerque, and New Mexico in general, because they are so numerous in relation to the population in total. So I like being there. There's a lot of Indian people there from all over the country, not just Pueblos and Navajos, and Jicarillas and Mescaleros. That's what makes it pretty comfortable. People are tolerant—it's not like that every place in New Mexico—because of the tri-cultural arrangement in Albuquerque. I feel ambivalence towards southern California because of the dense population. The pollution really disturbs me and that's one of the main reasons I left here. I couldn't stand to live in polluted air. It always made me feel bad. So I left.

BMc: Did you move to Albuquerque to get away from the painful aspects of southern California as much as the blue sky and the billowy clouds?

MB: I think I did. I worked with my dad out in Walnut and Fontana. There are a lot of great places in Fontana, but when the smog would move in, it was just very depressing to me, like a blight. So that was a good motivation for me. But I miss southern California at the same time. I miss seeing my old haunts. I loved Joshua Tree [National Monument], used to go [there] a lot. At the same time, I don't resent anybody's living here. I can understand why people want to live here. It's so beautiful and green, and lush and wet, with the beach so close by. It's a wonderful place to live. So I don't begrudge anybody coming here, even recent Chinese immigrants, who have pretty much taken over San Gabriel. They come from different places. I don't begrudge them their being here—because to say it was wrong for the Mexicans or the Spaniards, or anybody after us to have come here—you cannot reverse things. It started when Cabrillo got here, what was it, 1542? It's been a continuous—

VB: I'm just afraid, especially for San Gabriel, that in time it's going to lose its old mission look.

BMc: Burials are sacred to you. Is that a fair assumption?

MB: Well, they are sacred in the sense that human remains have to be dealt with with respect. But I don't think that they are sacred in the sense that they necessarily shouldn't be disturbed. I've dealt with those burials before. I dealt with a big relocation of an entire burial site in the city of Encino on Ventura Boulevard.* They were building a high-rise, and they contacted me and my uncle Sparky. As we got into the project, it became evident that there were more and more and more burials. I was a real estate developer. I was building condos, apartments, custom homes. I loved digging into the earth. I loved excavating; I loved clearing the land and making

---

* In 1984 and 1985, archaeological excavations in the city of Encino, California, near the intersection of Ventura and Balboa Boulevards revealed evidence of a Gabrielino community which included a site with human and animal burials. This may have been the ancestral village of Siutcanga. Radiocarbon dating revealed that Indian people had occupied the site since as early as 5000 B.C. Much of the site was destroyed by redevelopment, and only a small portion preserved under landfill.

room for a beautiful building. So I didn't begrudge these guys out in Encino. They wanted to build their building, and there was a burial site right there.

First of all, I didn't have the political or the legal resources to resist their development. I was a lawyer, but an inexperienced one, barely one year out of law school, and I didn't want that fight. So I worked with the archaeologists, and we got all the burials relocated to the state park across the way. Those burials were already being disturbed. [There was] a stream that ran right through that property into the lake that was located on the state park, and burials were already being washed down the stream. So it wasn't as if the natural forces weren't already doing the job of disbursing those burials and reducing these people and their bodies back to dust. But some were incredibly intact. Spooky, scary. You had people curled up in fetal positions and with the abalone shell on their head and dentalium [shells] around their neck.

I just depended on the archaeologist to excavate them. I specified that they be placed in buckskin wrap, and we moved them all across to the state park, where we could be more assured that in the decades ahead they would not be disturbed again. If I had known that there were fifty or sixty burials on that site—maybe there weren't that many. Maybe there were thirty or forty—at least that many. If I had known that starting out, I may have approached it differently. The developer and archaeologist might have been somewhat disingenuous with us in having suggested to us that the site was only a few in the beginning. It turned out to be not just a few. But, we worked with it, and we got them relocated in a respectful way, and it's the best we could do with the resources we had.

I don't think they are sacred in the sense that you say, "Well, you've desecrated the burial site of your ancestors by having allowed them to be disturbed at all." I don't believe that. Perhaps, if we had had the political and the legal wherewithal, we would have stopped the development if we had known in the beginning what we knew at the end. But I don't have enough time in my life for that kind of a crusade. I didn't think I had the resources or the experience as a lawyer to resist this multimillion-dollar development.

My perspective is colored in large part by the fact that I'm a Catholic, and I try to be a faithful Catholic. I do not practice native religion. I did at one time. I was away from the church from fourteen to the age of thirty-one. During that time you could say I was searching for my Indian roots or wanting to be with other Indian people. And I found them—with all of their virtues and their limitations. I was wanting to take the step beyond hand's reach and see the supernatural aspect [of the world]. I still enjoy that today, though with all of the responsibilities I have, making a living, seeing that my kids are well attended to, and paying the mortgage and all that, I don't have as much time to devote to the pursuit of that other-worldly sense [as I did] in college, when my dad was paying the bill.

I had a lot more freedom, could spend time in Padua Hills. I was an excellent student, could make the A's, so I had time. I used to watch the planets, study them. Not deep scientific study, but watch them with a telescope, and I learned where they were, how they were oriented to one another, their distances and sizes. I could see the rings of Saturn, the big red spot on Jupiter. I could see Venus through its phases. I could sense their relative distance.

I remember one time I saw Venus, Saturn, Jupiter, the moon, and the sun in the sky at the same time. I could feel them. The moon was not just [a] flat disk of light, but a globe. It was three-dimensional. It was right there. I could see its relative size. If you looked at it otherwise, it was just flat light, just like in its phases. I used to look upside down and I could see the globe. I would sit on the top of those towers where they have big fans that would blow the frost off the orange orchards and watch the moon come up. I was watching all the time, just walking around. On campus, I would notice that all the shadows were laid out in perfect orientation to the sunlight shining [with its] white light. I was watching my own shadow. I tried to tell my dad about it. "Oh, that's weird shit," he told me, "that's weird shit." I'd tell him, "Oh, it's just my observations."

I went to North Dakota, then came back to law school and met my first wife. Her father was from White Earth Reservation, in northern Minnesota. Her father's mother was [Sisseton-Wahpeton] Sioux, and her mother was [Sisseton-Wahpeton] Sioux, I think mixed with Anglo. She wasn't full-blood, but pretty darn near. I fell in love with her because she had those classic features—long black hair, a dark face, and beautiful features. But she was like the child for whom the Child Welfare Act was written, because she had lived in about five or six foster homes. Certain people, non-Indians, all cared for her in five or six foster homes, and along the way some were kind to her.

She grew up outside of her culture but always wanted to return. She was a Dakota, studied the language. She was very much into practicing Indian religion, and could write the U.S. Forest Service and they would send her an eagle. She'd pray to the grandfathers, or to Great Spirit, and so long as we were together and married, that was part of our religious outlook.

But the problem was I found out two things. First, nature is cruel. Funny—when I sat up there in the canyons, I'd come back covered with poison oak. I was always at the student health service having to get a shot of penicillin because I was covered with poison oak. "Nature is cruel in tooth and claw." We can't be too romantic about nature. Look at the tsunami. There's all this arbitrariness in nature. Our people had it easier than most, because they had the most wonderful, plentiful land [in which] to live and [the] sea close by. They had the land-based animals and the sea to feed them. But Indians in the Southwest, the Spaniards reported they were dying of starvation in places like where my grandma grew up,

Yuma and Sacaton, Mojave Desert. I realized that, and that I do believe there's a moral order to the universe.

If you do something that's contrary to the law of nature, you're going to suffer consequences, physically, emotionally, spiritually. I grew up in the sixties, in the time of sexual promiscuity, and it got me into real trouble. I came to realize that when you do things contrary to nature and things that are sinful, the wages of sin are death. If you do things that are counter to nature and counter to God's will, that you suffer consequences, including death. So that's when I returned to the Church. I realized that the Catholic Church, of all churches, has a strict moral order. And I need it. So I went back to confession in 1984. I was thirty-one years old.

I was getting near to a divorce, my dad had just died—I was finally having to grow up. I couldn't be out and about like I was before. I had a child, a career. I was trying to make a living. I couldn't continue on with nature as my god, because it can strike you down at any time. That's why I returned to faith in the [Catholic] Church and its founder. So now I'm a Catholic. Full out. But I think that that's part of our inheritance as well. I think there's a reason for it. So that's why I don't have any problem with the world changing. I love the idea of us as a tribal people with a common genetic inheritance where you don't have to explain, "Well, I got Spanish, I got Mexican, I got French." We navigated plank boats among the Channel Islands, and I love the idea of being a hearty people like that, and living on the land. But it's gone. It's not like that anymore.

CJ: What do you want for today, then, for the people who call themselves Gabrielino and live in Los Angeles?

MB: I don't know. I used to be involved in the politics, but there's always the politics. There were a lot of people who were really critical about the idea that an Indian would go back to being Catholic. They think that's giving in to a system that was repressive and brought pain and change and disrupted the traditional lifestyle. I've heard all those criticisms. But I don't care.

CJ: There's been a remarkable pattern of leadership that has run through your family. It's been recognized, but do you view it as your personal family legacy, a generational pattern of leadership, or something that just happened?

MB: I don't know. I think it's an inheritance from sometime long ago.

BMc: With your knowledge, professional position, your background, you are someone who, at least if you were living in this area, at some point, probably would be a Gabrielino elder, a Gabrielino leader.

MB: I could assume that position if I wanted to. I'm fifty-two. I can speak articulately. I have a lot more education than money. But I was involved before and didn't like it, because there was always squabbling, people telling you you're doing it wrong. I see that among all Indian tribes, of course. I work with Navajo people all the time. I worked in the government. Not in the [Navajo Nation] government, but I worked against the government, because of stupid things they would do. I just don't know that I have the time or the energy to be involved in Gabrielino politics again. Because it just gets petty right away. That's what turned me off about involvement in burial issues, intertribal politics, and the push for federal recognition.

CJ: Do you think it's important?

MB: I think it's important. But other things are more important. I just have to hold my own at home first and then deal with other things. I'm now heading the Indian Alumni Council [of the University of New Mexico Law School], newly put in that position. I'm a board member of the Navajo Nation Bar Association. I'm on the parish council at my church. Beyond that I'm stretched pretty thin.

BMc: Do the Gabrielino need leaders?

MB: Yes. What's the ultimate goal, though?

BMc: If they need leaders, what should those leaders be? What should their role be? What should their responsibilities be? You've seen the world from many different perspectives. You've had the opportunity to deal with the politics and the legalities of the non-Gabrielino world, see how it looks to the Gabrielino, as well as how other people view that group and the issues they are dealing with.

MB: I could come back to southern California and work on Gabrielino self-determination full time. No doubt. Sometimes in the past I thought I had to do that, but I didn't. In fact, I distanced myself from it because I just didn't want to be involved in arguing over things that don't matter a whole lot. I could have said—if we had poised ourselves strategically for federal recognition back in the seventies and had that today, had an identifiable tract of land, we could have opened a casino, and I could have been rich beyond my wildest. But now the politics have changed. The U.S. government is looking very critically at federal recognition on the basis of the intent of the petitioning parties as to gambling and establishment of gambling establishments. So it's probably a harder thing to achieve now than it was back in the seventies.

Not only that, there's a whole continuum. There's tribes whose culture is as decimated as ours is, even some that are more thoroughly decimated, with less identity and racial inheritance, less cohesiveness, all the way to tribes far more at peace. The Pueblo Indians, who speak their language from the very youngest to the very oldest, who lived in settled villages then, live in settled villages today, have this cohesiveness, racial commonality in villages that probably means they will survive another hundred years, easy.

My wife's tribe was the tribe that Lewis and Clark wintered with in 1802 and 1804, and yet there's one Mandan speaker left. When I visited North Dakota in 1979, her father, her father's brother—there were many Mandan speakers—a few, but quite a few. Now there's one man, the last Mandan speaker [just like] the rest who were the last Gabrielino speakers.

The Navajos don't pass on the language like they should. Some do, but not like the Crows or the Pueblos, where it's still integrated in society to pass on the language and culture. I don't think you can buck the tide. I was really gratified, at the same time, to see in *The First Angelinos* all the different attempts to preserve the language. My mom and I were going through and realizing that, out of those three or four or five different attempts, "hand" was the same word in about three or four of them. So we got it. We know how to say "hand" in Gabrielino, "aman."

But can we go back and revive that language? No. It's a moribund language. It's dead. It's gone. It will never be revived. Is my intent to go back and provide leadership so we can get federal recognition so that we can sing and dance and speak our language again? I don't think it's ever going to happen. I'm a Gabrielino, undeniably. But I can't go back.

BMc: What about different kinds of leadership—contemporary leadership, moral, cultural, political, legal?

MB: I'm not sure that we are even cohesive enough as a people.

CJ: Is that important? If not cultural tradition, not DNA, then what goes to the essence of Gabrielino identity for the native people who still live in this area?

MB: The thing is that we are just so racially mixed, too. I see it among all Indian tribes—Jicarilla Apache—I used to work for them. You look at photo albums of them when they went in 1896 to secure the southern tract of their land. They had feather headdresses, sat in those open Model Ts and drove all the way to Washington, DC, to petition Congress to extend their reservation. At that time they looked like all the members of the same tribe. They looked like Jicarilla Apaches. They were lean, and their faces had common physical facial features.

[Later Jicarilla Apaches] recount how they all traveled to Washington, DC, to give oral argument in [the 1982 Supreme Court case] *Merrion & Bayless vs. Jicarilla Apache Tribe,* involving Indian taxation of non-Indians for oil and gas production on their reservation. You see the photos of them—they are wearing cowboy hats and belt buckles. They've intermarried with Spanish, with other racial groups. This is who the Jicarillas are today.

Who are the Gabrielinos today? You can interview us, and people can trace their roots. We're all related. But there's no way we're going to be racially pure, have that same kind of identity. We are just not that people anymore. I thought I wanted to marry an Indian woman, and I did. But it's not so important anymore. We are who we are. My kids grew up in Albuquerque. They didn't grow up in San Gabriel.

Their grandma just died, she's ninety-three years old, Cora Young Bird. She spoke Hidatsa. She was one of the real old-timers. She had contact with people who lived in the Stone Age. Her grandma, She Kills, died when she was ninety-six, when Cora was eight. Cora was born in 1913. Grandma She Kills was born in 1825. So within the living memory of a person with whom I've had contact, another person lived the Stone Age life. I've seen this continuity. But it's winding down. It's changing.

And you know what? I've had some contact with Pueblo people. You might say, "Well, these are the people who have really preserved their culture and their language and their tradition," and they have. It's beautiful. But they have the most parochial, closed-minded, dogmatic people among them. I tried to work with them. They wanted me to set up an enterprise by which they could send out their people as construction workers. They could not get off the dime. So on the one hand, they were strong in their native culture, but in dealing with the outside [world], they had to keep that parochialism, that closed-mindedness, that narrow-mindedness in order to do it.

CJ: Why have you chosen to identify with this one aspect of your cultural identity? You're also French, you're also Mexican.

MB: Well, I also identify with my French identity. Our name, Barthelemy, is French, but it's Bar Ptolemeus, son of Ptolemy, son of an Aramaic. Ptolemy is an Aramaic word. We are Catholics through the Franciscans, but we're Jewish, we're like the lost tribes. Bar Ptolemeus. I accept all of it.

CJ: What is the "something more" about being Gabrielino that you're trying to communicate to the next generation about this community of people, who may work in many different communities?

MB: I've not even shared with my children what I've told you today. I think they probably identify more with their mother as Indian than me because I don't say much, tell them much. She's closer to it. When they go back there [to North Dakota], they've got Indian dancing, and they've got a lot of relatives, but they don't have as much exposure to Gabrielinos as they do with Hidatsas and Mandans up there. They go there and feel very much like they belong. That's okay with me, too.

They saw me speak to a whole room full of Indians on Friday night. I tried to impart a little wisdom to those other Indian law students and tell them what my experience had been in legal practice in the federal Indian law sector. I think they appreciated it, even though they said, "Oh, Dad, you're such a nerd."

I don't see that in the near future I'm going to take a leadership role again in Gabrielino politics. I feel other obligations have higher priority—my more immediate family, my law practice, and my church. I don't expect my involvement in Gabrielino tribal life will very soon bring me back to California. I mean, I love California. I love to visit. But it's really hard to make a living here.

All Indian people deal with that. All Indian people are between two worlds. For all Indian people, nostalgia is like the controlling theme of Indian life. They all hearken to the past. But if you're so attached to what was that you can't function in the present day, you're in trouble. You're giving up too much.

CJ: Are there things from the past that you do not give up? That is one of the issues that is at the core of this question of identity, at the core of "Who do we want to be tomorrow?" It's also a legal question.

MB: There's still something inside me that tells me I kind of wish Andre would marry an Indian. Andre is my oldest son. He looks like his mother. He's dark, he's got black hair. But I can't control that. I'm not going to step in and say, "Hey, you should marry an Indian like I did." I've hinted, but I don't think that it's all that important. You see, my wife can't go back and marry in her home reservation, because she's related to everybody on the reservation. My wife grew up at the Saint Anthony's Catholic Mission in North Dakota. I grew up in the San Gabriel Mission in southern California. Our greatest commonality is our Catholic tradition. Being Indian comes second to that.

Patty Roess: It's interesting to hear him articulate this because I have very much the same feelings. The thought of the land being destroyed by development hurts a lot. There's a burial site at San Mateo Creek that they gave to the Indians to move their remains there. They want to put a pillar for the toll road right on top of it, and we will have to move them again. It's not so much that it's sacred land, but it's "push the Indians aside." It's happening again and again. "Oh, they are just Indians, they don't have any money, they don't have any power."

They are not recognizing us as people—our connection to the land. When my mom and I were discussing her future, whether to come live with me [in San Juan Capistrano], all of a sudden the lightbulb went on. My mom can't leave her area. She is connected to that land, and it's a really strong connection. I'm connected to the oaks. I love those oak trees—there's this draw, it's an amazing thing. My life is as ruled by the freeway as everybody's. To stay at peace with it, I take time when I go try to see the trees, the landscape rather than the buildings. As I get older, I'm starting to feel different things connect me more and more to the land, to my roots—wondering, "Why do I think these things? Why do I see things in this way?" All I can say is—it's my heritage finally emerging.

One thing I felt really strongly about is the ridgeline. I can't stand to see houses built on top of the ridgeline. Why? I can understand people wanting that view. But it's the ridgeline, I think it's sacred. I love seeing the ridge of the mountaintops. That's just, I think, the ancestry.

CJ: If being a Gabrielino is a personal journey of recognition, is there also a need for someone to take it beyond that sphere? If it's only a personal journey, will there be a collective identity, a cultural community? Or is there a need for people to be elders, to continue the tribal struggle to protect and fight for larger concerns—whatever they are?

MB: Right now I feel okay with that. I may change, maybe in my older age, when these responsibilities are past. That's why I don't begrudge newcomers to the valley, and why I try not to concern myself too much with whoever my children will marry, because my ancestors before me didn't marry exclusively within their Gabrielino clans. I'm not so concerned about maintaining a cultural, a collective identity. I think we do have a collective identity.

Whether or not we meet formally, whether we have any formal organization to our people, there are others who continue to do that. That's fine. We have done that before. I used to attend meetings that my uncle Sparky called. We had a collective identity to the extent that we met and shared common ideas. I just see that cultures come and go. Cultures die. Languages die. As strong as these impulses are, as strong as these links to the past remain for us, and as painful as it is to us to see things change, I'm not sure whether there is much we can do to reverse the tide.

It doesn't change who I am. That's why the whole idea of having to justify one's "Indianness" relative to some blood quantum or federal recognition really rubs me wrong. "You don't speak your language?" Even among the strongest tribes, there's a real diminishment of a culturally, linguistically cohesive people. So I can say, "Well, you're on the continuum just like we are."

BMc: Do you think that the Gabrielino can be a community without land as a base?

MB: I think the land is real important. You take the Sioux people, for example. Their culture is dying or is threatened because their land base is so threatened. They started out—the range was all of Nebraska, South Dakota, Montana, North Dakota. Now it's confined to little reservations, pockets of poverty within those reservations, all the other land being leased to non-Indians. And this is the great Sioux Nation. They do have an active culture, they have Sun Dance, they have song, they have dance. Their language is greatly threatened, but they have, in the face of all those attacks, managed to preserve cultural identity. But it's ever-changing. It's not getting better.

I do think that any people, regardless of whether they maintain a collective tribal identity—the Indian worldview continues to influence, is part of American consciousness. Clearly Indian people's art, their dance, their worldview very much affect and influence American thought. Even though our country is so aggressive militarily and economically, there still survives this other worldview. It's even romanticized. In areas like Santa Fe and Albuquerque, it's put up on a pedestal and elevated to art. I'm encouraged by that. I'm encouraged that people sing and dance, have their powwows, have their gatherings, and it's not going away in too big a hurry. But you just have to sort of go with the flow and accept change as it comes.

CJ: When people, kids, pick up and read the paper, is one overwhelming contemporary definition of a native person as someone who owns and benefits from a casino?

MB: Gosh, I hope not.

CJ: How does native culture continue to distinguish itself from the larger definition of "American culture"?

MB: Well, unfortunately, many peoples inherit the very worst, sometimes, of American culture. They sell tax-free cigarettes, they are extremely prone to alcoholism, they have gambling establishments wherever they can on their reservations, all of which are vices to me, and now they just buy into all of these very negative things. I was glad for the opportunity to give you a sense of how I define myself as an Indian. But I sure don't have a solution.

CJ: What perspective might you bring to the table which might address the commonality of all cultures? "This is who I am. This is who you are. This is what we might share." It's important.

MB: Other religious values define for me our purpose for being here, and that doesn't have ultimately to do with being an Indian person. Certain perspectives on the world seem to be uniquely Native American. At the same time, the worldview that I inherited through the Franciscan influence and the establishment of the missions as much defines who I am as my Native American racial inheritance. That perspective informs me that I need to be concerned about maintaining racial purity or maintaining language and religion. My religious perspective informs me that all people are equal before God, allows me to embrace anyone. That's why this whole concern about "Indianness" takes a back seat for me now.

BMc: I think that part of the requirement for federal recognition is that you have to demonstrate a sense of community. Is there a Gabrielino community separate from individuals? Do you think that the Gabrielino can achieve federal recognition? If that came with casino development as part of that package, is that acceptable?

MB: I think that we do have a collective identity. If you talk to any other people who know that they descend from the Gabrielino people, you'll find common themes. In that respect, I think we have a community of thought and belief, and a common racial inheritance. I think that the history shows that we have maintained that common identity.

I don't like casino development. That certainly shouldn't be our first aim. I don't know that it should be our aim at all. There are certain Indian groups who have achieved federal recognition and then sought to develop casinos right away. They have become, some of them, fabulously wealthy for having done so. But that isn't my aim. I think our aim in securing federal recognition was two things: First, to secure the satisfaction, to arrive at a point where we are satisfied other people outside recognize us as an Indian tribe, not to be excluded and not to feel excluded. I think that's the primary motive. Second to that has been to secure whatever financial or whatever federal benefits flow from federal recognition in the way of health care, education, establishment of a land base.* Perhaps by that establishment of a land base, to better develop a sense of ourselves again as a people with common goals and a collective goal which have been lacking without the land base.

The casino development is an issue that's more recent. It's certainly not my goal. I think it's better avoided. I'd be content to waive any intent. They say they wanted us to state that we would not, and I didn't like that idea. Already in extending federal recognition they are putting conditions, placing conditions about what we will do. Because of the proliferation of gambling operations, they say, "You cannot do this, as a condition for our recognition. We won't extend to you this sovereign prerogative. We won't allow you to do this thing." That's what I didn't like. So that's the way we expressed our intent.

I think that federal recognition could be achieved with the proper effort, with a continuous effort. Whether it could be, whether it would be granted without stating flatly that we will not [develop casinos], as a condition of federal recognition, I don't know. The government could say that, but I don't know. It just doesn't sit well with me, this idea, "Okay, we will recognize you, but you won't do this." I don't need this on those terms. I don't need their recognition, period. Maybe some will say, "Well, that's foolishness." But I don't need federal benefits to be an Indian. If they want to so condition that, I would just say no.

CJ: You said that your uncle Sparky was an active Gabrielino leader with knowledge of the community. Do you have any recollection of him speaking about the local Mission Indian Federation?

---

* For more information on ongoing private and public assistance to the Native American community in the Los Angeles area, including the Tongva, refer to the conversation with Angie Behrns, in which the Los Angeles City County Native American Indian Commission is discussed, as well as the conversation with Anthony Morales, in which he refers to his work with the Native American Ministry affiliated with the Los Angeles Archdiocese.

MB: I don't. In fact, I knew very little about my uncle Sparky, my grandpa, or my uncle Joe's involvement in Indian affairs before a few years ago. But these amazing photographs [show] my grandpa and my uncle Joe dressed out in loincloths at Indian dances at the Santa Barbara Mission. They were dealing with people from the Santa Ynez Reservation, other, Chumash Indians who were involved in the same dances. I had heard that my uncle Joe had danced Indian, but I had never seen it. I mean, there were a few family gatherings where he would break out and start dancing Indian, but I didn't know they had actually danced at the Mission Days at Santa Barbara until recently.

VB: I started to dance in Santa Barbara when I was five, but when I was eight or nine they joined. They had the Indians up on the hill, the Spanish coming down on their horseback, and then they'd have the fiesta down on the stage.

MB: These are the events you used to dance Spanish dancing. The integration of Spanish and Indian cultures was so close, it was certainly not unexpected to see both at the same event. I think I've heard that my grandpa was very resentful, as were his brothers, of people making some judgments about their degree of Indian blood. It's not just me. A few didn't like what Tommy Temple told them about their limited degree of Indian blood. They knew they weren't full-blood, but looking at them, it's undeniable that these people were Indians. They just didn't like some outsider making some judgment about them that way.

My wife, my kids are enrolled up at her reservation. She wonders why I don't try to do more genealogical work to justify a greater degree of blood quantum for them or federal recognition. Again, why should I depend on others to recognize me? I don't really feel the need to. I think it goes back to my grandpa's feeling about the same issue.

BMc: Do you know when Temple was doing that, around what time?

MB: I expect about in the forties. I looked at Tom Temple's records. You no doubt know that he transcribed a lot of mission records and reduced them to his own writing. I pored over those records, and we compiled a genealogy based on those records. So I was aware that Tom Temple had had something to do with that. I think that predated anybody's concern about federal recognition. I think his interest was the history of San Gabriel, his family having gone so far back in San Gabriel. I think he thought he was somehow related, too. But it was just done in conversation. Nothing was ever put on paper or anything like that. Not that I know of. But I know they used to call each other cousins.

BMc: He was going to lots of missions and doing genealogies. I always thought the impetus was the 1928 enrollment, which put the idea in people's minds to trace lineage. But I've never known—within your family, were they questioning the accuracy of his work, or was it just a matter of not liking an outsider trying to tell them—

MB: They were questioning the accuracy of his work because he was telling them that they were of a lesser blood quantum than they believed based on what they had been told and what they observed. That's why they resented him making those judgments.

CJ: Is the community small enough, would you know who was Gabrielino? Would you take it at face value if somebody said they were Gabrielino?

MB: I wouldn't take it at face value. I'd be suspicious because of the casino issue. If they could tell us who their relatives were, who their ancestors were, and if they fell on our family tree, we would accept them as family. San Gabriel is the base for us. No doubt there are people who are very closely related, even at Cahuilla or Pechanga.* I know some of our people took land down at Pechanga. My uncle Sparky told me that at a certain point they were offered land at Pechanga, and they didn't follow up.

BMc: I'm curious how some families would be able to move, say, to Pechanga or Pala. To be enrolled on a reservation they would have to prove that they were Luiseño or Cupeño. Is it because of intermarriage? Or was it a situation where they could live there but not necessarily be enrolled on the reservation?

MB: My understanding is that other Gabrielinos were offered land tracts on Pechanga by virtue of their status as Gabrielinos, not because they married in with that band down there. At one time I felt kind of sore that Uncle Sparky and others didn't follow up and didn't accept the land. At the same time, I've heard tales for years about land in this valley having been deeded to our ancestors, but I've never followed up either. So I can hardly fault him for failing to do what I myself have failed to do. Maybe it's neglect. It would be great if there were a tract of land. But I can't imagine what kind of squabbling there would be if there was a tract of land ready to be divided up among everybody claiming to be a descendant. I suppose we'd take it. We would have to be formally recognized, and take it in trust on behalf of the tribe. But still, it would come to a question of who would have the right to live there. Then I suppose some would be pushing for casinos. I imagine that if at this late a date that offer was ever made again, it would lead to controversy for sure.

My grandma had pretty close contact with Morongo Indian Reservation.

---

* The 18,884-acre Cahuilla Reservation is in Riverside County, near Anza, but only 2,000 acres are common tribal lands; the rest are assigned. The reservation population is approximately 154 members, but Cahuilla also live on the Agua Caliente, Augustine, Cabazon, Los Coyotes, Morongo, Ramona, Santa Rosa, Soboba, and Torres-Martinez reservations.

Located near Temecula, California, the 5,500-acre Pechanga Reservation belongs to the Pechanga Band of Luiseño Indians, a federally recognized tribe. Established by the executive order of President Chester A. Arthur, Pechanga later increased in size. Today, Luiseño people also live on the La Jolla, Pala, Pauma, Rincon, Soboba, and Twentynine Palms reservations.

The 12,273-acre reservation for the Pala Band of Mission Indians is located in northern San Diego County, and home to Cupeño and Luiseño Indians. In 1903, President Rutherford Hayes enforced a Supreme Court ruling and ordered the Cupeño people to move to a reservation which had already been established for the Luiseño. Their descendants today consider themselves one people.

Even though she was enrolled at the Colorado River Indian Reservation and was a Pima, she lived close enough to know people there. Curiously, my wife's close relative moved there recently. He's a Hidatsa, speaks Hidatsa and lives on the Morongo Indian Reservation now. I was sitting up last night thinking about these connections. One time I was with my grandma at an Indian dance at Morongo, and Russell Means showed up. It was curious to see Indians from far-flung places show up in our home territory, essentially trying to make relations with local tribes. Of course, the southern California tribes have come much more to the fore now that they have money, power, and influence. But in those days they didn't—pre-casino days.

CJ: You are now arguing cases on behalf of Indian people against Indian tribal government.

MB: The issue is that Indian tribes enjoy sovereign immunity from suit. They have been recognized as sovereign governments predating the United States Constitution, and that concept is, was established by early United States Supreme Court precedents. Tribes have been exempt from civil rights protections extended to all of us. For example, the Indian tribes were expressly exempt from any provisions of the Civil Rights Act of 1964. That means they can't be sued for discrimination on the basis of race, religion, gender, age, or disability.

Because of the Supreme Court case *Martínez vs. Santa Clara Pueblo,* the Pueblos essentially have free rein to decide matters of enrollment and religion and housing without any interference on civil rights grounds from individual Indians. For that reason, any individual Indian people can be subjected to abuses at the hands of their own government.

Navajo Nation has a Navajo Nation Sovereign Immunity Act where they allow suit under limited circumstances. So there are more protections. But among the Pueblos, laws are largely unwritten, or if they are written, they don't afford civil rights protection to their people among the few Pueblo tribal codes that I've seen. That means that people, the Pueblo governor and the councils, can be pretty arbitrary in deciding matters of enrollment, for example. Also there are very few rights to redress against the Pueblo governments. That's why my perspective on individual Indian rights against Indian governments has changed.

CJ: You said you felt you were discriminated against. Did that take any overt form other than a feeling that you had?

MB: No, there was overt prejudice, name calling, that kind of thing.

BMc: Did the prejudice ever make you wish that you weren't Indian?

MB: No. I've heard that among other tribal groups, like the Navajos, for example,

I've heard that they went through a period of their time, during the boarding school period, for example, when they were given the impression and came to believe that they were lower or lesser because they were Indians. I suppose that could occur where you have a dominant group of non-Indians who are telling you all the time that you're worthless, you might get that impression over time.

But I always felt proud to be an Indian, which I found isn't universally accepted. If you tell somebody in Mexico, a mestizo, that you're an Indian, they wonder, because in Mexico Indians are so poorly treated—full-blooded Indians. There are more full-blooded Indians in Mexico than in U.S. America. The Indian people you see on border-town streets are the poorest of the poor. And they have a pretty cohesive tribal identity. Many of them don't speak Spanish, even. But if you ask a mestizo in Mexico whether they are Indian, if they look Indian, appear Indian, they don't want to hear that, because where they come from, being Indian is the lowest rung of society.

In this country because the non-Indians, the Anglos, are sort of patrons of Indian art and many romanticize what it is to be Indian, Indians have a different status, I think. Particularly in places like Santa Fe. In [other] places, forget it. You know, you're still just the lowest of the lowest.

But what I talked about before was just this idea that I was dark-skinned among all these other, light-skinned people, and I was singled out and called names. The teacher didn't back me up. I remember experiencing that and wondering about my skin color and being sensitive about my skin color. But I don't know if it was really linked to being Indian, necessarily, so much as just the color of my skin.

CJ: Are there things that we haven't talked about that are on your mind or that these conversations have provoked?

MB: There are a couple of things. One time I knew a fellow from law school, Woody Morrison was his name. He was from Alaska, and he had a friend from Alaska who was Eskimo—a great big guy, had blue eyes, but he looked Indian. One time I saw him lumbering across the lobby of the law school, and I could have sworn from the back that he looked just like a polar bear. It was just really striking that he lumbered in the manner of a polar bear. I thought, "There's gotta be something to this." I think it's because he's descended from a group of people who for eons have been pursuing the polar bear. They have come to so admire the polar bear and its power—they are so fearsome—that over time the Eskimo people have sought to emulate the polar bear in their manner, in their manner of walking. I know, for example, that among my wife's people, Hidatsa, a lot of the Plains Indian people dance in the manner of the prairie chicken. The men's traditional dancers move like a prairie chicken, the way they turn their head. It's meant to recapture or capture the movements of the prairie chicken that would sit on the ridgeline and do their mating dance against the horizon. It occurred to me that people inherit things genetically, but they also inherit sort of imprinted behavior. When you talk about my sister Patty's affinity for the oak tree, or my affinity for the dry chaparral terrain of southern California, I think it's sort of a long-imprinted connection.

I remember in those days when I used to go out and survey the chaparral around Padua Hills and Glendora Ridge Road, I used to walk on the firebreaks along the base of the Angeles Forest. When the storm would clear, the black clouds are in the east and it leaves these billowy white clouds across the valley. They move with the storm, but they trail behind.

I just happened to be up on one of those firebreaks one time looking out over the valley. I could see all the way to Catalina from up on Glendora Ridge Road. I could see downtown L.A., and all the clutter of man-made stuff, all the streets and the buildings sort of fall away. You can sort of see the vision of what the valley once was. As I was standing there looking out at those white clouds, white on top, gray on the bottom, moving ponderously across the blue sky, I realized that by standing there looking at the valley from this unique perspective, I was bringing that vision into being. I was both the subject and the object. I was indistinguishable from the stuff of my vision. I was the valley. I was the sky. I was the clouds.

It goes along with what I was saying about this Alaska native who lumbers in the manner of a polar bear. You become the stuff of your vision. It's inherited culturally and genetically, and there's something deep-seated and inherent in your vision of the world because all the people before you looked out and saw the same vision. You are the stuff of what you view. You bring it into being. It doesn't exist if you don't see it yourself. When I had that epiphany, that moment, I realized why the attraction, why the affinity for the southern California landscape, and why this continuing interest and concern over things ancient. Because I saw it in others. That other-worldly vision that I entertained in my youth didn't spring from me alone. It came from all those shamans. I don't like that word "shaman"—all those visionaries from our past. We were other-worldly people in our ceremonies and in our initiations into life. We were urged, we were drawn ceremonially to a place beyond hand's reach. There was nothing mundane about living that life.

People romanticize Indians because they can take that step beyond hand's reach, because they are a visionary people, and they are not stuck in the clutter of man-made manufacture. I think that we make accommodations, we drive cars, we use computers, but there's that connection to the land and to nature that non-Indians envy. I think that's the brilliance of Indian people, what distinguishes Native American people from other groups. I also think that there's universality among all people. This vision of life and nature is not unique to Native Americans. It's just that because of where we come from, that is the emphasis—that has been the emphasis.

T W O

A Connection to Place: Land and History

William McCawley

When I tell people about who I am...I tell them I acknowledge all my ancestors, but my identity is from this land, because that's where I'm from right now, that's my history.[1] — *Craig Torres*

LAND IS THE COLOSSUS STRADDLING THE GABRIELINO-TONGVA'S history, one foot firmly planted in their past, the other stepping uncertainly into their future. Land—and the memory of land—lies at the very foundation of their identity. It exists simultaneously in their cultural memory both as a thing taken from them and, paradoxically, as a thing that can never be lost. "We didn't give our land away. We didn't sell it. Remember that," cautions Angie Behrns.[2] In fact, the Tongva never abandoned their land, nor did they yield it through military conquest. Their legal rights to it were taken from them gradually, over time, as new governments seized power from old ones while ignoring the obligations of their predecessors, and as the officials of those new regimes allowed (and often abetted) the efforts of individuals to enrich themselves at the Indians' expense.

Land, and their connection to land, forms an integral part of the Tongva's individual and collective identities. Cindi Alvitre says, "I was raised in Orange County—Santa Ana, Huntington Beach, Newport, Fountain Valley....[That was]...the immediate identity my father linked to and my family discussed....I identify with the land." For her, Los Angeles exists as layers of history stacked one atop the other, each layer as real as the buildings and streets that stand today. In her mind, past and present coexist. "I don't see these rectangular blocks of asphalt and concrete," she says. "I see earth and villages."[3] Attitudes like this are rooted in the Tongva's traditions and history, a history fixed in the Los Angeles region.

Two centuries ago the Tongva relied on their deep connection to the land—an intimate knowledge of its seasons and moods, a constant awareness of its hazards as well as its potential—for their very survival as a hunting and gathering people. But when the Spanish arrived in the eighteenth century they brought a different view. Where the Indians saw seed-bearing grasslands as a vital source of food, the Spanish envisioned enormous pastures for their vast herds of horses and cattle. The Indians periodically burned off the grasslands to keep them productive, but the Spanish imposed laws that forbade the burning of such valuable pasturage.[4] Where the Tongva saw rivers and streams feeding wetlands teeming with life, the

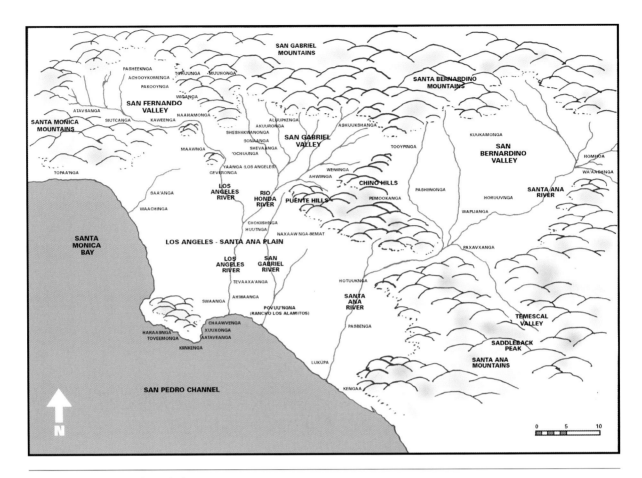

Gabrielino-Tongva villages on the mainland. Map by William McCawley, Drawing by William S. Wells

Spanish recognized valuable sources of water for their farms, vineyards, and orchards. The Tongva fished the rivers and gathered reeds and willows from the wetlands to build their homes; the Spanish dug irrigation canals. Where the Tongva saw ancient villages rooted in the land, the Spanish spied prime real estate. The Tongva memorialized their villages in songs and oral histories; the Spanish built ranch houses with adobe bricks cast from straw and clay and built ranch houses with them.

The gulf separating these two worldviews was immense. It took the Tongva several decades to truly comprehend the new world that was suddenly thrust upon them. Over time they grew accustomed to the novel ways. They became farmers, vaqueros, and ranch hands and formed new connections to the land. When the missions were disbanded in the 1830s, a fortunate few became landowners and received legal title to their properties (although they faced relentless and often brutal challenges to their ownership), while others without land had to go wherever work was available. Throughout the nineteenth and twentieth centuries their fortunes shifted as the economy of Los Angeles evolved from agriculture to industry, and ranchos gave way to citrus orchards and then suburbs. Yet the Tongva's deep emotional connection to their homeland survived, a connection to the hills and canyons and the place names they carry. It lives in them today, centering them in space and time regardless of where they live, linking them to their past and to a vision of their future that can never be taken from them, no matter how often the land is bought and sold, no matter how often it changes hands. Michael Barthelemy knows the connection well. "When I went to college I would seek out areas that I knew were pretty well undisturbed," he says. "Just south of Claremont College, I'd go up to Padua Hills and sit up in those canyons because I felt at home there."[5]

But today's landscape is a far throw from the one the Tongva's ancestors knew two and one-half centuries ago. Theirs was a land of broad rivers with winding channels cut through sandy beds, vast wetlands thick with willows and rushes, and dry chaparral-banked hillsides. Their villages were placed in carefully chosen locations near reliable sources of freshwater, where they would also be protected from the winter flooding that sometimes covered thousands of acres with a silvery sheen of water. There were approximately fifty major villages dotting the prairies and scattered along the seacoast and among the islands of their homeland. A few large ones held several hundred people, though most had more modest populations of perhaps fifty to one hundred and fifty Indians. Each village held a territory of roughly thirty square miles that included a diverse assortment of ecological zones—habitats—and provided an assortment of plant and animal foods throughout the various seasons of the year.[6]

One of these villages holds a very special meaning for the Tongva today. The village of Povuu'ngna crowns a low hilltop near the coast in the city of Long Beach, approximately two miles north of the Pacific shore and a mere half-mile inland from Alamitos Bay, in a spot that lies near the very geographical center of their historical territory. Take a map and draw a circle around the Tongva homeland with the center at Povuu'ngna. The top of the circle brushes the mountains to the north—the ones the Spanish called the Sierra Madre and that we know today as the San Gabriels—while the bottom of the circle crosses San Clemente Island. Only tiny San Nicolas Island, sixty miles out to sea, falls outside of it. Today many Tongva also regard Povuu'ngna as the center of their cultural and spiritual universe, thanks in part to its history and in part to important political developments in recent years.

The Village at the Center of the World

The places we honor are the ones that embody our most cherished values. The silent battlefields of Gettysburg and Normandy embody sacrifice and courage, the soaring arches of Chartres and Notre Dame cathedrals evoke piety and devotion, the simplicity and marble grandeur of the Lincoln Memorial symbolize justice and compassion. These places are more than mere real estate and architecture; they are sacred spaces that connect us to our past, memorialize those human qualities we honor most, and provide symbolic signposts to guide us into an uncertain future. For the Tongva, the ancient village of Povuu'ngna is just such a place. As Janice Ramos explains, "You have your myths, and your beliefs, and you have your faith, but...many people...need something tangible. They need something to see. And that's...what Povuu'ngna represents."[7]

Povuu'ngna is important because it represents a sacred center for the Tongva. Historian Mircea Eliade defines a sacred center as a place where religious truths are revealed and made manifest.[8] For many reasons, no other Tongva site meets this definition so closely. In his book *Chinigchinich*, Father Boscana explains how this village came to have such importance. Povuu'ngna was the home of Ouiot, the First Tongva Chief, a powerful ruler whose cruelty and abuse of supernatural power ultimately led his followers to assassinate him. It was also the place where the Tongva's prophet and spiritual being Chinigchinich first appeared. Chinigchinich was the creator god who formed the first human Indians out of clay scooped up from a nearby lake. He also selected the chiefs and shamans from the ranks of the First People (animal beings who lived on earth before humans were created) and anointed them with the authority to rule over the Indians. Chinigchinich set down the rules they were to follow in their daily lives, instructed them in how to build the open-air temple that was sacred to him, and taught them the dances and rites necessary to sustain life in this world. When his own death approached, Chinigchinich ascended to the stars, where he continued to watch over his people.[9]

> *You have your myths, and your beliefs, and you have your faith, but many people need something tangible.* —JANICE RAMOS

Today many Tongva see Povuu'ngna as a place of origin and renewal, although their interpretation of what this means is individual and highly personal. Cindi Alvitre asks:

> Is Povuu'ngna sacred?...Is it just a sacred symbol...or does it mean more?... And why is it important to protect the physical site of Povuu'ngna as well as the sacred symbolic significance?...Does Povuu'ngna offer a path for the future, and [a] place of renewing cultural ties within the community as well as reconnecting and reconciling with others?[10]

Craig Torres explains, "A lot of our families, they never mentioned the name 'Puvungna,' but they always mentioned, 'You are from here,' you know, 'This is where you come from.' And that connects us to Puvungna....My mother would always tell me that this is where we come from."[11]

The symbolic and religious importance was made clear when California State University, Long Beach, announced plans in 1992 to build a strip mall on an undeveloped parcel of land at the northwest corner of the campus. Previous archaeological work

Illustrated woodcut from the 1933 edition of Father Geronimo Boscana's Chinigchinich. *The original manuscript dates back to 1822. The 1933 Santa Ana Fine Arts Press edition was partially funded by Fred and Florence Bixby, the owners of Rancho Los Alamitos.*

on the parcel revealed a site with at least one prehistoric burial, and the archaeological site is listed on the National Register of Historic Places as part of the village of Povuu'ngna.[12] Michael Barthelemy recalls the events at the time the burial was discovered:

> In the late seventies, '78, '79, and then again after 1983, my uncle Sparky [Morales] and I were...identified by the California Indian Commission as the most likely descendants[13] of any ancient burials that were unearthed in this area. So whenever they were unearthed, we were the first to be contacted. On that occasion, there was a burial that was unearthed somewhere on the campus when a pipeline was being installed and excavated, and so we answered the call. We did a little research and we realized that there was a nearby village. I guess at that time I had been doing a little reading in the book...[Father Boscana's] Chinigchinich book, and I realized that this was a very important place...the place in which... Chinigchinich, a law-giver God, had emerged. I got the idea...that we would see to the reburial and that we would commemorate the spot by recalling that this was the place of Chinigchinich....[A] wood sign was made to commemorate the spot...I made that sign....It was an attempt to give some respect and honor to these people who lived here.[14]

> *We would commemorate the spot by recalling that this was the place of Chinigchinich. A wood sign was made to commemorate the spot....It was an attempt to give some respect and honor to these people who lived here.*
>
> —MICHAEL BARTHELEMY

Jacaranda Walk, Rancho Los Alamitos, 2008. CRISTINA SALVADOR PHOTOGRAPHY

Later, in the 1990s, following a lawsuit, a lengthy series of court hearings and legal actions as well as public protests, the university declared a moratorium on development of the parcel, although this decision is non-binding on future university administrations.[15]

TODAY POVUU'NGNA LIES BENEATH RANCHO LOS ALAMITOS HISTORIC Ranch and Gardens, the campus of California State University, Long Beach, a veterans' hospital, and a private residential community. Yet the signs of it are still there, if one knows where to look. Visit Rancho Los Alamitos and stroll past the tennis court in the cool shade of the purple-flowered jacaranda trees and you will see the evidence beneath your very feet, tiny flakes of white shell embedded throughout the dense, ash-gray soil, reminders of centuries of Indian life at this unique place. Although Povuu'ngna is not the largest Tongva village or even the best known,[16] it is very special nonetheless. One reason is its history; another is its location. Most Tongva villages survive as mere names on a map, roughly placed within the boundaries of the Spanish and Mexican ranchos that absorbed them in the eighteenth and nineteenth centuries. Rarely is there enough detailed information to stick a pin in a map and say, "There it is." But Povuu'ngna is one of the rare exceptions, thanks to historical, anthropological, and archaeological evidence gathered over more than two centuries.

The earliest information about the village comes from writings of Father Boscana (around 1822) and Hugo Reid (in 1852), both of whom located Povuu'ngna at this place.[17] Much later, in the early 1900s, Smithsonian anthropologist John Peabody Harrington visited Rancho Los Alamitos and observed how, "due east of the...Bixby house and downslope from it...in the alfalfa field...the ground is covered with shell debris—the remains of the ranchería of Puvú'." When he interviewed José de los Santos Juncos and José de la Gracia Cruz (a Juaneño from San Juan Capistrano), both men "equated this village and spring, and the ranch house on the hill upslope...to the Spanish name Los Alamitos."[18] Archaeological investigations carried out at Rancho Los Alamitos have confirmed that the heavy shell deposits seen by Harrington still exist on parts of the hilltop.[19]

There are no maps or drawings to show us how the ancient village once looked. The Spanish called it a *ranchería*, which suggests a relatively small settlement of one hundred to two hundred Indians (by contrast, they called the large

Craig Torres, 2006. Craig, a member of the Ti'at Society, is teaching students on the Jacaranda Walk at Rancho Los Alamitos, once the kitchen midden of Povuu'ngna. TY MILFORD PHOTOGRAPHY

Chumash villages along the Santa Barbara coast "pueblos," or towns).[20] Assuming each family had two adults and two children, perhaps twenty-five to fifty houses stood in the village. A spring of freshwater once flowed near the southeast slope of the hill, surrounded by a small grove of cottonwood trees.[21] It was this spring that undoubtedly first drew the Indians to settle in this place; the presence of freshwater also influenced how the village was laid out.[22] Houses probably stood on the east slope of the hill near the spring (where the ranch house and tennis court stand today) and down the hill past the jacaranda walk. This is where archaeologists have located the densest surviving deposits of shell refuse, or *midden*, a sign that the place was occupied over a long period of time.[23] This may also have been the spot where the chief and his council kept their homes.[24]

The rest of the village likely sprawled across the broad, gently sloping plateau,

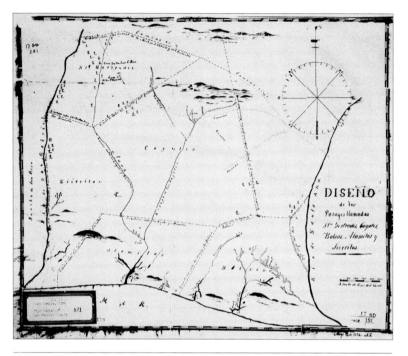

Diseño showing division of Los Coyotes into five great ranchos in 1833, Rancho Los Alamitos included Povuu'ngna.

although its overall size and extent remain guesswork. Two hundred years ago, when the water table was much higher, smaller springs may have flowed at other places nearby, and each of these could have had its own cluster of homes. On the campus of California State University at least ten different areas show evidence of archaeological deposits scattered amongst the buildings and walkways;[25] most likely, other nearby sites were destroyed when housing tracts were constructed throughout the 1900s. As Stacy Thompson comments, "I see...a key piece of it being there at Cal State Long Beach, but seeing it as a much larger area that probably moved, and so we could look at this whole area as being Povuu'ngna....[Because] you're not going to have just...one little hut right here. You're going to have to spread out. Why would you be so close when you've got so much room here?"[26]

IN 1771 THE SPANISH FOUNDED MISSION SAN GABRIEL APPROXIMATELY twenty miles north of Povuu'ngna (the mission originally stood near Whittier Narrows and was moved to its present site in San Gabriel a few years later); Mission San Juan Capistrano, thirty-one miles to the southeast of Povuu'ngna, was established in 1776.[27] Perhaps because of the distances involved, it was six more years before the missionaries recruited their first convert from Povuu'ngna; but in 1782 the first baptism of an Indian from this village was recorded at San Juan Capistrano. Between 1785 and 1805, thirty-two Indians from the village were baptized at San Gabriel, while another six were baptized at San Juan Capistrano between 1784 and 1788.[28]

The missions were not the only sign of the Spanish presence in the Tongva's territory. The Pueblo of Los Angeles was founded in 1781, and enormous land grants

Rancho Los Alamitos Hilltop and Ranch House, 2008. CRISTINA SALVADOR PHOTOGRAPHY

were also awarded to private citizens.[29] One of these went to Manuel Nieto, a Spanish leatherjacket soldier from the Portolá Expedition. In 1790, Nieto received the grant of Rancho de Los Coyotes, an immense three-hundred-thousand-acre tract that enclosed the village of Povuu'ngna within its boundaries. He used most of his land for grazing cattle and probably hired some of his workers from Povuu'ngna and other villages in the area.[30]

Originally the Indians may have worked as seasonal helpers. But as cattle raising expanded (and as more and more of the native plants and animals disappeared), the Tongva found themselves unable to rely upon hunting and gathering to support themselves and became increasingly tied to the ranchos and missions. In addition, the Spanish brought new bacteria and viruses that spread diseases for which the Indians had no immunities: European illnesses such as measles, tuberculosis, influenza, dysentery, and syphilis. Between 1803 and 1806 a measles epidemic hit the Indians living on Santa Catalina and Santa Cruz Islands and by 1806 the outbreak had swept throughout the entire chain of Upper California missions. Undoubtedly those Indians still living in the coastal villages also felt death's touch. It may not be a coincidence that the last baptism from Povuu'ngna occurred around this time, in 1805.[31]

By the early 1800s, cattle ranching was in full swing around Povuu'ngna. A small adobe ranch house may have stood on the hilltop as early as 1806.[32] Following Nieto's

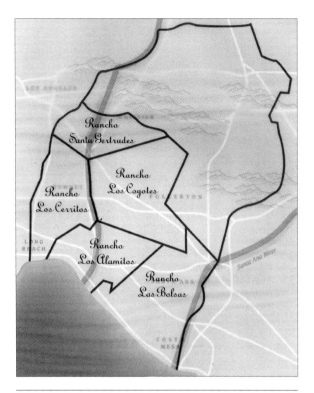

Contemporary map showing the 300,000-acre land grant awarded to Manuel Nieto. In 1796 the grant was split between Nieto and Mission San Gabriel. In 1833 the remaining Nieto portion was split into five ranchos. Rancho Los Alamitos included the Tongva village of Povuu'ngna.

death in 1833, Los Coyotes was divided into five separate ranchos—Los Coyotes, Los Cerritos, Santa Gertrudes, Las Bolsas, and Los Alamitos—and split amongst his heirs. Povuu'ngna fell within the borders of Rancho Los Alamitos, the "Ranch of the Little Cottonwoods."[33] Tongva and Juaneño Indians continued working at the rancho through the 1850s and perhaps later; the 1850 federal census shows thirty-three Indians living and working at Los Alamitos.[34] Juaneño José de la Gracia Cruz, who went by the nickname Acú, told anthropologist Harrington that he "had sheared sheep at Los Alamitos ranch house"; according to Harrington another Juaneño named Eustaquio also "used to shear sheep there."[35] An Indian named Eustaquio appears on a list of servants working at Rancho Los Alamitos from 1850 to 1854.[36]

Some Tongva still considered Povuu'ngna to be sacred land, long after barns and ranch buildings covered the hilltop and the village name was forgotten. Cindi Alvitre's father shared with her stories he remembered from his own childhood. "He didn't call it Povuu'ngna," Cindi says, although he knew it as a sacred place. Her father told her, "When we came through this area, this was very sacred, especially the ocean. When I was a kid, and my grandpa [Cindi Alvitre's great-grandfather] used to deliver hay to the Bixby family, we weren't allowed to speak because it was a sacred space. So you could only whisper. That's all."[37]

Today Povuu'ngna is sacred to many Tongva because it connects them to their history, their land, and their traditional religion and culture. These beliefs are deeply personal and vary from one person to the next, but they draw upon the same shared source. "It's a spiritual sense of the area...that connects what you feel," says Gloria Arellanes. "You explain it's a center of creation. You explain about...Chinigchinich.... And you explain about some of the stories that we have learned."[38] Povuu'ngna

Rancho Los Alamitos, near the hilltop of Povuu'ngna, 1887. RANCHO LOS ALAMITOS COLLECTION stands for continuity and tradition, but also for change. It is a place where the world can be viewed in fresh ways, where new meanings and expressions can be found in older traditions and values, and where new ideas and new visions can be shared with a broader audience. "Our identities are complex throughout the generations and they change," says Craig Torres, "but the connection to this place is always the same."[39]

Our identities are complex throughout the generations and they change, but the connection to this place is always the same. —CRAIG TORRES

Povuu'ngna is also important as a rallying point for the Tongva's efforts to preserve other sacred sites throughout their territory. The struggle to save the site at California State University, Long Beach, contributed to a growing concern for the destruction of other coastal sites, especially burial grounds like those at Playa Vista in Santa Monica,[40] Hellman Ranch in Seal Beach,[41] Bolsa Chica in Huntington Beach,[42] and Harbor Cove in Newport Beach.[43] Indeed, the Tongva's connection to Povuu'ngna is not only to the physical space, but to the many sacred spaces throughout Los Angeles and Orange Counties and the communities they represent, communities reaching back centuries into history.[44] As Cindi Alvitre says, "I don't live in the past. The past lives in me. Because I'm not just an isolated being. I am thousands of ancestors."[45]

Craig Torres, 2006. Torres, a member of the Ti'at Society, is walking around the altar at the Povuu'ngna site at California State University, Long Beach. TY MILFORD PHOTOGRAPHY

A Changing Landscape

Change is an inescapable fact of life in southern California, sweeping across the *sierras* and *playas* like a searing brush fire fanned by Santa Ana winds. Graders and earthmovers strip away the earth, reordering the countryside. Vacant fields become shopping malls; business parks sprout up overnight. Old neighborhoods are razed and reborn as townhouses and condominiums. The land is forever changed.

The Tongva have experienced these changes firsthand, sometimes with results that are emotionally devastating. "The significance is...everything has been destroyed," says Angie Behrns. "Our cemeteries [and] Ballona Wetlands." She remembers exploring caves near Topanga Canyon. "The last time I hiked down I didn't realize it was so large....I cried....[because people] have gone in there and totally destroyed [the petroglyphs]...the mortars were there [and] they put candles in [them]."[46]

By the 1830s most of the Tongva villages lay empty, except those attached to nearby ranchos.[47] The land had changed as well. The natural countryside, which the Indians had once partially managed through selective burning and other horticultural practices, had been transformed into vast pasturelands. But the changes went far deeper. An early history of Los Angeles County describes how the countryside from Los Angeles to the ocean was once covered with marshlands, thickets, and dwarf forests of scrub brush and trees.

Green River Pottery, Earl Campio's first pottery yard, 1945. He named his pottery shop "Grace" (Altagracia) in his wife's honor. COURTESY OF EARL AND DAVID CAMPIO

Rivers flowing through this thickly wooded place rarely reached the ocean, even during the rainy season. Instead, they fanned out across the land to form lakes, ponds, and marshes. But years of overgrazing left the countryside vulnerable to erosion by water and wind, damage that grew worse as farming and ranching expanded. According to one early history of Los Angeles County, beginning in 1825 the Los Angeles River cut a channel to tidewater and began draining the marshlands. The woodlands carpeting the countryside disappeared soon thereafter.[48]

The toll of this environmental damage became apparent in November 1856, when a fierce windstorm swept across Los Angeles, raising clouds of sand that blocked the noonday sun and bathed the city in an eerie dusk. Benjamin Hayes described the gloomy scene:

> At 10 a.m. a cloud of sand and dust from the seashore and plains overspread the city, rendering it impossible to see beyond 150 yards...and finally, about noon, making the sun wholly invisible....The dust penetrated into the closest rooms. The world without presented a most dreary spectacle....The wind had drifted the sand and light soil of the plain so as to efface all signs of the road for a great distance....The entire appearance of the yellow atmosphere gave me an unusual gloom. I thought of the shifting sands of an Arabian or African desert.[49]

These environmental changes paralleled equally momentous changes in the Tongva's relationship to their land. More recently, David Campio and his uncle Earl Campio experienced the anger, helplessness, and personal loss their ancestors must have felt countless times. Earl's father owned a pottery factory along the Santa Ana River and as Earl recalls, "we had our own water well and the Santa Ana River is right down the bank there. The river was our backyard."

> Where...[highways] 71 and...91 connect [and] the dam comes right there, and the river flows down....At the end...where the river is going down to the bottom, that's where...[Earl's father's] original house was....But if you go up here where the Santa Ana River flooded quite often...he said that was the...summer home where it was cool, [and] they would go up to...the caves... where they kept...their meat and things. And he even had initials carved in those caves where they used to stay.[50]

David remembers how all of this changed when Prado Dam was constructed across the Santa Ana River in the late 1940s.

> We'd always go down there and have family picnics, play in the river, about the sixth and seventh grade. We would just splash around....my...[uncle Earl] was on the banks...and we kids are swimming in the water. Next thing I remember is getting plucked from the water....We didn't know that we were all covered with leeches from the stagnant water. We've never been back to the Prado Dam since that day. The stagnant water carried the leeches. I just remember driving back—I was in the front of the old yellow Chevy truck with my...[uncle Earl]—and seeing him cry, "We'll never go back as a family to that river. It's not pure anymore. It's unclean, it's dirty, it's bad." And we never went back.[51]

I just remember driving back...and seeing [my uncle] cry, "We'll never go back as a family to that river. It's not pure anymore. It's unclean, it's dirty, it's bad." And we never went back. —DAVID CAMPIO

The construction of Prado Dam tamed the winter floodwaters of the Santa Ana River and opened up Orange County to development, but it also changed the character of the land forever.[52] Soon subdivisions and industrial parks replaced farmland and open prairie, and in that bittersweet transition one family lost its personal connection to the river and land.

Changing Laws of Land Ownership

The changes in the landscape mirrored legal changes in land ownership and land use under the Spanish and Mexican governments. Spanish and Mexican laws reflected attitudes formed largely on principles of property ownership, whereas Indian practices were based more on possession and usage. Under Spanish colonial law the Crown owned all of the land, while the missionaries held the Tongva's lands in trust. These lands would be given back to the Indians when the missionaries decided they were ready to manage their own affairs—that is, when they felt the Indians had became thoroughly Spanish in culture and lifestyle. Those lands the missions did not use could be granted as ranchos to private citizens as long as they did not encroach upon any existing Indian villages.[53]

The legal situation changed after Mexico won its independence from Spain in 1821. The newly organized Mexican government granted citizenship to the Indians in 1826,[54] but it refused to acknowledge their claim to their ancestral territories. In fact, the government's intent was to make as much of the mission land as possible available to non-Indian settlers.[55] The neophytes (as baptized Indians were called, to distinguish them from gentiles, or non-baptized Indians) retained the right as citizens to claim shares of mission lands, once the missions were converted into pueblos. Under this new legal system, mission land and property would be distributed to the neophytes and any remaining undistributed land would revert to the public domain. Smaller neophyte villages would be allowed to organize and claim legal status as separate communities.[56]

But reality was quite different from the plan. Once San Gabriel was turned over to civilian control, the mission fell deeply into debt, while living conditions for the Indians steadily deteriorated. The Tongva grew unhappy with the civilian administrators appointed by the government; they also realized that owning their own land was the key to their economic, political, and social survival, both as individuals and as a community. In 1846 they delivered a petition to Governor Pío Pico, signed by 140 of their members, citing their grievances against San Gabriel's civilian administrator and asking that the mission be converted into a pueblo and its lands distributed to them (neighboring Mission San Juan Capistrano was formed into a pueblo in 1841, the only California mission to be so reorganized).[57] In less than a month they had their answer. A government body set up to review such requests, *la comisión de misiones*, rejected their petition on the grounds that Mission San Gabriel had already incurred too much debt, debt accumulated under the civilian administrators appointed by the government.[58]

Tongva still had the right to apply for shares of mission land as individuals, but few benefited under the new system. Mexican governors routinely granted legal ownership of former mission lands to non-Indian settlers, while Indians living in villages and settlements enclosed by these new grants were denied title to their property (although Mexican law protected their rights to occupy and use their land). Indians who resided in small villages sought ownership of their land as they were promised under the law, yet they were routinely frustrated in their efforts. And despite their newly bestowed citizenship, neophytes were still forced to labor on public lands without compensation, much as they had under the missions.[59]

Indian Land Ownership under the Mexican Government

A fortunate few Tongva became landowners under the Mexican government. Indians could receive land through two separate processes. In the first case, Indians recommended by mission administrators or other officials could petition for ranchos like any other citizen. Those who were successful sometimes acquired ranchos that encompassed hundreds, even thousands of acres. In the second case, Indians could receive much smaller parcels as direct allotments from mission administrators. The difference between these two processes is significant: Indians who successfully petitioned for land got legal title to their property, while those who received allotments got no title.[60]

Anthony Morales's ancestors received the grant of Rancho Potrero de la Mission Vieja de San Gabriel. "It's up in Mission Viejo, Rosemead and San Gabriel Boulevard in Montebello Hills," he says.[61] Anthony's father, Fred "Sparky" Morales, spoke of the family's land in a 1980 interview. He explained that after the missions were secularized, the Indians:

> Already found themselves here and they stayed here. Like many of our families did. They stayed on the land. By that time...we had some property....
>
> [My] mother...was born on this rancheria. She was born at the old sub-mission, the sub-mission Verde. Where they have Potrero Heights now. That's along Rosemead Boulevard.[62]

Other Tongva also have ties to the Rancho Potrero grant through stories handed down through their families. Cindi Alvitre recalls:

> It's where the previous Mission San Gabriel was, that's Potrero Chico....It's where the original Mission San Gabriel was built....And, in fact, pieces of that land somehow persisted through time. My father's cousin—Lupe, I think—I don't remember her last name....She passed away in the late eighties and was still living on a portion of that land. I remember as a child going to El Monte to the ranches.[63]

Morales family at Grandma Modesta's home, 501 E. El Monte, San Gabriel, ca. 1920–1922. Clockwise from left: Hope Morales, David Morales, Virginia Morales, Fred "Sparky" Morales (father of Anthony Morales), and Joseph Morales. Seated is Olgeria (Modesta) Morales, the grandmother of Vivan Morales Barthelemy, Art Morales, and Anthony Morales. COURTESY OF ART MORALES

The brothers of María Giacomini Thompson Flores with their mountain lion kill, early 20th century. COURTESY OF STACY THOMPSON

Information about other Tongva land grants is preserved in *expedientes* (legal documents) from the Mexican period, as well as United States Land Commission Records, U.S. District Court Records, and early deeds from the office of the Recorder of Los Angeles County. In 1843, Governor Manuel Micheltorena granted Tongva Prospero Elias Dominguez a tract of land near San Gabriel measuring 466 *varas* by 266 *varas* (approximately twenty-two acres). During that same year another neophyte, named Francisco Sales, received a grant of fifteen acres. In 1846, Governor Pío Pico granted the Indian Simeon a tract near San Gabriel measuring twenty acres, while five other Tongva are known to have received Mexican grants ranging from seven to forty-nine acres in size.[64]

Victoria Reid, the wife of rancher and historian Hugo Reid, received in her own name the grants of Huerta de Cuati and Santa Anita, while another Tongva, named Samuel, received a tract of land northwest of Mission San Fernando. José Miguel Triunfo, an Indian from San Fernando, received the grant of Rancho Cahuenga from Mexican Governor Micheltorena, which he later traded for Rancho Tujunga. Ramón, Francisco, and Roque received the four-thousand-acre grant of Rancho El Encino in the San Fernando Valley, while another trio, Urbano, Odon, and Manuel, received Rancho El Escorpión.[65]

Other Tongva living in villages enclosed by ranchos did not get title to their land, although their right to occupy and use their property was generally protected under Mexican law by language contained in the grant documents. Indeed, having an Indian village on one's property was considered an advantage, since it assured a cheap source of labor for the rancho. This pattern continued for a decade or so after the American takeover of California in 1847. In 1856 Captain Edward C. Ord wrote how he:

> Visited all the Ranchos within twenty miles of San Bernardino, as well as that place, and I found, except a few left in their villages, to watch the crops, that the Indians are all quietly labouring on the farms, cattle ranchos, or in the villages, as servants to the whites, according to the laws of this state....
>
> Each of the large cattle ranchos near Los Angeles and San Bernardino has from fifteen to thirty Indians permanently occupied on it.[66]

The brothers of María Giacomini Thompson Flores working on a Bakersfield ranch, n.d. COURTESY OF STACY THOMPSON

The B. D. Wilson Report summarized the status of local Indian landowners in 1852:

> At the close of the late Mexican War, some of the old Mission Indians remained in possession of tracts of land, which they had held for a long time by occupancy and license of the Fathers, or under written grants from the Mexican Government. Some have since sold out, for trivial considerations— others have been elbowed off by white neighbors; so that, in the settled and settling parts of the county, there are not now fifty Indian land proprietors. They are awaiting the adjudication of the Commissioners of Land Titles. A league [approximately 4400 acres] is the largest tract that any of them claim; in general, their tracts do not exceed fifty or a hundred acres....
>
> They are anxious to hold on to their little homesteads, and resist all offers to buy as steadily as they can....[They] plant regularly from year to year. Some have a small stock of horses, cows and sheep.[67]

Indian Land Ownership under the American Government

Although the patterns of land tenure begun under the Mexican government continued for a while after the American takeover, the legal basis of land ownership changed dramatically under the new government. Mexican citizens living in California were granted American citizenship under the terms of the Treaty of Guadalupe Hidalgo, including the protection of their property rights. However, American officials chose to ignore or deny the property rights of Mission Indians, even if those Indians had Mexican citizenship.[68] Subsequent government actions further weakened the Indians' position. Before ratifying the treaty, the Senate deleted Article 10, which acknowledged the validity of Mexican land grants. Henceforth, all landowners would have to prove the validity of their Mexican grants. This single action placed many Mexican grants in jeopardy, since the legal documentation for these grants was often scanty or nonexistent. Grants that were not confirmed would revert to the public domain.[69] Next, in 1851 the United States passed "An Act to Ascertain and Settle the Private Land Claims in the State of California" and established a federal land commission to hear evidence from those claiming title to land under Mexican law, and to issue titles under United States law to those who proved their ownership.[70]

A few Tongva had their grants confirmed by the land commission. One grant, known as the "Prospero Tract," was confirmed to Rafaela Valenzuela, the widow of Prospero Dominguez, the original Indian grantee. Others were confirmed to the Indians Simeon and Francisco Sales.[71] According to anthropologist Florence Shipek, however, the commissioners for the most part "ignored all the evidence that once existed" pertaining to Indian land rights. The outcome for the Indians ultimately proved catastrophic; anyone whose title was not confirmed by the land commission saw his or her property revert to the public domain. These public lands were then open to homesteading by non-Indians (Indians did not have the legal right to homestead property until the passage of the Indian Homestead Act of 1883 and the Public Domain Allotment Act of 1887). "For legal purposes," writes Shipek, "the land was lost in 1851."[72]

Surprisingly, Indian land tenure appears to have continued relatively uninterrupted for the first two decades of American rule. The 1850 Act for the Government and Protection of the Indians passed by the California state legislature instructed sheriffs and other local authorities to mark the boundaries of lands occupied and used by Indians and protect them from encroachment by non-Indian settlers. As a result, sheriffs in southern California did make some efforts to protect Indian land rights, at least until 1865. Indians also continued to make up the primary labor force in the region for agriculture, stock raising, construction, and road building as well as other activities.[73]

But this changed when immigration to California dramatically increased following the close of the Civil War. Suddenly Indians found themselves facing a two-pronged assault on their properties. First, those with unconfirmed titles were often driven from their land by non-Indian squatters. Second, those who lived in villages enclosed by ranchos faced eviction because the federal land commission, when it confirmed grants, regularly omitted the clauses that (under Mexican law) had protected the Indians' rights to reside upon and use their land. As a result, Indians were evicted, encroached upon by white landowners, or simply forced off their land.[74]

One of the most notorious examples of such an eviction involved Rogerio Rocha, an Indian from San Fernando who lived for sixty years on a ten-acre tract of land in the San Fernando Valley. Rocha's land, which had a good spring of freshwater, was enclosed by a rancho owned by the de Celis family. When the family sold their rancho, the language protecting Rocha's residence rights was omitted from the deed. The new owners began eviction proceedings and eight years later Rocha and his wife (both of whom were eighty or more years of age), as well as several Indians living with them, were removed from their property. The removal took place during a winter rainstorm and Rocha's wife died shortly afterward from shock, exposure, and grief. Indian agent Horatio N. Rust recounted the story and noted that it "is only one case of the many that have been similarly treated in our vicinity."[75]

Recalling similar stories from his own family, Fred Morales told how they lost their property: "they were just driven out of their land....My people felt very bad... and they went to court about five or six times. Our lawyers just vanished overnight and we lost the case."[76] Fred's son Anthony Morales remembers hearing stories about their land as a child:

> From what I remember [from] my grandmother...in those days some local ranchers would dress like Ku Klux Klan, with the hood and torches, and go to the village and threaten them—[saying]...they're going to burn the village down. That's why they ended up losing their land grant. It was taken by force.
>
> There's stories that say they got my grandfather drunk and made him... [sign his name with] an X, and that's how he lost his land, but...it was really harassment and threats.[77]

Art Morales, Fred Morales's nephew, also heard these stories.

> My uncle Joe...he had stories my grandmother shared with him about guys on horses, with the hoods, that would come down and try to chase them out. They were trying to scare them off the property....They were probably defrauded...[out of] the property....It had to be in the...late 1800s....
>
> There are maps that reflect that my grandmother Modesta [and] her brother had a plot of land up near Montebello that goes back to the oil field area. So we do have maps somewhere reflecting his name. In fact, there [are] supposed to be two plots of land that show their names as having land, but it was all swindled away.[78]

Stories of how this land grant was lost have touched several families. Al Lassos heard his family's stories of how they were defrauded:

> You know where the Baldwin Hills are? All the oil wells there used to belong to my family. My family owned land from San Fernando Valley all the way to Baldwin Hills. [The oil company]...wanted to get a clear deed to that land, but they couldn't because it belonged to the Indians. So...they said, "We'll pay you off." They asked my mother and my aunts and uncles, "How

much would you take, for a clear deed to this?" They said, "Well, you're making all the money. There are five of us left, we'll take five million dollars, a million dollars apiece." They said, "Oh, no, no. That's way over our heads." They said, "We'll just wait until you all die. You're going to be dead anyway, pretty soon."[79]

Desirée Martinez's family knows these stories as well:

> There's Potrero Chico and Potrero Grande. My grandmother always said, "Oh, they used to live there." Then I came across some lawsuit documents. A lot of my family members, the Valenzuelas and Alvitre families, were suing because the land was stolen from them....
>
> There was a woman who died, and she was the great-niece of Valenzuela. When she died her estate went into escrow. Under that escrow they put her portion of the José Valenzuela estate since they chopped up the land grant between Alvitre and Valenzuela. I guess in the fifties they found all of the great-grandchildren of José Valenzuela—I want to say Temple [genealogist and San Gabriel City Historian Thomas Temple] was involved. There was some shady deal where there were eight grandchildren of Valenzuela. They got one of the grandchildren to sign away the rights to the whole land grant, which they didn't have rights to. They then, of course, found oil.[80]

They got one of the grandchildren to sign away the rights to the whole land grant.... They then, of course, found oil. —DESIRÉE MARTINEZ

Craig Torres is a descendant of Prospero Elias Dominguez, one of the few Tongva to receive a Mexican land grant, a twenty-two-acre grant near San Gabriel made by Governor Micheltorena in 1843. The tract was located north of the mission on what is now the Huntington Library grounds, on the lower east side, where the cactus garden is located.[81] Craig recalls his family stories of how their land was lost:

> The earliest memories that I have of my ancestor's land grant are from my aunt Stella Guzman and my mother, who were always relating stories about a woman who they called their Nanita...[who was] Prospero's youngest daughter, Candelaria Dominguez....The story is that Prospero was given this tract of land...because of his service to the San Gabriel Mission as a vaquero, a cowboy....He was granted this land...and it was in the family...up to his youngest daughter....I remember my aunt always telling stories about what Candelaria had told her...that when Candelaria was a young girl she remembers two, as she referred to them "Americanos," coming to her house and giving her wine and getting her drunk and making her sign an X on the actual deed and that's how they acquired the land. And I heard the story over and over and over again. The same story, it was never altered, it was never changed....[The] way it was told....it was done...underhandedly. And I think back about...what was going on at that time...the native people were... illiterate...and they didn't know a lot about the laws and these things, so it was probably very easy to [steal someone's land]....They didn't have any legal standing, so they couldn't do anything....

There was never any mention that I know of...of any money being exchanged or anything like that.

They don't talk about a year [when Candelaria lost the land]...my aunt...makes reference to her Nanita saying [it was] when she was a young woman. So, I believe she was born in 1851 or 1852, so it must have been in the early 1860s when this might have happened.[82]

Torres has researched what happened to the land after it left his family. "The land was later acquired by...[Benjamin D. Wilson] and given to, I think, one of his son-in-laws or daughter-in-laws as a marriage gift....So it definitely became part of that family." An entry in the County Records Book of Deeds for March 23, 1869, lists the tract as part of the land given to Maria Shorb, a daughter of Benjamin D. Wilson.[83] For Craig Torres, the stories he grew up with represent more than one family's loss. They document a bias that California histories have yet to fully confront: that the state of California failed to protect the property rights of Indian landowners. "The one thing that I've always wanted people to be aware of and acknowledge is what was taken from our people," he says. "Because even today...it's still never acknowledged."

> *The one thing that I've always wanted people to be aware of and acknowledge is what was taken from our people.* —CRAIG TORRES

Throughout the history of California...anybody who had any sense of power, or...any control, are the people...who've maintained ownership of land....[All] you have to do is look at...[the Tongva] compared to even some of the tribes that have reservations....At least they have a land base where their communities can congregate together, and we're so spread out...[we're like] orphans in our own homeland.[84]

Reservations

In the early 1850s, even as the federal government created a commission to investigate Mexican land titles, it also established a separate policy to remove the Indians of California from their ancestral lands and relocate them to less desirable lands further inland, where they would be isolated from the white population.[85] The creation of a reservation system in California had far-reaching consequences for Indian policy throughout the United States. For the Tongva, a reservation would have provided a land base and economic resources to help insure their integrity as a tribe. To implement its new policy, the federal government sent three commissioners to negotiate eighteen treaties with the Indians of California and establish reservations for them.[86] But the Tongva were not included in the negotiations. Desirée Martinez explains:

One of the men [who]...was designated to go and make the treaties—his memoirs stated that he didn't get a chance to go to L.A. One reason was because the Indians weren't causing trouble. They were pretty much doing what they needed to do to survive. They were blending in. They were just good workers and laborers. They weren't causing problems. So he didn't feel that there was a need to go and deal with them.[87]

The Senate eventually shelved all eighteen treaties when the California delegation opposed them on grounds that valuable land was being given to the Indians. Ironically, more than seventy years later, in 1928, California authorized the state attorney general to sue the federal government on behalf of the Mission Indians for the Senate's failure to ratify these treaties. The U.S. Court of Claims ruled in favor of the Indians in 1944. Additional claims were filed in 1946 and formed the basis for a 1964 out-of-court settlement between the Indians of California and the United States government.[88]

Despite the state's opposition to reservations, many people in California supported them as a solution to the growing "Indian problem," which was, in fact, a "settler problem" brought about by uncontrolled immigration during, and after, the Gold Rush. Some well-meaning promoters saw reservations as the best way to protect the Indians from white settlers who were stealing their tribal lands, destroying their food supplies, and even attacking them. Reservation supporters also hoped to shield the Indians from the most destructive and demoralizing effects of white civilization: alcohol, prostitution, and kidnapping. However, more self-serving individuals simply hoped to acquire the lands abandoned by the Indians once they were removed to reservations.[89]

The controversy reached a crescendo in 1852 following a brief and unsuccessful Indian rebellion led by Antonio Garra, chief of the Cupeño tribe living at Warner's Ranch in San Diego County.[90] In the revolt's aftermath the new Superintendent of Indian Affairs, Edward F. Beale, commissioned the B. D. Wilson Report, which detailed the conditions of the Indians living in the southern half of the state at that time and recommended the establishment of a reservation for their exclusive use. Beale subsequently created the Sebastian Military Reserve (or Tejón Reservation, as it is more commonly known) approximately sixty miles north of Los Angeles. The Indians living on the reservation were mostly Tejoneños (a mixture of Chumash and Kitanemuk) and Yokuts; few Tongva chose to go, probably because doing so meant losing their own lands to white settlers. Their misgivings proved well founded; the Tejón Reservation lasted only ten years before it was converted into a private rancho.[91]

DURING THE LATE 1800S THE INDIANS OF SOUTHERN CALIFORNIA struggled to hold on to their land, while their living conditions steadily deteriorated under relentless pressure from white settlers. In 1865 the federal government took steps to provide a minimal land base for these Indians by establishing reservations at San Pasqual and Pala. However, the lands set aside were too small and of too poor a quality to support the number of Indians planned for them. Also, the Indians already residing at San Pasqual and Pala objected to their property being overrun by newcomers. The executive order that created the reservations was withdrawn in 1871; however, a few reservations were created by later executive orders in 1875.[92]

In 1891, the federal government passed the Act for the Relief of the Mission Indians and established a commission (known as the Smiley Commission) to investigate Indian land tenure in southern California, and to make recommendations for removing those lands from the public domain and reserving them for the tribes' exclusive use.[93] However, once again the Tongva were ignored. Cindi Alvitre argues:

> Part of that political process was...they wanted the tribe to become extinct. They wanted an extinct status. Just like any other tribe in any other city in California— San Diego, San Francisco, and Santa Barbara—[where] you have [an] abundance of resources. If you want to take those resources...the best thing to do is eliminate the tribe, the people.... That could be...[done by] not making any efforts to really reach out and see who's there.[94]

The government's failure to provide a reservation for the Tongva not only denied them a land base, it also made them seem "less Indian" to other tribes that had land. As Bea Alva explained, "We used to go to these reservations like Pala and Rincon and they just didn't care for us. We were not considered Indians because we were not out of the reservations. They just didn't want to accept us as...Indian[s] because we were like people without a country."[95]

Some Tongva moved onto reservations established for other tribes. According-ing to Anthony Morales, "probably the thirties, the forties, [they] came to the urban area and...[said], 'You're allowed to go and live on the reservation.' That's how a lot of them made it on the reservations. That I know happened, because there is a family... going through some issues with enrollment."[96] Art Morales remembers that "there were points in our history where people from our tribe were offered the opportunity...to move to Pechanga....They moved...

We were not considered Indians because we were not out of the reservations. They just didn't want to accept us...because we were like people without a country.. —Bea Alva

and...[became] part of that reservation. Then there was a core that decided to stay in San Gabriel."[97] Michael Barthelemy recalls of one family from San Gabriel that "They were old residents....You knew they were of the old Indian people from San Gabriel. I think they were given land, that's why they moved to Pala":

> I know some of our people took land down at Pechanga. My uncle Sparky told me that at a certain point they were offered land at Pechanga, and they didn't follow up....
> My understanding is that other Gabrielinos were offered land tracts on

Mary Virginia Belarde Carmelo (great-grandmother of Virginia Carmelo and grandmother of Delores Deatherage) and her husband, José Ciriaco Sosa Carmelo, standing in front of their home on the Soboba Reservation next to their corn crop. Mary Virginia is pregnant with Daniel (father of Delores Deatherage). Their other son, Joe (grandfather of Virginia Carmelo), was also raised at Soboba. After José's cousin Pete Sosa married Rose Silvas, who was raised at Soboba, José and Virginia also moved to Soboba. They later lived in Orange, California. COURTESY OF DELORES DEATHERAGE

Pechanga...by virtue of their status as Gabrielinos, not because they married in with that band down there. At one time I felt kind of sore that Uncle Sparky and others didn't follow up and didn't accept the land.[98]

Cindi Alvitre tells of one woman who "lives out in Pechanga. She was from Rose-mead....Her great-grandmother received the allotment—people...[who] weren't Luiseño...received allotments too."[99] Virginia Carmelo's own ancestors resided at the Soboba Reservation. "My grandfather was raised at Soboba because his mother was the San Gabriel Indian. She was in the Riverside area when she married—her husband was Apache—[and] they moved onto the reservation."[100]

For many Tongva the choice was whether to remain on land they had occupied and improved for many years, land that had been in their families perhaps for generations, or to move onto largely unimproved reservation land that had no direct connection to their history or culture. A story told by Earl Campio illustrates their dilemma:

One day we got in the truck, and drove up to Pala. He [Earl's father] knew the elder and where the little church is. We went and talked to him about...my great-grandmother. He [Earl's father] said, "Your great-grandmother used to like Soboba better than she did Pala."...So we went up to Soboba....But boy, when we drove in and...[saw] this one water fountain—[and] everybody has to go there [to get water]....I don't think so. He [also] said, "It sounds good, but they [the Indians on the reservation] really have no drive. They were kept people....The ambition has been taken out of them," he told me.[101]

Sacred Stories, Sacred Lands

Land is sacred to most Tongva; it is a physical and spiritual link to their past as well as their future. Land is timeless and so their connection to it is without beginning or end. In David Campio's case, the sacredness flows from his family's stories about the land. "The Prado, Rincon area—old Rincon, new Prado, would be a sacred area for our family because that's where my grandfather lived [and] grew up—that's the foundation of his stories."[102]

Virginia Carmelo remembers a story about the land that her mother shared with her:

Mary Virginia Belarde Carmelo and her husband, José, ca. 1940s. They were married for fifty years. Courtesy of Delores Deatherage

> My grandmother Virginia used to need rides to visit different...family members out in Riverside and different areas. One afternoon they took her to visit one of her daughters, I think at San Bernardino. On the way back, she had them stop. I think it's Mount Rubidoux now, in Riverside. They went up to the top of the hill. I think it was her and her husband, and my mother, and my father. They said, "Look around, everything that you can see with your eyes was all our land, look at the entire landscape."[103]

Michael Barthelemy sees himself as part of the landscape his ancestors once knew:

> I remember in those days when I used to go out and survey the chaparral around Padua Hills and Glendora Ridge Road....I used to walk on the firebreaks....When the storm[s] would clear....I could see all the way to Catalina....I could see downtown L.A., and all the clutter of man-made stuff, all the streets and buildings sort of fall away....As I was standing there looking

Like the sound of *e* in
San Di**e**go (short, not stressed)
as in:

'e**v**iit
"awl"

This contemporary illustration by Jacob Gutierrez of an awl pictures a sound in the Tongva language. COURTESY OF JACOB GUTIERREZ

out at those white clouds, white on top, gray on the bottom, moving ponderously across the blue sky I realized that...I was bringing that vision into being. I was both the subject and the object. I was indistinguishable from the stuff of my vision. I was the valley. I was the sky. I was the clouds.... You become the stuff of your vision....

People romanticize Indians because they can take that step beyond hand's reach, because they are a visionary people....I think that's the brilliance of Indian people, what distinguishes Native American people from other groups....

That's what makes us really agonize over [the] destruction of the beauty of nature.[104]

A CONVERSATION with the Tiʼat Society and guests, including: Cindi Alvitre (Ph.D. candidate in World Culture at UCLA, faculty at CSULB, and board member, California Council for the Humanities); Gloria Arellanes (poet and writer); Linda Gonzales (cultural educator); Jacob Gutierrez (artist and storyteller); Janice Ramos (cultural educator and child care); Nicole Ramos (writer, nonprofit marketing and publications); Stacy Thompson (educator); and Craig Torres (graphic artist and cultural educator)

October 15, 2005
Rancho Los Alamitos, Long Beach, California

The Participants

THE TIʼAT SOCIETY IS AN INFORMAL EDUCATIONAL GROUP CREATED within the larger Gabrielino-Tongva community in 1989. The *tiʼat* was the traditional plank canoe of the Tongva people. In 1992 the Tiʼat Society and others helped Phil Howorth, a master boat builder, create the *Moomat Ahiko* for the Tongva community through a project funded by Phil Noyes. The first *tiʼat* to be built in almost two centuries, the *Moomat Ahiko* has come to symbolize the reclamation of Tongva maritime culture and the ongoing cultural memory of the people today. Reaching out to the native and non-native community alike, members of the Tiʼat Society explore the culture of the Gabrielino-Tongva people through creative visual arts and educational programs which highlight the maritime culture of the people. Its accomplished members draw upon their backgrounds as awarded artists and graphic artists, dancers and choreographers, native plant experts, scholars, writers, and educators to encourage and facilitate an ongoing dialogue among all people.

The Discussion

In the following conversation, members of the Ti'at Society share family stories and observations as they consider the sacred significance of Povuu'ngna, the ancestral place of birth (home) of the Tongva people. The discussion explores the renewing spirit of Povuu'ngna in contemporary times, the continuing definition of sacred in view of surviving cultural memory, and the identity emerging from the growing cultural confidence of the Tongva-Gabrielino community today.

Cindi Alvitre: How do we define Povuu'ngna? What is it to us? This process has never been done before. We've gone through these eras, especially at the end of the nineteenth century and into this era, where you had salvage ethnography. People were just capturing John Peabody Harrington's efforts to take the desperate few elements that were left in the culture.[*]

Now we are through this history of seeing the land transform, and yet here's Povuu'ngna. We're here. It's still as precious to many of us. Look at it becoming a place where there's a charter myth. By that I mean...mythology. Mythology is not the stuff of fairy tales, "myth" means sacred, the most sacred, most ancient of those narratives. Just as the Bible is to Genesis, that's what mythology is as opposed to legend or folklore. Here is where this charter myth, in other words, the dreams of the ancestors, emerged. It's traveled, it's been fragmented, piecemealed. Now we're attempting to look at it and say, "What is this place? What is it to us? Is Povuu'ngna sacred? How and why?" Is it just a sacred symbol, cultural memory, or does it mean more? Is it an actual place? Why is it important to protect the physical side of Povuu'ngna, as well as the sacred symbolic significance? Does Povuu'ngna offer a path for the future, a place for renewing cultural ties within the community, as well as reconnecting and reconciling with others?

I think you all sitting around the table know what Povuu'ngna is. When we had the Povuu'ngna lawsuit, people began to "re-know" Povuu'ngna.[**] It's become a new place for some people. I can't say that for everybody, because you all have your own stories, your own experiences with this space and place. That's where we begin thinking about this, so we hear from you, share this.

Stacy Thompson: We can't really talk for the community.

CA: No. You can only speak for yourself.

---

[*] Harrington was an early-twentieth-century anthropologist from the Smithsonian Institution who interviewed many Native Americans, including Tongva people.

[**] In 1944, 283.5 acres of Rancho Los Alamitos land was condemned to build Long Beach State College (California State University at Long Beach). Today both the Rancho and CSULB comprise the area known as the ancestral village of Povuu'ngna. Both the Rancho and CSULB are included in the "Povuu'ngna District" which has been listed on the National Register of Historic Places since 1974. In the early 1990s the California Native American Heritage Commission and plaintiffs within the Tongva community sued CSULB over the proposed commercial development of a known archaeological and burial site of Povuu'ngna on undeveloped university property. At the time the university declared a moratorium on any such further development, although the declaration is not binding on future administrations. For more information refer to the preface and the essay "A Connection to Place: Land and History."

Craig Torres: I know that, for a fact, not everybody knows about the significance of Povuu'ngna or even knows about Povuu'ngna.

ST: You have to remember there are people out there completely disconnected from any cultural knowledge at all, and don't have family stories passed down to them. I wasn't raised with anything but family stories which were not related to the culture, but just who lived where, who married who, who moved to different places, but not cultural knowledge.

Claudia Jurmain: So they wouldn't have spoken of Povuu'ngna in your family.

ST: No.

Janice Ramos: Not mine either.

CJ: When you speak about Povuu'ngna today, what are you communicating to people who have never heard anything about it before? Are you saying it's a "place," or does it represent something more?

ST: I would say both. To somebody who doesn't know anything, I'm going to give them the history I've been involved in. As far as the physical place, that's the twenty-three acres

Janice Ramos, a member of the Ti'at Society, in the Jacaranda Walk at Rancho Los Alamitos, 2006. The Jacaranda Walk was once the kitchen midden of Povuu'ngna. Ty Milford Photography

at Cal State Long Beach, and my interaction being a plaintiff [in the lawsuit against CSULB during the early 1990s]. That's where I would start. Unfortunately, beyond that relationship with that place, I don't have a family history with it.

JR: How many people's ancestors stayed pure, stayed in touch with their history and background as a Tongva, and how many assimilated into the culture? My family certainly assimilated into the culture. We never spoke of [it] at all. In fact, the only people that piqued the interest in my family was the federal government sending checks to descendants.* That's what really made us start looking into it. I don't know that it wasn't considered a positive, but to be an indigenous person wasn't really something that was talked about, proud of, the way that it should have been. At least in my family.

---

* In 1950 qualified enrolled tribal members received $150 each for claims resulting from the California Indians Jurisdictional Act of 1927, which authorized the state attorney general to sue the federal government on the basis of the nonratified federal treaties of 1851 and 1851. In 1972, seventy thousand qualified, enrolled tribal members received $668.51 each as part of an out-of-court settlement for lands not included in earlier claims. For more information, refer to the essay "Continuity within Change: Identity and Culture."

Stacy Thompson, a member of the Ti'at Society, Rancho Los Alamitos, 2006.
TY MILFORD PHOTOGRAPHY

CA: This cultural memory, this memory of who we are, has traveled through time. We can say that. There are certain spaces, certain places that are even generating—like you say, "a check" that motivated people, or piqued their interest and curiosity in their own identity.

JR: That is why I think Povuu'ngna is so important. You have your myths, your beliefs, and you have your faith. Many people need something tangible. They need something to see. And that's what Povuu'ngna represents.

Bill McCawley: Why did Povuu'ngna become so important to you that you wanted to get involved if you didn't have a family memory of it? What did it mean to you?

ST: Hmmm, that's a good question. I had been getting involved, going to meetings, and reconnecting with people for a couple of years before that. When I was told about it, I thought it was important, a way to reconnect with the culture. Seeing those things happening and other places being destroyed, I made a connection.

CA: What was the connection? Why was it that particular space?

ST: One of the things was the fact that there were burials there, that being such an important issue, a very tangible thing. We need to have respect for our ancestors buried in other places that have been desecrated. That's a common thing we've seen here with so much development. There are people buried here, they need to be left where they're not disturbed. That's such a basic human right. Understanding the history and the significance around the idea of Povuu'ngna, how it connected to the creation stories, then seeing that other people were also involved—I think it grew out of that, and the community. A lot of the community came together over that.

CJ: Where is Povuu'ngna?

ST: Well, I see a key piece of it being there at Cal State Long Beach, but a much larger area probably moved, and so we could look at this whole area as being Povuu'ngna. I find people say, "Well, a village was here, but where?" With

Povuu'ngna, you're not going to see a signpost. That's the western thinking—"Where is it? Is it exactly here, or is it over there?"

Gloria Arellanes: I also was a plaintiff in Povuu'ngna; it was an issue of turning twenty-three acres into a strip mall. You can go there and still see nature, the herons, the hawks, the foxes that used to be out there, but it's a spiritual sense of the area that connects what you feel. I really can't explain what I feel, coming from a family where my mother just absolutely used to tell me, "You're Mexican" because she grew up being punished for who she was, and had to deny who she was. That was our sense. I always felt like it was our generation that had to bring back the information once we started getting it, teaching people who were elders to us because they did not know these stories. In those times, there's an invested

energy that we put into the site. [During the early 1990s,] people slept out there for days and days and days, at night—out there for months enduring unkind things [because the issue was controversial and in the papers]. Yet it was a center where everybody came, and not only Tongva people, but other nations. Just by some of the burials and the bones [that] were etched, it's a spiritual sense that is here.

Gloria Arellanes, a member of the Ti'at Society, at Rancho Los Alamitos, 2006.
TY MILFORD PHOTOGRAPHY

CA: If somebody who knows nothing about it asks, "What do you mean by sacred? Why is Povuu'ngna sacred to you?"—

GA: You explain it's a center of creation. You explain Chinigchinich and the creation stories. That's the easiest way to explain Povuu'ngna—how it was named, why it was named, and what it means. It's a slow process. Information wasn't given to us. You didn't sit down with some wise person who told you everything. It was a long, slow process. Traditionally that's how we learned. In oral traditions you sit and listen to the elders speak. I learned one thing from my mother which was totally wrong because she didn't know how to be proud of who she was. Very sad. Yet her sister, until her passing, could remember things about being Indian. She would tell me, "My mother said this," and "My auntie said this."

CJ: The early Gabrielino-Tongva people had other ceremonial and trading sites within their fifteen-hundred-square-mile area. If I were speaking with another

María Giacomini Thompson Flores, n.d. An ancestor of Stacy Thompson, she was a direct lineal descendant of Manuel Antonio Perez and María Florentina Alvitre, both Gabrielino Mission Indians. COURTESY OF STACY THOMPSON

group of Tongva people who are not sea-, but inland-based, would they feel the same about the sacredness of Povuu'ngna, or would they be talking about another place?

Linda Gonzales: Even [if] it's taking on something new, it still always has the origin story. That heart, that's not going to change. How is it [people] can sit there after looking around, [and say] "This is a nice place, it's special. You can feel it." What brings them to that point? They've just been told it's an old village. Cindi used the words "silent knowings." I really liked that word to be used, or "silent knowing." My family was always proud of being Indian, so we didn't have that stigma that we had to be Mexican. Even if you don't know, your ancestors know who you are. There's always that "silent knowing" that somewhere [the memory, the knowledge], it's there.

CA: You're hitting the heart. What are those experiences that generate those kinds of feelings in people? Is it the physical space, the stories they have heard, something in their families? Is it a particular memory, a connection to the land, that region? This experience is not confined to people who have a link to Povuu'ngna, and have for generations, because that's not the reality of the history of this place. It's been transitional. People are constantly reconnecting with this space, and it's going to be different.

CT: What are people's earliest cultural memories? Like Stacy, we grew up with family stories—who's who, who you're related to. We didn't grow up with a lot of traditional culture, because a lot had disappeared. But those cultural memories, those stories connected me to [Mission] San Gabriel because that's what they were talking about, the community around there. I wanted to find out more—which connected me eventually to Povuu'ngna, where our people originated. Why is this land sacred? What significance does it have in our culture? Where was that learned? Where [do] the stories come from? Something inside—genetic memory, the ancestors talking—led me back to this place where it all began, where everything was laid down for our people way, way back. The knowledge and everything we needed to survive in this world came from this place. That trail, starting with my family history, and stories, led me to this place. That's where it begins with us—stories that stay within the family. We all know the history of what happened to our people. We didn't have a lot. A lot was taken away. Some of the last fragments we had to hold on to were those stories. For us that was the beginning connection to this place here [Povuu'ngna].

ST: As long as I can remember, about once a month my grandfather would get out all of the letters, genealogy, and paperwork that had been done by Tommy Temple, read it all to me, and interpret it. He was from the Temple family, the Workman Temple facility in Whittier, very connected to the Catholic Church, but a big genealogist, and did a lot of local families' genealogy.

JR: I have a letter signed by him.

LG: So do I.

CA: We all have those.

LG: Along the lines of family, Gloria was saying we have to teach the elders now. You have to be respectful. My dad still says "Mission Indians," and I want to say, "What were we before the missions? How did we exist before the missions if we're Mission Indians?" We know we were at

Craig Torres, a member of the Tï'at Society, Rancho Los Alamitos, 2006.
Ty Milford Photography

the mission, but because books have told us, "You're Mission Indians"—California Mission Indians—it goes in one fell swoop. He would say, "Well, we know that we're Mission Indians, but we don't know which tribe," until he did the genealogy. That's hard because I've tried to nicely say we're not Mission Indians, and yet that term [remains].

CA: That's the way that they identify, too.

LG: That's how they know themselves.

CJ: Then your sense of Povuu'ngna comes from your own work and your own self-identity, not your family?

LG: I don't even know how I first found out the name or heard the name. I don't even know where I was, or who would have said it. I don't know. I have no idea.

CT: I have to tell a little story—Linda and I, we met at Povuu'ngna. We connected our own family history at Povuu'ngna.

LG: That's kind of an origin right there. How many generations were silent in our genealogy until us, we two, by "divine coincidence" met there?...Craig was, "Oh really, Tongva—how come I don't know you?" Just like, "I don't know her, [it] must not be true, because we're so small." Craig says, "Who's your ancestor?" When I said, "Prospero Dominguez," he goes, "Well, that's mine." We found out that I'm from the eldest daughter, and he's from the youngest daughter.

JR: I never heard of Povuu'ngna until I spoke to Craig about it, until he told me about this book project. I had never heard of it before this year.

CJ: Yet you knew your own family story?

JR: Yes. Narcisa was baptized at the mission in the 1800s and lived at the mission, where she met a German storekeeper, married him, and went to live at Fort Tejón.* They operated a store there. I know that she was a wonderful horsewoman and supposedly could tame horses that no one else could. She had four daughters. I know she lived in Bakersfield until she died, and that's pretty much all that I knew of her.

 I met Craig [when] I was volunteering at a museum in Ontario, and they were having a Gabrielino [speaker]. I told her, "You know, I have an ancestor." She looked at me like "Who's your ancestor?" I said, "Narcisa Rosemyre," and she—"Oh, Narcisa the Talker." I was just amazed that people knew about her. In questioning my family, [I learned that] my grandmother died very young, and her sister did not want to be associated with Tongva-Gabrielino culture at all. She never talked about it at all, but I have my mother's cousin, who is ninety-one [and] actually remembers Narcisa living in back of them, or in front. In fact, Craig interviewed her. I was just taken aback—so much that he knew, I had no idea about. So this is all basically very new to me. We had the book, the Hugo Reid letters.** My mother and cousin had it; it was like a sacred book, almost. We brought it out and looked at it like a talisman, almost. But that was the only thing that I had, that I knew of her.

CJ: What is your identification with Povuu'ngna today?

---

* In March 1853, Congress authorized funding to establish five military reservations for California Indians on land to be owned by the U.S. government. Located in Grapevine Canyon, on the route between southern California and the Central Valley, Fort Tejón was garrisoned in 1854 as part of the Sebastian Military Reservation, also known as the Tejon Reservation. When the reservation closed in 1864, the fort was abandoned.

** Scottish immigrant Hugo Reid married a Tongva woman named Victoria who was the well-respected daughter of a local village chief. In 1852, the *Los Angeles Star* published a series of his letters, which revealed his close acquaintance with the Tongva community as he described their traditional culture and language, and offered rare glimpses of the Tongva during the early American era. (Refer to the essay "Continuity with Change: Identity and Culture" for more information.)

Linda Gonzales and Jacob Gutierrez in the Cactus Garden at Rancho Los Alamitos, 2006. Ty Milford Photography

JR: It's sacred...it was deemed so by our ancestors. That, to me, makes it sacred.

Jacob Gutierrez: Cindi, was it your brother who lived in the camper [at CSULB] during those lawsuit years?

CA: My brother occupied the land for eighteen months at Povuu'ngna at CSULB. He lived in the camper in the parking lot. It was 1993-94, because my father was still alive.

JG: At the time I [was] looking at "Indianness," you might say. I remember being out there, and that's when I was aware of Povuu'ngna. As far as Povuu'ngna's sacred spirituality, it really came from reading Bill McCawley's book and going to the World Song Fest in the last few years.*

I think back in my activist days, when your brother was there, was my first awareness of Povuu'ngna. But for me personally—my grandfather was a horse whisperer, and he used to find water with the divining rod. I used that for finding my spots [sacred places]. I really haven't quite found that in Povuu'ngna. My

---

* The book referred to is McCawley's *The First Angelinos: The Gabrielino Indians of Los Angeles.* The World Festival of Sacred Music is sponsored by the Foundation for World Arts and UCLA Center for Intercultural Performance.

brother bought a couple acres in Palos Verdes. He pulled up a tree stump, and there's five feet of shell midden. Rather than build a house there, it's become a sacred ceremonial site for our family. Things have happened there on the spiritual level for us—especially as we're learning our language, things are occurring. We're like this 360 by 360 complicated Chinese puzzle. It's like, "Whoop! Something fits over there, and something fits here!" It's always been underneath us, the information, and tying into it, I think part of us has always known we've been here. My great-grandmother, who has a photographic memory, who died at 105, said, "We've always been here." I don't have any documentation. All I have is [that] she said that "We were here," that "My mother was here," and on and on and on. That's all I have to go with, and my own personal sensibility.

CA: It's oral tradition.

CT: We're talking about Povuu'ngna, cultural memory, the stories, and how people came to know. A lot of families never mentioned the name Povuu'ngna, but they always mentioned, "You are from here, this is where you come from." That connects us to Povuu'ngna. My mother would always tell me that this is where we come from: "We didn't come from Mexico, that's your dad's side—we come from here." She was always stressing that to me, growing up. That connects me to Povuu'ngna, just that fact, even though we didn't know the name.

BMc: Was she talking about a specific place?

CT: She was referring to the San Gabriel Mission because that's where our people were taken, but that's what she knew. She knew San Gabriel Mission, being Gabrielino. So to me, that connected me to the land, to the whole place.

CA: San Gabriel Mission really becomes another place of origin as far as [a] historical place where people are connected to, to some people a sacred space.

LG: I have a different background than Craig. We always hated any acknowledgment of San Gabriel. I know you feel connected to it. We feel the opposite. We have a revulsion. Usually if it's mentioned, or any of the missions, it would be with a sneer from my parents.

JR: That was all the little I had. That was the only connection I had until now to Narcisa. So that, to me, is a very important place.

Nicole Ramos: Obviously I have the same story as my mom. Growing up, visiting the mission was the only thing we knew and the only connection we really had to that part of our background. I feel a little embarrassed at my ignorance. It reinforces Povuu'ngna's importance because I feel there are other people [who], like me, don't know a lot and need a place to start. Like my mom was saying, we had a book and a few papers, but that was really it. I think another way Povuu'ngna is important is just awareness. It's somewhere for people who want to get involved, want to get an interest, and want to know where to start. It's something to grab on to physically as well as spiritually.

JR: The mission is pretty much a dead end. You find out that your ancestor was there, but that's all you're going to find out.

CA: I think that everybody is going in this direction. You're experiencing part of the process where people have been very disconnected from having a continuum of culture. As Nicole said, that's really heartfelt to me, because I think we've all experienced what you're experiencing—the shame, the embarrassment, the silence. Knowing that, what we haven't achieved is being able to honestly discuss these things as part of that healing, because we know these fragments of history, but how do they connect?

JR: As negative as the missions were in so many ways, they allowed my great-great-great-grandmother to survive. They gave her the skills to survive in the world that was becoming. She had to. They gave her that ability, and the ability to speak the language, so she could tell you some of the stories, and translate things. That's what the mission gave her. As negative as it was, it was still a meeting place where we were together. So this land has to be sacred to my family because it allowed her to be with her people—

CA: Part of the healing is not to be ashamed of any of the stories, not to have to deny [the] part of us that was connected to the south in Mexico, the connection to the mission, that we don't have our language, that we don't have a lot of things. That's what pushes people into the "vampire syndrome." We start attacking each other because we feel comfortable expressing [our anger] with people we know we can attack. Nobody talks about these things. The significance of this book project [O, My Ancestor] is, if it comes out as a publication, we'll be amongst the first people to really say, "You know what, we're not ashamed of who we are. This is our reality. We're not going to manufacture. We're not going to invent." There is a certain degree of reconstruction, or renegotiating, your identity, and being able to have the freedom to feel proud.

JR: Very proud. We were the first people here.

CT: But also to acknowledge that very turbulent history because it's part of who we are. My mom connects to the San Gabriel Mission because that's all she knew. To her it is a sacred place, what she grew up believing, that's her reality. For me and my generation, it's different because of what I know, but I still consider it a very important place in our history, and that's what I tell people. What happened is very important because it's part of our healing, but go on from that point. We also have to acknowledge that there were families who were never brought to that place, who have somewhat of a different history.

CA: Does Mission San Gabriel become another place to regenerate this coming home, the foundation of the mythology? Just as with the sacred stories, it's become a comfortable place, a place to be able to be who we are, and maybe rebuild our stories, to release our stories. Is that what it becomes?

LG: Well, I can see that some families would want to use that [Mission San Gabriel] as another Povuu'ngna, because that's their origin, almost. That's where they came into. You have it on paper that that's where you were. So I can understand. I don't think my family could ever be that good-natured about it.

JG: We are having an elders' gathering right now at Angel's Gate [Point Ferman, San Pedro, California] from all over the country. Anyway, they had busloads of children coming and we had a map [of Tongva villages]. I was trying to explain different locations on the map, to give people points of reference. People that have lived here for a long time didn't realize how many villages, sacred sites we have.* I'm out there trying to put ourselves on the map, to get rootedness. It's just blooming, our seeds, for me anyway. There are a lot of people who have been entering cultural education, but there was an opportunity for me to express who we are and who we still are.

CA: Well, that's the question. Who are we? Who are we today? Povuu'ngna has become a bridge from this fixed-in-the-past image. Many people have gotten stuck in this time warp of "who we are," not able to go comfortably about "who we are today," that this is us, we're mixed. We don't know everything. It's impossible. We are unique from any other tribe that is here, in what I call the Indian diaspora—all the relocated tribes that overwhelmed and saturated our area.** There is a conflict between us and out-of-state Indians. What does that leave? I think it's the land. Some people are only Tongva on the weekends, some people don't talk about it, but keep it in a very sacred space inside. There [are] different levels of reality of being Tongva, none of which deserve to be judged as being inauthentic by anybody.

GA: In reality, we get burned out a lot, and we get beat up a lot. Sometimes you have to decide what you want your energies to be. I've reached a point in my life where I don't feel I have to prove to anybody who I am. Either you accept it or you don't.

---

* There are about fifty documented Tongva villages, according to William McCawley's *The First Angelinos*.

** During the 1950s and 1960s, federal policy sought to terminate government responsibility for Native Americans, moving Indians into "mainstream society" by breaking up tribal reservations through individual allotments and payments, ending federal services, and retraining people for outside employment. The government established nineteen urban centers around the country, relocating 160,000 to 180,000 Native Americans from reservations to cities. By 1995, the Native American population of Los Angeles was approximately 100,000, the largest urban Indian population in the United States.

CT: One of my healing points is going back to history, going back to the origin, knowing these stories. What the first people went through with each other is the same thing going on today. Those are the lessons that I learn. I'm not significant. Who am I to complain about this? The same thing has been going on for thousands of thousands of years.

LG: That also gives you strength to go on again because you're standing on their shoulders and they're waiting for you to begin.

CT: Again, I remember those stories, where they originated from and the place. It's always pulling me back to this place, it's the origin. It creates a balance within me that centers me and makes me realize "You're doing what you have to do. Stop complaining."

LG: You have to pick your battles, because a lot of the times the environmentalists will use you. You get called two days ahead—"Day after tomorrow there's a meeting and we're trying to save this site. We know there was a village there, and we want to see if you can come down." How many times do we get that one? We have to see how much strength we have, and how much we're going to take off of work. They use you as a last resort rather than the respect of giving you the first resort.

CA: I couldn't even live like my ancestors lived. We probably would all be horrified by some of the things they did, my family. I know I would be. But we live in a new time. There's technology. There is electricity. There are computers. There are all these things. I want to be able to push our people out of the funk, into the other place where they can really contemplate, be reflexive about who they are, feel proud about it, and generate other ways of expressing, not only to teach the world, but to teach our own people. These are the tools we have now. Let's look at the tools. Let's acknowledge what's happened. Let's be able—and that doesn't mean to put the past away—[to] get over it. I don't live in the past, the past lives in me. I'm not just an isolated being. I am thousands of ancestors. We all are and we sense that every day. I won't invest my time in a lot of things anymore, because I don't have the energy. But I have to look at the value of my investment, not for myself, but for [the] community, for my grandchildren, for my great-grandchildren, and for the larger public, too. When you gain a cultural confidence, which I think we have lost and we're slowly regaining, then you have the ability to influence people. Then you're not threatened by being influenced by things like technology, and computers, and those kinds of things. You're able to stay cool.

CJ: Do elders within the community have stories? What is their sense about Povuu'ngna, or identity and place?

CA: There are wide ranges of stories—the sacred, very ancient stories to folktales, or legends connected to history, historical figures. I know people have stories about their family during the mission era, or with wild characters like Joaquin Murietta.* People just have all kinds of stories. We're saturated with them.

ST: We have to look at our whole family. In my family I get most of my understanding of where we came from, and the history, from my grandparents, from my grandmother, who is not Tongva. But that's where a lot of the Tongva history comes from—that was "her place" in the family. She tells me about my grandfather's family from things that she knew about San Gabriel. You put it all together because we can't separate all those pieces out.

CA: Let me just use a map [of the region] as an example. If you take my family's stories, they're probably going to have the connection up to where San Gabriel is, up in this area. My family's range of stories are going to be here extending to Catalina Island. You're going to get little circles from different regions, but some are going to overlap. You may have common stories and that becomes a common link to families, and generations. Our generation, we've lost that. I know your mother still remembers those stories, your grandmother does, my father did. We don't have that memory, those like, "Oh, I knew your mom and your father. We used to play violins at the fiestas, and go to Corpus Christi Days at Pala." But there [are] still stories that some people have held on to. There are people in the community that we do not know yet, still part of that silent knowing, maybe embarrassed because they feel they have to perform or behave in a certain way to be accepted. That's not true.

ST: How other people perceive you can be very interesting. I started a new job recently and I took stuff into my office, some pictures of baskets, and things like that. The first day I came back, several people ran up to me, "Oh, are you Indian?" I said, "Well, I'm California Indian and Mexican," and just made a general statement. Couple months later I'm talking to someone and they said, "Well, you're a full-blooded Indian, aren't you?" "No, did I tell you that?" It was just out of context. "Why are you even asking me that question?" Or I'll have people say, "What do you mean you're Mexican? I thought you said you were Indian." "Well, I am." If you just leave it there, people really are not comfortable. They want other people to be clearly defined so that they feel comfortable with it.

CA: I don't know, in my family they talked about "Indianness," we heard more "you are home, you are home." There was a generation, perhaps, that [was] proud of saying we were home, but they lost being proud to say that they were Indians. They became closet Mexicans, or closet Indians and practicing Mexicans. Where was that transition?

---

* Joaquin Murietta, the legendary California bandit of the Gold Rush days who was born in Mexico, has come to symbolize resistance against oppression.

CT: I think each generation of our people identify themselves differently according to new influences, what is influencing you. One thing is becoming really clear—Povuu'ngna has always been the same for all of us. It's an origin. You go back a hundred years—it's going to be the same for our ancestors. This place is going to be significant as we continue to relay stories and the songs to the future generations. Our identities are complex throughout the generations and they change, but the connection to this place is always the same because of what has come from the place.

LG: People don't accept that you can also be more than one thing. I don't identify with only being [one thing]. You have to identify with everything of who you are, otherwise you're denying half of what you are. You shouldn't be embarrassed—they are your past, just as the ones you want to acknowledge are your past, too.

CT: I think my take is a little different. I understand what you're talking about, but when I tell people who I am, I tell them I acknowledge all my ancestors, but my identity is from this land, because that's where I'm from right now, that's my history. That's where everything I know derived. My dad's side is from Mexico, and sure, I acknowledge that.

LG: But you don't deny it.

CT: No, I don't deny it, but my identity is here. It's not Mexican.

CA: There is this lack of knowledge [about] the history of our tribe. In order to continue population, you had to marry into another clan. You weren't allowed to marry within your clan. Identity changes. If you were Coyote, you didn't marry into a Coyote clan for five generations, otherwise it was considered incestuous. You were always part of another. Then that changes you, you become part of that. That's the reality of our ancestral way.*

CJ: What would each of you hope for Povuu'ngna for today and tomorrow because it means land, place, and emergence?

CA: Our mentions, as Tongva people, have been as footnotes—[at] an occasional blessing of a building, or a table—"Let's give you a cultural center that isn't yours, you can come on one day and set up your [exhibit] tables." It's been good for education. It's not a criticism, it was a necessary process, but I'm over that phase. I want to see something more. It's time for us to keep moving on. What will future generations have to access? What's going to be the memory of the Tongva

---

* Gabrielino-Tongva culture consisted of kinship or related groups known as lineages which were traced through the male ancestors. Lineages owned and protected their territories, and determined where someone had the right to hunt and gather. Lineages were made up of individual family units, each with a common ancestor. Tongva lineages were, in turn, divided into two groups of people, the Coyote and Wildcat moieties. During festivals and ritual ceremonies, people from the two moieties would come together since neither group possessed all the elements (perhaps a song, dance, or ritual item) required for a successful ceremony. Such occasions supported trade, the distribution of food, and the regional economy.

Paddling a traditional ti'at *along the north shore of Catalina Island, Ti'at Festival, 1998.* FRANK MAGALLANES AND ALTHEA EDWARDS PHOTOGRAPHY.

community? I speak more for the Ti'at Society and the direction we're headed because we are very much about education, about creativity, about creating projects that might be interpreted as very academic to very artistic. We've made a commitment for our generation. It's so hard to see how long that's going to continue, because you have these phases of interest. They have their peaks. My fear, honestly? If we continue the way we are right now, people just fighting, nothing is going to be there. We've just about completely become even beyond less than a footnote.

LG: I see it as more hopeful. I'm sure you're getting asked to do more and more demonstrations, booked into next year, people are looking ahead to have you come back. Even if our children don't take up the flag and go, you still have kids, and school kids from the future [who] will know us.

CA: That's been going on since the eighties. As long as there are active people, that's one way to maintain. But do you keep it at that level, or do you expand on it, and train young people to do these things?

GA: In the time that you've been doing that, you have to say it's grown—because a lot of people have exhibit tables now in different cultural areas. So it has grown and will continue to grow.

JG: You know, [the *ti'at*, the rebuilding of the traditional plank canoe]—the continuation [of] that ancient crossing is so healing, revitalizing. I see a long, long prosperous future for us because it's land and the ocean. The songs and storytelling, it's just so wonderful.*

---

* The first *ti'at* in almost two centuries (see introduction to this conversation) made its maiden journey on September 1995 as its crew (which included Cindi Alvitre and others from the Ti'at Society) paddled a symbolic fourteen-mile journey along the coast of Catalina Island, from Two Harbors to Avalon. Since then the *ti'at* has been taken out to sea on several occasions, most recently at the World Festival of Music held on Santa Monica Beach in September 2008. Watching the *ti'at* travelers paddle through the ocean waves is a mesmerizing, timeless moment, both old and new.

The Moomat Ahiko *entering Avalon Harbor at the Ti'at Festival, Catalina Island, September 1998.* FRANK MAGALLANES AND ALTHEA EDWARDS PHOTOGRAPHY

CT: Right. That's the whole point of what we're trying to do. For our people, I wanted to bring back these stories and songs and put meaning into them, to show, to make people understand why they're important to us, why they were important to our ancestors, why they will be important to the future genera-tions. This [Povuu'ngna] is where it began. This place is significant and things happened here. There's no point in dressing up to wear this or that if you don't understand the significance behind it. If you just get a skirt, put feathers on it, and wrap it around your waist, it's not going to mean anything unless you know the stories connected. That goes back to the stories and the songs, and it goes back to this place. We come into this earth in a certain place, and we leave very much the same way.

CA: I think that amongst people in the state, the Tongva are not looked upon as being authentic. They are not. We've heard it. We've heard the comments. I've heard the comments from everybody. Yet there is this endurance, this very deep pride. I think I've heard it expressed by an Iroquois elder, many, many years ago, who told me the Tongva are like wild horses. They haven't been domesticated. They weren't put on reservations, just stuck into the system. He says, in some sense, it's like these wild horses that are still running through the hills and refuse to be captured. We have a freedom that others don't have. We've already been inserted into the worst nightmare that could possibly happen to people in the world. We've lost everything, almost, except our spirit. We are bicultural. We adapt well. We know our culture and we know the other culture.

When we acknowledge that we can do anything we want—this is where we need more people besides the handful of people we have at this table who are active. We need to more encourage the next generation to become involved. And like with education, what does it mean for a fourteen-year-old? They're going to have a cultural confidence we didn't have. You're not going to hear, "You guys are extinct. You're not real. You're just Mexicans," all the rhetoric. My children are already born into learning about *tí'ats*. I didn't have that. We didn't have those messages, so we're already nurturing the next generation. We can do anything that we want. We make those decisions, we make those choices at this point. Honestly, I see us as being a very, very, very powerful and influential people of cultural scholars. I do. It's putting ourselves into another setting that says, "Damn it, yes, we can do this," and, "Yes, we do have the opportunity," and I have made a choice to be here and I will do it.

ST: I don't think that's the context of how most native people are defined—"Are you federally recognized?" That may not be the reality for us. That shouldn't be our goal, our only focus, or a barrier to continuing to do things that we want to do.

LG: What will the future generation be? My daughter, when she was growing up, would say, "Mom, I'm having something at school, and please don't come Indian." It hurt my feelings, but all I could do was pray that there would be a day that she would change. Well, about five years ago, maybe more, she got a bumper sticker and it says, "Native American and proud of it." When I saw that, I was just, "Oh my goodness, my prayers have been answered."

CT: I know what I want, what motivates me is to have a new generation of culturally confident people who will be able to know who they are. You're not going to let anybody tell you who you are, or define who you are. You're not going to let anybody intimidate you spiritually, or in any other way. You're confident who you are, and that encompasses everything—teaching this, teaching that.

CA: Who are culturally confident, and because they have confidence, are inclusive and not exclusive.

LG: That knowledge—not just the confidence, but the knowledge, makes it so that I don't have fear.

BMc: Is the goal of educating people common among all Tongva groups? What common goals are there that you all share, or is that specific?

ST: What information they're giving is different. What they want, what information they want to put out there, is not the same.

LG: There is some information that's incorrect. There are some things that— an educational group that might look at the past and say, "This was used for—" and it might not even exist in this area. We have to decide what is native to this land...

CA: What point in time are you going to go to determine what is authentically native? Because it transitions.

ST: With the *tí'at*—I've seen newspaper articles where it will say it's a replica. Well, do we consider it a replica? No. Was it made with traditional materials and traditional tools? Well, not really, but is that relevant?

CA: That's a running argument.

CJ: Are there any examples when someone says, "This represents a certain belief, and a certain way of being," and you would say, "I don't think that's who we are"?

GA: I think so. It is so new to so many people. They jump on it very fast and don't take the time to really learn things that were here so long ago. I'm scared at what people do in ceremony. I see people getting sick and injured, and it really frightens me.

LG: I don't think it's fair to start bringing in others' things because that will fill in this blank right here from another culture.

GA: I've come to realize, first there is an evil spirit world and there is a good and positive spirit world. We don't believe there's a hell in our spirituality, but I do believe things can happen to you in a bad way. I think if you don't balance that in your spirituality, it can hurt you. [Ceremonies] have been evolving. I'm not going to say whether it's good or bad. I can only say what I'm comfortable with, what I'm not comfortable with, and when I hear how something is done it makes me cringe.

CA: When we did the reburial of the ancestors in Carson, we went to the family of Janice Ramos and asked permission to use their songs that we knew were funeral songs.* But we really don't know the context in which those songs were sung. We had somebody who we could directly consult with and ask permission. Other songs you don't know so it could become "dangerous" if you don't understand how it was really done. We don't have a sense of that unless you go to the reservations and see [other traditional ways]. Those elements of danger can bring

* In September of 1998, the remains of approximately fifty Gabrielino-Tongva were discovered during the construction of a power station at the Arco refinery in the city of Carson, in Los Angeles County. Thought to be approximately two hundred years old at the time, the site was unusual because some of the individuals within had met a violent death; moreover the burials did not reflect traditional custom. The ongoing archaeology and reburial were completed in cooperation with the state's Native American Heritage Commission and the designated "most likely descendant," who supervised the excavation work and the reburials on behalf of the Gabrielino-Tongva people. For more information about most likely descendants and excavations, see the conversations with Michael Barthelemy, Vivian Barthelemy and Art Morales, Earl and David Campio, and Anthony Morales.

harm because that's a belief system. That's what has survived—a belief system that some things are dangerous. People have this longing for the past—a craving—and they want to bring it back in this form.

ST: Some of us are going to say, "I don't feel comfortable trying to bring that back." We respect that ceremony. We're not doing that. Somebody else may say, "I have the right to do that, and I'm going to do it."

CA: Part of bringing, acknowledging, or respecting those ceremonies is not to bring them back. That's a very strong position of people. They don't have the ceremonial houses [*yovaar*], because nobody has the knowledge, the responsibility, to manage those houses in this contemporary setting.* Otherwise it gets out there and becomes "commodified," like a lot of other things.

CT: You don't have cohesive communities as we did back then. Everybody is fragmented today, and you don't have that trust within your communities that people really do things with pure intent. Today, what would you consider artistic interpretation and how would you differentiate artistic interpretation from something that's just created within, something that you're making up? Where is your information from? Those of us who have been doing this all our lives barely understand certain elements of our culture. Then you have people who have been around for a couple years creating ceremonies, and we're asking, "Where did it come from?"

CA: As far as I'm concerned, the sacred stays sacred. Beyond that, whatever you do is interpretive stuff, that's different.

ST: What if the sacred has a gap [is not known]?

LG: As far as the sacred stuff that we don't have, that we've lost forever, for me it's a heartache that hurts. You can't say, "Well, then we'll make this up because we have to find something to do."

JG: But that's an answer, too. That wanting, that need is also part of the creative aspect of being a person, especially that fourteen-and-a-half-year-old. They're going to experiment no matter what you say to them.

CA: Well, if they learn the difference between what is sacred, and what is appropriate and what is not. The difference is, and I think where you can begin to draw the line, is who you're doing it for, and what's your purpose? I dance. Do I dance as a public display? No. It's artistic creativity, it's expression. Who do we do it for? I do a lot of things that are for [me] or for my family. If you take it out to the public, you're getting paid money. It is promoted as traditional, that becomes the controversy. I think creativity is tradition. Creativity is sacred. Tradition is not stagnant,

---

* An unroofed enclosure, the ceremonial *yovaar* stood in the center of every Tongva village. This is where the secular met the spiritual world, for inside was a representation of Chinigchinich, the sacred being of the people. Inside one encountered the sacred, and for that reason all entry to the *yovaar* was controlled.

otherwise it would cease to be. Traditions are things a community deems valuable and important. They hang on to it. It is perpetuated through time.

LG: But we have to make sure [of] the difference. The sacred needs to remain. The tradition will always change.

CA: Who defines that? That's the challenge, who defines that? Everybody is making a value judgment based on only a limited amount of knowledge. When it comes down to it, what is really, really authentic? That's where the education really becomes important, because how many people really understand that core intent?

CT: Your heart aches because of the ceremonies we'll never have. But what is it that we really need? Something I always carry inside me is the eagle dance. I never understood what it meant, but as I became older, I understood the symbolism more and more. Other ceremonies I know that I don't know, [they're] not important to me. What did we do it for? The eagle dance teaches young people something. When they see it performed, they're seeing a part of our creation they wouldn't know otherwise unless somebody sang the song to them, unless somebody told them the story. But if they're seeing it visually, they're seeing that whole story created, performed in front of them, and that's the connection.

Craig Torres, a member of the Ti'at Society, reflecting at the altar at the Povuu'ngna site, California State University, Long Beach, 2006. TY MILFORD PHOTOGRAPHY

CA: Teaching them how to see again.

CT: Teaching them how to see in a different way.

CA: Beyond the textural, beyond the visual, there are other ways to see and [be] symbolically literate. Let me give you an example with the Tongva people. We were all lashing people—we bound together our nets, baskets, canoes, houses, everything, without using nails. Those lashing patterns are two-dimensional; but how do you teach that to somebody? It just looks like a bunch of rope wrapped around.

There's a well-known sculptor, Felipe Tohi, who's Tonga.* In his culture the lashing patterns used on houses, canoes, and more are decorated with symbols and stories. Tohi uses similar patterns in his sculpture. He creates three-dimensional lashings which imbed traditional symbols of his native culture, but in a new way. He makes a large lashing, then places a smaller and smaller one inside, each painted with traditional symbols until all the individual lashings create a new three-dimensional whole. It's to point out—"Do you see these symbols take new form—is this a creation story—or is it a maze of lashings?" He's demonstrated very sacred narrative, brought it into contemporary form, into what he feels is a safe way to show the sacred.

CT: One thing lacking today is that people really [don't] know the reasons behind what they're doing. When you did have that responsibility, and you carried that in your community, it was major. When you pass on anything, you pass it on with etiquette. Today I see people passing on and teaching but they don't do it with etiquette. Etiquette, that's my way of saying, "I've given this to you, but here [are] the guidelines and use them. If you don't, then whatever comes upon you, that's your choice." People don't understand that today. That's what separated the elders from the rest of the community. There was a wisdom. You carried knowledge, but there was a responsibility with passing that knowledge on. You were supposed to teach protocol. If you didn't, then it was just anybody saying whatever they wanted to say.

CA: We can't assume that we have this way of seeing what is sacred. You go to other tribes and it's not the same thing. We did a pine nut gathering last month, month and a half ago. Somebody asked for somebody to do a prayer, and [someone said], "Well, we don't do that." Another woman [who had] been immersed in this other type of learning—sometimes they consider it to be New Age—said, "I'm going to do this because I feel the need to do it." But the others said, "We don't do that, that's personal to us. We never do prayers in public." You've seen this [reaction] with all the folks on the rez. It's a completely different way of looking at things. People start perceiving praying in public as being very urban Indian.

CJ: I think the sacred brings us full circle, because the first question we asked you is, "Why is Povuu'ngna sacred? Is it just a place, or is it a place where you can come together and experience renewal?"

CA: The truth of the myth exists and continues to live. It takes on its own energy. Once it's unleashed, it just continues.

---

* Felipe Tohi is from the Kindgom of Tonga, also known as the Friendly Islands, which is in the South Pacific Ocean, about two-thirds of the way from Hawaii to New Zealand.

A CONVERSATION with David Campio and Earl Campio (uncle of David Campio)

March 18, 2006
Rancho Los Alamitos, Long Beach, California

April 2, 2006
David Campio Studio, Ontario, California, and Campio Pottery Shop, Ontario, California

The Participants

IN HIS PROFESSIONAL ROLE, DAVID CAMPIO ENCOURAGES AND ASSISTS minorities interested in higher education. In his hobby and role as a "cultural educator" and the family "apprentice" potter, he has created a cultural resource center on the history of clay use along the Santa Ana River. In 2008 he was appointed to the Ontario-Montclair School District Board of Trustees.

A retired aerospace engineer and project manager for Litton Industries, Earl Campio worked at his father's side in the pottery shop, creating his own signature style. Today, he and David are documenting family stories and reestablishing the historic Campio Pottery Shop in Ontario, California, as an educational facility and working pottery studio.

The Discussion

Identifying themselves as the "Clay People," David Campio and his uncle Earl Campio describe how their native identity and family legacy have evolved from "clay to concrete." As they express their family's longtime affinity to the native inland environment, the two explore the native influence and difference between the pottery of Earl G. Campio (Earl's father and David's grandfather) and the

David (left) and Earl Campio (right) standing by three pieces of pottery made by Earl Irena Grijalva Campio, 2006. Top to bottom: Indian fruit basket, ca. mid-1940s; a water jug with a the signature "snake spout"; and a piece made for growing strawberries. Ty Milford Photography

master potter José Jesús Manzone, from Mexico (Earl's grandfather and David's great-grandfather). Earl Campio reveals how his father's native background influenced his life, and recounts how he created pots and piñatas for Hollywood sets, Disneyland, and historic Olvera Street, in Los Angeles. David connects his family's past to the larger native community, commenting on the archaeology of native pottery, nature of sacred things, and changing times, native identity and recognition, and cultural education. The following brings together two conversations occurring on different dates, one with David Campio, and one with David and his uncle Earl.

David Campio: My name is David Campio. My family is from the Santa Ana River. We're part of the river people. We're from the San Bernardino area, Corona area.

Claudia Jurmain: Have you always known that your family was Tongva? Do you say Tongva or Gabrielino in your family?

DC: There's really not a name for us. We have our own identity. If we were going to say anything—we're the Clay People. We've always had a foundation of clay from time immemorial. I've known I've been Indian as long as I can remember.

When I was little, my grandfather had a pottery shop probably about two orange groves away from where my mom lived. I'd get up in the morning, and I'd want to go to the pottery shop to visit my Indian grand-father. So my mom would walk me down the concrete sidewalks, and then I would take off and run through the orange fields, picking up oranges on my way. When I got halfway through, I could see my grandfather waiting there for me, and of course, I'd start to run a little bit faster. I'd have my shirt filled with oranges, and we'd sit there on his benches, and eat the oranges together at the pottery shop. He would tell me the crazy stories of our people, about how we all came from clay. Then he would make a frog and say, "Well, the frog woman killed our first deity." He was constantly making these little clay figurines for us and telling us stories when I was little. That's how I know I've always been Indian, stories from my grandfather.

His name was Earl Campio, Earl Ireno Grijalva Campio. He was born in 1916 in Prado, California, which was actually Rincon when he was born. His parents died of tuberculosis, so he was orphaned when he was one or two [and raised by his grandmother until he was about twelve.] He was [then] taken in by another native family and forced to live in the barn and wash the feet of the people he lived with. You hear these stories when you're little…"I was barefoot, I had to walk to school and had it rough"—those are stories everybody hears.

When I started my research, I found some photo-graphs of the early schools in Prado. My grandmother was able to identify him [Earl G. Campio]. She moved from Mexico to the area about 1920, and remembers him as the only child without shoes, and he lived in the barn. So I was able to identify him in the school picture—he is the only kid without shoes on. He ran away and found some uncles in the El Toro area. He got a job hunting squirrels, was able to go back to Prado. He worked in the pottery studio and shop of José Jesús Manzano, married his daughter (my grandmother), and became a successful potter of the area.

So my earliest identification of being Indian is growing up in the pottery business, going back to the time my grandfather told me stories while we shared oranges together. I find out later my grandfather was allergic to orange [blossoms]—but he would sit there and eat them with me. If you look at the history of the orange groves, what it did to the native population and agricul-ture in this area, sometimes I wonder…Did he taste the bitter sweetness of oranges the way I do today?

Earl Campio working at his potter's wheel in the Azteca (Ontario) pottery studio, 1956. His massive, rough style of pottery often revealed his native heritage and set his work apart from the style of his Mexican in-laws. With vivid reds, yellows, and black, Earl used traditional native symbols found in nature and stories, including animals and reptiles. He often made snakes and frogs "grow out of" the pottery, and according to his son Earl, he used flowers everywhere. COURTESY OF EARL AND DAVID CAMPIO

Altagracia Manzano and her cousin Frank standing in the Prado Pottery Studio, 1932. The studio was owned by her father, José Manzano, a master potter from Jalisco, Mexico. Earl Campio met and married Altagracia when he worked at the studio as a potter. Courtesy of Earl and David Campio

CJ: Do you think he chose to be a potter because of the meaning of clay?

DC: I think it was survival. He was orphaned, had very little education, but it's ingenious the way he created molds, how he made them, manufactured them in the market economy. I have no idea how he learned the skills. My grandmother doesn't know, but she came to the Rincon area in the 1920s [with her family from Mexico]. There was already a family member who was living in Prado doing pottery and he had a tile company. They knew the clay deposits from the Prado area were nice to work with. Her family moved, started a pottery business, and the business really boomed out there.

   My grandfather went to work for her father at a young age because he already knew how to process the clay, make pottery and tile. So they hired him and he ended up marrying my grandmother. My grandfather moved his pottery business in 1938 (when they built the Prado Dam) to Santa Monica for a couple of years, one year. Later, my grandfather started a new pottery business at Green River Parkway where the 91 freeway is now. When they built the freeway and the government moved them off, they bought a piece of land in Ontario. That's why we still have a pottery shop in Ontario.

CJ: You told me earlier that your family was at Mission San Gabriel?

DC: Yes, Mission San Gabriel and San Juan Capistrano, through two missions.

CJ: What is your profession today?

DC: I'm a college director educating minorities to go to college. I have opened up a cultural resource center on the history of clay use along the Santa Ana River. That's a hobby. I have a great teacher, my uncle [Earl], who I would say is [the last] native potter of the Santa Ana River—out there digging up the clay from the river—and manufacturing it. The pottery story is ultimately how [I've] moved through [the] history of our family.

I remember when I was in the third grade or fourth grade, when the teacher started talking about the San Gabriel Mission, I stood up proudly and said, "I'm Gabrielino Indian." She laughed at me: "There are no Gabrielino Indians left. Sit down, be quiet." I got sent to the principal's office that day. Well, I went home devastated. I don't think I ever told my mom, but I did tell my grandfather. He said, "You're going to get that the rest of your life. If somebody asks you, just say we're businessmen. We'll keep our identity here in our backyard in the pottery shop." That's just how it was.

Azteca Pottery Shop, 1965. Earl Campio Sr. built his Azteca Pottery Shop and studio on Holt Street in Ontario after he had to leave his Green River Pottery studio when the 91 freeway was built. Now closed, the pottery shop remains a period piece, with the interior filled with old merchandise and the pottery yard in working order.

COURTESY OF EARL AND DAVID CAMPIO

My mom was also a single mother raising three kids. That was frowned upon. When they identified us as Indians—the school sent out counselors, and pretty much forced us to go to Catholic school. The next summer me, my brother, my sister all find ourselves in Catholic school. Fortunately, or unfortunately for me, the first day of Catholic or catechism school, I had a massive asthma attack and had to be rushed to Pomona Valley Hospital. I was in an oxygen tent for days and never had to go back.

After the attack, I ended up spending all those years with my grandfather in the pottery yard, but my brother and sister had to go to Catholic school, catechism, made First Holy Communion. Well, I got my lessons from my grandfather in the pottery yard, working with my grandfather. I think that's why my [Gabrielino] identity is stronger. Ask my brother and my sister what their identity is—completely different. My sister identifies with the born-again Christian community, my brother with more of a Chicano identity. My mom laughs about it. She says, "I have three kids—I have a Chicano, an Indian, and a white girl."

Bill McCawley: What years did these events take place?

DC: About 1974, '75. I was humiliated, degraded. I didn't know what to do, because my whole identity up to that point was what my grandfather was teaching me. I walk into a school and they're telling me, "No, you're wrong." I don't know how I dealt with it. I just know we were forced to go to catechism. I got really sick. I didn't have to go anymore. I got to play with the pottery shop. I was a happy kid.

I worked as an ironworker before I went to college, for twelve years, and was a welder. You know, you're proud, [but] sometimes you're ashamed. Are you Indian for the money? Where is our language? Are we too lazy to twist our tongues to the old-time manner anymore? The self-inflicted abuse we put on ourselves, alcoholism, drug addictions, have all run through our families. But that's the reality of being Native American—identity crises, dealing with the Bureau of Indian Affairs, not dealing, being terminated, being "unterminated," having a roll number—what does it mean? Who's Indian and who's not? Our whole family—we all know we're Indian, but how are we going to self-identify and when is it appropriate? That's a survival issue for our family.*

CJ: What stories did your grandfather tell you about the Campio family?

DC: Remember, all his parents and grandparents died at a very early age. So what he held on to was the knowledge, history of clay. The frog woman, the creation stories—because he was orphaned, we're not sure where he learned all those stories from. When I was real sick with asthma, he would sing these songs to me. At one point I asked him, "What were you singing to me?" He said, "They're healing songs."

Because I was sick, I always stayed in the background with him, doing pottery. At that point it wasn't even pottery. We started doing cement fountains because

---

* After the 1927 California Indians Jurisdictional Act was passed, the state attorney general sued the federal government on behalf of Indians over the eighteen nonratified treaties negotiated by federal commissioners in 1851 and 1852. California Indians were required to document their native genealogy and tribal association and enroll with the government to file a claim and receive an award. Over the years not all eligible Tongva have chosen to enroll, either because they did not wish to be associated with the federal government, or because native people believed they knew who they were without having the government define their identity. Other enrollment papers were lost in the process. However, enrollment papers, like the old mission records, have come to be viewed as an important and "officially" recognized verification of native family lineage. But not all native people entered the missions or have chosen to enroll. For their descendants today, this is a difficult historical paradox.

During the 1950s and early 1960s, the federal government sought to sever the historical legal relation between Indian tribes and the U.S. government by eliminating reservations and tribal government and ending all federal programming and financial aid, and through relocating reeducating and assimilating Indians into mainstream society. No longer would Indians be "wards" of the government under the BIA, but rather full citizens with rights and responsibilities. In 1953, House Concurrent Resolution 108 with the Senate supported the new "Termination" policy, calling for the immediate termination of several tribes, including all those in California. Public Law 280, which passed in 1953 without tribal consent, gave certain states, including California, most civil and criminal jurisdiction over reservation lands. The California Rancheria Act of 1958 led to the termination of twenty-three rancherias and reservations between 1958 and 1970. In 1983, seventeen northern California tribes regained federal recognition and the tribal status held before termination as a result of a class action suit settlement, *Hardwick vs. United States*. Other individual suits prevailed as well, leaving twelve terminated California tribes to date.

From 1953 to 1964, 109 tribes in the U.S. were terminated, 1,365,801 acres of land removed from protected trust, and the tribal affiliation of over 13,000 Indians taken away. During the 1950s the federal government established nineteen urban centers around the country, relocating 160,000 to 180,000 Native Americans from reservations to cities. By 1995, the Native American population of Los Angeles was approximately 100,000, the largest urban Indian population in the United States.

In 1974, the Indian Self-Determination and Education Assistance Act was passed. Reversing termination, the government's new policy emphasized "maximum Indian participation in the Government and education of Indian People." Indian tribes could now negotiate their contracts with the BIA, assume control and responsibility, and administer federally funded education and social programs in their best interests. Since the disastrous policy of termination was abandoned, U.S. policy, in general working theory, supports self-determination; Indians tribes are to govern themselves.

he couldn't go down to Prado anymore to get the clay. He was still able to get clay, but the city passed ordinances; he could not have the outdoor burning kiln anymore. He turned all these pottery molds and clay molds into concrete molds. So it went from clay to concrete.

When I went to college, I took a Native American studies class. I started reading federal Indian law, Indian policy dealing with federal regulations and said, "This is what happened." I increased my studies, reading and writing law and policy from a native perspective. When I started up at Humboldt State University, I studied under two tribal attorneys and one tribal psychologist. I started relating all these studies to our family history, to my master's degree. I'm a law-and-policy kind of guy—I like to read and write policy and law for regulations. So I get to UCLA and my advisors don't want me to do that! "Do something more cultural." That's where I got the idea to write "Clay to Concrete," the history of clay use and how it eventually turned into concrete through my family line.

CJ: There's a younger generation in your family now. Who do they identify with if your brothers and sisters more strongly identify with other cultures?

DC: My sister is in church, but she still does check the box "Native American," and so does my brother. I mean, go back to the pottery yard, and we're all Indians.

CJ: Who's the storyteller in your family now?

DC: I guess I would have to take that role along with my uncle Earl, that responsibility, and that's why I am documenting all the stories. My grandfather had four sons and a daughter. We have about eighteen cousins, rough estimate, and everybody has kids except for me. A lot of us are in the Ontario, Montclair area—all the way down to San Diego and all the way up to Yuba City. Then a couple of us ended up in Arizona.

CJ: You have your family Tongva identity and there is also a larger political movement. Is there a link between the two? Do you see a need to have a larger political identity since you work in the realm of native law, policy, and regulations?

DC: It's just a thing I enjoy doing. Our identity is the Prado Dam area, the Corona area. All the stories my uncle [Earl] tells us are from Prado because that's where they were raised, were born. That's where my grandfather was buried, raised, born. As a political movement—I would write for federal recognition just to beat the system, as a personal challenge.

How much money do we get out of it? That's not the issue for me, for my uncle. Our home, what we have held on to, is a simple little pottery shop in Ontario on about a quarter-acre of land. We're still fighting now because the city wants to take another thirty-five, forty feet of it so they can widen the road. We

Earl (left) and David Campio (right) standing in front of the pottery shop on Holt Street in Ontario, 2006. Ty MILFORD PHOTOGRAPHY

had that happen in 1940. They took fifty yards to make Holt Boulevard without any compensation. It's trying to hold on to what little we have left, which is the pottery shop. It's closed, but all my grandfather's old stuff is there. I've recently taken many of the items from the shop and rented a studio where I have a little cultural center on pottery. It's more about trying to hold on to that [pottery shop], maybe getting landmark status, than federal recognition. "Am I Indian for the money or for who I am?" The identity thing—you see that throughout the country.

CJ: There are native people from many different tribes across the country in the Los Angeles area. Do you see a need to find and seek out Tongva community leaders or do you think it's enough for your family to identify themselves as Tongva?

DC: We weren't a big tribal group. We were based on the moiety system, very small family units.* Trying to bring everybody together as one single tribe is a huge slippery slope. That's not the system we had here in California. It has to stay within family, each has its own leader (ours is Uncle Earl). That's more historically correct from my perspective than people running around saying, "Oh, I'm the Gabrielino elder." In our family we try to stay out of that. We say our identity is here.

---

* Gabrielino-Tongva culture consisted of kinship or related groups known as lineages which were traced through the male ancestors. Lineages owned and protected their territories and determined where someone had the right to hunt and gather. Each lineage was made up of individual family units who each shared a common ancestor. All lineages were divided into two large groups, or "moieties" (a term used in anthropology), Coyote and Wildcat. People from both moieties came together during festivals since each moiety only knew or possessed some of the required elements for a successful ceremony; maybe a song, dance, or ritual item. The resulting mix helped support trade, food distribution, and the regional economy.

CJ: What if another community advances a Gabrielino-Tongva cause under their banner that might impact you?

DC: They can do whatever they want to, it's a free market. It will never take our identity. We are strongly identified with the historical use of clay, the pottery shop, the Prado area, the Corona mountains. To fight over a casino, who's going to be enrolled, not enrolled—that's a nightmare. We have decided as a family not to play that game.

BMc: What does recognition mean to you in the larger sense? Is it important that non-Indian society recognize your family has been out here, has the special tie to the land? Is it important other Indian people in the Los Angeles area see this special tie?

DC: No, because that's just self-ego, not important. We know who we are. I do get invited to lecture; I'd go out on other issues, too. It's what they do in L.A., what they can do in L.A. Out here we're a different branch. I work with other local tribes. They know our family history and identify us. We already know we are Indian and we don't need L.A. people to tell us that. I think they do need to open their eyes up a little bit.

CJ: Does it matter that most children are taught in the past tense? As an educator, do you want children to know the Tongva people are an active part of the community today?

DC: That's one of my favorite lectures I do for people who become teachers, for fifth graders, second graders, third graders, or college. I have the kids or the adults draw a picture of an Indian. Hatchets, liquor in our hands, bloody arrows, the feather—adult or child, they're drawing the same image. Then I have them draw a white person. They'll draw a man in a suit and tie, his hair parted on one side. Why have Indians been locked in time? I'll show that. All the pictures, from third graders and college students, they're the exact same thing.

CJ: The judgment constantly applied against the Gabrielino-Tongva community is that you no longer know your own native culture. You may exist genetically, but you don't have a culture.

DC: It's been a forced change. When you get your knuckles slapped every time you do something, if things are taken away from you—you can't do it. You find other ways, other means. Like the rattle. When they started using cans, they altered the music. Some tribes up in northern California—you see old pictures of them doing their dances, but they would have the American flag blowing back there. They were allowed because they had the flag. It's a lie. It's completely different. When your cultural identity is taken away from you, you're forced into a different identity, you have to alter. That's survival.

CJ: What wasn't taken away?

DC: Our identity—our use of the clay, our knowledge of the earth.

CJ: Does your sense of sacred come from the land?

DC: When all the land was taken away—it's hard to say that sacred land is still there when you see what's happened to it. Sacredness is in the stories.

BMc: Do you use the term "sacred"?

DC: Absolutely, absolutely. I don't throw it around as loosely as a lot of people do, although the reburials are sacred and it's a sacred ritual to rebury. Sacredness comes from within. What you find sacred is completely different from what I find sacred. It's internal, not physical. I say my family is sacred, my grandfather is, my mother is sacred. The things they taught me are sacred.

CJ: How, or is, your sense of family different than my sense of family?

DC: They could be very similar in nature. Sure, we've been here a long time and have documented our family history, but what you might find sacred, and what you're going to teach your kid is sacred—the Prado, Rincon area—old Rincon, new Prado—would be a sacred area for our family because that's where my grandfather lived, grew up—that's the foundation of his stories. Now, he might say the San Bernardino area, up on the Santa Ana River towards the Highland area, would be a sacred spot for him, because his parents told him stories about that area, or the horse and buggy rides he would take down to Pala, up to San Manuel to visit family members on the reservations. I think the sacred sites are based on stories that he told us.

But it's changed—land, the clay, and the water. We'd always go down there [Prado] and have family picnics, play in the river [about the first or second grade], just splash around. My uncle was on the banks, and we kids swimming in the water. Next thing I remember is getting plucked from the water. My uncle just laid me on his lap. We didn't know we were all covered with leeches from the stagnant water. We've never been back to the Prado Dam since that day. I just remember driving back in the front of the old yellow Chevy truck with my uncle and [hearing] him—"We'll never go back as a family to that river. It's not pure anymore. It's unclean, it's dirty, it's bad." And we never went back.

BMc: Did your grandfather speak any of the Tongva language in addition to Spanish and English?

DC: He didn't even speak Spanish [to me], but he did sing me those songs when I was sick in the hospital. One he remembered was when his parents were dying. They would come in and sing those songs to him when they were sick. My uncle and I are working on those songs to get them down, to remember them. He's trying to tell me as many stories about things my grandfather taught him. I've been documenting it, writing. My uncle won't talk on tape, so it's all about me writing it down and having him go over it—"No, no, no, what are you talking about here? That's too much, too romantic. That's not what happened."

CJ: Federal recognition for some is a healing issue, making up for some of the past abuse, the hideous things that have happened in history. Words such as "healing" are used as much as "sacred," "identity," and "sovereignty." Do these words have meaning to you?

DC: The definition of sovereignty is the right to power and authority to govern. Title 25 CFR (Indian Code of Federal Regulations) is one of the biggest code books in the United States government.* It's the only race of people that have to live by a code of rules. So sovereignty doesn't exist for me. It's an unrealistic, romantic term even the native populations really don't understand.

Sovereignty, federal recognition—what really comes with it? If you seek federal recognition, what are you really biting off?** Now, our family is fine. What would happen if we all wanted to move on a one-mile by one-mile stretch of land together? We can't even make it from Thanksgiving to Christmas without arguing. Who's going to write the grants? Who's going to deal with the policies? That's a big project. I've worked as a housing director for tribes, been their cultural resource person. That's a huge responsibility. It's not an easy task to all of a sudden get your federal recognition and try to develop your education policies, housing policies, government. If they can pull it off, have a game plan, more power to them.

I'm focused on getting our pottery shop historical landmark status and using that as an educational facility. We don't do a lot of pottery. I'm still learning my technique, but there's a lot we have to show our identity—talk to kids about it, have educators come over and see.

You can look at the way my grandfather took pottery in the 1930s, 1940s, and

---

* The Code of Federal Regulations includes all the regulations issued by federal agencies that have "general applicability and legal effect." Federal statutes authorize and limit the regulations. Title 25 includes all the chapters and subsections defining and detailing acts and statutes pertaining to American Indians, including the criteria for federal recognition and gaming, definitions of language, mineral rights, and education and health benefits, among many, many other issues.

** In order to receive federal recognition, a tribe must meet standards set by the Bureau of Acknowledgment and Recognition within the Bureau of Indian Affairs. 25 CFR Part 83.7 lists the criteria, some of which may be mitigated if "previous acknowledgment" by the federal government can be established. For more information on federal recognition, refer to the essay "The Enduring Vision: Recognition and Renewal," as well as the conversations with Anthony Morales and Virginia Carmelo.

see a trend going back to ORA-64.* Beads, pinch pots—all different types of pottery techniques are there. Spanish, Mexican rule—that's the first time you really start seeing coil-type pottery in this area. It's nondecorative, just water bowls, ollas, pots here and there. Also, in that coil pottery you're still seeing pinch-pot style at the top.** It's a transition. You start seeing more decorative stuff because now people are permanent.

With American rule, you start seeing a [growing] market economy. You don't see the coil system anymore. You don't see pinch pots. You start seeing decorative molded pottery you can mass-produce. Take a mold called a hump mold, pat out a tortilla-type shape, put it over a cylinder, and pop it off—you have your pot. Then they would take the coil technique, put it on top, and make the top. So you're seeing many different styles based on different movements and societies moving into the area. That's our family history.

CJ: What's your grandfather's contribution in that historical evolution of pottery?

DC: He made these molds so he could survive and mass-produce the pottery. His potter's wheel that I have in my studio right now is an old wagon wheel.

CJ: What was his style, his signature in the pottery?

DC: Using a simple fork. Go back to ORA-64 and they describe a fork, a four-pronged instrument used to put designs on the pottery.

I have four pieces left and over 150 molds. One piece my uncle received back [from] some lady out in Arizona who collected native pottery. Upon her death, in her will, she said these pieces go back to the family. So we received one back about ten, fifteen years ago. He would do huge clay chimneys for people, and pottery demonstrations. One day he was hired at Knotts Berry Farm and did Indian pottery. He did that for a day and said, "Never again would I go back and do that."

Those are the stories my grandmother tells me and I'm documenting. I haven't seen any pieces at LACMA [L.A. County Museum of Art], but my grandmother, she knows they're there. He never signed anything, but you can tell his work because his hands were huge. So when you create these flowery tops—his things—you can tell it by his hand size. My uncle would do the same thing but they're smaller.

---

* ORA-64 was the sixty-fourth site in Orange County on a nationwide list of archaeological finds, but today a gated community sits on the bluff overlooking Newport Bay where once there was a Native American site estimated to be 4,000 to 9,500 years old. In 1972, very small, fired-clay ceramics were unearthed, dating between 6,000 to 7,150 years old, perhaps the oldest decorated, fired-clay ceramics in the Western Hemisphere. In 1995 and 1996 an estimated six hundred human burials and thousands of cultural items, including ceramic cylinders, stone spheres, and balls, were excavated during the development construction of the thirty-acre site. Attempts to place the site on the National Register of Historic Places were not completed, and a ballot measure to save the site failed. The development company followed all due legal process, was willing to sell, and worked with the Native American Heritage Commission, site monitors, and the designated "most likely descendants." However, the project remained controversial due to the cultural and scientific significance of the site, one of the largest and oldest on the Pacific Coast. The unearthed burials were reinterred per the wishes of the native participants involved, without DNA testing or radiocarbon dating. The process followed the letter of the law, the California Environmental Quality Act, but several scholars rued the scientific loss of irretrievable information, while many in the native community were not fully aware of the process until later. For some, ORA-64 represents a failure of the system despite adherence to the law, and the loss of scholarly information, and for others, the desecration of another native cultural site.

** In coil pottery, rolled lengths of clay are placed on top of one another and shaped into a vessel. Ollas are earthern jars or pots used for storing water, seeds, and food, or for cooking. In pinch pots, the clay is pinched into a shape.

The glaze he used was chunks of real poisonous stuff. They would dig it out of the Corona mountains. We still have his old meat grinder. He would take big pieces of lead, grind it up, make a slurry, and glaze the inside.

CJ: Who is the next generation of potters in your family?

DC: My uncle. He's the next generation, and I have another uncle who is a really good artist and potter out in Arizona, and two of his kids. I'm making some tile right now for Hupa and Yurok tribal members. They've been sending me carved acorn paddles out of the redwood trees, and artwork. My cultural center is based on various tribes throughout California—I want to show some of their original pieces. We'll show pottery there, but I'm trying to get other tribal members.

CJ: Would you live anywhere else? Your family's identity is rooted in this region, so is it essential for you to live here?

DC: At my age, what I'm trying to accomplish, I don't see myself moving. My uncle's getting older and we have something we have to protect here. It's the foundation of our family, the pottery shop. I have to get my little nieces and nephews in there. I've got to teach them the stories, show them. The stories might take on new meaning because we are documenting everything. One of my nieces is in college and she likes history. "Okay, here's history for you, come on."

BMc: Do you know your family's connection to Mission San Gabriel and San Juan Capistrano?

DC: I've heard that we made shoes. I've heard another story that we did the tile.

BMc: You mentioned you had traced your genealogy back as far as one person born in 1864?

DC: Their parents were, are buried in the San Gabriel Mission. We were taught the missions were good. Now, study the subject. Pick up two different books and

David Campio at his grandfather's potter's wheel, 2006. Earl Campio made the unusual potter's wheel from the wooden wheel and axle of an Essex automobile, ca. 1920s. The "maseta" (big pot) sitting on the wheel once sat on the roof of Earl's Azteca Pottery Shop, to advertise its wares.
TY MILFORD PHOTOGRAPHY

you got two different stories. What's the correct one? You have to find a balance in there somewhere, and I think I've found the balance. Some of my cousins are very strong Catholics, identify with being Indians and Gabrielino. I'm not going to take those stories and bash them, bash the church, take away their identity. Their identity was already taken away once. They're happy. They're fulfilled. They have that in their lives. They still identify with being Gabrielinos. It's just a difference of opinion.

CJ: Do you think your family has something unique and special that many, many others within the community don't have, because you have the pottery studio?

DC: Absolutely. Clay, the history of pottery, the history of clay use—it ties us back to the land. My grandfather started doing concrete work and fountains after he couldn't do the pottery anymore—that is a continuation of our culture. So what if we're doing concrete? It's still a native art, still continuing our culture. We just can't build the kilns anymore. We can't have outdoor burning pollution, but it continues. My grandfather used to always make cement beads for us. All of us were running around with our cement beads—we were Indians with cement beads. How often do you see that? We'd play in the sand, and he would say, "Whoever is being bad is going to have to go swimming with those beads on."

BMc: What do you feel about the Tongva culture in present time? Is it living through your family, changing from day to day, or does it feel that you're trying to recover something that has been lost?

DC: Using these molds is tough, but I've been on the potter's wheel and I can throw pots now. Now, is that a continuing? I can't do it—well, I can do it. I'm going to get it down just to show my uncle I did one! Everybody will say Indian culture is based on a circle worldview. My thing is a spiral—different things in life will come around and alter, but knowing who you are from the beginning, and continuing this.

 I use clay as a metaphor, clay and concrete. We are in the concrete phase. I'm—we're—using concrete, trying to reintroduce the clay aspect. A culture, any indigenous group throughout the world is altering daily. I see Indian tribes or Indian people—"This has to be, because I can't change." No. The seasons change, everything changes. You can't lock yourself in—you'll miss out on a lot.

CJ: Your family has found and kept its ongoing sense of identity based on your evolving pottery studio and story. You have made it relevant today, in some new way, without losing yesterday, because it still means the same. How do other people find that?

DC: I think it's through education. Even when I show some of my research to my uncle, I have to sell it to him. He's still locked in time—this is the only way we can do pottery—using these molds. He says, "You need to use this first before you go on to this step." But he learned that. He didn't learn the coil system my grandfather knew. He learned this. Well, I'm learning a different way, but I still want to do the same type of pottery. I'm just using different methods. I think it's going to happen through education.

CJ: Do you feel as if you're caught in your own heritage?

DC: I accept it. I enjoy it. My uncle and I have hundreds of conversations. We sit there with my grandmother sometimes and she'll look at us like we're just nuts. My grandfather had these old plaster molds that he did, really crude. Basically take the clay, wad it up and just cram it in there, bust out the mold, and you have different various frogs. For the life of me I can't do one. I just can't. I've tried about a hundred times, probably lost about four pounds trying.

CJ: Do you have people from within the community, or outside, come back and say, "Your grandfather did this for me"?

DC: Even adults about my age will come back and say, "Oh, I remember going through a tour of your pottery yard and your grandfather making pottery for people."

CJ: Was he recognized within the larger Tongva or Gabrielino community as a Gabrielino potter?

DC: No. He taught me he was better off to say that he was a businessman. My grandfather didn't know a lot about his identity. At times I think he wished he knew more, but he did share with me what little he did know. It's just what happened—he didn't get all the stories. Who knew what all the stories mean anyway? He was a strong Indian man—that's what he was.

CJ: If you meet someone who is a coastal Gabrielino, do you have any affinity with them at all?

DC: No. I'm cool with them. I don't know what the heck they're doing with those canoes—something about the ocean and paddling! I think it is good any time you can educate anybody. I'm not one to judge and tell them, "You're doing it wrong." They can put out what they want, their story—that's great, but let's not forget about us inside.

BMc: Your grandmother, she's ninety?

DC: Yeah [eighty-seven]. When she came over from Mexico, they had a vacation pass, and I guess her father was working for the railroad. They came to Prado, got off, and set up house there. On his [great-grandfather's] documentation, they have him listed as an "alfareo," which is a potter from Mexico.

CJ: When is the first time you heard about Povuu'ngna?

DC: Probably ten, fifteen years ago.

CJ: Because of the political activity at Cal State?

DC: No, not at all. Didn't hear about them—just education, reading, writing, researching. It really didn't resonate with me, wasn't part of something I was looking into. I was more interested in the inland tribes.

CJ: Do you think of Povuu'ngna as a cultural rallying point?*

DC: I still don't see it out there. Within the communities, you really have to dig deep to look for it. So, rallying point? Good—whatever brings people together, but you have those internal battles. It's more about the people and personal power within the whole community, and the hierarchy structure. You hear about those battles more than Povuu'ngna in tribal communities all the way up the coast—people battling down here over something—federal recognition they don't even have yet.

CJ: Is the issue money and casinos?

DC: Absolutely.

CJ: Are there other issues?

DC: Absolutely. Who knows more? Who is the ritual leader? Who knows how to do this ceremony and that? It's never going to be the same. Take what you have, work with it, work together. It's not that "I learned this from so and so, and I am the only person who can do it." How much can you really take back to what it was before contact?

We have purposely stayed away. We don't want to join any of those people, don't want to be part of it. We don't really go out there and tell our stories a lot.

BMc: How old was your grandfather when he died?

DC: Sixty-eight.

CJ: What do you want to pass on to a child about who you are and why you feel that is unique? What distinguishes your people from another tribe?

---

* During the 1990s the Native American Heritage Commission and plaintiffs from the Tongva community filed suit against California State University at Long Beach to prevent commercial development of an archaeological and burial site of Povuu'ngna on university property. The university administration declared a moratorium on developing the site and protected the open space. The moratorium was not binding on future administrations. For more on Povuu'ngna refer to the essay "A Connection to Place: Land and History" and the conversation with the Ti'at Society.

DC: Clay—the land along the Santa Ana River. The history of our family has been the land along the river. I would teach my nieces, my nephews, and the generations that we are the Clay People. When we were little, we'd run up and down the pottery yard, and it seemed like a big place. We'd get really thirsty. We wouldn't run for soda—we had that clay olla. Drinking that water, that clay taste, that earth, was just so cold on those hot, sunny days. Tasting that earth in water nourishing yourself was a powerful thing.

BMc: Has your connection to the land and to your heritage there become more important as you've gotten older? Changed?

DC: It's a prominent, important force in my life now, continuing to grow or decrease, but a continuum. I don't think I would have that if I didn't go out there—college, graduate work, write, upset my grandmother by asking her tons of questions—"What about this?" Just my persistence…tell the story.

CJ: Is your wife Native American?

DC: No, she is Jewish. I'll tell you this story because it's kind of funny. Our first big argument was a big cultural standoff. We got into this argument—she was cooking dinner, and she was mad. This is when we were still dating. She goes, "Here's your dinner." I said, "I can't eat that." "What do you mean you can't eat that?" I said, "Well, I was always taught when you cook, you're nourishing somebody's body, and you're supposed to cook with a good heart and good mind. You know," I said, "I can't eat it. I'm not going to eat that. That's like eating poison." She's a clinical psychologist, so she looks at me and says, "Well, I'm Jewish. We argue. You're supposed to break the bread. I'm making amends—here, eat it." And I said, "No, you're poison."

That was our first big argument. Breaking bread was a healing thing, but no, I was always taught if you're cooking and eating, you're supposed to be good-hearted. I have to cook now! But it was interesting, [we] ended up laughing about it. It was a cultural standoff—really got there—and we've worked beyond it.

CJ: Is the family pottery shop in Ontario still open?

DC: The pottery shop has not been open in twenty-five, thirty years. It's just sitting there, all kinds of real neat little objects everywhere. We want to have it be a studio—anybody in our family can come and make a fountain, make a pot—and have tours come through. That's where we want to go with it. Of course, if they want to come over, they have to listen to me tell the stories! We're passing it on.

Before European contact, they would go gather the white clay—put it on their hair, wash their hair with clay. They made native pottery with the red clay. The red clay or the adobe was sometimes pulverized and used as red pigment for making

Prado Pottery Studio, where Earl Campio worked for José Jesús Manzano, who eventually became his father-in-law, 1932. Manzano, a master potter from Jalisco, considered Earl the best potter he had ever known, and of all his sons, "the one that had it." COURTESY OF EARL AND DAVID CAMPIO

paint for ceremonial purposes. The Santa Ana River people [were] upriver, downriver. ORA-64, Newport Bay Harbor—clay ceramics have been uncovered there—beads, simple pinch pots and effigies, ear plugs possibly, globular balls—people don't really know what these were for, probably a child's game or gambling game.

[At this point in the conversation, Earl Campio, who is David's uncle, joins us. Earl Campio is the son of potter Earl G. Campio, David's grandfather.]

Earl Campio: It ties in with what my dad used to say when they took him to Soboba.* My grandmother lived in Prado where the Campio farm was. My dad, his parents died when he was one, two years old, and his grandmother raised him [until he was around twelve]. She used to take him to the reservation in Soboba because she loved to gamble, and they had a game that had a clay round stone. They would make a fire pit. They chose sides, took the ball [round stone] and handed it from one person to the next. Then they would throw sawdust and things into the fire to make it go up. They let the fire go down, look at each other's eyes, and gamble money. Who had the stone? He said they would play for hours. The buggy ride took two days to get there and two back home. They would go there at least once a month. That's why I think this [the globular balls at ORA-64] might have something [to do with gambling].

---

* Located at the foothills of the San Jacinto Mountains in Riverside County, Soboba Indian Reservation was established in 1883, one of six federally recognized Luiseño-speaking reservations in southern California. Soboba has also been home to the Cahuilla, but today most residents are Luiseño.

DC: ORA-64 was the largest collection of all known clay specimens. The vessel rims were simple pinch pots—the oldest ceramics of the New World—seventy-seven hundred years old. The clay used during the mission system is altered for adobes, water canals, pottery, and tile. But during Mexican occupation, some archaeological findings along the Santa Ana River, [you] still see globular balls, effigies, and beads and tubular beads out of clay. All these natural runoffs of the Santa Ana River eventually drop into Newport Bay Harbor. Between Newport Bay Harbor and Alonzo Creek was all marshland, so there weren't a lot of habitats there. The families there were the Manzanos, the Arreolas, the Grijalvas, and the Campios. Those were big pottery families—all one family.

EC: Cousins.

DC: The José Jesús Manzano family—about 1938 they had a big pottery company in Prado. [José Jesús Manzano and his wife, Francisca Arreola, are the great-grandparents of David Campio and the grandparents of Earl Campio. Jesús Manzano (his common name) was a master potter from Jalisco who established his successful pottery studio and shop in Prado, which was at the time the foremost center for making pottery, tile, and bricks in southern California.

Earl Campio Jr., 2006. Earl learned the art and craft of pottery from his father, Earl Campio. Although he pursued another line of work, Earl helped out in the pottery studio throughout his life. Today he lives in the house his father built by Azteca, the pottery store and studio on Holt Street, Ontario. TY MILFORD PHOTOGRAPHY

Earl G. Campio (Earl Campio's father, David's grandfather) already knew how to process clay and make pottery and tile when he went to work for Jesús Manzano. There Earl G. met and married Altagracia, the daughter of Jesús Manzano and Francisca Arreola. In time, Earl G. Campio and his wife opened their own pottery studio and shop, first at Green River and then in the city of Ontario.]

CJ: Did the pottery style of Jesús Manzano reflect their new home in Prado or where they came from in Mexico?

DC: I think it's unique to the area, but it has its foundation in Jalisco, Mexico.

EC: I went to the town where they came from, but the pottery they had there was not the same because the clay kind of dictates the style. This [Prado] clay

Water jug made in the mid-1940s by Earl Campio, 2006. Bright green with yellow, black, and red trim, the jug illustrates Earl's traditional native colors and symbols. The snake-like pouring spout distinguished his work from that of his Mexican in-laws, who considered snakes evil and never used the motif on their pottery.
TY MILFORD PHOTOGRAPHY

will take a lot of abuse and some clay won't. The difference is in the finishes and the glaze.

DC: In 1941 the [Prado] dam was completed. Everybody had been moved off the land in 1938, 1939 for the dam construction. My great-grand-father Jesús Manzano did briefly go to Santa Monica. [Jesús Manzano moved his Prado Pottery Studio to Santa Monica when the Prado Dam project began. However, by this time Earl G. Campio had already married Altagracia and left his father-in-law's pottery studio, and was subcontracting out to other pottery studios in the area. Because Earl G. and Grace Campio eventually had four children to support, he went to work for Douglas Aircraft. He then became a gardener and was drafted during WWII. After he returned, health issues forced Earl G. to leave the ocean air climate. He decided to go back to his roots. He and his family headed back to the Prado area to start making pottery again.]

EC: 22nd Street and Olympic, behind the home— strictly a manufacturing place. They made a kiln, made pottery in the back and sold it to different places.

That's when they came back to Green River. That's right down from Prado [Dam]. There's the clay and he went back into the pottery business. He and my mother just sold everything, came to Green River, and put up this pottery yard.

DC: 1945.

EC: Right around there. The kiln was back there, we had our own water well—the Santa Ana River was our backyard. We'd get the clay at Prado [Dam, since it was all an open area then], bring it down and make pottery. Later [archaeologists] did a dig, found pottery and didn't know where it came from. It was our pottery yard at Green River.* When the 91 freeway went through, my father started looking around. He came to Ontario, was fascinated by the mountain, and that's where he put his next pottery yard. That's why we ended up on Holt Boulevard in Ontario.

---

* The location for "Grace's," the pottery shop Earl G. Campio opened on the Green River, was a good business move at the time. The shop was located on Highway 91, the main two-lane road leading from the desert into Los Angeles.

DC: My great-grandfather, José Jesús Manzano, he's the master potter. You really can't describe his pottery as just Mexican pottery, because it takes all kinds of influences to have current pottery. They're digging up [excavating] some of the impressed designs and stamps, and Mexican pottery, but if you see designs, it's the same. Just saying "Mexican pottery from Prado" really limits the history behind the pottery of a certain area. The Manzanos came from Mexico and set up a pottery shop, but the laborers are Indian. To identify it as Mexican pottery is a stretch for me. You have to give everybody credit because all these different people created pots. It's just the times.

EC: It's the person doing it. Anything my grandfather [Jesús Manzano] made was never like my father made. My father had his own massive rough look in the pottery he made, and the way he made it. My grandfather used to make all these little fine things, which I think was more Mexico. It's the person and the clay.

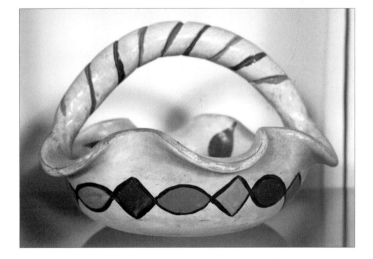

DC: My grandfather's style [Earl G. Campio]—he'd like to do snakes and a theme of animals coming out of the pieces of pottery. He was Indian. I wouldn't even consider the pottery Mexican. I would consider it from Prado, because there were no snake deals in Mexico. This was his thing—snakes. A water jug—it's the mouth of a serpent and the water pours out of it.

EC: He never talked about those designs, but I remember my grandfather saying, "I would never make [a snake]." That might be because my grandfather—they're all religious Catholics and my dad was not. To him a snake was a good thing, but to my grandfather, the devil probably.

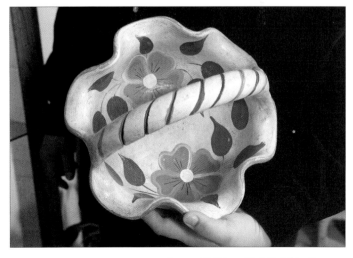

DC: The water jug—if you go back to the pieces they're digging up [ORA-64], it's kind of the same thing.

EC: Where 71 and 91 connect, the dam comes right there and the river flows down. Going down 71 to 91, on the left, you'll see the main part of the dam. At the end where the river is going down to the bottom, that's

Earl Campio called this piece he made in the mid-1940s for his wife an "Indian Fruit Basket."
TY MILFORD PHOTOGRAPHY

Francisca Manzano and her daughter Altagracia at the Prado pottery studio, 1932. Earl Campio, an orphaned, Indian potter at the studio, married Altagracia despite her mother's opinion. COURTESY OF EARL AND DAVID CAMPIO

where my father's original house was [the Campio homestead]. But if you go up where the Santa Ana River flooded quite often, he said that was the summer home, where it was cool. They would go up to the caves where they kept the meat, their meat and things. He even had initials carved in those caves where they used to stay.

CJ: Where did your father learn to work with clay?

DC: Growing up in that Prado area with clay deposits, he picked up the trade as a child. So he went to work with my grandmother's father and ended up taking over the business.

EC: [He also married] the daughter [Altagracia ("Grace") Manzano Campio]—not that he didn't have a big hassle from my grandmother—she didn't like him. He was an orphan, he was Indian, and Mexicans have their own ways too. He didn't have any money. She thought they were like aristocrats—Manzano is a French name. They were French, Mexican, Jewish and very light-complected. My mother had red hair, and here's this Indian boy that didn't have a pair of shoes until he was sixteen, courting the daughter—that was a no-no.

CJ: Did he present himself as an Indian?

EC: Yes, he always told us we were "wild Indians." He didn't go to church. My mom said he was an Indian and he didn't care who knew about it.

CJ: When people came to your pottery shop, either the one on Green River or later in Ontario, did they know they were buying pottery made by a California Indian or did they think they were buying Mexican pottery?

EC: It's really hard to tell, because the pottery shop in Ontario was called "Azteca," and the one in Green River, "Grace's Pottery," after my mother. I don't know if my grandfather's pottery studio and shop in Prado had a name. I don't think they named their businesses. In Prado, the labor was Mexican, Indian, but my dad never hired Mexicans. My dad hired kids, guys I went to school with, my brothers. I worked there until I went into the service. I'm an aerospace engineer, but this never got out of my blood. When I was sixteen, I was buying and making molds. I started making stuff, selling it to my dad, selling it to places in San Fernando, Sylmar, Simi Valley. I never signed it.

CJ: Even though your dad was orphaned, did you get together with his other family?

EC: Maybe once every two years he said, "You know, we're going to go see the Indians, your Indian cousins, because I want you to know that you do have people."

CJ: Did your father speak any of the language, know any words?

EC: He knew words when they got together, but he never told us any. My father was fluent in Spanish, he never taught us Spanish either.

CJ: Was your father's goal to run a successful pottery shop, be an artist?

EC: He was a businessman. He wanted to work for no one. Disney came to the pottery yard and offered him a place at Disneyland, and he talked to them. When they said Disney would have control, he said, "I don't need you." They came, sent people, and he went down and looked at the Mexican Village at Disneyland. He could have had that one corner, the whole thing. When they sat down and told him what the rules were going to be—they wanted this and that—he said, "No, I'm in my own business. I'm my own boss."

We made pottery for the movie studios. They used to send us tickets to go see the movie. One sticks in my mind—an Arabian movie. I remember them breaking every piece of pottery, and there's a big old fight. We were watching and my little brother gets up, "We made that!"

CJ: When he gave pottery demonstrations and spoke with people, did he ever weave in his background? Was he proud of his own legacy and heritage?

EC: When Miss Bebe, a family friend, came, he'd talked to her about the Indian heritage, making the pottery. She always wanted him to go and talk, and show this type of pottery at the University in Arizona, but he never did. My daughter, we would send her to my father's pottery shop (Azteca) in Ontario. Shoes were optional—in the summertime nobody wore shoes. My daughter must have been maybe about six, seven, [and] my father says, "We are going to make you some Indian shoes because it's really getting hot out there and burning your feet. I used to wear these." He took a bicycle tube, cut the size of her foot, slit the top, and she put those on and she walked. She wanted to go to school with "Grandpa's Indian shoes."

My father started wholesaling. We used to go as far north as Solvang, and as far east as Phoenix, and south to San Diego, where we were making pottery and cement things. Piñatas were all made for Olvera Street. Before they started making them out of papier maché, we made them out of clay. You had to make them very thin, as thin as possible, because when they hit them with a bat, they would just explode. We used to make hundreds.

CJ: Did your father encourage you to leave the pottery studio and shop in Ontario?

EC: My dad had a sign in our bedroom that said, "18 or out of school—you're gone." Go do your own thing. You could work with pottery or whatever. I decided to go, to get as far away from California as possible. I went to sign up in the Army. My dad wouldn't sign the paper. I was seventeen. He [the Army recruiter] said, "We have a radar school in New Jersey." That's how I ended up in electronics—[manager of inertial guidance systems and gyroscope lab] for Teledyne and Litton Industries for twenty-nine years.

I ran the Ontario pottery yard—my sister worked for me, we would come here, do pottery on the weekends and engineered during the week. Always came back—I retired, wanted to open it back up. The city said, "You can't." Tomorrow if I opened that gate, you'll see the pottery is still all in there, unused since. [Today the Ontario pottery shop is a period piece filled with retail inventory and "collections" from the days when the Azteca pottery shop and studio of Earl G. Campio were open for business.]

When I was in grammar school, my dad had some pottery he had made when he was a kid in Sherman Institute.* He had always told me if I wanted to go to an Indian school, I could go to Sherman. When he was talking about Sherman Institute one day, he said, "Remember the stories about going to Pala?"** I said, "Yes, why don't we go live on a reservation?" He said he was thinking about teaching the Indians how to do cement work—"I could give them a few molds and show them how."

One day we got in the truck and drove up to Pala. He knew the elder and where the little church is. We went and talked to him about his grandmother, my great-grandmother. He said, "Your great-grandmother used to like Soboba better than she did Pala." So we went up to Soboba, where he said, "You know, this reservation we could really live in."

But boy, when we drove in and see this one water fountain—everybody has to go there—and we're living over there—I got it. "I don't think so." He said, "It sounds good, but they really have no drive. They were kept people." I asked him,

---

* Opened in 1902, Sherman Institute was a vocational training school run by the Bureau of Indian Affairs in Riverside, California. For more information, refer to the essay "Continuity within Change: Identity and Culture."

** Located in northern San Diego County, the 12,273-acre reservation for the Pala Band of Mission Indians is home to both Cupeño and Luiseño Indians.

"How come you didn't go back to the reservation?" "The ambition has been taken out of them," he told me. They just lived there. The government gave them their money. He talked to some about making pottery, if he could help them set up something. They weren't interested.

That was it. That was life. I guess most of them grew up and joined the military. That's why my dad hated it when I told him I was going into the military, because "You're voluntarily going into something that to me is detrimental." I said, "But I'm going there to get an education."

He was drafted [in WWII]. He was twenty-six, twenty-seven years old and had four kids. They sent him to Texas. As soon as the train got to the border of Texas, all the Mexicans and Indians, they want them to get to the back car. There was a big riot between the California Indians and Texans. Nobody moved anywhere. He said that was really the first time he ever really felt discrimination.

In Prado and Corona, there's bitterness. My dad never went to "The Plunge"— the swimming pool. The Mexicans and Indians could go there only on Fridays because they emptied it on Saturday. My mom's sisters really remember that. But my dad never had discrimination because nobody really knew what he was. We didn't live with Mexicans. We had a business. He wasn't a gardener, a construction [or] field worker. He was always respected because of the business. I don't think discrimination bothered him. He didn't have an accent—my mom didn't because they didn't speak Spanish at home. My mom looked French. She had red hair and light freckles. And "Campio"—everybody thought we were Italians.

I traced our family history by going to the mission—finally decided, "Okay, Dad, we're Indians, you're telling me the real truth. I'm getting on that roll." I said, "I'm going to do it," and he said, "I don't want nothing from the government. They already took the land we had there. If you're going to do it, you have to do it yourself." He said, "This is what I can tell you—what's been handed to me. Your [great] grandmother was Mission Santa Barbara, and your [great] grandfather was from San Bernardino Indians." He wouldn't go with me. My mom went and we talked to a priest. He said, "What background—what can we look for?" My mom, she knew stories. She said, "This is what my husband told us." We started looking page after page, and boom, there it was. My great-grandmother and father were married Indian tradition, with the thumbprint and X. That's on their marriage certificate.

We did find my grandfather's plot in Corona. I could trace my [great] grandmother—once we got that, we got a number for the roll. I put my brothers, David, all our kids on the rolls. I sent it all in, got all the paperwork done. The numbers were issued to us and sent back to me. That's where we finally became, we can say, true Indians. I think my daughter may be more Native American than I am. My daughter's mother is San Carlos Apache from New Mexico, and my daughter looks probably more Indian than I do. I know that she's Apache. She has higher cheekbones than we do, and the whole works. Who knows what is what?

DC: Remember, the "enrollment" name is Arballo. They're on the original roll.* You find them on the Pala Reservation nowadays. You see some up on the Soboba. On the papers my grandfather would sign, sometimes he would say that he was Cahuilla, which puts a little twist in it all. But the San Bernardino area sounds like the four corners of all those tribes, so it could go either way.

CJ: How would you describe your father's unique style?

EC: It's his character. It's macho—his designs, his colors. I saw pottery my grandfather painted and it was more the Spanish fancy soft colors. My dad is more Indian—red, yellow, and black. The redder the better, something that stood out. When he would paint a frog, it's the same frog. You could tell he painted it. Plants, he had flowers everywhere, the colors he chose.

CJ: Would he have lived somewhere else?

EC: No. Never. No place outside of California. No place out of this area.

CJ: The clay was his identity, this place.

EC: Yes, I think so. The heat. He didn't care about money. He really didn't. He didn't need money to have a good time. He liked being his own boss and creating things. My [Mexican master potter] grandpa said that my dad was a better potter than anybody he had ever known. My grandfather always said, "None of my sons could ever make a pot, and here he is—he's the one that had it."

---

* To qualify under the 1927 California Indians Jurisdictional Act, claimants had to be descended from an Indian living at the time of the 1851-52 treaties. The Campio family descends from Guadalupe Arballo, who was living in California during this time. Every claimant was then required to submit an "Application for Enrollment." In 1933 the Secretary of the Interior approved the first enrollment (1933 census list) based on the applications. In 1940, 1948, and 1950 Congress amended the 1928 Claims Act to add new eligible names and remove enrollees since dead. The new rolls were completed in 1955 and 1972. Refer to the essay "Continuity within Change: Identity and Culture" for more information.

A CONVERSATION with Desirée Martinez

January 15, 2007
Rancho Los Alamitos, Long Beach, California

The Participant

DESIRÉE MARTINEZ GREW UP IN BALDWIN, CALIFORNIA. SHE ATTENDED
the University of Pennsylvania, where she received her B.A. in Archaeology with a
minor in Religious Studies, Folklore and Folklife. She is completing her dissertation on the relation between native people, archaeologists, and cultural resources
for her Ph.D. in Archaeology from Harvard University. She is also the codirector
of the UCLA archaeological field school on Catalina Island, which views the landscape and the ancestral cultural objects within from a native perspective. In the
summer of 2008, Desirée began the Pimu Catalina Island Archaeological Project,
a five-year effort designed to describe the social and economic relation between
the island and mainland Tongva of southern California over time. Desirée's lifelong goal is to write the cultural history of the Tongva people. Her lifelong dream
is to open a cultural center to explore and explain the history of the Tongva to all
"newcomers" in the Los Angeles region.

The Discussion

The conversation with Desirée Martinez discusses her family's relation with Sherman Institute, a vocational training school opened by the Bureau of Indian Affairs
in Riverside, California, in the early twentieth century. She speaks to her own
family's memories, as well as her academic and personal quest to protect cultural

resources in the practice of "indigenous archaeology," archaeology viewed from the perspective of native cultural belief, including the power of sacred places. Her views on federal recognition express her thoughts on the need for unity within the larger Tongva community and her commitment to protecting the land and the story of its people.

Desirée Martinez: My name is Desirée Martinez. I'm originally from Baldwin Park, California—currently a Ph.D. candidate at Harvard University—and also have Tongva heritage.

Claudia Jurmain: When did you first find that out?

DM: Since I was young.

CJ: How did you know?

DM: My grandmother, and the way that my family was. It's my maternal grandmother who's Tongva, and both of her parents were also Tongva. She grew up in Montebello, California. My grandmother was one of seven children, and five of them went to Sherman Indian School in Riverside. My grandmother and her youngest sister were too young at the time so they didn't get to go, which was a good thing, I guess.

CJ: How were they identified as Indians at the Sherman Institute at the time? They weren't part of the San Gabriel [Gabrielino-Tongva] community, or were they?

DM: No. My family, because they converted to Catholicism, really didn't participate in a lot of the traditional ways of the community. We were more family oriented. When my great-grandmother died at age forty-three, my grandmother was eleven, all family gets scattered. She died in 1934. She was forty-three years old. I know that because my [great-]aunt Mary was the one that spent the most time at Sherman. She was there for eight years. She didn't graduate from Sherman because her mother had died and she had to come home and take care of my grandmother and her youngest sister.

CJ: What was the link between your family and Sherman Institute? How was that connection made?

DM: From what I understand, my great-grandfather knew one of the dorm women, and she was a good friend of the family's. They went in 1926 to Sherman. It was really difficult to feed the family, there were seven kids. So they're like, "Okay, give them a good education, give them food. Is there any way you can get them in?" She got them in.

Desirée Martínez in the Jacaranda Walk, Rancho Los Alamitos, 2008.
Cristina Salvador Photography

CJ: Was it a manual training education?

DM: The boys learned carpentry. The girls learned home domestics—my aunt's a good cook—and cleaning. She always says she learned to do all that at Sherman. I did an oral interview with her about 1994 for one of my projects for college. They had the "outing system," where she would go and work for a white family as a domestic, the maid, and things like that. Most of what was happening there was vocational, trying to train the students to do manual labor.

CJ: She saw it as a good experience, or was it mixed in retrospect?

DM: When I talked to her, it was all positive—"I got a good education, three square meals. While I was sick they took me to the infirmary." So I took that at face value. But her children and grandchildren remember her talking about how she got beat. She had a little doll and they stole it from her. They told her, "You can't be a baby."

CJ: Who is "they"?

DM: The people at the school. I guess the dorm mothers. I can't remember in particular. These stories—she never told me. She said, "It's a good education." I happened to be in school at the time, too, and education is a big deal in my family. I don't know if she was trying to forget everything bad that happened or not. My own research on Sherman [showed] some harsh discipline handed out to the kids. Other people I know who went there around that same time, and in the decade before, liked their experience as well.

CJ: Was Sherman Institute a high school?

DM: At the time, it was all ages, from third grade to high school. After the Merriam report* came out, they switched it over to late middle school, high

---

* The 1928 Merriam report, edited by Louis Merriam, was prepared by the Institute for Government Research (the Brookings Institute) at the request of the federal government. Documenting the disastrous economic and social conditions of Indians, the report led to the Indian Reorganization Act of 1934 and revised federal policy.

school. That's why my grandmother and her youngest sister didn't get in, because they made the cutoff dates for birthdates higher.

Bill McCawley: When your family was at Sherman, were they identified as Gabrielino-Tongva? I noticed in some of the records they kept note of which tribes were there.

DM: Right. I haven't looked at those records. But from what I understood it was always "Mission Indian," but we always said "Gabrielino." My family never said "Tongva." In fact, my grandmother refuses to use the name "Tongva." She's always identified herself as either Mission Indian or Gabrielino.

BMc: Both her parents were Gabrielino?

DM: Yes. They were born in the late 1800s, so it was after the Mission Period. From what my grandmother tells me, they bought the house in Montebello in 1907 and were married a couple of years before that. I understand they used to live in a traditional Ke^ch [Tongva word for "house"] when they first got married, up in the hills of Montebello, which is called Potrero Chico. There's Potrero Chico and Potrero Grande. My grandmother always said, "Oh, they used to live there." Then I came across some lawsuit documents [from the Superior Court of the State of California in Los Angeles, in the matter of the estate and real estate property of Antonio Valenzuela, who died in 1860]. A lot of my family members, the Valenzuela and Alvitre families, were suing because the land was stolen from them.

BMc: Who were they suing?

DM: Well, there were a couple of lawsuits—let's see if I can remember. There was a land grant that was given to José Valenzuela and Juan Alvitre which was the Potrero Chico portion.

CJ: After the mission closed?

DM: Right. Those two people are my relatives, my maternal great-great-grandfathers, or whatever. There was a woman who died, and she was the great-niece of Valenzuela. When she died her estate went into escrow. Under that escrow they put her portion of the José Valenzuela estate, since they chopped up the land grant between Alvitre and Valenzuela. I guess in the fifties they found all of the great-grandchildren of José Valenzuela—I want to say [Tommy] Temple was involved. There was some shady deal where there were eight grandchildren of Valenzuela. They got one of the grandchildren to sign away the rights to the whole land grant, which they didn't have rights to. They then, of course, found oil. That was the lawsuit for forty million dollars. The thing is, who do you sue? When you try to figure out what the land title is—they couldn't even figure out how big the grant was.

CJ: We've heard this story from others we've talked with.

BMc: Different pieces of it. And we've seen pieces of documentation for the land grant through census records and through mission records, but no one actually had a copy of the lawsuit—or available anyway.

DM: I have a copy of the lawsuit. [One of the members of the Gabrielino-Tongva tribe] is related to a woman who was named in the lawsuit. Her aunt hired lawyers to see if there was any viable claim anymore. It's just too complicated because of the titles. There are too many discrepancies and it would take, I think they said, ten million dollars. And this was in the seventies.

CJ: Your family identified as Gabrielino, but did they keep their identity to themselves, or were they involved in a larger community?

DM: My grandmother tells me stories of when she was young. She tells me also, "I wish I would have paid attention when I was younger." When she was younger [she didn't tell me how old she was], they used to go to San Gabriel and Alhambra. They would knock on doors and visit the cousins. They would also visit the Alvitres. They would just go from door to door knocking.

CJ: Did they go to mission festivals also?

DM: I don't know. I never asked. But I know my grandmother identified with the mission a lot. She considers that home. I remember stories, back in the fifties they would have meetings regarding the lawsuit, the California Mission Indians versus California—the payment for the land.*

CJ: Was your family enrolled?

DM: Everybody is enrolled, except my grandmother's oldest brother because they sent it to the wrong address.

CJ: Who did that for your family?

DM: My grandma. My grandmother is considered the genealogist in the family history.

CJ: Did she work with Tommy Temple?

---

* Indians filing claims under the California Indians Jurisdictional Act passed by the state legislature in 1927 were required to submit an "Application for Enrollment with the Indians of the State of California under the Act of May 18, 1928." In 1933 the Secretary of the Interior approved the enrollment (1933 census list). In 1940, 1948, and 1950 Congress amended the 1928 Claims Act to add new eligible names and remove enrollees since dead. The new rolls were completed in 1955 and 1972. Claims filed in 1928 were awarded in 1944, and in 1950, a payment of $150 was distributed to each enrollee. Additional claims for land not previously included were filed in 1946 and an out-of-court settlement reached in 1972. Each enrolled California Indian received $668.51. Refer to the essay "Continuity within Change: Identity and Culture" for more information.

 Eligible, documented California Indians had to enroll in a tribe and be formally listed by the federal government to share in the settlement coming as a result of the California Indians Jurisdictional Act. Some Tongva did not wish to be involved with the government, others' enrollment papers were lost. The last award distribution to enrolled Indians came after the final settlement in 1972.

DM: Yep. We have all of that documentation. She got all that stuff together. I was born too late so I don't have a roll number. Most of the kids in my generation didn't have a roll number. All of my grandmother's siblings, I guess, except the one brother, are enrolled—or they all have the numbers.

CJ: Back to your grandmother. Did they visit the reservations? Did they have family?

DM: My grandma goes to all of the Indian casinos. She tells me stories of how they used to get into the car and they would go to all the reservations. Whether they visited people—I never asked. That's what they would do on a Sunday, they would go out to the rez—I don't know what they would do out there. I've never asked her. This would have to be when she was in her twenties and teens. She was born in 1922, so it would be the thirties or so.

BMc: Did you have any family members living on the reservations that you know of?

DM: Not that I'm aware of. From what I understand, all of my family lived in the Montebello area. They now live in Whittier and Brea and like that, but we've always lived around this area.

BMc: Did your family, prior to your grandparents, back in the early 1800s, grow up in the mission?

DM: Stories about treatment in the mission didn't come down because my great-grandparents separated. My great-grandfather went off to Los Angeles and left my great-grandmother in Montebello taking care of seven kids, which is one of the reasons my family would send them to Sherman. She couldn't take care of them by herself. She would do washing and ironing and cleaning for all the people around the area. My grandmother tells me stories about what a wonderful cook her mother was. She used to do beading. She used to make all of these—I don't want to say Indian crafts, but she remembers her beading these purses, belts, and hats.

There's a story that one of my grandmother's brothers actually spoke "Gab." He would speak a language that no one understood. He went to World War I and they thought, "Oh, maybe it's German." He died in the fifties, so I never got to meet him. They think that that's what it was, but I'm not sure. Just like some of the stories my grandmother would tell me about the meaning of, like, birds. She would talk about how her mom was in the living room ironing and a little bird came to the window, talking. She would say that her mom would ask the bird, "What are you trying to tell me?" It turned out that somebody had passed. Same thing with owls, white owls, the bearing of bad things, death, be careful of that.

CJ: Do you assume those are traditional ways of communication that she learned from someone else?

DM: Yes. That's the kind of thing that I'm trying to document, and my whole family is—stories, ways, and beliefs that never have been told to me. But the more I interact with other Gab people, the more I talk to other people, it's like, "Oh, you don't believe that?" My grandmother has a big fear of spiders and snakes. [If you] see those things as a traditional belief—"They're bad, stay away, they're harmful"—not just that they can kill you, but spiritually. What is it? What's the story?

CJ: What has your mother passed on to you that is important about being Tongva, something that would identify you differently from someone else of another culture?

DM: My mom doesn't really identify herself as Tongva. She was born in '47, so there's that disconnect. Most of the stuff that I was taught was from my mom. Also, my grandfather was Mexican, but he considered himself American. He didn't care how people were raised. They were trying to raise their kids as American.

CJ: Is your mother also trying to learn what it means to be Tongva?

DM: She is a total disconnect. She supports what I do, but she doesn't feel the type of attachment my grandmother or the rest of the family does. My grandmother's youngest sister's kids, who are the same generation as my mom, are totally into the Gab stuff. They would go to powwows and sometimes we would meet them at powwows. Mary, my grandmother's sister, my grandmother, and Mary's kids were together all the time. They lived in the same house for a long time.

CJ: Did your grandmother volunteer this education to you, the passing of cultural memory, or is that something you asked her to do?

DM: No, it was always prevailing. I remember I was in junior high. They were trying to do a census of all the ethnic backgrounds of the students. The teacher would go one by one, "What are you?" and it came to me. "Oh, I'm Native American, Gabrielino." She's like, "Well, your last name is Martinez." From the very earliest times I always had to fight against this idea that I was Mexican.

BMc: What was the earliest age that you recall saying, "I'm Gabrielino."

DM: Maybe in kindergarten. One of the reasons I got into anthropology was because in the fourth grade we went to the Southwest Museum and they said the

Gabrielinos were extinct. A lot of my friends didn't believe I was Gabrielino, because they would look at the dioramas and see that they were living in traditional housing and half naked. They're like, "Well, you're one of us. You live in a house, you wear clothes, so you can't be Indian." I've always known. I can't tell you when they told me.

BMc: You knew it as Gabrielino, not as Indian?

DM: Right. My grandmother would say, "Oh, we're Indian, too." In fact, she will only use "Indian." She doesn't like the term "Native American" or "indigenous." She rolls her eyes at those. It was always Gabrielino.

CJ: What did your father say about all of that?

DM: Nothing. He was in and out of my life the whole time. His mom never liked my mom. I think at one point my mom told my dad's mother that she was Gabrielino. And she piped back, "Well, we're Yaqui," which, I don't know if it's true or not. She passed away before I was able to ask her anything about that. But obviously, my mom at one point used that identification.

CJ: Since cultural memory is not intact, what in the twenty-first century distinguishes or identifies a group of people as Gabrielino-Tongva, other than this place? "You don't exist, you're many things." How would you answer that?

DM: I answer that question a lot, because I talk to so many people from other unrecognized tribes. I try to explain that California is just mixed up because of the history, because of the dispersion of people, because of the way that we originally lived in extended families. That was the thing, it was about extended families. It was never about the large, overarching tribes. Because of missions, because of the fact that you had bounty on heads for being Indian, you didn't want to proclaim as much. I remember asking my aunt Mary, who went to boarding school, "Did you ever tell anybody you were Indian? Did you ever proclaim or talk about it?" She never did. She never volunteered the information. Everybody just assumed that you were just like everybody else.

It was only with my aunt going to Sherman that they started to get a little bit of pride in the heritage. Actually, people who were prideful about being Tongva didn't go to Sherman. The youngest brother of my grandmother, who currently lives in Oklahoma, moved from the family forty years ago to Oklahoma and changed his last name from Martinez to Martin. I've never talked to him. He stayed seven years at Sherman. He taught there for a year after he graduated, and he did carpentry. He left in 1936, if I'm not mistaken. He never wanted to identify himself as Indian. Now in Oklahoma, he's actually known as "Indian Joe," which is really funny. Oklahoma is full of native people. He wanted to discount that part of his family, and he ends up identified as that now.

CJ: There was never a larger structure over all Tongva people, or one unified people. The same is true today. People who criticize the Gabrielino-Tongva for not being a single community at large really do not understand their heritage. Is that accurate?

DM: Definitely. You also have people who have been brainwashed by the U.S. government in terms of how to deal with people. The U.S. wants to deal with groups of people as efficiently as possible. So if we can draw a ring around all of the natives, and then create a policy to deal with all of the natives, work is done. A lot of people have bought into that way of thinking about people and groups, and unfortunately, it doesn't work. Within native communities, what works for one native community doesn't work for another because of the way history is. That's the problem with BIA acknowledgment.*

CJ: How does federal recognition relate to a community that is many communities within?

DM: No California group has gotten federal recognition through that process that they created since 1978.** They will never get federal recognition unless there's some united voice. The government wants to identify one group because one of the characteristics states that 50 percent of the people on your list have to have lived in the same general area. But you have all of these people—historical dispersion—who had to go to Fresno to feed their families, they had to go pick fruit, or you had other people who got chased because of history. Up in Santa Maria, they're Gab, and they want to be part of the community, and they had their own community up wherever they were.

There's a Tongva community in Santa Maria. The grandmother was telling the story about how her family got out of [fled] Santa Maria. Her family—their village was being rounded up to be sent to Sebastian Indian Reservation.† When they got rounded up in the Hollywood Hills there was a massacre. The soldiers, instead of taking them to the reservation, slaughtered all of those people. So the people that survived ran, and they ran to Santa Maria. That's where they've been since that time. The grandmother telling the story was saying that it was her grandparents who were telling them the story. And when they were telling it [they said], "Don't forget, this is why you should never go back. Don't forget the story. Tell everybody." Any time she can get any Gab person, she tells that story because that's how that family got there [Santa Maria]. Because they had to run away, they survived.

---

* Only Congress has the power to recognize tribes, but since 1978, it has delegated the task of "acknowledging" which tribes meet federal recognition requirements to the U.S. Department of the Interior through the Bureau of Indian Affairs.

** One California tribe has received federal recognition since then. In 1983 the Timbisha Shoshone Tribe of Death Valley petition for federal recognition was approved by the Branch of Acknowledgment and Research in the Bureau of Indian Affairs.

† In March 1853, Congress authorized funding to establish five military reservations for California Indians on land to be owned by the U.S. government. Located at the southern end of the San Joaquin Valley some sixty miles north of Los Angeles, by Tejon Pass, the Sebastian Military Reserve (also known as the Tejón Reservation) closed in 1864.

BMc: Back to the federal recognition process. You were talking about the fact that it has very narrowly defined rules—like where people reside. But at this point that's the only way to get recognition, correct?

DM: No. There's a congressional recognition. Congress can just say, "We recognize you." That's also called restoration. During the fifties [federal] termination [of Indian reservation land and sovereignty] was going on. People who say that they were unjustly terminated without due process—the BIA will restore their standing. Basically you want to show that the government always recognized you as a community, and at one point extinguished that recognition without any due process.

CJ: What is the "we don't recognize you" date for the Gabrielino-Tongva?

DM: What's interesting is they did recognize Gabs. In the historical record, one of the men that was designated to go and make the treaties [in 1852]—his memoirs stated that he didn't get a chance to go to L.A. One reason was because the Indians weren't causing trouble. They were pretty much doing what they needed to do to survive. They were blending in. They were just good workers and laborers. They weren't causing problems. So he didn't feel that there was a need to go and deal with them.

BMc: Also, the local landowners didn't want them to come to Los Angeles, because they didn't want them to have a reservation. Because then they would leave Los Angeles and all the laborers—

DM: Right. Because all their workers would be gone.

CJ: That would be the last official federal recognition of the Gabrielino-Tongva people?

BMc: 1852.

CJ: Are you aware of others?

DM: A friend of mine who's Yokuts has been looking at the history of Yokuts, at all of these documents that she found at the Southwest Museum, but there's a whole bunch of stuff on Gabs as well. Restoration has to be through the San Sebastian Indian Reservation—they were going to take a Gab village to San Sebastian. Obviously, that's a group of people that they [the U.S. government] identify as Gab. So if they were supposed to be one of the founding communities of the reservation, then [the government would not have to] deal with them anymore [as a separate group]. I think that would be the last one, but I'm not sure.

CJ: Is it essential to have federal recognition for your identity today?

DM: No. Being an Indian has nothing to do with what the government says. The only reason you would want federal recognition is to be able to tap into the federal programs and special rights that federal tribes have because of that recognition. In particular, I'm thinking about NAGPRA [Native American Graves Protection and Repatriation Act], about HUD Housing, health care—it's better than nothing. To tap into that is why a lot of community members are going to federal recognition. I can care less. The government's done everybody wrong anyway, and they have nothing—I don't want to say nothing—to offer. But you know, I guess you're sleeping with the enemy.

BMc: I can understand recognition would have value in terms of the programs that it would make available, but if you have a community that is separated into different groups, it's going to be difficult for them to take advantage of those programs. How will the different groups of Gabrielino-Tongva that exist now recognize who's Gabrielino-Tongva? Some are very strict, some are less strict.

DM: I really do think some type of unity needs to go on. Ideally, I would like to see, like, each group recognized on their own merit. Because of the way that recognition works, it's never going to happen. It behooves the government not to say anything. When you start having people discount each other and declaring, "They're not Indian," that works against any type of recognition. I talked to a friend of mine who's Hopi and he was asking me, "How do you know you're Indian? Why do you see yourself as Indian?" There are people who found out they were Indian when they were forty years old, because they were going to get money, et cetera, and they're now learning, which is fine. But when they start to proclaim that they're the only ones who know or that they're a leader, or they start pointing fingers at other people, I think that's just wrong.

CJ: If you found out at age forty that you were Indian, that means you've probably identified with many other cultural ways along the way. So why does "Indianness" come to bear now?

DM: In talking to, or just listening to people, those people who learned when they were older want to be different, not like everybody else. Society is now holding "difference" as the key to being somebody. The same with white people who want to be Cherokee, have a great-great-grandmother who is Cherokee. If they cannot be what they are, they can be something else. Everybody wants to be a minority because minorities get these programs and special treatment when, in fact, in some instances, they don't.

CJ: How has being Tongva affected your life?

DM: It's directed my career protecting archaeological sites. My grandmother used to chop out all of the articles about not only Indians, but Gabs. A lot of the articles were "this site is getting destroyed and there's a protest." She kept it in what she calls her "Indian book." It has all of her genealogy and history. Those areas are the last visible demonstrations of our community in terms of archaeology. That past stuff, those villages—protecting those is going to bolster us in the present. So when I was introduced to archaeology in the sixth grade, I was like, "That's what I'm going to do. I'm going to use archaeology to protect the sites and prove that the Gabrielinos still exist."

BMc: How is being Gabrielino different than if you were Yaqui or Hopi or Navajo? What difference does that make to you?

DM: If you were to dig up my house right now, it would be typical middle American. Well, you would see all of my grandmother's pictures, Indian stuff, and things that were her brother's, like spears, but in other portions, just like any other person's house. In terms of differences between the Gab community and other communities which are more cohesive (although a lot of them are not as cohesive now), I guess it has to do with the feeling, connection to the area. When I was back east for school I missed my mountains. Those are my mountains—tell me who I am. I always knew I was going to come back to southern California. I can't leave. I don't want to say the land is calling to me, but this is where it is, this is where I am. This is where my heart is. I think it's that kind of feeling. You can't learn it, you can't be taught it. It just is.

CJ: How important is federal recognition relative to obtaining land again?

DM: We can just buy land. My dream is to build a Gabrielino cultural center. Do research in Gab history, collect oral histories. Create business plans in order to get this thing going. And I can't do that by myself.

CJ: Are you working with different groups within the larger community?

DM: That's what I'm doing now. That's the point of unity, to be able to say, "Okay, we all have to agree that this is what we want to do." We're never going to get the ancestors back, because we're not going to be recognized unless we all agree that this is where, how, and what happened.

UCLA moved the archaeological collections from Hershey Hall last summer to a new building. We contacted everybody, saying, "We have your ancestors, we're moving them into a new building, how would you like us to handle them? Any ceremonies? Anything you want us to make sure?" People came out [saying], "We don't want women touching it. We don't want this." We created a community—a committee out of all of those different [Gabrielino-Tongva] factions—and said, "Some of them are Gab, but a lot of them were other tribes. Because this is our land, we need to be the caretakers for a community that can't come and take care of their ancestors." I told each person, "These are other people's ancestors and we have to be mindful about that." We all came together, made this plan, and created ceremony, dancing and song, as all the ancestors were being moved.

CJ: Do you mind telling us how old you are?

DM: I'm thirty-four. Any time you talked about Indians—[in] the fourth grade in California you learn about Indians and the Mission Period. In the sixth grade, we were learning about California history, and they were teaching us about the Chumash. They always focused on the Chumash—the biggest, most wealthiest tribe. So we were learning about the Chumash, about archaeology, and were watching movies about Richard Leakey.* I came to realize that people looked to anthropology, looked to scholars for information. They are the authorities. I don't know how it clicked, but it was like, "I'm going to be that person. I'm going to be the authority. I'm going to change all of the information that has been stated about my community and show that there's a different version, there's a different story." So I decided I was going to be an archaeologist.

Yep. I got a full ride to the University of Pennsylvania as well as Harvard. I got scholarships and fellowships, had to work a steady job. I went to my first archaeological field school the summer before my senior year in high school, at an Anasazi site in Colorado City, Arizona. It was the last day of the dig—it always happens on the last day of the dig—I'm cleaning up the floor of a house, there's a hearth, and I actually went all the way through the floor and found a pot. It was a whole pot—you never find whole pots. We dug it up. Inside the pot was another pot, and inside that pot was a baby. It was a skeleton of a baby. I knew I had to protect that baby. I happen to have had a younger sister who died when she was nine months. So when I found that baby, I was just like—you know, I wouldn't want anybody digging up my sister. I need to protect it.

CJ: In that case, what happened to the baby?

DM: They covered it up. We covered up the whole site, actually. I don't know if they ever went back and dug it up or not.

CJ: What's your Harvard Ph.D. dissertation topic?

DM: The relationship between Native Americans and archaeologists. To me it's changing the practice of archaeology so that it incorporates how native people want to have their cultural resources dealt with. We're creating what's called "indigenous archaeology." The way a community is going to use archaeology is different depending on their cultural beliefs. Because cultural resource laws dictate consultation, there's always this dichotomy between native point of view and

---

* Richard Leakey is a noted paleoanthropologist and conservationist, and the son of renowned archaeologists Mary and Louis Leakey.

an archaeologist point of view. I want to make sure that my research is applicable to native communities. You use the tools, methods, and theories of anthropology to solve a community's problems. Because you have this dichotomy between Indian perception of the past and archaeology/anthropology perception of the past, you can't get at what you need to do, either to protect sites or get ancestors. You're fighting history and preconceived notions of what the other person is doing. You can't get to the table and say, "This is what we need to do and this is the plan that we need to have."

CJ: How does it take tangible form in this area? One is bringing people to the table.

DM: Right.

CJ: I'm assuming identifying sacred areas would be another.

DM: Right. The whole idea of "sacred" is different and I believe there are different levels of sacredness. I think there's a misunderstanding about what sacred is and what isn't. Things can be sacred at any time. You can make them sacred at any time.

CJ: What practical things can you take from these theories and apply to the Tongva community if necessary?

DM: I use a lot of social psychology as well as negotiation studies, communication studies. A lot of conflict is all about communication, about preconceived notions of the other person. You had all of these people in this area, the cultural material is similar but there's something different, there's something that separates those communities. And that hasn't really been looked at yet.

CJ: Had you ever heard of Povuu'ngna? When is the first time you heard that word?

DM: The early nineties. It was in the newspaper.*

CJ: Did you know it was the Tongva place of emergence and belief?

DM: That wasn't something that my family believed in, because we were Catholic. My grandmother has an attachment to San Gabriel Mission, and sees that as a point of origin, if you want to think about it technically, because Gabs didn't exist until the mission was created. I mean in terms of that identity. She always looked towards that as the thing on the landscape.

BMc: That ties in with your ideas about sacredness. Maybe you could talk to us for a minute about that.

---

* The press coverage was because of the legal and political activity at the Povuu'ngna site at California State University, Long Beach. For more information refer to the essay "A Connection to Place: Land and History."

DM: You need to create an environment which the community will be able to use now in its ceremonies and its gatherings, but that will also support the sacredness already there, the power there. That's what "sacred" is. "Sacred" to me is a place that has power. And that power and that place give you a connection to something greater than yourself. Whether it's to the great spirit, to other spirits, to a historical moment in your community that has been passed down—there's power. There's something intangible when you stand there; you know something great happened. Or something bad happened, because sacred places have power, good and bad. And those places need to be stayed away from.

CJ: Do you have sacred places?

DM: You know, I tell you, all archaeological sites are sacred. I will accept other people's identification of other places that are sacred if it's from the community.

CJ: Who determines the criteria?

DM: Nobody does. That's the thing about community and that's one of the problems. Everybody has their own definition of what's sacred, what's not sacred, what's an archaeological site or not, or what should be protected or shouldn't be. Each individual has their own idea, it's a sensibility. There are people in the community who I talk to, and I respect their words. And there are other people who are respected by the outside community who I'm just like, "You're dumb." You don't want to get involved in that because that's going to bring something bad to you.

BMc: For you sacredness is something that is rooted in the place?

DM: It can also be rooted in an object. Places can also lose sacredness, particularly if you desecrate it and the power goes away.

BMc: So you feel that the sacredness of something is not dependent upon the people, it's rooted into the object or the place?

DM: It's greater than us.

CJ: Perhaps one way of saying this would be that it's always there, discovered and rediscovered in different times and different ways?

DM: It becomes revealed to you when it's your time to know.

CJ: All the activities of different people and groups within community—do you bring that together in some place?

DM: That's one reason I want to open up a cultural center. I would have it on land that has no [institutional] connection. It should be a grass-roots thing. I've always wanted a Gab museum, a Gab cultural center where people can come together. It has to be on land, a place in the middle where everybody can come and feel welcomed, have other people teach other community members about their culture because they have lost it, create that sense of community again because it's so fragmented. There are so many people who, because of their background, because of history, have lost touch. And they shouldn't be discounted because their family made choices.

CJ: Again, that's one of the issues—people who have had this other identity their whole lives, and then suddenly at age forty, they discover they're Tongva.

DM: Depends on your heart. I was very involved in the Harvard Native American Program, and we used to have people who were native participate in events because they are true of heart. They don't want to use that identity for the public—they're just interested. You know those people. You know that they come to it out of good sense, and they're not about to proclaim that they know everything. They're going to be respectful. I don't know that you can teach them, but they're going to be mindful about what they're doing. I'm not about to turn those people away.

CJ: You have an optimistic sense of the future. Is your number-one priority to bring the community together, and maybe obtain federal recognition?

DM: Yeah. That's my whole research. One of the big things about Gabs not getting federal recognition is cultural continuity—this idea of finding the community through time. So my deal is to show culture continuity through archaeology and oral history. I was talking to a Zuni elder ten years ago and he talked about shells in California. As late as 1960 he would drive all the way to southern California to the beach to gather the shells he would use in sacred ceremony. Along the way he would stop at Indian families' houses and give gifts, et cetera. If you can document recognition not only by the government of that community, but other Indian communities identifying you as a group, then there's your cultural continuity.

I didn't ask him who he was visiting, but if he went all the way to southern California, he's visiting Gab people, Gab families. Again, you're recognizing the family as opposed to the larger [group] entity. I can document trade objects going here and there through time, because you have people still practicing ceremonies even though they're Mexican Catholics. They're still doing all those traditional things at night while they're still having those relationships with other people. So bring it forward. Use archaeology to trace everything and understand the different communities through time, but also to see connections still going on.

BMc: Do you believe there has been cultural continuity for the Gabrielino?

DM: Yes. I can't point to it, but I know there are certain families who have done ceremonies, who've had their cultural practices, things that have been done in the past. There are other people who have created things in light of what they know and what they've learned through scholarship, through the "ethnic" historical record. They're private family things—baby-naming ceremonies, weddings. People gather at funerals, ancestors' poles, mourning ceremonies.*

CJ: Let me ask a question because I know we are coming to the end. What do you think about casinos? It creates a great bias against the community today because many think it's the only agenda underlying federal recognition.

DM: Right. I think it's shortsighted. Community development, cultural development, language preservation—those are the things I think are most important and, yeah, you need money. Win the lottery, go to huge foundations. You do like everybody else. You write grants. You hope to get a rich benefactor. That's how you do it. I don't want to say it's dirty money—the thing is, that's what ends up happening. There's so much focus on getting a casino, you forget everything else.

CJ: Why are you doing this?

DM: For the ancestors. It's always been about them—being treated with respect and being remembered for who they are, and what they did. The biggest thing for me was that not only did people not identify me as Indian, but that they're discounting my whole family, my ancestors, my history. They're not mindful of that. You're celebrating mission and California history, but you're not going to celebrate the people who were originally here? You're not going to acknowledge the people who built the missions? You're not going to acknowledge the people who died making your clothes, making your candles, killing your beef? You're not going to acknowledge those people? Those people deserve to be remembered and deserve to be treated with respect. That's the whole thing. It's never been about me; it's always been about making sure that those who came before me are given their due.

BMc: What do you think the Gabrielino leaders should be doing today?

DM: They need to start strategizing together, start building alliances with other groups of people. That started to happen back during the sixties. There was a grouping of the Chicano movement and Indian rights. People were supporting each other at that time, and that got dispersed. You need to gather the skills and the knowledge throughout the community, come up with some strategic plan, do stuff together. Each community has an idea of what they want to do, but then they cancel each other out. You have one group here lobbying for a casino and

---

* According to Craig Torres and Cindi Alvitre of the Ti'at Society, today Tongva ancestor poles are memorials, and places to honor those who have recently passed on. However, they may also honor the spirit of the living, the longtime dead, the land and sea, or other natural elements. Only the ancestor poles honoring the deceased are painted black, white, red, and gray to represent parts of the body. Other ancestor poles are decorated with symbolic designs. The ancestor poles made by Tongva people today express contemporary form and use within the spirit of the past, not exact tradition.

another here lobbying for a casino. When you're so dispersed, our community doesn't know what to do because you have so many different stories going on.

Because it's all crazy, people are not going to go with you, because they don't want to support the wrong people. Who you support is political. Who you talk to and who you're going to help is a political move. Because this is such a political world, cultural groups are going to be wary. That hurts the Gab community. Everybody has the same bigger picture. They want recognition, whether it's at the federal level or just local. They want to make sure that if they don't know the culture, they learn the culture. If they have participated in the culture, they want to continue to pass that down on to the next generation. Everybody has the same goal. Take the casino issue. They want the money to do all this other stuff.

You get together and you realize that everybody has the same goals. Let's get together and create a unified way of going about it. You can still be separate communities, but if you can unite in this one way for one thing, then that's going to work. That's what I hope. Repatriation and archaeology—that will be that focal point so people will come together. I don't know if it's going to happen. This is what I care about, this is my goal, this is what I want to do. I want to collect information. I want to write the book. I want to document that history. And no one is against that.

BMc: Getting recognition is a common goal and knowing the culture is a common goal.

DM: Preserving the culture and passing it down.

BMc: What about the land? Who's protecting the land and dealing with the land? Is that a goal that the larger group shares?

DM: Definitely protecting open land. I shouldn't say "isn't developed" because the land in southern California has been developed, but any open space, trying to protect that, even space that has been built over—protecting cultural sites, archaeological sites. It has to revolve around recognition, whether it's on the federal level, or within schools, within the greater community. You know you're being identified as a group of people who were here before all of this, people who had to participate in a horrifying history because of the ranchos, because of the Californians. That history shouldn't be forgotten. You know that the economy of southern California wouldn't have existed without the blood, sweat, and tears of the community—[and] respect for those [native] people who are newcomers so they understand that history. They contribute to the new history, part of modern society, but [they] have a link, a further link to the past, and a link to the land.

THREE

The Enduring Vision: Recognition and Renewal

William McCawley

Being an Indian has nothing to do with what the government says.[1]—*Desirée Martinez*

In 1903, ON THE CUSP OF THE NEW CENTURY, anthropologist C. Hart Merriam traveled to the small town of Bakersfield, eighty-five miles north of Los Angeles. He went to interview Narcisa Rosemyre, an Indian woman born near Tehachapi of a Serrano father and Gabrielino-Tongva mother. Mrs. Rosemyre, whose maiden name was Narcisa Higuera, was raised at San Gabriel and was a singer in the church in her youth. Later she married James Vineyard Rosemyre, a store-keeper at the sprawling Tejón Ranch, where they raised six children in an adobe house near a spring that became known as Rosemyre Spring.[2] Janice Ramos, a descendent of Narcisa Rosemyre, tells us, "I know that she was a wonderful horsewoman and supposedly could tame horses that no one else could."[3]

During their visits, Mrs. Rosemyre shared with Merriam her knowledge of her culture. She recited the Tongva language for him and described their rituals, especially their ceremony of the dead. She told how the workers rose early in the morning and cut down a tall pine tree to use as a grave pole, then carried it back to the village, where they trimmed and painted it and decorated it with baskets before raising the pole in the cemetery. She told how the mourners prepared themselves, painting their faces and bodies and dressing in ceremonial skirts and belts covered with beads and feathers. They filled a large bag sewn from sealskins with their most valuable possessions—beads, shells, cloth, acorns, bread, even gold and silver money—and burned it as an offering to the dead, even though many of them were very poor. In Narcisa Rosemyre's memory

Narcisa Rosemyre, Bakersfield, California, July 1905. C. Hart Merriam Collection of Native American Photographs, Y. Tongva Stock 24a. Courtesy of The Bancroft Library, University of California, Berkeley

Mrs. Jimmie Rosemyre with her children (left to right, identified in Latta 1976, p. 140) Mary, Virginia, James, and Rosalina, an unnamed male relative, her daughter Stella, and Stella's son John, 1887. Narcisa Rosemyre spent her childhood at Mission San Gabriel and later lived at Tejón Canyon, where her German husband ran the commissary and general store. She died in Bakersfield about 1912. Fluent in the Tongva language, she provided invaluable linguistic and ethnographic information to J. W. Hudson and C. Hart Merriam in the early 20th century. PHOTO BY CARLETON WATKINS, COURTESY KERN COUNTY LIBRARY

the ancient Tongva world still lived, and as she shared her stories with Merriam, the anthropologist copied them all down in his notebook.[4]

Merriam also took several photographs of Rosemyre, iconic images that stand as some of the most striking portraits ever made of the California Indians. In one of them she sits straight in her chair, wearing a long-sleeved blouse with a dark tie, her graying hair pulled back from her handsome face, arms resting at her sides and her bright eyes looking off into the distance. Was she gazing back into her people's past, or peering ahead into their future? Or could she have been looking both ways at once, Janus-like, guarding the trail that leads the Tongva from yesterday to tomorrow?

TODAY THE TONGVA COMMUNITY COMPRISES SEVERAL BANDS OR councils—political organizations representing their own individual memberships—including the Gabrieleno Tongva Tribal Council of San Gabriel (sometimes also called the Gabrieleno Tongva Band of Mission Indians of San Gabriel),[5] the Gabrielino-Tongva Tribe,[6] and the Gabrielino/Tongva Nation.[7] All three of these organizations share a common goal of achieving federal recognition, although their approaches to this are quite different. There are also other groups (with overlapping memberships) devoted to programs for cultural preservation, education, or public outreach; these include the Tongva Dancers, the Ti'at Society, the Gabrielino/Tongva Language Committee,[8] and the Gabrielino/Tongva Springs Foundation.[9]

Trial by Ordeal: Federal Recognition

Who decides what constitutes an Indian tribe? Who decides which tribes Congress recognizes and which ones it does not? Who sets the standards for recognition and what are they? What benefits does recognition bring to a tribe and its members? And what part does tribal gaming play in the process of gaining federal recognition?

Only Congress has the power to recognize tribes; however, since 1978 Congress has delegated the task of "acknowledging" which tribes meet the requirements for federal recognition to the Department of the Interior. Since that time, recognition by Congress and "acknowledgment" by the Bureau of Indian Affairs/Department of

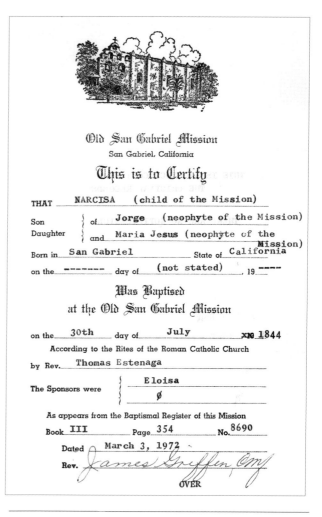

Old San Gabriel Mission
San Gabriel, California

This is to Certify

THAT _____ NARCISA _____ (child of the Mission)

Son } of _____ Jorge _____ (neophyte of the Mission)
Daughter } and _____ Maria Jesus (neophyte of the Mission)

Born in _____ San Gabriel _____ State of _____ California

on the ____-____ day of _____ (not stated) _____, 19 ____

Was Baptised
at the Old San Gabriel Mission

on the _____ 30th _____ day of _____ July _____ XX 1844

According to the Rites of the Roman Catholic Church

by Rev. _____ Thomas Estenaga

The Sponsors were { _____ Eloisa
{ _____ Ø

As appears from the Baptismal Register of this Mission

Book _____ III _____ Page _____ 354 _____ No. 8690

Dated _____ March 3, 1972

Rev. _____ *James Griffen, O.M.*
_____ OVER

Certification of baptism for Narcisa Rosemyre at Old San Gabriel Mission on July 30, 1844. COURTESY OF JANICE RAMOS

the Interior have come to mean essentially the same thing.[10] But federal recognition/acknowledgment does not create tribes; it recognizes entities that predate the United States and acknowledges that a trust relationship exists between them and the federal government. It also entitles recognized tribes to certain federal benefits, protections, and sovereignty.[11] The requirements for federal recognition are rigorous. In fact, some contend that they are unrealistic given the culture and history of the California Indians. The process requires petitioning tribes to document that they have had a continuous social, political, and cultural existence over an extended period of time; successful petitioners must provide documentation that they have existed as an American Indian entity since at least 1900.[12] Desirée Martinez contends:

> The government wants to identify one group because one of the characteristics states that 50 percent of the people on your list have to have lived

Janice Ramos's mother, Gloria, and aunt Mary at Mission San Gabriel, ca. 1940s. Both were granddaughters of Narcisa Rosemyre, who was baptized at the mission in 1844. COURTESY OF JANICE RAMOS

in the same general area. But you have all of these [Tongva] people—[who experienced] historical dispersion—who had to go to Fresno to feed their families, [or] they had to go pick fruit, or you had other people who got chased [out of the area]....Up in Santa Maria, they're...[Tongva], and they want to be part of the community, and they [also] had their own community up wherever they were.[13]

Virginia Carmelo sees the federal process as seriously flawed. "Federal recognition wants to have these guidelines for every single tribe from the eastern coast to the western coast," she says. "Well, I'm sorry, it doesn't work, because California has always been unique as a state, and...[its] history has been unique, even in how... [it deals] with the rest of the United States."[14]

According to a Bureau of Indian Affairs statistic cited in 1997 by the Advisory Council on California Indian Policy, a group created by Congress and headed by Indians and their allies, as many as two-thirds of all California tribes remain unrecognized. In fact, since 1978 the Branch of Acknowledgment and Research (BAR) in the Bureau of Indian Affairs has approved only one petition for federal acknowledgment, the Timbisha Shoshone of Death Valley, in 1983. The BAR averages one petition review per year; as of 2005 there were 188 petitioners.[15]

To be acknowledged, a tribe must meet the criteria defined by the BAR. The Code of Federal Regulations (25 CFR Part 83.7) spells out the mandatory criteria for acknowledgment and items that must be submitted:[16]

- A statement of facts establishing that the petitioner has been identified from historical times until present on a substantially continuous basis as "American Indian" or "aboriginal."

- Evidence that a substantial portion of the petitioning group inhabits a specific area or lives in a community viewed as American Indian and distinct from other populations in the area, and that its members are descendants of an Indian tribe which historically inhabited a specific area.

- The petitioner has maintained tribal political influence or other authority over its members as an autonomous entity from historical times until the present.

- A copy of the group's present governing document, including its membership criteria.

Surrounded by members of the Ti'at Society, the Moomat Ahiko *comes into Santa Monica Beach at the World Festival of Sacred Music, September 2005.* FRANK MAGALLANES AND ALTHEA EDWARDS PHOTOGRAPHY

· The petitioner's membership consists of individuals who descend from a historical Indian tribe or from historical Indian tribes which combined and functioned as a single autonomous political entity.

· The membership of the petitioning group is composed principally of persons who are not members of any acknowledged North American Indian tribe.

· Neither the petitioner nor its members are the subject of congressional legislation that has expressly terminated or forbidden the federal relationship.

They let us attend Sherman Indian School....We got reimbursed for some lands. You also registered us. You gave us roll numbers....We've complied with the law, and this is the law that the government imposed on us....And now here we are and the government is still denying us. That's not fair. —ANTHONY MORALES

For California tribes such as the Tongva, the BAR's acknowledgment process constitutes a de facto denial, more than two centuries of governmental efforts to de-legitimize their authority and deprive them of their land.[17] This denial continues to the present day. For example, although the Tongva participated in the California Land Claims cases and received financial settlements, the United States government does not accept this as evidence of value in acknowledgment

Studio portrait of Virginia Belarde Carmelo (great-grandmother of Virginia Carmelo) and her husband, José Ciriaco Sosa Carmelo, 1908. Virginia is holding her son Joe Belarde Carmelo (the grandfather of Virginia Carmelo). José is holding their son Daniel C. Carmelo. This portrait was probably taken at San Jacinto. Virginia Belarde Carmelo's mother and father were Tongva and baptized at San Gabriel, as stated on the application for the 1928 California Judgment Roll. José Ciriaco Sosa Carmelo was Diegueño and Apache. COURTESY OF VIRGINIA CARMELO

proceedings, because in both the 1928 and 1946 cases all of the claims were consolidated into one claim on behalf of the Indians of California, rather than filed as individual cases. Although participants are regarded as persons of Indian blood, and although they had to be enrolled on the California Indian Rolls and state a tribal affiliation to share in the settlement, they are not considered members of tribes.[18]

This is just one illustration of the confusing and contradictory government policies that anger many Tongva. "Way back, my dad received the first amount of money," says Vivian Barthelemy. "He and his sister, and...brothers, and then I...and my children....How can we receive...money if we're not recognized?"[19] Anthony Morales echoes her frustration with the government's inconsistency:

> The government has allowed us into all the federal programs. They let us attend Sherman Indian School back in the twenties and thirties when they became government schools. You've [the government] allowed us to get some of the government programs. You've allowed us to sue you [in the California Land Claims cases]....We got reimbursed for some lands. You also registered us. You gave us roll numbers....[We've] complied with the law, and this is the law that the government imposed on us....And now here we are and [the government is] still denying us. That's not fair.[20]

The benefits of federal recognition are substantial and include the repatriation of burials and grave goods, religious and cultural protections, federal housing aid, educational aid, trust lands, and the right to own and operate casinos.[21] As valuable as these economic and material benefits are, for many Tongva there is something even more important at stake. Justice. Although individual attitudes toward federal recognition—how to achieve it, and the part that Indian gaming and casino development should play in it—may vary widely, the demand for justice cuts across all political and personal boundaries. As Michael Barthelemy explains:

I think our aim in securing federal recognition [is first]...to arrive at a point where we are satisfied that other people outside recognize us as an Indian tribe, not to be excluded and not to feel excluded. I think that's the primary motive. Second...to secure whatever financial or...federal benefits flow from federal recognition in the way of health care, education, [and the] establishment of a land base....[And] to better develop a sense of ourselves again as a people with common goals and a collective goal.[22]

Virginia Carmelo echoes his thoughts.

To me it's important in that the federal government chose, for whatever reason, not to recognize us for a lot of years, [for] political reasons. The importance of it is justice, justice, justice for who we are today. Justice for our ancestors and that history we have behind us....In the bigger scope, for me it's an injustice that Los Angeles is such a big...urban area, and most of the people here don't know who the indigenous people are.[23]

The three current Tongva tribal councils exist in large measure because of the passionate debate over recognition and how to best achieve it. One important aspect of recognition is deciding how a tribe's membership should be determined. Setting membership requirements can be difficult and divisive, as many California tribes have discovered to their dismay. Virginia Carmelo, tribal chairperson of the Gabrielino/Tongva Nation, believes that membership should consider the special circumstances of the Tongva's history. "We want to be inclusive of any person who has Gabrielino-Tongva lineage, and not just here within our own [geographical] area, but even [for Tongva living] in other...tribal [territories]....We will not use blood quantum. The decimation of our tribe has been so great that it would be ridiculous to do that."[24]

Tribal funding is another important subject of contention. The recognition process is long and very expensive, particularly since the Tongva tribe is a landless urban tribe that lacks its own sources of revenue. To fund such an endeavor, the tribe must obtain outside financing either from grants or investors. The Gabrieleno/Tongva Tribal Council of San Gabriel previously pursued federal acknowledgment through an ANA (Aid to Native Americans) grant with the University of California, Los Angeles. That effort was suspended when the funding ended. "Basically we're just researching different avenues to pursue," says Anthony Morales. "We haven't given up, no."[25] The Gabrielino-Tongva Tribe and the Gabrielino/Tongva Nation are both currently pursuing recognition with funding from private investors, including those associated with the gaming industry. Virginia Carmelo, the tribal chair for the Gabrielino/Tongva Nation, says, "We are now on a course toward federal recognition....[The] next step is for economic self-determination

> *The importance of it is justice, justice, justice for who we are today. Justice for our ancestors and that history we have behind us.* —VIRGINIA CARMELO

which would be establishing a casino project which would basically allow us to be economically self-sufficient."[26]

Not all Tongva agree that casino development should be a priority. "That certainly shouldn't be our first aim," says Michael Barthelemy. "I don't know that it should be our aim at all.... It's certainly not my goal. It never was our aim for as long as we have been talking about federal recognition....I think it's better avoided."[27] Desirée Martinez has her own concerns about casino development. "I think it's shortsighted. Community development, cultural development, language preservation—those are the things I think are most important....There's so much focus on getting a casino, you forget everything else."[28]

Anthropologist Sarah-Larus Tolley suggests that the Bureau of Acknowledgment and Research has effectively become the gatekeeper for Indian casino development; in other words, the stringent federal requirements were designed to prevent tribes from getting recognized and operating casinos.[29] "Now the politics have changed," says Michael Barthelemy. "The U.S. government is looking very critically at federal recognition on the basis of the intent of the petitioning parties as to gambling and establishment of gambling establishments. So it's probably a harder thing to achieve now than it was back in the seventies."[30]

> *What works for one native community doesn't work for another because of the way history is. That's the problem with BIA acknowledgment.*—DESIRÉE MARTINEZ

Regardless of the reasons, the petitioning process moves with glacial slowness. In 1997 the Advisory Council on California Indian Policy concluded that the federal acknowledgment process does not work in California because the Bureau of Acknowledgment and Research's definition of what constitutes a tribe contradicts the history of California's Indians. Furthermore, the federal acknowledgment process places sole responsibility for proving "Indianness" on the tribes themselves, while accepting no responsibility for governmental actions during the past two centuries that have left them unrecognized.[31] As Desirée Martinez notes:

> The U.S. wants to deal with groups of people as efficiently as possible. So if we can draw a ring around all of the natives, and then create a policy to deal with all of the natives, [the] work is done. A lot of people have bought into that way of thinking...unfortunately, it doesn't work....What works for one native community doesn't work for another because of the way history is. That's the problem with BIA acknowledgment.[32]

An Interview with Anthony Morales

Anthony Morales sits at the conference table in the Tongva Youth Center, his son Andy Morales Guiding Young Cloud and his niece Kimberly Morales Johnson, the tribe's archivist, at his side. Anthony is the elected tribal chairperson of the Gabrieleno/Tongva Tribal Council of San Gabriel. On this day he is dressed in dark blue, his full face framed by his dark hair and moustache.

The Tongva Youth Center is sparsely furnished. The conference table—an old dining table with chairs—fills an open space near a small hallway. Unframed posters and prints of Indian art are pinned to the walls. The building also doubles as an after-school day-care center run by Andy Morales. There is a Ping-Pong table at one end of the room and an old leather couch in a corner beside some shelves filled with children's books. The Tribal Council does not own the Youth Center; they lease the building with a block grant from the county of Los Angeles. The irony is not lost on the soft-spoken Morales:

Anthony Morales, tribal chair of the Gabrieleno/Tongva Tribal Council of San Gabriel, 2006.
TY MILFORD PHOTOGRAPHY

> We have nothing, and at one time we were up with the most prosperous tribes in real estate. Just look at our territory. We're from the west deep into the Santa Monica Mountains, to the north all along the Angeles Crest National Forest, to the high desert...all along into Orange County...and then all along the ocean and islands....That is our territory. I don't like to refer to it in the past tense [with the] word "was" because it still is. It's still our territory. We were an urban tribe. We were settled in some prime real estate. This is why I feel that...[the government] doesn't want to recognize us....[You] think they're going to give this prime real estate back to us? I don't think so.[33]

Not all Tongva recognize Anthony Morales as their tribal chairperson. As noted earlier, there are other tribal organizations, each with its own leaders. There are also some Tongva like David Campio who question whether it is necessary or even appropriate for the Tongva to recognize tribal chairpersons:

> I think you get into a very slippery slope when you seek out community leaders because we weren't a big tribal group....We were...very small family units....It has to stay within family, each has its own leader. That's more historically correct from my perspective.[34]

Andrew Morales, Tongva cultural educator and dance captain for the Gabrieleno Tongva Tribal Council of San Gabriel, 2006. TY MILFORD PHOTOGRAPHY

Viewed from a historical perspective, the Gabrieleno Tongva Tribal Council of San Gabriel has the oldest continuous link to the Tongva community of San Gabriel; it is also the first Tongva tribal council to be organized.[35] As Anthony Morales explains:

[The] community has always been here. It's been ongoing. The evidence of that...[is] the attendance of everybody at parties, barbecues, fiestas, baptisms, marriages, funerals....

[My] knowledge of our traditional community has always been deep rooted here in San Gabriel....[Our] ancestors are part of the mission.... [We've] been here since then, way before then, and we're still here....

This community did the actual suing of the government....[in] Docket 47 [and] Docket 80[36] ....We made history by joining with the other bands of Mission Indians from the high desert and other areas...to sue the government for the land that was taken away from us....

To me...[San Gabriel is] the main tree trunk.[37]

One of Anthony's main concerns is protecting Indian burial grounds.[38] He considers archaeological sites, cemeteries, and burial grounds to be sacred:

All this land is sacred to me because this is our territory. Any portion or parcel within our territory [which] has human remains—that is sacred—artifacts uncovered during development...[those] to me...[are] sacred, all these artifacts and the human remains. When they say, "They could be reburied,"....No. Reburials were not meant to be....That is what sacred means to me...never to be disturbed, never to be desecrated.[39]

In 2006, the Tribal Council, under Anthony's leadership, cosponsored Assembly Bill 2641 along with the San Manuel Tribe and other tribes from the high desert.[40] The bill, which protects Native American burial grounds, was signed into law later that same year. Anthony is proud of AB 2641 and what it will mean to his people and to the Indians of California:

Morales family cousins at the San Gabriel Mission, 2006. Left to right: Anthony Morales, Kimberly Morales Johnson, Vivian Morales Barthelemy, Art Morales, Andrew Morales. Ty MILFORD PHOTOGRAPHY

> I've been working on this bill for three years and finally this year Assembly Member Joe Coto from San Jose introduced the bill...[with] Senator Denise Ducheney...she represents the San Diego tribe. They cosponsored it....Now there's a bill...to protect all burial grounds that pertains to the whole state of California.[41]

These days much of Anthony's time is spent working with city councils and other government agencies to promote awareness and understanding of the Tongva's history and culture. "Like the Forest [Service]...now lets us go on the land to gather sage and basket-weaving materials and medicines."[42] He also works to collect and preserve the memories of Tongva elders for future generations and to educate the public about the Tongva people, their culture, and their history. Anthony credits his family, especially his wife—who is not Tongva—with giving him much of the strength to carry out his duties. "It's her support," he says. "She shares my vision and my dad's vision."[43]

Anthony inherited the title of tribal chief from his father, Fred "Sparky" Morales. He also holds the position of tribal chairperson, to which he was first elected in 1997. The chair position is not hereditary; under tribal regulations the chairperson must stand for reelection every two years. Nor is it honorific; the duties are demanding, both spiritually and emotionally. How long does he wish to hold the job? Sitting at his side, Anthony's niece Kimberly draws a breath. "I'm scared of the answer," she admits. Anthony speaks quietly, effortlessly, without a trace of hesitation:

Modesta Morales and her children, ca. 1940. Back row, left to right: Arthur (father of Vivian Morales Barthelemy and Art Morales), Virginia, Modesta, and David Morales. Front row, left to right: Joseph and Fred "Sparky" Morales (father of Anthony Morales). COURTESY OF ART MORALES

To tell you the truth, I'll take it on as long as it's in the best interest of the tribe, and the best interest of the membership. [If] they feel that I'm good for another two years, if they elect me, I'll do it as long as I'm strong, and healthy, and able to do it, which thank God I am right now….I'll do it as long as they want me to do it. I'll continue.[44]

Renewal and Recognition

Federal recognition is a shared vision and aspiration of the Tongva; however, this goal does not limit or define them. Cindi Alvitre asks:

Do we continue to have generations struggling for federal recognition? Is that your identity? Or do we really start doing what we should be doing: laughing, telling stories, sharing them in the community, getting together and doing as our grandparents did. [That means celebrating] the fiesta, not in the Mexican sense, but in the sense of acknowledging our holidays, or our holy days, that have been lost in Americanism.[45]

There are other types of recognition besides federal recognition; these include recognition from state and local governments, from other Indian tribes, and from the general public. In 1994 the Tongva were formally recognized by the state of California and also by the city of San Gabriel.[46] And while political organizations like the various tribal councils work toward federal recognition—each in its own way—other groups, like the Ti'at Society, the Tongva Dancers, the Gabrielino/Tongva Language Committee, and the Gabrielino/Tongva Springs Foundation, devote their efforts to public education and awareness, cultural preservation, language studies, and the protection of sacred sites. "Everybody has the same bigger picture," says Desirée Martinez. "They want recognition, whether it's at the federal level or just local. They want to make sure that if they don't know the culture, they learn the culture. If they have participated in the culture, they want to continue to pass that down…to the next generation." Of course, these efforts cost money, and federal recognition—along with casino development—would help, but as a means to an end, not an end in itself.[47]

In 1992 members of the Ti'at Society of the Tongva people helped build the first traditional ti'at (plank canoe) in almost two centuries. In September 1998, the Moomat Ahiko (left) was launched at Descanso Beach on Catalina Island accompanied by a Chumash tomol (right) and ended its journey at Avalon.
FRANK MAGALLANES AND ALTHEA EDWARDS PHOTOGRAPHY

For many Tongva, recognition is also a personal journey of discovery and renewal that brings with it a growing sense of confidence. Cindi Alvitre has seen this firsthand:

> The past is that starting point, it's that connection.... And over time you will see people relax and say, "I didn't have to do all that. I don't have to wear twenty eagle feathers tied in my hair and wear ribbon shirts. I'm okay. I can wear a Target sweat suit and it doesn't change the intimate part of my identity.[48]

"We don't have to prove that we're Indian," says Angie Behrns. "I don't have to prove I'm an Indian anymore, prove traditional ways....I know I'm a Tongva. I know my children are."[49] This confidence extends to all parts of a Tongva's cultural inheritance, as Virginia Carmelo explains. "I'm not full-blooded Tongva. I have all of these other lineages...and I don't separate them. I don't say, 'Today I'm this, today I'm that.' To me it's always there. It's all been part of my experience."[50]

Do we continue to have generations struggling for federal recognition?...Or do we really start doing what we should be doing: laughing, telling stories, sharing them in the community, getting together and doing as our grandparents did?

—CINDI ALVITRE

Earl Campio is standing beside the potter's wheel of his father (also Earl Campio) with his nephew David Campio looking on. Earl Campio made his unusual potter's wheel from the wooden wheel and axle of an Essex automobile ca. 1920s. The "maseta" (big pot) sitting on the potter's wheel once sat on the roof of Earl's Azteca Pottery Shop. Ty Milford Photography

Education has been, and continues to be, a crucial part of the recognition process, helping to acquaint the public with the Tongva's traditional culture. Andy Morales believes that dance is symbolic of the Tongva's journey. "The stories change, the dance patterns change. We grow from that. It's not stuck on one specific step. It's...a continuous growing circle of life."[51] Education can also help to dispel the racial stereotypes that still exist. "That's one of my favorite lectures I do for people who become teachers," says David Campio:

> [I do this] for fifth graders, second graders, third graders, or college. I have the kids or the adults draw a picture of an Indian. [They have] hatchets, liquor in...[their] hands, bloody arrows, the feather. Adult or child, they're drawing the same image. Then I have them draw a white person. They'll draw a man in a suit and tie, his hair parted on one side. Why have Indians been locked in a time frame?[52]

The protection of sacred lands is another core principle that unites many Tongva. Sites like Playa Vista, Povuu'ngna, Hellman Ranch, Bolsa Chica, and Harbor Cove have become rallying points for many Tongva who see the loss of these sacred places as part of the destruction of their culture and heritage.[53] Desirée Martinez has devoted her career as an archaeologist to protecting such archaeological sites. "It has to revolve around recognition, whether it's on the federal level, or within schools, [or] within the greater community," she says:

> Those areas are the last visible demonstrations of our community in terms of archaeology. That past stuff, those villages— protecting those is going to bolster us in the present....To me it's changing the practice of archaeology so that it incorporates how native people want to have their...[cultural] resources dealt with.[54]

Angie Behrns has worked since the early 1990s to preserve the site of Kuruvangna Springs. The Gabrielino Tongva Springs Foundation, which she helped found, holds a twenty-year lease from the city of Los Angeles on the two-acre historical and archaeological site. Here, on the campus of University High School, amidst classrooms and administrative buildings and athletic fields, students come face to face with the Tongva world of the past as well as the present.

The Spring in the Hollow: A Visit to Kuruvangna

On a warm June day we follow a white SUV down a narrow street along the south side of University High School, in West Los Angeles. Buildings sprayed with graffiti line the right side of the street; on the left, a tall chain-link fence encloses a small field. The truck stops and Angie Behrns steps out of the vehicle and unlocks the gate. We drive inside and turn right to park on a narrow cement apron.

The afternoon is warm as we step out of our air-conditioned car; a dry breeze rustles dead, brown stalks of grass in the field gone to seed. Nearby, a small pond lies shaded under some trees. Two green-feathered mallards rest among the white-flowered calla lilies at the pond's edge; Japanese koi flash silver and gold sunbeams in its dark waters. A narrow stone channel runs from the pond back toward the spring that feeds it. This spring, the "lower spring," looks unremarkable—just a shallow pool a few yards in diameter enclosed by a low rock wall. The surroundings are equally unremarkable: bungalow-style classrooms straddle their cement foundations; an upturned bench with peeling paint lies abandoned in a patch of straggly brown weeds. But two bronze plaques, almost hidden beneath the wide acanthus leaves at the pool's edge, hint at something more here than meets the eye.

Angie Behrns at the sacred springs at University High School, Los Angeles, 2006.
TY MILFORD PHOTOGRAPHY

Something very special.

The bronze markers proclaim the history of this place: in 1769, Captain Gaspar de Portolá and Father Junípero Serra passed through here on their march north to Monterey during the first European land expedition to cross California.[55] We look up and gaze about in wonder. Could this truly be the place Portolá and Serra visited in that defining summer more than two centuries ago? Father Juan Crespí, the expedition's diarist, recorded the day in his log:

> Friday, August 4.—At half-past six in the morning we set out from the camp....At a quarter of a league we came to a little valley between small hills, and continued over plains of level land, very black and with much pasturage....[We] stopped at the watering place, which consists of two little

Angie Behrns with students from University High School, Los Angeles, at the site of the sacred springs, 2006. Ty Milford Photography

springs that rise at the foot of a higher mesa. From each of the two springs runs a small stream of water which is soon absorbed; they are both full of watercress and innumerable bushes of Castilian roses....We made camp near the springs, where we found a good village of very friendly...Indians, who, as soon as we arrived came to visit us, bringing their present of baskets of sage and other seeds, small, round nuts with a hard shell, and large and very sweet acorns....I called this place San Gregorio, but to the soldiers the spot is known as the Springs of El Berrendo ["the deer"], because they caught a deer alive there, it having had a leg broken the preceding afternoon by a shot fired by one of the volunteer soldiers, who could not overtake it. The water is in a hollow surrounded by low hills not far from the sea.[56]

The ringing of a school bell snaps us back to the present. We hear voices to our right: young students—teenagers—speaking Spanish. Seven girls with long, dark hair flowing over their shoulders stream down the walk leading toward the bungalows. Angie and her daughter Dalfine greet them and the girls immediately pool around them and begin talking. Angie speaks with her hands as much as her voice, her gestures punctuating the air, until the school bell rings again and they say their good-byes and the girls walk to a nearby building. Angie heads in the opposite direction, following the path that sweeps gently to the left toward an open gate; she motions for us to follow.

Angie is a founder of the Gabrielino/Tongva Springs Foundation and president of its board of directors. She also formerly served as a commissioner on the Los Angeles City and County Native American Commission.[57] On this day she gives us a personal tour of the springs site, which lies on the campus of University High School. Following her along the asphalt walkway, we leave the lower spring and walk out onto the main campus. On our right the hillside rises steeply to a terrace covered with school buildings; on our left it drops down to a broad, grassy athletic field. "There are several springs on this site," Angie explains:

> I don't know how big the school is, but the springs site is about two acres. There's a little spring, and it constantly bubbles up. It produces twenty-two thousand gallons of water a day. When they built the school, they made a little stream. It goes into a pond, then into the drain, and into the Santa Monica Bay. On this area, and this school site, there is also a waterfall. There are many other springs that have been turned into manholes.[58]

She points toward a large, gymnasium-size building on the far side of the athletic field and tells us that a seismic fault runs through the property and the building has been closed several times due to earthquake damage. The Spaniards also experienced earthquakes when they came through here in 1769. On August 2, just two days before reaching the springs, Father Crespí wrote, "we felt three consecutive earthquakes in the afternoon and night," and the next day after fording the Los Angeles River he noted, "We felt new earthquakes, the continuation of which astonishes us. We judge that in the mountains that run to the west in front of us there are some volcanoes."[59] Crespí guessed wrong; there are no volcanoes. Had he asked the Indians, they would have offered him their own explanation for the tremors: the earth is supported on the shoulders of seven giants and whenever they move or shuffle their feet, the ground shakes.[60] Happily for us, the giants are at rest on this peaceful summer day.

Angie leads us to the place where the upper spring gushes forth from the hillside, just a few feet below the asphalt pavement of the schoolyard, forming a small waterfall that spills into a channel and winds its way through rocks and greenery as it flows downhill toward the athletic field. The water runs clear and sparkling and makes a gentle, splashing noise as it slips over the smooth rocks. A student sits on the hillside a few feet away, textbook open in his lap, studying quietly; behind him, four girls dressed in blue jeans and brightly colored summer blouses talk softly, their schoolbooks cradled in their arms. Other boys and girls mill about the campus between classes. Their faces mirror urban Los Angeles: Asian, black, Hispanic, white. Some linger for a few moments before moving on, the springs drawing them close with their cool, soothing presence, just as they did in Father Crespí's day.

The Spanish soldiers named this place El Berrendo; Father Crespí called it San Gregorio, perhaps in honor of Saint Gregory of Nonantula, a Benedictine monk whose feast day is August 3rd.[61] Sadly, the priest did not preserve the Indians' name for the springs or their nearby village. In the early 1900s, Tongva interviewed by anthropologist J. P. Harrington vaguely recalled Kuruvangna as a place somewhere in the Santa Monica area, yet that name does not seem to appear in the mission registers kept by the Franciscans at San Gabriel.[62] Perhaps the missionaries overlooked the little Indian village in their endless search for new recruits.

Or perhaps this little hollow with its springs and wild roses was simply too wondrous and beautiful a place to forsake for the uncertainties of mission life.

JUST BELOW KURUVANGNA SPRINGS ON THE UNIVERSITY HIGH SCHOOL campus is a garden laid out in the shape of a medicine wheel—a large circle with stone and gravel pathways radiating out from the center like spokes from a hub. Yellow monkeyflower, blue-eyed grass, and golden California poppies spray the garden with color, like a desert hillside in spring. This is no showcase planting, laid out like a spread in *Sunset Magazine*; it is a living part of the school, just like the springs. Angie says they once had several landscape specialists study the garden and make recommendations on how to improve it, but the consultants advised them to tear out all the non-native plants. Angie shakes her head. They wouldn't do that, she vows, because there are birds living in the bushes and trees by the pond.

A young teacher in jeans and a blue work shirt, clipboard tucked under his arm, approaches Angie, followed by a small group of students. He tells her that they are adopting the medicine garden; each week they will come and pull weeds and tend and water the plants. All of these students are new arrivals at the school and speak little English; working together in the garden will ease their transition to their new surroundings. In a few minutes there are twenty boys and girls standing around the medicine wheel. Angie launches into an impromptu lecture, speaking in Spanish, stepping carefully between the rows of flowers as she talks to the students. Afterwards she tells us:

> I do talk about my culture. But respect—that's one word I always throw out to them. I'll ask, "Do you know what respect means?" And they listen. You have to start from a very young age, by the time they're eighteen, nineteen, it's too late.... You've got to really teach them when they're little. Respect is a big, big, big word for us.[63]

For Angie and many Tongva, land is a symbol of respect; respect for land and respect for people go hand in hand. Some of the students follow Angie's words carefully; others appear lost in their own thoughts on this soft, warm afternoon. A girl with brown eyes and long, dark hair stands behind her boyfriend and wraps her arms around his waist and whispers to him. He smiles, the two of them alone in the crowd in this peaceful place. Angie finishes up and quickly steps away from the garden, and the teacher gives the students their assignments. Watching from the sidelines, it is

---

Respect is a big, big, big word for us.

—ANGIE BEHRNS

Virginia Carmelo (left) and Cindi Alvitre (right) demonstrating dance movements in the Jacaranda Walk at Rancho Los Alamitos, 2006. TY MILFORD PHOTOGRAPHY

hard not to wonder what the future holds for these young people and for this garden and springs. The Los Angeles Unified School District owns the property and the Foundation must renew its lease every twenty years. Angie and her family hope to continue as custodians and guardians of the site. "Hopefully my children will continue...so they can leave a legacy to their children," she says. "That's what I would like to leave to my children, because everything has been lost."[64]

The spring site is a living part of the Tongva's cultural memory. It is an urban heirloom that enriches our daily lives as it connects us to the past and carries us into the future. The bronze plaques near the koi pond anchor this place in history, but the high school students connect it to the present. As our visit draws to an end we feel a twinge of sadness at the thought of leaving this place and we wonder: Did Father Crespí feel the same pang of regret as he headed north for Monterey on that summer day so long ago?

A Future Rooted in the Past

For more than two centuries non-Indians have viewed the Tongva through the prism of their own preconceptions. Missionaries, census agents, newspaper reporters, historians, and anthropologists: all have framed and then answered their own questions, defining the Tongva by their own standards while rarely considering how these Indians defined themselves. Too often these learned (and generally well-meaning) men have oversimplified the Tongva and reduced them to stereotypes; too often they have been wrong.

The Tongva culture has always been a rich and diverse blend of cultural influences. Long before the Spanish arrived in California, they were many separate communities with a shared identity, united by language and culture. Their homeland, with its varied geography and resources, helped foster this diversity. The establishment of the missions in the eighteenth century created a new identity for the Tongva, one that blended Spanish Catholic religion and culture with traditional Indian beliefs. Later, during the nineteenth and twentieth centuries, the Tongva adapted and assimilated to the new conditions thrust upon them by Mexican and American societies. Throughout this time the familiar pattern continued: diversity within a shared identity; continuity within change.

It continues to this day.

The quest for federal recognition is a deeply rooted dream for the Tongva. "That runs deep," Art Morales says softly. "It would mean a lot. It's hard to describe, just the fact that we would be federally recognized. There doesn't have to be anything else to go with it, just the fact that we were recognized."[65] Anthony Morales sees federal recognition as a fundamental right that the American government has denied to his people.

> It's a shame that we have to prove our right, to prove our title, to prove our history, and to earn the respect of our government. Our government has acknowledged us, and continues until this day, but has failed to [formally] recognize us even though we have been in existence in our ancestral lands for thousands of years.[66]

The road ahead is a difficult one, filled with uncertainty. "Sometimes I really don't know what to expect for the future," says Craig Torres:

> I think one of the things I always try to hold on to is hope....It's not so much trying to enlighten or educate our own people about their own history and their responsibility for all their relations and for the land...[but] we don't live here by ourselves anymore. And other people don't always feel that same obligation and those same responsibilities that we do. And that's when I start to think about my ancestors and what they must have felt....[If] they could survive what they did back then, when it was much, much worse, what makes me think I can't survive anything today?[67]

The Tongva will ultimately achieve their goal. Federal recognition will come in time and with it, finally, a chance to reclaim a small part of the homeland that once—that still—belongs to them. The Tongva will achieve this goal because they are a patient people. Patient over lifetimes. Patient over generations. Their resolve remains unshakable.

But it would be a mistake to think that federal recognition defines them. The Tongva do not need recognition, federal or otherwise, to define who they are. They define themselves and always will. As Art Morales explains:

> Ever since I can remember, I've always been Indian. That's just who I [am]....Even though there weren't specific stories, or other things that went along with it, I knew I was....It somehow continues through at one point or the other....It's like a river, it just keeps flowing. No one is going to stop it.[68]

A CONVERSATION with Cindi Alvitre

May 16, 2006
Rancho Los Alamitos, Long Beach, California

The Participant

IN 1988, CINDI ALVITRE BECAME THE FIRST APPOINTED CHAIR OF THE Gabrieleno/Tongva San Gabriel Band of Mission Indians. An advocate of cultural awareness, education, and scholarship, as well as the creative arts, she was a founding member of the Ti'at Society, which was established to encourage new communication and expression throughout the native and non-native community. In addition to developing traditional educational curriculum, she is a composer, choreographer, and performer of music and dance which explores and interprets Gabrielino-Tongva culture. The recipient of a Chancellor's Fellowship at UCLA, Cindi Alvitre is a Ph.D. candidate in the Department of World Arts and Cultures at UCLA, and a faculty member in the American Indian Studies Department at California State University, Long Beach. An active leader in the Tongva community at large, she serves on the board of the California Council for the Humanities.

The Discussion

The conversation explores the existence of cultural memory and the definition of Tongva identity in view of current issues and trends within the native community. As she shares her family stories, Cindi Alvitre connects the identity of the Tongva to the changing landscape while noting that genealogy is the common thread throughout the larger contemporary community. She discusses cultural discrimination and identity within the larger native and non-native community alike,

Cindi Alvitre in the Cactus Garden at Rancho Los Alamitos, 2006. Ty MILFORD PHOTOGRAPHY

commenting on federal recognition, tribal politics, the validity of cultural memory, and the growing dialogue and cultural confidence emerging throughout the larger Tongva community today.

Cindi Alvitre: My name is Cindi Alvitre, Gabrielino-Tongva descendant.

Claudia Jurmain: How do you know that?

CA: That has come down through genealogical charts and oral history, also Bureau of Indian Affairs documents. Actually, that's not Gabrielino-Tongva, that's Cahuilla. I'm not an enrolled member of any tribe. I grew up identifying as Gabrielino-Tongva, linking to culture which is non—federally recognized—very interesting [the] non-status of non—federally recognized tribes.

Bill McCawley: Why do you identify with the Gabrielino-Tongva culture?

CA: As opposed to Cahuilla? Probably geography. I was raised in Orange County—Santa Ana, Huntington Beach, Newport, Fountain Valley. Always the descriptions of the land, the immediate identity my father linked to, my family discussed, reminded us. The Cahuilla was put in the context of "cousins over there," but as I grew up, I became more connected—not identity, but geography again. When I was going to University of California, Riverside, I became involved in working on the *Cahuilla Voices* exhibition, active with basketry, the language, the bird songs.

The Cahuilla link became more clear—what culture was, the difference between Cahuilla and Gabrielino-Tongva—one a non-status tribe, the other active, struggling, but well marketed, and a much different status—reservation versus non-[reservation]; language, at least some fluent speakers, versus an extinct language; bird songs versus having very few songs. It was a way to learn about this other lineage of mine, also develop my sense of what was meant by Gabrielino-Tongva. It's not a racial identity—this is my opinion. It's not a biological identity. It's absolutely a cultural, socially constructed way of perceiving yourself in relationship to a certain space geographically, and to a particular lineage of history in California. I identify with the land.

We're here at Rancho Los Alamitos. This is where my grandparents, or my grandfather, spent a lot of his life, in Orange County. My [father's] grandfather used to deliver hay to the Bixby family, Midway City, Garden Grove—all agricultural. So the whole notion of Povuu'ngna being sacred was discussed. Not in the sense they would go back and recount the creation story, just to remind us kids when we would take these rides. My father was fantastic about—every Sunday—going for a ride someplace. Wherever we drove, he would have a story about that piece of land. "Here it was...This is where...This was a very sacred place...This was where Grandpa would come with his wagon train. I was just a little guy and would lay at the bottom of that wagon train and feel, hear the wheels moving, and smell the dust. Everybody would, all of a sudden, get very quiet. As we got closer, my father would tell us, 'You don't talk loud around here because this is a *tierra sagrada*—sacred land, holy land.' You always respect and talk in a very low voice." He had a different sense—was more respectful, conducted this quiet persona, I always noticed that his personality changed. That was interesting to me. Otherwise, he could be wild, boisterous and crazy.

When we would go to Tujunga Canyon my father told us that our families were from that area, from the Tongva villages of Tuju and Siba, where it seemed that land was very saturated with stories.* He told this story of ponds, and places of water, where there were water witches and the rock could sing to you. There are a lot of stories of witchery in the family. The Santa Ana Mountains, my father talked about a lot because [he] was born to two parents who probably should have been his grandparents. My grandmother was near fifty when she had my father, and my grandfather was well into his fifties.

---

* Tujunga Canyon is located in the northern part of Los Angeles, in the Crescenta Valley. Also known as the village of Shevaanga, Siba was located near the site of Mission San Gabriel today.

My father was born in 1926. My grandmother was born—I don't remember the exact year—1880, my grandfather 1870. I believe that's close. He was from that older generation. They had their own cultural values, their own way they dealt with people, their own sense of the land as he knew it. It was very early in the development of California, but there was still a lot of open land. They lived off of Euclid and Westminster [city of Westminster]. There was what they refer to as a *colonia*. They explained that to me. First, you had the villages that existed in those areas, and people started to move around with the missionary activity and everything else. Then, eventually, little communities began to emerge. When those *colonias* first started, the land was even more open.

My father was born in a little adobe house there at home. My grandfather was an herbalist. I don't know what he did outside, maybe physical labor. Outside of that he really had no occupation, but he always had a place where he had his herbs. He would take off into the Santa Ana Mountains for days at a time, sometimes a week, sometimes longer, usually with my great-uncle Vidal, his brother. He would go gather herbs, medicine, bring them back, and dry them out. People would come and see them. My father was still young. In the process of telling where he gathered the medicine, the herbs, he would tell other stories about Whole Legion Canyon, Trabuco Canyon—I want to say Black Star Canyon. There was a village site, and my grandfather claimed that when he slept there at night, you could hear the voices, hear the battle going on. You could hear the cries of Indians—something very bad that happened there.

There are different places in Anaheim Hills known as Five Palm. Right off of Imperial Highway is an adobe where ghosts used to travel by. Atwood towards Placentia—there was a story that if you went at certain times of the night, this door opened, a spiritual door, and this ghost would come out. But he was more like a *Tacquich* [a witch]. My grandfather talked about *Tacquich*. *Tacquich* were bad. *Tacquich* from the Cahuilla. Interesting my father used the term *Tacquich*, and that he was also present in the lowlands here. He would even come and confront you if you were walking on the streets at that time of night, and could harm you. So *Tacquich* was very, very present. We were never allowed to look at the first shooting stars when it was starting to get dark. My father would refer to them as *Tacquich*, or witches that could take you away forever. We never looked.

Every place had a story. The Santa Ana Mountains were immersed in old spirits because some historical activity had happened there. There is a story about Maria Susweta, a spirit that appeared to my grandfather when he would gather up in the Santa Ana Mountains by himself. He had no fear of being out there in those hills—walking was normal for a man, to be out like that. I don't think a woman would do that. It would take a lot of courage because there was this belief—a lot of spirits, unknown things out there that you just didn't mess with. Men had the bravery to do that. When he was out there, this woman, Maria

Susweta, said that she wanted to talk to Vidal, his brother. She didn't have any interest in talking to my grandfather. She wanted to talk to Vidal because she had something to tell him about gold, and if he came up, she would reveal this wealth so he wouldn't have to struggle anymore. My grandfather went again, and she appeared again. Finally he convinced my great-uncle to go, but when getting closer and closer to the place where he knew she would appear again, he chickened out. He went back.

We heard these stories repeatedly as kids. Here's a gold story again, here's Maria Susweta. All I heard was "Maria Susweta." I didn't know if this was a real person. I was doing genealogical research through the San Juan Capistrano Mission Records, and I found a Maria Susweta related to Alvitre, a carpenter at San Juan Capistrano Mission. She was a real person, which startled me. I always had my different sense—"You listen, you don't deny it could happen because you don't dare. That will curse you forever." But living in the contemporary setting, you're always saying, "Is this real? Is this real?" Then you start getting these little things—like at Tujunga—the sense of it being a very special place.

At UCLA, the curator of archaeology and I were going through collections from Little Tujunga Canyon, Big Tujunga Canyon, looking at the quality and kinds of artifacts found. She and I started mapping one of the sites where there was a lot of soapstone, island stuff. They had taken pictures or drew exactly how they found these artifacts, and there was a soapstone pipe. I wondered where this pipe pointed to on a map. It was pointing right at the island of Catalina, to Two Harbors! You're not going to get that quality of soapstone here on the mainland, you're going to get that on the island, and it had traveled to Tujunga. Could be from people who were from the island and lived in that village site—could be a number of things.

Harrington mentions water babies, spirits who lived in still water, in his notes.[*] When the water moves, you can hear their voices. In Tujunga Canyon there were always these ghost stories. Harrington's stuff is very different from the way I heard it because it's told more in the context of spirits. But you don't think of them as ancient spirits, you think of them as people, or spirits that existed around the turn of the century. That could be in my own head. It could be in the way people retell stories, or their cultural memory—how they're recalling it, how they're interpreting it in the context of their present.[**] How I'm interpreting it in my present becomes very different.

CJ: Do you think cultural memory is more about the future than the past?

CA: I think cultural memory travels—something that is situated in the past and

---

[*]   J. P. Harrington was a Smithsonian anthropologist who interviewed many Native Americans in the early twentieth century, including extensive work with the Tongva. His notes from the 1930s and 1940s reflect his earlier field research.

[**]   For more on cultural memory refer to the essay "Continuity within Change: Identity and Culture."

travels to the present—perhaps to create unknowingly, unconsciously, a future for the protection of a culture. Maybe this unconscious activity we participate in, especially people like Gabrielino-Tongva who are struggling just for acknowledgment, but also passionately, sometimes desperately clinging to the very, very little that you have.

CJ: Can the Tongva people have acknowledgment without political recognition, without some formal organized body of people?

CA: Oh, absolutely. I believe that. Sure you can. A lot of energy is wasted for the political, legal acknowledgment by the Bureau of Indian Affairs. Not that that's not significant, not important. I think it's an acknowledgment, the principal argument—something critical as tribal people who have occupied a space for generation after generation after generation. To obtain a legal status is significant because first of all—just the respect. Not only from the government, but from other tribes, which Gabrielino-Tongva do not always have. They're probably one of the most criticized tribes, or questionable. "Are they real? Are they playing Indian?" I hear it all the time. I deal with all the rest of the tribes too. I'm so immune to it. I understand where they're coming from. It's not something that I take personally, but it's part of that. The principle of being acknowledged, for the government to, in legal terms, admit something occurred that was unjust, and not recognize Gabrielino-Tongva, was wrong. Part of that political process was because they wanted the tribe to become extinct. They wanted an extinct status.

Just like any other tribe in any other city in California—San Diego, San Francisco, Santa Barbara—you have abundance of resources. If you want to take those resources which are significant—we know that today L.A. is one of the world's richest areas—the best thing to do is eliminate the tribe, the people. That could be through political genocide, not making any efforts to really reach out and see who's there. Research still needs to be done—how involved certain players within the Gabrielino-Tongva were, like in the Mission Indian Federation, or groups dealing directly with the Bureau of Indian Affairs, or any of the unratified treaties [of 1851 and 1852]. I don't believe people have taken the time to really look at those individual treaties. Who was involved and not involved? What was each step to that point where they reached a treaty, or the discussion of a treaty?

So a lot of history has not been done in the process of attempting to obtain federal recognition. It's focused on genealogical stuff to demonstrate that there's a cultural continuum, a historical continuum, to the Bureau of Indian Affairs because that's one of their criteria. Other people have done it. We know it's a huge amount of work. It's so, so expensive—hundreds and hundreds of thousands of dollars' cost can be accumulated just seeking acknowledgment. The federal, legal, political acknowledgment is one thing, but this is my opinion—we as a community lack cultural confidence.

You're constantly told, "You don't exist. You're not here. You guys are playing Indian." Other people have done ethnogenesis commentary. There's validity to what they're saying, but they've completely ignored the very particulars, specific complex complicated details of each of these cultural groups, like the Gabrielino-Tongva. To establish that, validate a political status—it's important. At the same time, so much energy has gone into that, just taking care [of the] land basis and development, support mitigation of [damage to] archaeological sites. We know that mitigation doesn't mean, "Oh, we won't build here, Mr. Indian,"—pat you on the back—"No, we won't do that, because we honor and respect what you have." That's not what happens. Mitigation is also a developer's means of eliminating an attractive legal nuisance since they must protect places and cultural material of value to the native community from the impact of their project and its economic development. Get rid of it—put it in the archives of UCLA, Cal State Long Beach, in their warehouses, whatever.

That still doesn't contribute to cultural confidence. Right now we're at this bridge crossing. This process we're participating in at Rancho Los Alamitos, I think, has contributed significantly to get people off the defense about having to prove who they are. Back to Tongva identity—what is it? Well, everybody is going to have a different response. Some people may perceive it as biological identity, this genetic thing. Some people will see it connected to the land. Some people will see a constructed, recreated, revitalized community of people that you call Tongva.

BMc: Do common threads run through all of those groups you perceive?

CA: I think the common thread is genealogy. We're a group of people if you look at all our genealogies, people that don't get along, and all related. Beyond that, people are still trying to define what common link keeps us together. It might be a wider expanse of the land. The traditional land base would be the other link. People also have their own sense of the land, depending on where they're raised. The ones that left Los Angeles entirely and ended up in Tejon, or maybe out at Morongo or Soboba, perceive it different because their experiences are. If you're situated in the city, downtown, post-secularization, end up living in an urban area, it's going to be a very urbanized notion of the land. My family, we're coastal island—very immersed in the land because the landscape wasn't changing as dramatically as the city. If your family intermarried and resided at one of the reservations, you start accumulating this different sense of what it is to be California Indian.

There is starting to be change. A lot focused on protecting our cultural resources, the land, on federal recognition. But now as you emerge into revitalization, renewal of culture, people begin to build culture confidence, saying, "What do we need to survive into the future?" Do we continue to have generations struggling for federal recognition? Is that your identity? Or do we really start doing what we should be doing: laughing, telling stories, sharing them in the community, getting together and doing as our grandparents did? That's the fiesta, not in the Mexican sense, but in the sense of acknowledging our holidays, or our holy days, that have been lost in Americanism—even Flower Day, which we just had. It is an annual tradition to return to the cemeteries each May to clean the graves of family members and ancestors. That's when you went out, cleaned the cemeteries, left flowers, and did your respect. We did that as kids. A simple thing like that—that's very historical, very recent, but people aren't doing it. Or the *ti'at* (the plank canoe of our people)—the renewal of maritime tradition has been very significant. They do relate to the boat.* It's generated new interest in ocean maritime activity all the way from paddling to "You did this, you built the *Moomat Ahiko*, but were there other ways they built these boats?"

BMc: Over the last thirty years or so, certain events have provided unifying threads to the Gabrielino-Tongva—the struggle over the Povuu'ngna site; federal recognition; and the ongoing struggle to preserve lands that are sacred, have human remains, or represent cultural significance. These things have almost emerged, not so much as a rallying point, but as a catalyst for pulling together individual group interests. What other things could bring the different groups within the larger Tongva Gabrielino community together?

CA: Things have created a common thread and rallying points—as we've gone on through time we found that they're not complete. In fact, some have created separation within the tribe, like the struggle over development, which became complicated when you have Native American monitors at economic developments and construction sites. Strange as it may be, you have competition for those jobs. Or federal recognition—having people who want federal recognition and people who do not, or individual groups competing. This is very difficult to answer—I'm basing this on the experiences I've been having in the last six months with tribal members—we've not talked to each other. There has been friction, I won't say anger—a disconnect between us. Suddenly within the last six months, the tide is changing.

We're starting to ask each other this question. "This is what we have experienced in the last thirty-plus years, what has happened?" Some things have created unity, some more separation, more disaster than necessary. We're here, we're older, what do we build now? What kind of a foundation do we create to take people into the future?

We are looking towards cultural elements supporting the language. The language has always been very difficult. Within my [Ti'at] community we're becoming very active in education, into this level of philosophical and intellectual

---

* Alvitre is referring to the *ti'at Moomat Ahiko* that the Ti'at Society built in 1992. For more information, see the conversation with the Ti'at Society.

exchange—the process of identifying, deciding, and defining who the heck we are. It's actually very traditional—going back to the creation stories, entering discourse, then sharing the stories, your own knowledge, but regaining understanding, and creating an environment okay to talk. Romanticism has generated, throughout the world but in particular here in the United States, the Pocahontas image. Everything is fixed in the past and we're frozen in time. We're not doing what our ancestors did. Just basic human nature—being able to discuss these things.

CJ: Does the larger Gabrielino-Tongva community need an integrated hierarchy or mechanism for leadership that acknowledges an overall leader for the entire community, with or without political/federal recognition?

CA: I think there always is. That contributes to cultural confidence. People have somebody you can look up to, run things by, or ask questions. You get some sense of a response, some direction to identity, history, and where are we today. My father was very much about that. He was more of an elder, more of an adviser. Fred "Sparky" Morales was considered the chief. Not a hereditary chief, a leader of the community, an active person. He kept things going. Sparky, my father, and other people wanted to formalize this social activity that had been going on for generations, become more political. It was needed at that time as development and other things [came to the fore].

I was appointed by Sparky as tribal chair, not elected. I was their first tribal chair after the formalization of the San Gabriel Council. He wanted a younger person to take a role in the leadership, that's how he saw me. I was passionately involved in culture with the Cahuillas, crazy about anything fixed in the past, romantic. I wanted to be like my grandmothers and my grandfathers. We were playing this role, all of us. It was part of this whole sixties kind of scene. We wanted to live off the land—we would do anything to live off the land. Our kids suffered immensely. We tortured them regularly! They had to be Indian whether they liked it or not—speak to us in the language, eat roasted grasshoppers, spend all the time at sites, hiking. We laughed about this the other day. A lot of people at this really essential time had gone through—whatever. In the sixties and seventies, we weren't going to be like our parents. We were going to take an active role in preservation of culture. How these poor kids were raised, where they grew up as teenagers—"We want nothing to do with this. We are over this."

BMc: "Mom, not grasshoppers again, please!"

CA: "Do we have to do this? We know the songs. We know this." Our kids, who are all adults now, went through years of saying, "In addition, I don't like the fighting, the politics. I don't want to do that. I just want to be a kid, a young person." Now, as adults, they'll all come back and say, "Why aren't you doing this?"

My son saying, "I know that song. If I have to..." He will get up there and sing. So it's in their heads. It's good.

CJ: What is the dialogue today relative to educating others about the Tongva past?

CA: It's important too. It all makes contributions at different levels, and we've been doing that for many years. People are very, very active.

BMc: What role does the past play, going forward beyond obvious public outreach and providing important symbols for people to mentally carry? Does it belong to genealogy, bring people together around a common thread?

CA: I hope it does. There's obviously a tragic memory, a tragic history—that's the passion. We are all struggling and fighting to obtain some acknowledgment and recognition, whether it's political, legal—to keep the memory of our grandparents alive. Romantic images of the past—I don't think that's a bad thing, because we probably have thousands of descendants from the tribe in L.A. and throughout California who identify. The past becomes the process of reestablishing identity. I've lived through this, experienced it. But I've also tried to take it apart, analyze it, and say, "What's really happening?" People, for the last thirty years, are all of a sudden reconnecting—"I am no longer Mexican, I am no longer white—I am now Tongva." The past is that starting point, that connection. Maybe it's an honoring of their ancestors or grandparents, saying, "Oh yeah, Abuelita, Juanita—she was at San Gabriel Mission. I never thought of her, but now I'm honoring her by acknowledging that I'm this particular identity." And I can be sure that Abuelita, Grandmother Juanita, is damn proud of me for carrying this identity above anybody else's in that genealogical pool.

CJ: Do you want to exclude your other identities, other genetic cultural heritages?

CA: It's very strange. I don't know that people really think about it. Everybody is mixed—I don't know of any full-blood. I just object to any notions of racial purity on the planet. The world is much more intellectual, much more complex and much more beautiful than that. I don't see it as a negative thing. I think people do reject it because I don't think they see it the same way I do. This is my own personal perception that's developed over time because of where I come from, where I've been placed, not only culturally, politically, and socially, but also academically.

Sparky and elders said, "You know what, you're smart. You need to get your butt in school." I'm so passionate about my people, I said, "I will go. I will do this." Not only that, it's interesting, it fascinates me. But I've traveled way out of that scope. I'm an insider, but in some respects I've become an intentional outsider. I'm very capable of being a political leader, asserting and inserting myself anywhere I want. Now, I have to influence people into thinking, gaining confidence, saying, "It's cool, okay that you're mixed. It's not our fault. It's okay to go outside your community, see how other people, other tribes, other cultures function, and reexamine your identity. It's okay to participate in things not considered legitimately traditional because in reality we really don't know. Tradition is something that morphs over time, influenced by everything that's happening around you." I'm only answering for myself, because everybody you ask is going to give you a different answer.

People who just came back—all-of-a-sudden Gabrielino-Tongva—we know what the motivations are—probably the promises of casino and economic gain. If you ask them that question, they say, "No, I don't know all the rest. I know nothing about Catholicism, nothing about Mexicans or Europeans in my family. This is all we are." When people convert religiously, it's the same thing. They go through this extreme period. You can describe it kind of as a fanaticism, a fundamentalism. People just want to immerse themselves in this identity, this thing they've never known. Some people pull out of it. Some give up, "Screw this, I'm not interested." And over time you will see people relax and say, "I didn't have to do all of that. I don't have to wear twenty eagle feathers tied in my hair and wear ribbon shirts. I'm okay. I can wear a Target sweat suit and it doesn't change the intimate part of my identity."

That's where we're at now—being able to share that with people—a kind of outreach. I'm speaking about the Ti'at Society. This is a conversation other groups are attracted to, to our ability to change and say, "We know who we are, we don't have any anxiety about it anymore." That's the difference between our community and a lot of other communities. We don't have that anxiety, we want to have fun. We're in the midst of creating a major dance performance influenced by other performance artists, telling our stories in our own way using audio-visual technology—crazy stuff.

To communicate to the public or your own people, you have to communicate in ways familiar in the present. That's the thing linked with cultural memory. So the [exhibit] table serves elementary—almost like flash cards. Going beyond that, to people who have a sense of, still retain this strong creative presence—doing performance pieces is another way. For intellectuals—you have to appeal to that, too.

CJ: That dialogue provokes the question—what is being communicated? Sometimes it's just an idea, a thought. Sometimes its culturally or historically inaccurate based on what is known. Again, is there a need for a larger ongoing common identity, or is the definition of identity whatever any individual says about his sense of being Tongva/Gabrielino?

CA: I think absolutely you have a need for a larger identity—

CJ: Where does that come from in a community no longer rooted in an intact traditional culture or an agreed-upon common hierarchy?

CA: We have to have a larger cultural identity that is an amalgamation of all the above—a lot of work, communication with people. Right now we're trying to work with Anthony Morales's group [Gabrieleno/Tongva Tribal Council of San Gabriel] and anybody else, to get people together and say, "Okay, you are really into the political. We support you this week." Anthony is trying to get through this cemetery bill—we're supporting him.* At the same time, members of his community are dancers. Sunday we did some stuff and I choreographed this piece that's related to canoes. They're like, "Wow, I want to do that." So you start small.

Communication, supporting each other, acknowledging each other, especially what's happened over the last thirty years in respect to cultural resource management—the communities want to do the right thing to come together, communicate, and create a larger cultural identity and strength. You create a central agency, entity, that says, "We have to have some ethics involved, and some accountability in people who are going to be monitors. There has to be training. The money should be distributed this way—a percentage needs to go into a collective fund." This is just an example of the conversations we have in monitoring. We create classes and talk about cultural identity. It's a regular educational setting. We do ceremonial things that include everybody—*ti'at* ceremonies, *ti'at* festivals have really brought everybody together. So you're seeing all different elements creating a larger cultural identity.

I'm feeling very positive about it—better than I've felt in many, many years. Oh yes, absolutely, because I think people are breaking ground. People are still trying to bang their heads through a brick wall, but do you spend energy fighting people? Do you spend energy going up against people, trying to reprimand them? Or do you put more energy into creative activities; acknowledging people; new strategies; and dealing with agencies, community, every type of social, political group that we interact with. Or do you spend all this time, as in the past, just struggling like hell to get something done—two steps forward and five, ten steps back. You know, it hasn't been successful. That's sad. We lost a lot of time. I think that's just cultural communities attempting to have some sense of identity—how it occurs. I say this all the time—"We are unique. We are not Mexicans. We are not white. We are not any other ethnic group. We have a very unique identity, a very unique history, and a way of seeing the land around us." That in itself is very important.

CJ: Many people are attached to the land, wherever you go. What makes the Tongva perspective different?

CA: With Tongva identity you peel away the contemporary layers—say Los Angeles downtown, the high-rises and the asphalt. Beneath that, you will know,

---

* Effective January 2007, AB 2641 further protects Native American cemeteries in California.

or be very familiar with, where the village site of Yaanga [present-day Los Angeles] may have been. That carried a significant history—it was a refugee village. Essentially, you're looking at the landscape. I don't see L.A., I see Yaanga. I don't see Catalina Island, I see Pimu. I don't see Long Beach, Cal State Long Beach, Rancho Los Alamitos, maybe a little bit, Los Altos Shopping Center—I see Povuu'ngna. I don't see these rectangular blocks of asphalt and concrete, I see earth and villages. I see stories played out on this land that did not have any of the contemporary structures or elements.

I'm always looking at the land around me, other countries too, but when I go to New Zealand, I'm in Maori territory. I don't know the stories of the land, where the cemeteries were, where the creation stories emerged from. I don't know the significance of the highest mountain. Here I do. I have very deep familiarity with the Santa Ana Mountains, Mount Orizaba on the island of Catalina, with the wetlands where L.A. Harbor is—seeing ecology changing, understanding my father saw it different. My grandfather, the way he described it was different. Less developed, it wasn't polluted, little islands off where L.A. Harbor is now. Keep going back and the land is changing back. You take a snapshot of a piece of land. Then that snapshot changes because people are telling you, "Look at that chair. Before that chair was there, you would drop [through] the bottom of this trailer because this trailer wasn't there. Then take away the asphalt and let's move back a hundred years. You're probably going to be in the middle of some scrub oak. Maybe fifty feet around here you would have had a grandmother, or maybe there's a bedrock mortar where she was grinding acorns."

You begin to reexamine underneath the trailer, underneath the plants, all these little hints and pieces of natural landscape. Some of them still exist, they're there. You can't move a big, huge rock as easily as you can tear down a tree, you know. Old trees, how long have these trees been there? There's one over in Little Tokyo—very old, old tree. My friend, he's a Chicano music historian. We go to Little Tokyo, and he loves to just hang on to that tree. He says, "I'm from Boyle Heights. I've watched this tree all my life," and he tells me, "It's hundreds of years old." I said, "It's not hundreds of years old. It's old to you in your sensibility. Plus, it's a *Ficus*. *Ficus* wasn't indigenous to L.A." Those are examples of how the landscape is perceived differently by people.

BMc: Looking at leadership in the broader sense, not cultural, who are the leaders of the Gabrielino-Tongva today?

CA: That's a good question. Anthony Morales, myself. People are leaders of councils, but I don't know about their leadership. Maybe they fall more into the roles of elders or community leaders. Every group has their own thing.

CJ: Do the councils represent geography?

CA: That's the way I perceive them. I don't know how they see it. People have attempted to create councils to embrace all the communities, or all Gabrielino-Tongva. It doesn't work out that way. Logically, people live within a certain area, certain motives, and goals they want to accomplish. You can see I already created a hierarchy of who I would consider to be real leaders, and below that, if we're going to get into directional things. Other people are leaders at a different level—elders, older people who still have that memory, that link to the past. There are a lot of elders over at San Gabriel, but a lot of them are passing away, who also play their role in leadership. Active is different—there is a hierarchy already.

CJ: Is the hierarchy trying to reconstruct a common memory to enact a contemporary agenda? That could be the definition of cultural memory in some way because it's as much about today and tomorrow as the past.

CA: Yeah—that hierarchy is. I believe it's unconsciously been established. It's not conscious to the people. To some, it's starting to become more conscious. They say, "No, this is the way we are." If you're asking somebody who is Gabrielino-Tongva, "How are you organized?"—it's not a formal organization. It's just the way it happened. There was a master narrative, and there are holes in the narrative. People are inserting themselves, filling gaps within organizations.

Each story is different. Another woman who is Tongva lives out in Pechanga.* She was from Rosemead. Her great-grandmother received the allotment—people that weren't Luiseño received allotments too. I don't know if that was because of the tribe.**

I don't understand the whole disenrollment that's happening with the casino tribes. They're trying to get rid of families who were either allowed to stay there, they received allotments, and their descendants are all still living on the reservations. Now they're saying, "You need to leave because you're really not Luiseño." Then you get people saying, "No, I'm Luiseño because I live on the reservation." That just complicates the whole thing when they're not really. Their lineage is Tongva, but they relocated into those areas. Some were intermarriages with families at Morongo and Soboba but won't admit it now. They don't want to. They're more comfortable being inserted into a legitimate tribal body.

BMc: Leadership has evolved, and grown over time—be it political, cultural, or simply rising to an occasion in the given moment. Given that, does leadership carry responsibilities?

CA: We all have to be accountable. I think there has to be checks and balances. Sometimes we need to be reminded what our responsibilities are, who we are

---

* The reservation for the Pechanga Band of Luiseño Indians, near Temecula, California.

** For more information on the Tongva people who moved onto the reservations established for other tribes, see the essay "A Connection to Place: Land and History" as well as the conversations with Anthony Morales and Art Morales and Vivian Barthelemy.

accountable to. We're in a very transitional point. It's difficult to answer because we do need to address important questions that the community is beginning to ask and we have not yet answered. Obviously, there is a responsibility and need to construct something more formalized at a larger level, I believe.

CJ: You said a new dialogue is starting.

CA: I'll admit I'm pushing for it. It's in people's minds, but they're not quite sure how we go about this. Again, you start identifying those cultural links, common concerns, issues that require support from the communities to give us more unification, more power, more strength, more voice—acknowledging that the vampire syndrome does exist.

The vampires are wounded and infect people; rather than outsiders, you attack your own. It's what people are experiencing, it's not this detached, completely political thing. It's psychological, and very much the result of cultural historical trauma that transcends through the generations, part of cultural memory—you remember pain and you're wounded. You have this identity, but here in this city, you might as well be invisible, be one of those ghosts your ancestors, your grandparents and my father, talked about. You might just as well be Maria Susweta trying to tell somebody there is gold. Because nobody is listening, and nobody really gives a damn.

BMc: We talked about federal recognition and what that would convey, but there are other kinds of recognition as well. What other kinds of recognition are the Gabrielino-Tongva striving for today beyond federal recognition?

CA: I think they're playing with some settings where you would obtain recognition and acknowledgment, including the international level where people aren't really concerned about federally recognized tribes—the forum of the United Nations—people are listening to your concerns; providing strategies to protect your resources, revive, renew aspects of your culture [language programs, maritime culture]; accessing land—actually acquire some land base so you can reestablish a sense of community, have educational facilities, practice your rights to be buried, die, or be born in a more traditional sense.

CJ: Some don't need federal recognition because their identity resides in their own family; most don't need anyone else to tell them who they know they are. Some want it as a matter of respect, or "I was there first." Other people need something else. Is part of the concept and strategy to create enough strains of identity so that no one has to adhere to another's singular definition of what is Tongva? All of these ways happen at the same time. The new dialogue allows that possibility to exist. You're no longer saying, "I'm either going to get federal recognition or fail." You're saying, "No, we'll try, but there are many different ways to be Gabrielino-Tongva together, with or without recognition."

CA: Absolutely right. There's more beyond the very direct cultural connected identity amongst tribes. Why don't we have writers who are regularly writing contemporary pieces and have a column in the *L.A. Times*? Why don't we have contemporary Native American or California Indian dancers who are doing things besides powwow dancing? Why do we not have astronomers or astrologers saying, "Look, I can play your science, but I'm also going to insert my beliefs," who are comfortable in their settings? Back to the cultural confidence—part of it.

Everybody has a longing for community, some personal longing that's going to fill that hole, that gap within not yet fulfilled. Every contribution is valuable. Multifacets make up the jewel. When you're competing for one particular type of acknowledgment, you're sure to have friction. Even the notion of conflict is interesting. Creation stories illustrate conflict, something that changes face, a duality. They constantly challenge our notions of a fixed reality. What is one way can be another. Conflict generates change, but we've been socialized into thinking that it is this other kind of thing. Relaxing and saying, "This is our reality. I see you, acknowledge, and thank you for your contributions." Seems very idealistic, but I think it's a basic way of neutralizing conflict within the community. Just asking, "You're really good at that, do it. I don't have to, don't want to do it." Very interesting time right now, we're going to see a lot of transition. I'll probably be gone, all of us, we won't be here. Change takes a long time through generations of patience.

Absolutely fascinating—just the acknowledgment that we may be a very small little community within the midst of this immense monster called Los Angeles. But this happens time and time again throughout every piece of human history throughout this planet. People struggle. People are always struggling. And people resolve issues. Some people fail, some people succeed. So if you want to know people at the bottom of the food chain, how they survive...Actually sometimes it's not a bad thing to be at the bottom of the food chain rather than the top—it requires a lot of intermixing, reaching out to everybody else

I became tribal chair—probably '87, '88, around the late '80s. Prior to that there was one whole collection of Gabrielino-Tongva working with the Chumash or Sparky Morales. Everybody was working together, having meetings. Prior to that people were still communicating but didn't really start getting active in cultural resources until the seventies. Bea Alva was one of the elders. Bea was interesting, a very intelligent woman. In fact, I was going through some of my notes the other day and I found a bear song that she had sung for me and I wrote down the words.

CJ: Traditional?

CA: She said it was. She had this particular type of knowledge. But she was smart, she wasn't going to get stuck in how people had repeated it. She was a very independent woman. She knew the history of the land, and was involved in a level she could be at the time. Political activism is very different from my generation to my father, Sparky, Bea Alva's generation. I don't think there was an environment possible for them to be movers and shakers—Malcolm X, Martin Luther King—those kind of people. That didn't really occur until the sixties.

BMc: It seems that in the forties, fifties, maybe even thirties, it was more a matter of working within the San Gabriel community rather than the Gabrielino-Tongva community.

CA: With the fiestas there, yeah. They were actually reaching out too, because people would meet at Corpus Christi Day at Pala or people would kind of migrate.* It was more familial—"Okay, this is going on in San Juan Capistrano, or over at Pala." People would talk about the history. However, in San Gabriel you had the mission presence, which changes how identity is constructed, or how it would have remained. They had the plays, the mission festivals. As far as really understanding tradition, tradition in the sense of the past, I think they were just living. They enjoyed their life, loved their life at that time. The stories are all about people. People go through the generations and they're comfortable with the setting.

Everybody is going to have a different experience. What does happen to the next generation beyond the civil rights movements? Obviously, people are going to be thinking differently. Segregation plays into that because this is your world right here. My parents loved where they lived in Orange County and it was beautiful [even though they knew events in the larger world were not always as peaceful or good]. Even my own childhood, being raised in Orange County, having the land to run around on, the beaches and the citrus groves—we were in heaven, but all hell is breaking loose around you. I talked to my mother about this. I said, "I had a fabulous childhood." I don't remember—of course, as a kid you don't focus on those things, it's all generational. But in San Gabriel they have wonderful stories. "Remember they used to wash with the coyote melons? They would wash your clothes during summer and the little stickers stayed in. When you put on the clothes, you knew your auntie had washed with those damn coyote melons." "Remember when Auntie got bit by a wasp and so-and-so peed in the mud and put it on her wasp sting?" These kinds of things—it's so saturated with all kinds of experiences.

CJ: Do you believe in cultural memory? Do you think it's a valid expression? Or does it accommodate your own personal needs based on what you think the past has done to you?

---

* Located in northern San Diego County, the Pala Reservation was established for the Cupeño and Luiseño Indians, and it is home to the Pala Band of Mission Indians, who still celebrate Corpus Christi Day. This traditional Catholic feast and procession commemorate the body of Christ and take place the eighth Sunday after Easter.

CA: "Cultural memory" [as a term used] in the same sense as racial memory and genetic memory—I do believe in it. There's something that stays with us—that makes sense to me. Something inside of me still exists in my head from some other source I can't articulate. When you have dream time about certain things, like me with the *ti'ats*—why did I dream the boat? I never saw one of those boats before. I have no connection—nothing, nothing! Why did I dream these boats? Where did that come from? That's why I believe in cultural memory. With me it's dream time. Things come to me that I never had any connection to, and they made me believe.

CJ: You believe cultural memory is more than simply objects or memories passed down to you from your family?

CA: Yes. I believe the other way, too. That's obvious, but I believe it's something even deeper.

CJ: You believe in knowing things that you don't know?

CA: Right. What did Georgiana Sanchez say about stories? I knew that story before I heard it.

A CONVERSATION with Angie Dorame Behrns

June 13, 2006
Los Angeles, California

The Participant

A FOUNDER, AND THE CURRENT PRESIDENT, OF THE GABRIELINO/TONGVA Springs Foundation, Angie Dorame Behrns is also the editor and publisher of its newsletter, "Kuruvungna." She is a past appointee to the Los Angeles City/County Native American Indian Commission, and an active cultural consultant. She has also appeared in numerous documentary videos and television interview shows, and has had her poetry featured in a documentary on the Santa Monica Mountains.

The Discussion

The conversation with Angie Dorame Behrns, a founder of the Gabrielino/Tongva Springs Foundation, explores the significance of the sacred springs to the native and non-native community, past and present. Her comments express her commitment to the restoration and preservation of the site, her views on its ongoing sacred significance, and issues of respect, as well as her ongoing political activity on behalf of the larger native community. Her stories about growing up underscore the meaning and legacy of family within the Gabrielino-Tongva community. In 2008, the Gabrielino/Tongva Springs Foundation received a grant from the Santa Monica Conservancy to create new wetlands and replant indigenous material around the springs.

Angie Behrns at the sacred springs at University High School, Los Angeles, 2006. TY MILFORD PHOTOGRAPHY

Angie Behrns: My name is Angie Dorame Behrns. Grew up in West Los Angeles.

Claudia Jurmain: Did you sense you were part of a larger community when you were growing up?

AB: Always knew—we'd go to San Gabriel about once a month, on Sunday—just visit family. You knew who was getting married, who died. My dad was traditional, but I didn't understand that. I used to consider him superstitious, but now that I'm older, I understand. He was traditional. We'd go to the old cemetery that was right next to the mission. There were little wooden beat-up crosses, worn, ready to fall apart. I remember he would make us stand there and [he would] make the sign of the cross. I don't know how long. It seemed like forever. He wouldn't say much, "Let's see, I believe this is my great-grandmother, this is my great-great-grandmother." That's all he would say, but every time we'd go to the mission, we'd go through this ritual.

CJ: Was your mother's family also Gabrielino?

AB: No. My mother is Mexican. My mother used to call them "los Indios de San Gabriel." I was three, four, but I remember back in the forties, we'd also go to Rancho de Los Marquez, in Santa Monica Canyon, where the old families would gather.* The

---

* In 1839 Ysidro Reyes (the grandson of Francisco Reyes, who had been given Los Encino) and his friend Francisco Marquez were awarded the Mexican land grant Rancho Boca de Santa Monica. The 6,657-acre tract included contemporary Santa Monica Canyon, Pacific Palisades, and part of Topanga Canyon. The Marquez family continued to live and farm there, but by the 1870s, the oak- and sycamore-filled canyon had become a "resort" for Los Angeles. Family members were buried in the Pascual Marquez Family Cemetery in Santa Monica Canyon from 1848 to 1916. The site is now a registered cultural-historic landmark.

old oak trees no longer are there—I remember climbing them. Everybody took a main dish. It was just a wonderful time and all the old families knew each other. Like in San Gabriel, when they gathered.

CJ: Do you remember people coming from long distances? The San Gabriel community is a core, but what about people who lived in Orange County, or other places?

AB: All I remember is that we did. I've always been into the history of the Indians. I was proud of my heritage. I don't know why. My mother would tell me a little bit about my dad's family, about my grandmother, and I was just proud. When I was in the third and fourth grade and we were taught California history, I wanted to raise my hand so bad and tell that teacher, "I'm one of those people that you're teaching us about." [They] never told us, "Don't ever say you're an Indian," but we kind of felt it. We knew. We just felt it inside. So you didn't say that, but in third grade, I would get goose bumps when they would teach all of this.

But my dad always told us who we were. There was no question, we knew we were Indians. My grandmother Clara was Gabrielino, she was half. I always knew I was a Gabrielino. My dad was in his heart—San Gabriel was very important to him. He didn't sweat there, but he'd sweat in the bathroom, and he'd say, "I've got to get all this poison—all this bad stuff out of me."*

We'd go to Topanga.** That was our Disneyland when we were growing up. I don't know why he'd take us there. He would take us up to the mountains—you know kids, we're all over the place. We'd find artifacts. One time we came across a pestle. He went bananas and made us take it back where we found it. We had to dig a hole and rebury it. He says, "You never, never take that stuff. Never. If you take that, you're going to get sick. You cannot do that." Later on, I'd go to museums and start crying. I became almost anti-white, anti-Caucasian. Here I wasn't allowed to keep it, and they have all the artifacts and everything my dad said we couldn't have.

CJ: Did he ever talk about why this would make you sick, or what the meaning of "sacred" was?

AB: I came to the conclusion that maybe these people died of a contagious disease so their clothing, their instruments, what they had, was probably buried with them, or broken, because they knew this was contagious. Remember, they didn't have doctors back then. They thought, probably, a curse was put on you, but it wasn't—it was some contagious disease. She [Grandmother Clara] died of

---

* In Native American tradition, ceremonial sweat lodges (saunas) are used to cleanse, purify, and heal.

** Topanga Canyon is in the Santa Monica Mountains, in western Los Angeles County.

tuberculosis. A stagecoach left San Bernardino every day to Arizona. They would take her to Arizona and that's where she met my grandfather. She died when my dad was seven, but this is a sad history. She was raped right before she died. My dad was very prejudiced against white people—very, very. It goes both ways, believe you me.

CJ: Who in the community, other than your father, did you look to, to find information about your family?

AB: When Chacho [Maclovio Grijalva, great-uncle] got older, I called him up. I don't know why. I said "Tío, Tío," because we'd mix Spanish [and English], "I want to find out—were we Gabrielino, or were we Serrano, or what?" [Aunt] Luisa registered us Diegueño.* "I was a little boy and I don't remember much," he says. "As far as I know, we've always lived in San Gabriel. We've always been Gabrielino."

I'm very proud—I don't have to hide anymore. I don't have to be a closet Indian. When I was little, my dad's uncle, my great-uncle, lived right here in Culver City. They talk very little. I would think, "What's wrong with them?" I'd get frustrated.

CJ: Does being Gabrielino mean something different than being Cahuilla or another group of native people?

AB: No, it doesn't make me any different. I consider them cousins. My sister, for instance, her first husband is Morongo. Her daughter is probably full-blooded Indian. Her sister-in-law was married to a Gabrielino. We seem to have the same values. We gravitate to each other.

CJ: Do you have any thoughts about the mission in relation to the community?

AB: I feel you have to forgive and go on. My husband is German. My dad wasn't too happy when I married him. He didn't like my husband. He is white, he is Anglo, European. He didn't voice it, but he showed it. I don't know if it was just the values of my mother we were taught, because I'll be honest, my dad was an alcoholic. I didn't want my life like that, I wanted to better myself. But I was taught, "He's your father, and no matter what, you respect him. He tells you something, you do it." My dad always taught us, "Don't lie, don't steal, pay your bills on time, and work hard. You've got to prove to these people that you can do something with your life." He was always trying to prove himself.

CJ: Was there a community of Gabrielinos here?

AB: No. The Lassos lived way north of Wilshire, but we knew each other. We all

---

* The traditional lands of the Diegueño, or Kumeyaay, people are in San Diego County and northern Baja. The Spanish named the people "Diegueño" because they lived near the San Diego River.

went to the same high school, but you didn't come out and say, "I'm an Indian," or "I'm Gabrielino."

CJ: But your dad didn't grow up here.

AB: No, he grew up in Arizona. His mother went there because she had tuber-culosis. I don't remember what year, but he was thirteen years old. He drove his grandmother back to San Gabriel. My great-uncle lived right here in Culver City.

They called my sister "Chinoko." They threw out the word at the tribal coun-cil, and you know what it means in our language? "I don't feel so good." My sister was always complaining. Little things, you find out. I thought they made up this name just to call her that. My sister was at the tribal council. We looked at each other and started laughing.

CJ: When you went to those meetings at San Gabriel, who did you think were the leaders? Were you aware of any women leaders?

AB: No, my brother is the one that said, "You should get involved with the tribe in San Gabriel. They have meetings. You should go." I knew about Sparky [Morales]. I remember going there. Sparky was a very likeable person. My brother has pictures at the sacred springs [at University High School in Los Angeles]. My dad and Sparky would sit and they were laughing. I think they were talking about old times—old men in their eighties and nineties, close to nineties.

CJ: Federal recognition has been a consistent quest for the tribe for a long time, still is. What are your feelings?

AB: When I started to attend the tribal council meetings—the San Gabriel meetings—I started crying, because I thought, "God, I never fit in." My friends were Jewish, most of them in school, or Japanese. I didn't really relate to the Hispanic for some reason. When I went to San Gabriel, they knew who I was. I didn't remember them. I felt like, "I've found where I belong." Even now it just breaks me up because they knew me, knew my father. They knew who I was, and I didn't know who they were. Sparky came up and hugged me. I was in my fifties. I had never had people do this before.

CJ: What would recognition mean to you? Why is it important?

AB: It's important to me—we have opened up our arms to people from all over the world. We're still welcoming them. We're the original people. We give these people education. We give them medical. I want to help people, but it hurts. I've had to work, we've had to work, fight, and struggle for education. My family—we're a proud family. We've never been on welfare. We've never asked the gov-ernment for any help. My dad was an Indian—he was deathly afraid of authority so he wanted nothing [from the government]. In the thirties, my mother took in three girls that were orphans. He went to the school, because he couldn't feed us all, and said, "Can I do the lawn? In exchange can you feed my children and three girls I've taken in?" The school agreed. That was in grammar school. But my dad would never, ever ask the government [for help], and there were eight of us, eight children plus those three girls he took in.

CJ: We've heard this from others—"We know who we are. We keep it silent." Did you keep it silent, except for going to San Gabriel and your family, until you were in your fifties?

AB: I kept it silent until I got involved in the nineties with trying to save the springs. Then I realized being an Indian might not be so bad. We might get what we want. That's when I started changing, was a little militant. I think all Indians go through that stage—I mean, I was bad. It's a good thing I had children, because they kept me in line—I would have done very radical things. [My daughter was in the Indian program at Venice High School.]

CJ: What is the significance of the springs to you, or to anyone?

AB: I was raised in a farmhouse on Federal and Olympic. We're not even sure if that is [the village of] Kuruvangna. We know Kuruvangna is around someplace [by the springs]. The significance is—look at this area, everything has been destroyed—our cemeteries, Ballona wetlands.* My dad took us to Topanga. We went to the Ballona wetlands before it was paved. He took us there for reasons. We would get sand and bring it home—he had a nursery—and we'd wash the salt water out of it. Maybe we'd go to Topanga and get the leaves from the oak, acorn trees and make mulch.

CJ: What do you call the springs?

AB: I just say "the sacred springs."

CJ: Is "sacred" a word you've given the springs, or has the word also come down through time?

AB: To the Tongva from this area, they're sacred because they're life. You look at this area, everything has been destroyed. Here these beautiful springs bubble up.

---

* Both Ballona Wetlands and the ancestral Tongva village of Saa'angna have been affected by the 1,087-acre residential, commercial, and open space Playa Vista development located in the Westside of Los Angeles about one mile from the ocean. During the Phase I residential development, human burials were uncovered and removed, examined, and packaged by contract archaeologists despite native community protest. In 2004 the city of Santa Monica, the Ballona Wetlands Trust, the Ballona Ecosystem Education Project, the Surfrider Foundation, and the Gabrieleno Tongva Tribal Council of San Gabriel filed suit to block the Phase II commercial development of the project. The California Second District Court of Appeals in Los Angeles overturned all city approvals for the Phase II commercial development in 2007. In March 2009, subsequent discussions between the developer and the designated "most likely descendant" of the Tongva people resulted in the reburial of over 1,320 bundled ancestral remains in Playa Vista, in the village area known as Guahasna.

Angie Behrns at the sacred springs at University High School, Los Angeles, 2006. Ty Milford Photography

There wouldn't be plants, there wouldn't be animals, there wouldn't be you and I without water. Life. And because I was born near the area. I don't think it's confirmed, but the village of Kuruvangna is near the site at University High School. It is an archeological and historical site. We're now trying to get it on the National Historical Register. There are several springs on this site. I don't know how big the school is, but the springs site is about two acres. There's a little spring, and it constantly bubbles up. It produces twenty-two thousand gallons of water a day. When they built the school, they made a little stream. It goes into a pond, then into the drain, and into the Santa Monica Bay. On this area, and this school site, there is also a waterfall. There are many other springs that have been turned into manholes. If you see this area, you will see it shouldn't even belong to LAUSD [Los Angeles Unified School District]. This area should be protected.

We lease it—that alone was a miracle—for a dollar a year, the two-acre site to be used for educational purposes. But we've had memorials, had weddings here. What happened was I went to a University High School reunion picnic. My whole family went to University High School. At that time my husband was [a producer] on *L.A. Law*. This is the most beautiful campus in L.A. Unified. I talked him into going. I said, "Let's walk down, I'm going to show you this beautiful area." When I walked down—have you ever had that sick feeling in your gut? I couldn't believe it. I was so upset. I called my brother: "Have you been to Uni?" He says, "I have, but that's nothing. There aren't going to be any more springs. There are community people getting involved to fight the development." I said, "That's a historical site. They can't do that." He says, "Get involved." I started going to the meetings with the community—Brentwood homeowners. There were heroin addicts living in there. I was there when my brother had them escorted out. We found all the paraphernalia, it was disheartening. That was in the nineties, beginning of '91, I think. I got involved. Then I went to the tribe. I said, "We need your support." "We'll support you." I don't think Indians were that vocal—just barely.

CJ: In some ways it's a new sacred place.

AB: No, it's not new. That was an Indian village for many, many years. You have to remember—this is where I get militant—we didn't give our land away. We didn't sell it. Remember that. In 19—what is it—seventies—we got $664, our share for the California Judgment Fund. That's a joke. But I was smart, I bought this house with that money. But I don't like that when you say that [the springs are] new.

CJ: It is a new way of interpreting the meaning of sacred. You have taken a piece of land that was yours, and restored it to its natural, pristine setting with some change, and told people to use it to suit your life in new ways.

AB: Right. We've not only told Indians, we've told—

CJ: Everybody. What is the meaning of sacred? It changes as people change through time because it has to.

AB: It's sacred because of the water. It's life.

Bill McCawley: Is it a thermal spring or just a spring?

AB: No, it's a cold spring. Rancho Los Encinos is a thermal, but they have covered theirs. It's another village site, but it's not sacred in the form of "We're going to stand there and pray over it, or pray to it."* You have to remember we are Christian Indians. I think that we're there to share with everybody. But it's sacred in a sense that it hasn't been destroyed, hasn't been built over.

Everything in L.A. has been built over. Everything. This is one of the few places—thank God for LAUSD, that's one good thing they did. But our lease is only for twenty years. It's going to be up in four years. They may tell us to leave.

---

* Los Encinos was once the thriving Tongva village of Siutcanga. Its natural springs provided year-round water, attracting many to the freshwater and thermal pools. Located in the San Fernando Valley, the village disappeared when San Fernando Mission was completed, in 1797. To obtain their mission site, the priests exchanged 4,460 acres of land with property then ranched by Francisco Reyes, who used the same name, Rancho Los Encinos, for his new property. He was later accused of mistreating his Indian workers at his rancho, and in 1845, Governor Pío Pico granted Los Encinos to Tiburcio Lopez and three Indians who never gained title. In 1851, Vicente de la Osa, the next owner, sold the property to the first American landowners in the San Fernando Valley. In 1949, the valley, the surviving core area, the de la Osa adobe (1850), Garnier house (1871), blacksmith shop, natural spring, and pond became Los Encinos State Historic Park.

We haven't really restored it. We have cleaned it up because the school used to dump everything there. I've taken out pigs, chickens, rabbits.

CJ: The springs seem to be a place where people find "home," much as you did when you were in your fifties and first went to the San Gabriel meetings.

AB: Right, two months ago the Latinos from Santa Monica had a sacred run. They called me, "Can we—the springs have been chosen as one of the places we want to stop at." I said, "No problem." They said, "Can you get somebody to do a blessing? This is the first time we've done it. There's not going to be that many of us." Well, lo and behold, it was a bigger crowd, but we got somebody from our church, an ex-Marine, and he did a prayer, a regular prayer.

We don't have to prove that we're Indian. I don't have to prove I'm an Indian anymore, prove traditional ways. Yes, I respect it. I respect certain aspects, but I resent it when Anglos call me up and ask, "Can you do a blessing?" They don't want a blessing, they want a show. They want an Indian to get up there and burn the sage. I resent that so much, I can't tell you.

So this Marine from our church was Hispanic, and I'm glad, because the runners were all Latinos. There were Indians, too, and it was beautiful. We gathered around the spring and Mark did a prayer. I realized I don't have to have somebody burn sage. I don't have to show them who I am. I know who I am. I know I'm a Tongva. I know my children are. I'm tired of putting on little shows for everybody. I won't do it. Believe you me, I get plenty of calls and I'll question them. I'll say, "What do you want?" They just want somebody up there dressed like an Indian.

CJ: What would you like people to know about the community today, the people who are Tongva today? You do educational programs—what is your message?

AB: Respect. Whether you are Chinese, African American, Japanese, Iranian, Arab, Muslim, I don't know what you are—love one another, respect one another. That's a message I give to the kids. Those kids know that I care, love them. It's not just a show and I do talk about my culture. But 'respect'—that's one word I always throw out to them. I'll ask, "Do you know what 'respect' means?" And they listen. You have to start from a very young age, by the time they're eighteen, nineteen, it's too late. They're beating each other up. You've got to really teach them when they're little. Respect is a big, big, big word for us—whether you're Christian, Jewish—doesn't matter.

BMc: Do we know what was going on at the springs before they became school district property?

AB: First, it was part of the rancho [San Vicente y Santa Monica]. It belonged to the Sepúlvedas, and then, I understand [a sheep ranch].[*] There was a drought [in the 1860s] and they brought them on the hill, because there are springs, to graze. Then the school was built in 1925.

BMc: Do we know how many springs? You said some are covered.

AB: I know the lower springs and then [another] one popped up. About two years ago, because it's built on a fault, they had core sampling. They went down—it wasn't two feet—and they hit water. But there's the lower springs, and an upper springs with the waterfall. But then Lolly [Dolores Lassos] told me springs will pop up sometimes and then go away.

CJ: Are your children involved?

AB: My daughter is vice president of the springs. Sometimes I think, "What am I doing here?" In fact, I didn't want to be president of the foundation anymore. It's like running a small business. In four years we have to renegotiate. They might just say, "You're out of here," because we've done so much. I make sure that I know all our politicians [involved]. A lady [Loretta Ditlow] was very instrumental, really encouraged me, she's been my teacher. Hopefully my children will continue. That's what I would like to leave to my children, because everything has been lost.

CJ: When you meet people who say they are Tongva, and they are not from the San Gabriel community, do you accept them?

AB: Well, I accept them as Tongva, but I don't understand why they don't get involved—like they don't support the springs. It's only when somebody is going to hand them something—"Look, we have something for you." That's so degrading, to me. Hey, get in there and do something. Get in there and help preserve our history. I mean, there's one God, he loves us all—we're one family, but we still have traditions. Let's keep our tradition, let's keep our families together. But they don't get out there and work. Why don't you come out to the springs, come and help us maintain the area? Never.

But in a way, yes, I accept them. They're Tongva. I know they're Tongva, but they're not really part of the community, and they don't participate. I don't go to all the tribal council meetings, but if Anthony was to call me and say, "Angie, I can't go to this meeting," or "I can't go to UCLA, can you?" I'm there like that.

---

[*] Francisco Xavier Sepúlveda, founder of the leading southern California family, was a soldier from Mexico who was buried at Mission San Gabriel in 1742. His son Francisco established the Los Angeles branch of the family and was the acting alcalde (judicial and administrative leader) of Los Angeles in 1815. In 1839, Governor Juan Bautista Alvarado granted him approximately thirty-three thousand acres, named Rancho San Vicente y Santa Monica. The land was sold in 1872 to Colonel Robert S. Baker and his wife, Arcadia Bandini Stearns (the widow of Abel Stearns, who had once owned Rancho Los Alamitos, which contained Povuu'ngna). They thought it would make a good sheep ranch, but sold part of the property in 1874. During the early 1860s southern California suffered a series of natural disasters, such as grasshopper plagues, floods, and an extended drought that ruined many ranchers already in an economic recession. Likely the area around the sacred springs provided better grazing and some relief from the natural catastrophes of the decade.

CJ: So to be Tongva, you believe in the larger obligation of family and that is part of your definition of being Tongva?

AB: Of being a true Tongva.

BMc: You prefer the name "Tongva" to "Gabrielino"?

AB: The only thing that bothers me is, if I teach third graders, fourth graders "Tongva," they go to the library and there is no Tongva. So I have to use the name "Gabrielino."

CJ: Do you recognize everything you are? You are Gabrielino, but you are also Hispanic, and other things. Do you celebrate those heritages also?

AB: We never have at home—did we ever celebrate Cinco de Mayo? We just didn't. I think because of my dad. He grew up traditional. His mother was traditional. I took my daughter to the mission. As we go out the side door, I said [to the friar], "Correct me if I'm wrong, I'm either going senile—but that was a cemetery and Indians were buried there. We'd go and stand there at this grave site. That was my dad's great-grandmother." He says, "Oh, no, we dug up all the bones—you want to go see the monument? We put them in one. We don't know who they were." Ordinarily I have a big mouth, real sarcastic, but I couldn't even talk. He says, "You want to go see where we built the monument, where we put them all?" I didn't want to see it, because I knew if I went, I would say something that I shouldn't. I was very upset, very, very upset. They dug up all the Indians in the old cemetery and took the remains and put them in one burial site—I didn't see it.

BMc: This is at San Gabriel?

AB: San Gabriel.

BMc: Was your mother along on those trips? Did she stay home?

AB: My mother was old-school. She would tell my dad constantly, "Oh, Ricardo, you're so superstitious, change your ways." He'd do just a lot of little things. I don't know if it was Indian things or if it seems like it was—don't wear a red shirt or you'll get shot.

My dad was a hard worker, but my mother was the business head—third grade education because she came here from Mexico during the Mexican revolution. She was a beautiful woman. She always taught us, "Respect your dad," but she's the one that put a stop to going to San Gabriel.

My dad had very low self-esteem. There was reason for it. He went through a lot. For instance, his mother died when he was [seven]. Right before she died she was raped by three Caucasian boys—German. He knew who they were. My grandfather picks my father up. My grandfather is part Apache and Mexican.

His mother was Indian and father was Mexican. He's going to establish a ranch, start a new life. He buys some cows. He has horses, chickens. He couldn't build a house—so it's a tent. My grandfather goes to get provisions—two horses and the flatbed—left my dad and my uncle there alone. Some Apaches come riding hard, and the horses are sweating. They look around, water them down, and they leave. Twenty minutes later the U.S. Cavalry comes. My uncle was scared, but my dad was out in the middle. They asked him where the Indians went, and [he] tells them. He could tell they were riding hard, apparently they were chasing the Apaches. They water their horses—they kill every cow, every chicken, burn down their house—it's canvas—left the kids there, hot sun in Arizona. My grandfather comes back, he just starts crying. Puts them in the flatbed and they left. I think they went to Tucson. I don't know. My dad was afraid of authority, and you wonder why? When he was ten years old, he ran away, jumped the train. Cowboys were going to throw him off—hobos jumping the train. They're cowboys, they wear guns back then. It was a boxcar, somebody was sleeping in the corner all covered up. He didn't know who this guy was. There were three guys, Anglo. They picked up my dad. They said, "You blankity blank." They called him a Mexican and were going to throw him off. This big guy stands up and he's an African American black man. "Big," my dad said, he had big arms. The man says, "Before you throw him off you throw me off." My dad says, "You never saw African Americans in that part—I don't know what this guy was doing there." The guys put my dad down, walked away, just went to their little corner, sat there, and my dad went and sat next to this man.

CJ: Your mother told his story.

AB: She wrote a book, but it was not correct. She loved my dad's history. When she came [here], she adopted this country. When we were little, we might have been Indians, but we went to the Veterans Cemetery in Los Angeles (Westside) for Memorial Day. The big line of us, we'd stand there and have to salute. This was her country. So we were raised—you respect authority. When I got older, I went through that militant stage. I said, "Oh, mother, respect—they're a bunch of crooks."

CJ: Are you optimistic about what is happening now?

AB: Yes, I think things are going to happen, but I don't think they happen easy. Everything is hard obstacles.

BMc: Do you think that the tribe will achieve recognition at some point?

AB: I don't know. Why can't we work together? But the Tongva—until they lose that jealous spirit, they're not going to accomplish anything. They have to let that go. I don't know if that was brought on with the Europeans—I don't know.

CJ: What would federal recognition do for you?

AB: Education. Maybe we could get grants and start educating, start teaching our children their language. My daughter—I took her to the tribal council meeting in San Gabriel. She says, "Mom, this is so sad. We were the richest tribe in California and this [the building where the council meetings take place] is all we have?" I said, "We don't even have it. They lease it. They rent it." That is pathetic. That word I told you before—respect—it's about time. It's overdue. It's time [for the federal government to] show us a little respect. Help us get educated, help us get ahead. It's sad. We prospered because we were blessed, and focused. Thank God my mother raised us the way she did.

CJ: There are many important places, but certain ones resonate in people's life—Povuu'ngna for example. Even though it's a sacred place, people often are more familiar with its political history. Are the springs more personal?

AB: I really don't know how [people] feel [about it]. I know we had one Indian—would come and get water from the springs. I used to call him Indian Joe because he always wore that red hat, a real character. He would always come and get water because he wanted that water.

BMc: What does or can the springs mean to the non-Indian community?

AB: Education again. You'll see it's environmental because of the water, the animals. It's historical, it's Hispanic history. Besides, let's face it, all these rancheros were from Mexico. They were from Sonora, they weren't from Spain. Half of these rancheros were married to Indians from way back when Queen Isabella gave permission for the soldiers to marry the Indians. But they always say Spanish, Spanish, Spanish, and I don't like that.

A lot of the Anglo community, when we went in there [said], "Oh, the Indians want to take over." It wasn't about taking over, never has been. That's why we had teachers on our foundation. It's not a big foundation, very little. It's amazing what we've accomplished. We've joined the Brentwood Chamber of Commerce. We just marched in the Memorial Day parade. Not all of us can do this, so the ones that show up, show up. Money is power. My idea is, "They [the chamber] asked us to [march] in their centennial parade—we have to do that because we're going to be visible to the community of Brentwood. And they're the ones that have the big bucks, right?"

CJ: Did you know one of your roles would be to become a politician?

AB: It takes that. When I went to the Clinton inaugural ball when I was a

[Los Angeles City/County Native American Indian] Commissioner, I took my husband.* I said, "You're white, so I'm going to introduce you as my publicist. Take your camera and take pictures, just don't argue with me. You're my publicist, that's all. Don't ask questions." So we went to lobby for some [federal program] money which funded the American Indian Clinic alcohol and drug program, which had been diverted, for some reason, to a federally recognized casino tribe up north. The tribe called us and said, "We don't need this money. You need it in downtown L.A." So we decided to lobby Washington and at that same time we'd go to the Clinton inaugural ball—all we Indians. I've got to get to know these Indian attorneys. I may need them some day. [As a result of the lobbying effort, the federal funding for the American Indian Clinic was restored.]

The inaugural ball—this was so interesting. They had drummers, [but Indians] don't dance like the Anglos do to the fifties music. The Indians are drumming around. My husband comes out, he's looking for me, and I said, "I've got to network with these people. I've got to let them know who I am, who the [Gabrielino/Tongva Springs] Foundation is." I said, "I'll be there in a minute." Because, you know, Indians in Washington have their own office buildings.

I'm thinking, "They have to know who the Gabrielinos are," because I had the Gabrielino/Tongva Springs Foundation, but it's "Gabrielino/Tongva, they don't even know who we are. I've got to pass information out." Anyway, my husband comes out, so I said, "Well, I better go in—poor thing, he's here, he's the only white guy here, blonde hair," and he was much taller than everybody. So I stand at one of the entrances and all I could see was this blonde head going—he was dancing with the Indians. He just made himself at home. I was very happy he did that, because when you don't feel part of it, you want to leave. He's German and Scotch ancestry, but he's supported me all the way, and I'm really thankful for that.

CJ: There are native people who question the authenticity of the Gabrielino-Tongva as much as some non-native people. How do you feel about that?

AB: I went through that as a commissioner. I know the politics. When I was a commissioner, the commission was very active, very different than it is now—very strong. That's the Los Angeles City/County Native American Commission. They support other native groups. But you have to understand our history. There were very few of us left. Then in the fifties, what does the government do? Tells Indians to come to L.A. for jobs. One mother told me, she was from Colorado, "The United States Government told us to come out here and get jobs because

---

* Created through the effort of the Los Angeles American Indian community and the Los Angeles city and county governments in 1976, the Los Angeles City/County Native American Indian Commission works with federal, state, and local agencies to promote programs and services needed by the urban Indian community. An advocate for legislation and policy benefiting the urban Indian community in mainstream economic and social arenas, the commission advises the board of supervisors, the mayor, and the city council. Members of the Los Angeles City/County Native American Indian Commission are appointed by the board of supervisors and the city of Los Angeles (mayor), and elected from the Los Angeles Indian community. The commission is meant to reflect the diversity of Indians living in Los Angeles city and county.

they're expecting us to make a mass exodus out of our tribes' [land]. The old people are going to stay and die off, and then the United States government is going to go in and take over our land. That's what they want to see." She says, "Angie, you cannot believe. They go out there and preach to us and tell us to leave. They give us information. They tell us where to go, but we've caught on. I go back every year and I register [as a member of my reservation]. And my kids are going to go back every year. We might be here, we might be working here, we might live here, but we're going to go back and we're going to register because we're wise."* Now, whether that's true or not...But you know what? I wouldn't doubt it.

And so those Indians [who came from outside the region and the state] outnumbered us. Those policies made by the Los Angeles Native American Commission were all made by non-natives from Los Angeles. I believe I might have been the first commissioner that was Gabrielino-Tongva. Believe you me, I took my job serious. I was elected—the tribal members all voted for me. We have different areas where we vote. Nobody on that commission was from California. Later on, there were some from San Diego. But they didn't really care about us. They were more or less focusing on their issues. Maybe it's a little different now because we've become more vocal and stronger.

When I became a commissioner, I had one commissioner—very powerful, had been a commissioner for many years—she didn't ask me at that meeting, but when we got down [to the parking lot], she says, "I want to see your card, I want to see your blood quantum."** I was so insulted. I never do that to the Indian. If somebody tells me they're Indian, I'll take their word for it. I'll just ask, "Well, do you have a roll number?" Half of the time they say, "Oh, no, what is that?" So then I kind of know maybe they're one-thousandth of an Indian or something. But I still respect them because at least they say they are Indian, have Indian blood. The Gabrielinos—when Wallace Cleaves was involved, he gave everybody a card with their picture on it.† It was a tribal card. I don't even know if they [still] exist, but I keep everything. I kept that card, but that day I didn't have it with me. And she didn't believe I was an Indian. This was in the nineties, I believe.

CJ: Did you have an agenda of issues you wanted to address on behalf of the Gabrielino-Tongva?

---

* During the 1950s and 1960s, federal policy sought to terminate government responsibility for Native Americans, moving Indians into "mainstream society" by breaking up tribal reservations through individual allotments and payments, ending federal services, and retraining people for outside employment. The government established nineteen urban centers around the country, relocating 160,000 to 180,000 Native Americans from reservations to cities. By 1995, the Native American population of Los Angeles was approximately 100,000, the largest urban Indian population in the United States.

** Tribal cards ("proof of identity") and the criteria for tribal enrollment are determined by individual tribes, not the federal government, although the government establishes standards for Indian identity pertaining to federal legislation, usually 25 percent. However, each tribe has the right to set its own standards for enrollment. According to one expert, about two-thirds of all federally recognized tribes specify a minimum blood quantum in their tribal enrollment criteria, often 25 percent. But other federally recognized tribes require no minimum blood quantum. Instead, enrollees must be direct descendants of another tribal member. Because of their unique history and early urban culture, the ancestry of the Gabrielino-Tongva people is based on the latter criterion and adheres to standards for federal recognition for documentation of ancestry.

† Wallace Cleaves, now a lecturer at the University of California, Riverside, University Writing Program Department, wrote an early set of bylaws for the Gabrielino-Tongva Band of Mission Indians at San Gabriel which was later rewritten under an ANA (Aid to Native Americans) grant with UCLA.

AB: Yes. The reason why I became a commissioner, I wanted to bring recognition to our tribe. So I was very serious. I was on the Self-Governance Board.* I felt it was a conflict of interest, but that's beside the point. I asked questions. Recently I said, "I'd like to serve as a commissioner again, are there any openings?" "Oh, they're all taken, Angie." I ask too many questions. I don't want to write a letter just to write a letter. I want to know why, when, what, where? I know a lot of people, so I can get appointed easy. But I thought, "If I'm not wanted, forget it. I am just going to go in there and stir up a lot of worms." I get more done here.

---

*   The Self-Governance Board of the Los Angeles City County Native American Indian Commission funds American Indian service agencies to provide emergency services to eligible American Indian families and individuals.

A CONVERSATION with Virginia Carmelo

August 24, 2006
Rancho Los Alamitos, California

The Participant

VIRGINIA CARMELO RECEIVED HER DEGREE IN ETHNIC STUDIES FROM California State University, Fullerton. The mother of six, she is the director of Xipe Totec, a traditional Aztec dance group including members of her own family of dancers and musicians. In addition, she works with other Gabrielino-Tongva, and with linguists from UCLA to reclaim the native language. An active cultural educator, performance artist, and community leader, she is the tribal chair of the Gabrielino/Tongva Tribal Council of the Gabrielino/Tongva Nation, one of the organized groups of the Gabrielino-Tongva people today.

The Discussion

In her role as the elected chair of the Gabrielino/Tongva Tribal Council, Virginia Carmelo discusses the purpose of the recently formed organization. She comments on current Tribal Council issues related to federal recognition and casinos, as well as the effort to include, bring together, and culturally assist all those who know, or wish to find out more about their Gabrielino-Tongva heritage. She speaks to her childhood family identity as "Mission Indians," her emerging native identity as a student of Ethnic Studies during the 1960s and 1970s, her evolution as a traditional Aztec dancer whose creative visual interpretations express native cultural memory and language, and her calling as a community leader. Circumstances within the Gabrielino/Tongva Nation have changed since the original 2006 conversation. The bracketed statements reflect most recent circumstances based on comments made by Virginia Carmelo in July 2008.

Claudia Jurmain: When did you find out you were Tongva, and do you say Tongva or do you say Gabrielino?

Virginia Carmelo: I say both. Gabrielino, I usually try to explain that's our Spanish name from the mission era, and then the Tongva or Tongvet. Because now I'm working on the language, we know that it's probably Tongvet. We just say that "Tongva" would be the English pronunciation and "Tongvet" would be the pronunciation from our language.

CJ: They often added "vet" or "vit" to the end of the village names, which means "I am from"—that's what you're referring to?

VC: Correct. I always knew since my first memories that I was Mission Indian. I just remember—my parents, my grandparents—on some of my family and my dad's side, they would talk about being Indian, or being Mission. Sometimes joking, they just refer to each other as Indians. But I really remember the name came up, "Mission Indians," so always my earliest memories are saying, "I'm a Mission Indian."

I grew up in Fullerton, California. The elementary school I went to was segregated, so there were other Indians from other Indian groups. Sometimes some of the children would say, "I'm Indian, too," and that was it. That was the length of our conversation. In those years it was de facto segregation. People could only buy a house in certain areas, and in the area I lived, there was only one elementary school. Everybody was brown. There were a few blacks, a couple Asians, and here and there, one or two whites.

CJ: Did the other kids know their background?

VC: Some of them did. Some would just say, "We're Indians from here." "We're Indians from Mexico." That was the difference. But I remember one young boy said, "We're Indians from the desert," and that was it. Some children did say they had relatives on reservations, and we did, too, in Soboba.* We went quite often to Soboba because my grandfather was raised there and his cousins were living there. Our family—my uncle and their family, all my cousins—were there quite a bit. We would go visit the family and stay overnight.

Bill McCawley: When your family said "mission," were they talking about any mission in particular—San Gabriel, Capistrano? Do they have stories or memories along those lines?

VC: I remember them saying that Uncle Dan was married to a Mission Indian from San Juan Mission, but at that time I had no idea what he meant.

---

* Located at the foothills of the San Jacinto Mountains in Riverside County, Soboba was established in 1883, one of six federally recognized Luiseño-speaking reservations in southern California. Soboba has also been home to the Cahuilla, but today most residents are Luiseño.

CJ: Did your family visit other people, for example, at the San Gabriel Mission community, or become part of that community, when you were growing up?

VC: No. My contact with the mission [was] with our family and that was in Soboba. When I was younger, my grandmother would take us to other reservations. I went to Pala, but I don't remember what for.* We would visit families in Santa Ana, but I don't remember who they were, what their Indian background was—I was thirteen or fourteen—until the time I kind of [said], "I don't want to go with you guys."

CJ: When you say family—?

VC: I'm talking aunts, uncles. My father's brothers, definitely.

CJ: Lived in Soboba?

VC: No. It was my grandfather. None of us lived in San Gabriel. We weren't in San Gabriel. But my father and my grandfather still had cousins, probably first or second cousins, third cousins by that time, living at Soboba. So everybody, the elder people, we called them aunties, and the other people were just our cousins. Now, as an adult, I know that

Virginia Carmelo demonstrates a dance movement in the Jacaranda Walk at Rancho Los Alamitos, the kitchen midden of Povuu'ngna, 2006.
TY MILFORD PHOTOGRAPHY

they were probably second and third cousins, I believe. I'm not too sure, but my grandfather was raised at Soboba because his mother was the San Gabriel Indian. She was in the Riverside area when she married—her husband was Apache—they moved onto the reservation. Then his—the Apache grandfather—first cousin married a Soboba woman. That's how those two families were there.

I remember asking one time, maybe when I was twelve, what kind of Indians we are, and hearing again, "We're the California Mission Indians. We're Mission Indians." That was it. I didn't ask again until I was eighteen or nineteen, then asked my dad again, "What kind of Indians are we?" He said, "I think we are San Gabriel." And you know, that was it. That was the length of the conversation.

---

* Located in northern San Diego County, the 12,273-acre Pala Reservation was established for the Cupeño and Luiseño people, who now are known as The Pala Band of Mission Indians.

That's when I started asking questions of my grandmother, who knew a little bit more. She did say, "Yes, we were San Gabriel, and we were Apache." She showed me some of the things that belonged to my grandmother, including a basket. She just gave a little bit more information. She wasn't the San Gabriel Mission Indian, but she did know because I could talk to her more. So, that's my first concrete [identity]—"Oh, San Gabriel Mission Indian," then going back, saying, "Okay, there were different people in different areas. We were all Mission Indians."

BMc: Was your father not really interested in talking about this?

VC: They were not interested. When they referred to themselves, it was just "Indian." They never classified themselves. I don't think there was pride. I think it was a matter-of-fact thing—that's who we are—[but] not a sense of something to be ashamed of. In terms of the time, of that era, it seemed to me that it was not of great importance. But I was the one asking the questions, so it was important to me.

We're talking early sixties, and I was involved in some of the social movements of the time. In '68 I was eighteen. That's about the time when I started getting involved, about the time I really remember my father saying, "I think we're San Gabriel." He never used "Tongva." Actually, my grandmother, who was not Tongva, signed the 1968 judgment.* She was the one gathering the information from my grandfather. She signed up all of us cousins. We just knew Grandma was doing it. She was the one taking the application and writing down the information. My great-grandmother did do it [enrollment] in '28. We have obtained copies of her application. It's interesting to me, had it been left up to grandfather, even though he was literate, he probably would not have done it, but she took the initiative. My grandmother was born in Chihuahua. She was a Tarahumara Indian, raised in Pasadena and El Modena, and the city of Orange, where she met my grandfather. A lot of the information I got through her. I would just ask questions, and she seemed to know the answer.

BMc: In the 1928 enrollment form, was your family just identified as Mission Indians? Have you looked at the forms?

VC: I looked at the forms. She identified herself as "San Gabriel." She identified both her parents being born at San Gabriel Mission. The thing that's impressive to me is that there's a question on there that says, "What lands do you claim as your traditional land?" [She answered], "All the city of Los Angeles," which at that time was a lot bigger than it is now. I thought, "Okay, this woman knew something." She

---

* The 1927 California Indians Jurisdictional Act authorized the state attorney general to sue the United States government on behalf of Indians over the negotiated, nonratified treaties of 1851 and 1852. To submit a claim, California Indians had to document their genealogy and tribal affiliation, and submit an enrollment application to the federal government. In 1950 each enrolled California Indian received $150 for their claim. However, by then additional claims had already been filed in 1946 over lands not covered in the earlier award. The 1972 out-of-court settlement resulted in an award of $668.51 for about seventy thousand California Indians who enrolled. For more information, refer to the essay "Continuity within Change: Identity and Culture."

understood, yes, yes, she did. So, yeah, she identified herself with the San Gabriel Mission. Virginia Carmelo. I'm named after her.

CJ: Do you have a sense of what might distinguish the Gabrielino-Tongva from other southern California native people?

VC: In my experience, I think we're similar to a lot of coastal cultures—definitely the language. Some of our languages are different, but we share a lot of words. I think that makes us quite similar. I have a close Juaneño friend; I see that culturally, even today, we are quite similar. We both have that Indian tie to the land and we have that Mexican mix in us. We were talking one day, just casual talk with a few other native Indians, about food, and it came to salsa. We don't say "salsa." That's what people say today. All our family says "sarsa." That must be a California thing because all our mothers and aunties, everybody says "sarsa." We all recognize it and we don't know where it came from, but I just attributed it to that. I definitely think that some items just come down and still connect us. Today, [what] might make us different is how we identify ourselves in terms of our actual land base, and what became of the land base.

BMc: You talk to your Juaneño friends about that?

VC: Yes, definitely, we have discussions, but it's pretty much [about] previous [times]—this is [the land] we claim, and this is what you claim, and it's not agreed upon.

CJ: Do you think of your family as a coastal people? They seem more inland.

VC: I think when my great-grandparents left the mission, they just went into survival mode. Probably would have preferred to go coastal, maybe not, but they headed out towards what was the Riverside area. That would have been 1880 or so, 1887. At that point in time, aside from San Gabriel and Los Angeles (which was then already established), Rialto or Alonso was the next biggest community. I think they went out there to live and just stayed. Myself personally—[I] identify a lot with the coast. My son, he always wants to go to the ocean, to the beach all the time, even when it is cold. I always tell him that's the Tongva coming out.

CJ: When did you meet Cindi Alvitre? Was that a political introduction?

VC: No, more of a cultural thing. She, at the time, I believe, was living in Corona, in that community out there. I had just started dancing. I also do traditional Aztec dancing. I had just begun to dance, probably that year. And the group went out to Corona in an invitation to dance. Probably would have been 1975 or 6.

CJ: Why didn't you develop a traditional Tongva dance group?

Virginia Carmelo (left) and Cindi Alvitre (right) demonstrating dance movements in the Jacaranda Walk at Rancho Los Alamitos, the kitchen midden of Povuu'ngna, 2006. Ty Milford Photography

VC: I don't think you just make up your mind, "Oh, today I'm going to go dance." And in our terms, I feel that I was called—dancing came to me. For whatever reasons, I was in that place at that time and that teacher was there. There was another teacher previous to that who actually did a lot of preparation with me and the other students. That would have been in 1969, in school. At that time, because of the social movement, we were trying to bring teachers in who would teach us about ourselves. "We don't want to learn about other things." In doing that, we actually got a dance teacher, a traditional from Mexico. He brought the other teacher, the Aztec dance teacher. That's how I met him, what was available at the time. The Gabrielino dances, they haven't been done for many, many, many years. A big part of any Indian community is the dancing and singing that goes on. What we're looking at today—as we speak—is bringing back those dances. How do we bring them back when we don't have any teachers to show us what they were like? Well, nobody says that people are stagnant. We still have that creation, and we have that memory. We're feeling the sense of that dance coming on. I can only look at what experiences I've had as an Aztec dancer, what experiences I have shared with my other California communities and their dances, and just bring the two together and mesh them. We've had times when we go to many other different tribal dance groups. Sometimes there are fifteen or twenty different tribes coming together to do dances in some of the invitations I've had. In talking with these people, in sharing, there are certain lines just in all of the dances. Whatever I know because I've been an Aztec dancer is going to come across somehow, because those things are like just there.

CJ: Like design, common motifs around the world.

VC: Yes, correct. In dancing it is the same thing. There are different styles, but it's going to come across. Not too long ago, there was a song being sung, and I was just standing there, and I had to move. That's dancing. Before, I would have just said, "Oh, that just happened," but now I look at it and I say, "We need to bring back these dances." If they start with little moves, that's the way it is. Historically some dances will start off this way and go through little changes over the years as people with different abilities—

CJ: Do you have a collaborative group of dancers?

VC: I have my family. Well, I have six children, and they have been raised [as] dancers, as musicians. They were singers. We've done some presentations now for Tongva gatherings. We gather together and we sing. This has already been going on for maybe two or three years, saying, "We need to dance." I have two boys and four girls. Of course I would like to involve some of the other community members—

BMc: What dances are you working on now? What Tongva dances are you focusing on?

VC: What I'm focusing on is creation, creation of dances. Lot of times in the Indian community, certain dances stem out of needs in the community. The dance I am taking on is what I call the basket dance. I'm going to give it its Tongva name. The basket dance—it's just a sense of taking work done by women, very fine basketry work, and putting it into motion so that people get the idea, because this was important for our people.

BMc: Do you consider that to be a new dance that never existed before?

VC: It might—I don't know if it existed. I haven't done the research, but yes, it will be a new dance. We have new songs our people are coming out with. That's part of my belief—some things maybe have lain dormant, but we as Indian people can be creative and bring it out. The test of all that is going to be—does it stick? Or, do people pick it up and say, "Yeah, this is part of us." Or do they not? That's the test in the community. When people pick things up, then you know it's taken in to that person and the community.

CJ: So the test is, does something new express a genuine spirit that has traveled through time?

VC: Correct, yes.

CJ: So when you create those dances, and you work on the songs, you are trying to make a message—

VC: Yes. It is connected to our past because I feel it's like coming out of some memory from someplace. I don't know what that memory is. That's my sense that it's coming out of some memory.

CJ: Tell us about the ongoing effort to recapture the Tongva language.

VC: There's a lot of information. I am working with a language group. I have been now for several years.

BMc: Are they all Tongva?

VC: Yes, they are Tongva. We gather once a month, and we have a linguist from UCLA. She gathers with us, and we do different things. We prepare— she prepares, sometimes, lessons for us. She started off with like little baby steps. Now, two years down the line, we're actually doing simple sentences. So it's a lot of work, but from this, you know, sometimes it's just a word or two that will catch, and next thing you know there's a song. It's very exciting. It's really even hard to explain because it's an honor to be called upon to do that. It's quite a responsibility too, because you put yourself out there [when you create new songs or dances]. There's always going to be the criticism [that they're not authentic], but like I said, I'm not really concerned with that. If a new song or dance takes, then it's part of us, and if it doesn't, then it's lost and something else will come up. I'm confident of that, something new will come out. Songs and dances in any community are kind of like that little gel that brings people together.

CJ: When you were in school, the civil rights movement also included the Latino struggle, and the need to recognize the rights and significance of its culture. When you were in school did anybody recognize the surviving "Mission Indian" culture, or did most believe, as books said, they all disappeared?

VC: Yeah. I think that as a child, and then as a young person, that was very puzzling for me. I remember the fourth grade, and opening this big heavy book that I can barely lift up, California history. I turned to the first page, and we're reading a sentence something like, "The Mission Indians used to live here and now they don't." I remember just looking at the picture—I think it was a woman with a willow skirt, grass skirt, sitting down, with her back to me. There was this man standing off someplace and a child. The whole picture was just very small. Just little. They just didn't give enough of what it was. I looked at it, and I thought,

"This is like who we are, me." I'm trying to find myself in that picture—me, my family, who we were, and it just wasn't enough.

CJ: Did you ever mention it to the teacher? We heard other similar stories, but it takes a great deal of courage to stand up to a teacher and say a book is wrong.

VC: No, no. At that age I didn't. Then, I wanted to turn the page and find something more, but it went on to the next section of history. Okay. That was it? What's come to me now over time—that made such a horrible impression on me, something I've always remembered. I don't remember a lot of other things, but I always remember looking at this [book], continuing to look, and trying to find something. That's not enough. Later on, as an adult student, that's when I was more open to saying things to my teachers. For instance, when I was in college, we had a teacher who was, I think, a Choctaw from Oklahoma. At that point I was just learning how to speak Spanish. I was in his class, and I think somebody said something to me and I said one word in Spanish. [The] next session he made some comment about how California Indians didn't have any culture, they were identifying with Mexican. Of course I took that as an insult, because had he known anything about California Indians, he would know that we interlaced with Mexicans. I mean, the Mexicans were here, so a lot of Mission Indians have that connection. And a lot of Mission Indians speak Spanish. Other Indians from other places don't really understand that [connection].

CJ: Many people are both California native as well as Mexican through the history of intermarriage—that's the community, that's what was going on. How did you identify yourself in college when the Chicano movement was so active?

VC: The people I was around had a new term they used among each other—we called them "Chican-Indio." You're Chicano, you have that Mexican, but you have Indio, which is the Indian. We used that for a long time. We found that to be a little bit more to our liking because we realize as Indian people that we had more ties to the land, not just our own land, but the whole landscape throughout the southwestern United States.

BMc: Do you feel that your family ever did lose its identity?

VC: No, I don't think so. I feel that my father, my uncle, just accepted the fact that the mainstream was kind of overpowering them, but they knew who they were, and they just had to do what they needed to do to live day by day. I don't think, at that point, there was an issue of, "Oh, we have to maintain our culture." I just think they, in some way, accepted [that] things were changing and mainstream had taken over.

I have only one uncle left, and he left the area. We've had some discussions—

"Do you remember any dances? Do you remember any songs?"—to see what he comes up with. I think he was past that era too. But, he did make one comment: "I always knew I was Indian. I always knew it." That's what I feel too. I always knew it. Maybe I couldn't capture all of it because a lot was lost, but that sense and knowledge was there. And he knew it because, he said, his dad, my grandfather, let it be known. The people, family that was around—it was just known.

I think there were some family stories. For instance, one day they were making beer, my grandfather and his sons and uncles. They were talking about how on the reservation they used to do that, back when—I imagine during Prohibition. My grandfather and his cousins would talk, his cousin used to tell stories. I don't recall them, I must have been too young, but I remember we'd be under an oak tree. He'd be talking, but I know he was telling stories.

Wait, I have a good story. This story was told to me by my mother. She was saying that my grandmother Virginia used to need rides to visit different parts of the family, members out in Riverside and different areas. One afternoon they took her to visit one of her daughters, I think at San Bernardino. On the way back, she had them stop. I think it's Mount Rubidoux now, in Riverside. They went up to the top of the hill. I think it was her and her husband, and my mother, and my father. They said, "Look around, everything that you can see with your eyes was all our land, look at the entire landscape." Then she started talking about how some relative had been hanged for being a horse thief. I don't know when, and I don't know who the relative is, but it was back in the days. They were saying that that was our land, but yet they were caught. You know, accusing us of being thieves.

CJ: Many people in San Gabriel worked with Tommy Temple to trace down their genealogy. Did your family have help with the 1928 enrollment process?

VC: What it looks like to me, from my grandmother's application, there were agents, or whoever the people assigned to do this work, going around. The application is not actually in her writing, only the signature. I think that there were people going around to different communities. She was in Santa Ana, and I think they were just taking people's information down. Since both of her parents were born in the mission, maybe she had some kind of information about that documented. I don't know. But it didn't seem they were requiring a lot of documentation.

CJ: Were people from the Bureau of Indian Affairs going around to help them?

VC: Well, that's what I'm wondering, too. California had different situations; how it treated the Indians was [different] than other states. So it seemed to me like it might possibly have been a state agent. I'm not really sure.

CJ: When is the first time that you remember realizing there was a larger extended family of Gabrielino-Tongva community outside your immediate family or your relatives at Soboba?

VC: Probably when I was involved in the social movements. There was a Chican-Indio community on campus. I went to Cal State Fullerton, and we did have some interactions with other state colleges. There was also a really small Native American group, which I also participated in. The only thing is that most of those native people were from other places, a couple Navajos and one Hopi. The only other guy, a Luiseño who was also California native, we had a connection.

CJ: Did they recognize you as Indian?

VC: Well, like I said, there was only five or six of us. There weren't very many. But, you know, they did. But I think it was difficult to recognize the group because they weren't very cohesive. At that time I also identified myself as Apache, so they did recognize Apache right away because that's more well known but—

CJ: Did you do that because it was better known?

VC: No. I think it was—that was around the time I finally asked my father, "What kind of Mission Indian are you?" So it wasn't intentional. It's just what I knew. When I started to find out, to ask my dad what kind of Mission Indian we are, he said San Gabriel. I checked with my grandmother, or somebody, just to verify. And yet, you know, it's San Gabriel, but at that time I didn't really try to find out much more. I remember getting a book or two that said very little about the San Gabriel Mission Indians. But since some of our families was married to Juaneños, I had kind of identified, it was very similar with San Gabriel. Even at that time I was still thinking all Mission Indians are the same, which they're not.

BMc: Is your family religious?

VC: Yes, all of our family is Catholic, the kind of families that went to church every single Sunday, and took confession. I went to, like, ten years of catechism, plus I went to Catholic school. I do practice Catholicism, do attend church, but I attend a Christian church, and it's nondenominational.

CJ: Do you incorporate your traditional beliefs?

VC: Yes. I do sweats sometimes, or other traditional practices, but for me it just comes down to—there is only one creator, and that creator comes across in any practice. There is no difference. That's kind of interesting because as far as the mission tied to the Catholic Church—I don't think it's by chance. I had to learn about the Catholic Church in order to understand my background. What I do in the Aztec dance, that's also tied to the Catholic Church. Had I not known all

I know about the Catholic ways and beliefs, I would not have learned the same way. So all of this plays together in my own personal experience—how, you know, all these things come together, how I perceive things, and how I'm able to take from them and bring them together in my native community and work.

CJ: How did your family feel about the mission experience? Was it a negative view?

VC: Not from my family, but there was a period where I was very much against the Catholic Church because of the genocide that took place, the way it was used in bad ways to take over the people. I don't think they came in with a definite idea—"This is what we're going to do." I don't think they realized so many people would get sick and die. I think it was different. There were good and bad leaders, just like we have today. But for myself, at some point I came to the knowledge that it's just like anything else. There are people who will use it for bad and people who will use it for good. So it's not the religion per se, it's the people who are, I guess, running it, or in charge, and how they're using it.

BMc: You had a period where you had bad feelings and then that passed for you. How?

VC: I think really it came about because of my dancing, because, like I said, Aztec dancing is very much tied to the Catholic feast days. Because I had a good knowledge of Catholic practices, and their beliefs, I could see all of this is really just ceremony. That's all it is. It's just a way of practicing. I came to that under-standing—it's how one practices, it's not how somebody, wherever, is running the Catholic Church. That's not what it's about. It's about the belief and the ceremony. I came to terms with it and that's why I still do support and practice Catholicism, because I understand what the ceremony is about. I understand how the Indian people were able to take it on, and it became integrated into what had been their own religious beliefs for centuries, how they were able to take on parts of the Catholic religion and say, "Okay, this is, like, the same work." That's exactly what I did, too. You have to look at it with the right view in order to accept it, and say, "That person, who is also a Catholic, may be run-ning the Catholic Church, or that community may think a little bit different, but that really doesn't concern me."

BMc: What do your children think about religion? Do they think of themselves as Tongva?

VC: Yeah, they all do think of themselves as Tongva. Their dad is Mexican. My son is funny because, of course, the male will always identify with the male. For a while he kept saying, "No, I'm Mexican. I'm Mexican." Then he would do certain things like say, "I want to go to the beach." I would say, "That's the Gabrielino coming out in you." It's come full circle. He really is the one coming out with the sense of the dancing, too. He's making his elderberry flute. He may be one of the first people to bring back the elderberry flute, the first Tongva to bring back the elderberry flute.*

I think they're able to do somewhat like I've done. I'm not full-blooded Tongva. I have all of these other lineages, and we're kind of just coming into who I am. I don't separate them. I don't say, "Today I'm this, today I'm that." To me it's always there. It's all been part of my experience. I think that that's what I'm seeing in them, too. They have these different backgrounds, taken from all of them, and integrating them. They're using their own creativity to express what that is.

CJ: After you joined your community at Cal State Fullerton, how did you become part of a larger community of people working on behalf of this larger Tongva community?

VC: It was more recognition at that point. I really didn't start working with the community until my children were all grown, and that was sometime in 1994, I believe.

CJ: Were you aware of Povuu'ngna, for example, that people were protecting a site?

VC: Yes. At that time I was. I was right away—you know what happened during this time, of course. I was busy raising my children, so I wasn't out there a lot. Not as much as I would have liked when I did make intentional time, saying, "I'm going to go see what's out there." I knew there were several communities out there. I decided to go with the San Gabriel group [Gabrieleno/Tongva Tribal Council of San Gabriel], and so that was my first exposure to that community. I was aware there was a community in Riverside, and there was a community out here in, I guess they called it West L.A. I knew that Cindi, I think she might have still been out in Corona. I don't know where she was. I knew Cindi wasn't with that [San Gabriel] group anymore. Very funny—when I went to their first meeting, that's one of the things they talked about, the other groups. So, I had an idea there were other groups out there.

BMc: What were those groups doing besides meeting? Were you just getting together to talk?

---

* The traditional, precontact flutes of California Indians were made of dry elderberry (*Sambucus*). Elderberry oil is toxic and green wood to be avoided. Handcrafted and often decorated, an elderberry flute was an open-ended tube with four to six holes, tuned and played to an ancient musical scale. Some were played from either end, which produced different scales. Simple to make, but without a mouthpiece or block, genuine elderberry flutes defy even practiced musicians. Experts say that the true California elderberry flute is the key to understanding the indigenous music of North America.

VC: I think my sense at that time, overall, they just seemed like people were gathering because people wanted to get federal recognition. It seemed like that was the base, it seemed like an important issue. To me it's important—the federal government chose, for whatever reason, not to recognize us for a lot of years, political reasons. The importance of it is justice, justice, justice for who we are today. Justice for our ancestors and that history we have behind us. The government needs to turn around and say, "We don't just recognize you for your lineage, but we recognize what was done to you and your people." In the bigger scope, for me it's an injustice that Los Angeles is such a big city, urban area, and most of the people here don't know who the indigenous people are. That's the big injustice. It's just something that we need to correct.

CJ: If somebody said they were Tongva, would you believe them?

VC: I think so. What I've found, generally, is that it's like the same thing that happened in my family. You don't really know a lot, but you know you're Indian because somebody said it to you, and it was an important thing to pay attention to. They didn't just say it casually. It was like, "You know, we're Indian. You know, you're Indian." Something was said that caught you. I'm finding this because I am meeting a lot of new people I didn't know were Tongva. It's like the same thing comes across, they say they are because somebody—their grandmother, whoever it was—said they were. So they knew they are. Of course that's one thing for them. But I think it's like that sense of who they are. They can tell you, "Oh yeah, so-and-so said that." That is the tie, the family tie that's always runs across, all of these people that I meet. And secondary to that is getting the documentation. A lot of people don't have documentation. Really funny thing, we heard about, "When those people came around with the 1928 judgment application," my grandmother said, [they said,] "'I don't want to have nothing to do with that.'" That's totally a good response, doesn't do much for the family today.*

But that recognition of one's self, those family ties, are really the strongest things. It brings us across. It's always funny, 'cause somewhere down the line we're connected, we're all connected. "So-and-so was your aunt? Oh, yeah, well, that was my aunt, too." Something like that always comes up. It's amazing, even people who have gone in different directions, they're living in different places, those family ties, they're still there.

[Our group] the Gabrielino/Tongva Nation—it's a group of people that joined together who then split. We're in different areas. We're not situated in any one place. We're all over. Basically, we are mainly gathering together to try to, well, do a lot of things. [After federal recognition] one of the biggest things is to establish

---

* After the 1927 California Indians Jurisdictional Act, and over the years, not all eligible Tongva have chosen to enroll, either because they did not wish to be associated with the federal government or because they believed they knew who they were without having the government define their identity. Other enrollment papers were lost in the process. However, enrollment papers, like the old mission records, have become accepted documented verifications of native family lineage, despite the fact not all native people entered the missions or enrolled. For their descendants, this is an ongoing problem of a "documented identity" and a difficult paradox of history.

an economic base so that we can have money. [It] takes money to do everything, to move forward in other areas, such as culture, economics, health, education, welfare. So we've gathered—we're increasing our membership because a lot of people are Gabrielino, they're Tongva, but they really haven't been part of some group, or they have been part, and want to work with us. So we are standing on the 1994 state recognition of the Tongva people as the indigenous people of Los Angeles, and taking that to move forward, to move the entire nation forward.

CJ: Can you explain the 1994 recognition?

VC: It was a state resolution passed by the Assembly and the Senate of California to recognize the nation, not any one group or band, but the entire nation as the indigenous people of the Los Angeles Basin.*

CJ: How many people have you brought together in your group?

VC: Our membership started at eighteen hundred and is growing. [There are some people in my own family who are not on the membership list right now, who should be, of course, but it's growing. I see it as taking baby steps because there are people who have been around forever in some of the other groups, but there are a lot of new people. We're on the Web now, so people have said, "Oh, I saw you on the Web, and I know I'm Gabrielino." So then, you know, they're coming in. The general catalyst was so that we can seek federal recognition and develop a casino like the other southern California tribes do, and northern California.
  [In the summer of 2008, Virginia Carmelo updated her comments, stating that "After we had the conversation in August 2006, some members separated from our group, but we retained the majority of the membership, about twenty-two hundred people. At some point we might need to temporarily cut off membership."]

CJ: If you took the casino out, would you still be interested in federal recognition?

VC: I would, definitely, yeah. Like I say, the casino, it's just the base to get from where we are to where we need to go. And certainly, the timing, because the other tribes are doing this too.
  [She also noted in 2008 that "The original investment money in the tribe is now gone, but we are actively pursuing interested investors. We are not a 501(c)(3) nonprofit group like the San Gabriel group."]

---

* In 1994, the state of California recognized the Tongva in Assembly Joint Resolution 96, chaptered by the California Secretary of State as Resolution Chapter 146, Statutes of 1994, as follows: "Whereas Gabrielino tribal territory encompasses the entire Los Angeles Basin and the Channel Islands of Santa Catalina, San Nicholas, and San Clemente...Whereas the State of California recognizes that the Gabrielino Indian community existed and has continued to exist without interruption to the present day...Resolved by the Assembly and Senate of the State of California, jointly, that the State of California recognizes the Gabrielinos as the aboriginal tribe of the Los Angeles Basin and takes great pride in recognizing the Indian inhabitance of the Los Angeles Basin and the continued existence of the Indian community within our state; and be it further Resolved, that the California Legislature respectfully memorializes the President and Congress of the United States to likewise give recognition to the Gabrielinos as the aboriginal tribe of the Los Angeles Basin..."

BMc: How is the Gabrielino/Tongva Nation different from the Ti'at Society or the Gabrieleno/Tongva Tribal Council of San Gabriel? Can someone belong to all three groups or do people generally choose a group?

VC: In our group, sure, you could belong to all three groups. There will be no problem. I'm not sure about the Ti'at Society, how they work. I've never really been part of them. I've been supportive at a couple of their events but I would imagine they probably wouldn't have any problem. The San Gabriel group—you can't belong to any other group. I think what makes us different is that we want to be inclusive of any person who has Gabrielino-Tongva lineage, not just here within our own area, but even in other tribal groups. Definitely because of the casino issue—we're seeing that here in southern California. It's a very negative thing where people are actually being thrown out of their own tribe.

CJ: On what basis do you let people come in?

VC: Because of what's happened to our tribe historically, because the dissemination, the decline was so fast, the impact was so hard. Because of our history, we are actually looking at several different things. One of course would be the BIA records, which are there. Another thing would be the mission records. Now, with the Huntington coming on line, that's going to be an asset.*

The next thing would be oral history, which many other tribes are not accepting. It's the opposite of direct lineage—you can find directly who you're related to from going down the generations. But we have another method which we're using, which I think is called "lateral." Say my grandparent is the one that's on the 1928 judgment roll. Say, for instance, her sister decided not to go on it, and that great-grandchild from that person has no way to prove their lineage. Well, we can go back and do that lateral genealogy, and find out they are related. That's very common. When you hear the people talk and the anger coming through, it's totally understandable. One of the things we're looking at is to make our own determination. We don't have to depend upon the government. I think that's part of our own self-determination. You have to be Gabrielino-Tongva. You have to have the lineage to be either on the council, or a member, or a voting member.

[In 2008 Virginia Carmelo indicated that the qualifications had changed, stating that "All membership in the Gabrielino/Tongva Nation is based on the BIA's guidelines so that we meet the criteria for federal recognition. Our membership is not based on blood quantum, which is impossible because of our unique history, but all members must provide proof as stated by the BIA, including government, BIA, historical, court, or census records."]

BMc: Do you elect a chairperson like they do in San Gabriel, or is it a different situation?

---

* The Early California Population Project of The Huntington Library offers public access to all the information contained in California's historic mission registers.

VC: The elected *pco'tskome* (council) decided to appoint me as the chair. So right now we are appointing. That could change. Basically, the chairperson is to represent the tribe in a lot of different avenues, to be out there as the leadership. I think there are a lot of important issues we should work together on—the issue of Povuu'ngna, things that are happening locally within the county, definitely federal recognition, eventually.

[In 2008, Virginia clarified her position as tribal chair, stating, "I was originally elected to the tribal council in 2005 and then appointed tribal chair, but now I am the elected chair of the Gabrielino/Tongva tribe as led by me. The membership at large elects the tribal council, the *pco'tskome*, who in turn elects the chair.]

CJ: Have you submitted a petition to BIA for recognition?

VC: Yes.

CJ: Where is it in the process now?

VC: It's in the infancy. We know that the process is not meant for completion. Very few tribes have gone through it and actually achieved federal recognition. We started the process because we want to put our foot everywhere we can to get there, and hopefully we will. We think we can. I think we're out there in the different areas of the Los Angeles Basin letting people know who we are.

CJ: Do you do educational programs, for example?

VC: I personally do them. Unfortunately, in the community at large, and not just our council, there are very few people doing anything. I think that [when] we connect more, our younger people are going to take it on. Right now the younger people are not doing it, and I think eventually they will. That's what we're looking at. The more we're out there, the more we're out there. I'm coming across so many people who say, "Well, I never knew who the Indians were in this area. I never knew there were any Indians in this area." Even the Indians say that, you go to the powwows and they say that.

CJ: Why did you want to create this council, as opposed to working with existing ones? Why did you want to assume such a huge task of leadership?

VC: Like I said, I'm not going out there seeking these things. I think I was called upon to do it. I think I've come through a lot of different—I don't want to say just experiences, because that's not just enough—but maybe teaching and connections with people to be put in this place. I feel I just have to stand up to the plate and say, "Okay, this is what I'm supposed to do. This is what I'm going to do." We have brought together in our council [six] of the [nine] groups that were out there at that time. Now there are other groups out there. There's a group out in Beaumont. There's a family out there. There is a group in Riverside. The one in Beaumont, they are a family. I don't really know the one in Riverside. I would think they are a family. Of course, there's the San Gabriel group [Gabrieleno Tongva Tribal Council of San Gabriel]. It's not that we wouldn't want to work with them, we would want to work with them.

CJ: Why did you form this group instead of joining one of the other existing groups?

VC: When I decided to see what was going on in the Gabrielino community territory, I looked and found that there were several groups out there. I decided to go with San Gabriel—seemed like a good thing to do. [Then I and others] decided to come out of there and form our own group.

Indian politics is a horrible thing, worse because we're families. You can go to whatever community—there are a lot of people working together, but they're not cousins, aunts, and uncles who have these grudges that go back. When things started happening, I took a look at it. I said, "All of this is really detracting from the focus." At that point, I saw the focus was federal recognition, and time was passing and nothing was being done. I know the process is slow, but these other issues started coming out, and they were based along family lines. I said to myself, "This is not going anywhere." I wanted things to go in a different way. I was ready to pull back, and other [outside] people were saying, "We are going to bring everybody together under this [idea of seeking federal recognition and then a casino under a state resolution]. The idea of unity is what I liked, and I said, "Let's work for unity. This is what this tribe needs. This tribe has been scattered all over, everywhere. We really need to come together." That's what the basis of this group was—unity.

We brought five six of the groups together (beyond the San Gabriel community). I don't like to call them factions because "factions" has that tone of negative—somebody doing something different to undermine us. I don't think we're doing anything that different. We just have a different idea as far as how we're going to work. We want to continue to work in a unified manner and bring people together. Our council meets at least once a month. Our membership meetings have been twice a year so far, but we're planning to increase the membership meetings, probably to three times a year. One of the family groups meets on a monthly basis, and so we meet with them. That's in the Fresno area. So I've gone up there a couple of times to meet with them. Everybody is opening up. I guess there were three sisters, and all of those sisters had had children, and they were raised in that area. I did ask a couple people why did they go there and nobody knows yet, but I'm sure it will come out. We know there are people in the Bakersfield area. It's amazing, people—they're calling to get their membership in, and they're just everywhere.

[In 2008, Virginia added that "The entire membership of our Gabrielino/ Tongva Tribal Council group meets quarterly now. We also have small meetings with individual families."]

CJ: What's your best hope for your children?

VC: Of course a mother always wants their child to just be well developed in every aspect that they choose to be in. I certainly feel very happy that they have a firm knowledge of their Indian background, of their other backgrounds. Not even just the knowledge. I think it's just part of them. I feel very happy that's there, because I know that here with all the influences around us in the urban area, that's different, that's unique. It's not the norm. I can't say that I've worked to do it, but it's definitely been in the forefront. I think I would look at them to be leaders in the community at some point, to take it very serious and important, not let it go and set it aside. Always, my hope has been for them to have a very firm spiritual base, including our Indian background, and to be able to settle, to base themselves on that.

BMc: What do you see as the roles and responsibilities of the leaders in the community?

VC: Always of course the protection of who we are as Indian people, inclusive of everything—the culture, the environment. But I think in any Indian community, basically you're looking out for each other. The leadership is looking out for everything, making sure things are going as best that they can, and bring in the people to move forward together, in whatever aspect, whether education or economic.

CJ: Do you think if you took the casino element away that many of your membership would have come forth?

VC: I think they would have. Definitely, of course, it's an attention getter. When I've met with people in the meetings, certainly it's an important thing, but it's not like it's the only thing. It's not, it's just not. What comes across are those family ties, the sense of people wanting to help out, not necessarily towards the means of the casino, but just in terms of the general community—what can I do? I'm seeing people want to know more about the culture. People want to learn the language. People want to learn the song. People want to learn the dance. That is much more important to me.

CJ: Has your council done anything to record and document the new stories you are hearing to add to the cultural memory of the people?

VC: Not necessarily in those terms—the cultural memory—but we definitely talked about recording some of the people we would say are elders. [Now we are recording oral histories.] Of course, like anything, the problem is funding. These things come up, especially as we meet more and more of the people. One of the things I'm doing personally is, every time I meet somebody new, I always ask them, because I'm involved in the language, "Do you know, do you remember hearing any Tongva words?" "Did anybody you know, your elders, speak them?" There is a lot out there. I think just even—we have names, we have people, and it's okay there's other people out there. And I think they felt the same way—"We thought we were the only Gabrielinos."

BMc: How do you fund the things that you want to do?

VC: We really haven't had funding available yet. But, as we speak, most likely I think it's something in place. So when that does happen, then, yes, we'll be able to do something. [Today our original investor funding is now gone. We now have generous sponsors.] But interestingly enough, there are community members that want to donate their time, their money to progress this. We have one man who wanted to start a nonprofit right away so we can do cultural things. We have an office, but we want to establish another. That office is in Santa Monica, but so far we're only using it for our council meetings. [Our office is now in downtown Los Angeles.] We have had our council meetings at other areas, but our membership meetings so far have been in public areas. We're looking to have another membership meeting right here at Povuu'ngna pretty quick, hopefully.

Some of our members in Fresno are working out of the TANF office in that area. We're in talks with TANF, which is Tribal Assistance for Needy Families, but they have many different programs run through Torres-Martinez tribe. They actually came to the L.A. Urban League service to Native Americans with different programs—food programs, education. Torres-Martinez is a reservation, it's a tribe. They took over the TANF program. It's like a welfare program, but it's much more because they offer other programs. So they are now serving the L.A. urban community. We're talking with them about doing some other programs, for instance our language program, and other things, but you need to establish a center, which we would like to do. We're looking at different places, like Cal State Long Beach.

BMc: Who do you see as the leaders throughout the Tongva community?

VC: Barbara Drake, Ernie Salas, Cindi Alvitre, Jimmy Castillo. Anthony [Morales] is a leader. It's a few. Of course, the people in our council come from different groups. But, of course I think in terms of culture—Craig Torres—because the culture is important to me. There are different kinds of leaders, but definitely, I would include those people who have been out there teaching or sharing.

BMc: What do you see happening for the future?

VC: I see my membership continuing to grow. I see the culture developing more and being shared more, and maybe young people picking up and taking back their roots and their identity. And politically, I see the machinery moving forward to take us to that next level closer to recognition, certainly within the state—moving us to that level where some of the other tribes are. Here in California we have over two hundred tribes and only about one hundred of them are federally recognized. It's not just us, it's other tribes, too.

BMc: Do you think you'll achieve federal recognition at some point?

VC: I think we will. I don't have a time frame. It's kind of funny, because there have been tribes who totally didn't expect to receive federal recognition from one day to the next, even after they had petitioned, [and] you know, then they heard "federally recognized." That's the best thing that would happen.*

CJ: So if your group does gain federal recognition, who will be allowed to be added to your membership rolls? You will have to determine your own mandate. On what basis would that be?

VC: Our council stands on what we initially came together with, which is unity and being inclusive. We will not be exclusive. We will not use blood quantum. The decimation of our tribe has been so great that it would be ridiculous to do that. [But now we require everyone to prove their Tongva ancestry by using the criteria set by the BIA.]

CJ: But when the casino is an element, how will you deal with that?

VC: What we're talking about, we haven't put this into place yet, but that's why we're trying to increase our membership now, before any of this happens. Once that would take place we would probably have a freeze on membership for a period of time, but of course—

CJ: And what if somebody from San Gabriel, for example—the people who you already know, would they be invited in?

VC: Our council has determined we would be open to them. They are going to be included. One of the things we know, because of the Juaneños' recognition coming up, is [that] their three groups have been told they must come together. [We were all shocked when their application for federal recognition was denied in December 2007.] So we know it's an eventuality, and I feel really good about it. I feel it's going to be hard to go over past these hurdles, maybe. I just always

---

* Indian gaming is an economic goal of the Gabrielino/Tongva Tribal Council and their potential investors. In 1994, the state of California passed a resolution formally stating that it is "Resolved by the Assembly and Senate of the State of California, jointly, That the State of California recognizes the Gabrielinos as the aboriginal tribe of the Los Angeles Basin and takes great pride in recognizing the Indian inhabitance of the Los Angeles Basin and the continued existence of the Indian community within our state…" According to Virginia Carmelo, this state resolution of recognition is the basis on which the elected tribal council, Gabrielino Tongva Nation, is pursuing its economic objective, not necessarily federal recognition, since gaming compact agreements are negotiated between the tribes and the governor of California, not the federal government.

keep in mind that it's the tribe. It's the focus—what's going to move the tribe forward? It's not about an individual family or an individual place, or an individual idea. It's about a tribe, about a community, and it's about building that up, not doing things to knock it down.

CJ: Who or what brought that group together originally?

VC: The politics was just getting to be too inborn. And I think, of course, the issue of the casino was one of the driving points, because Anthony [Morales] at that point was saying no, he didn't want it, and somebody was out there saying [to us], "You know, we can help you do this." But that wasn't the driving point. The driving point was the unity, the unity, the unity, the unity.

When I started working with the San Gabriel group, as far as I knew, there was only five groups out there. When I came away from them there were nine groups out there. I said, "We can split into fifty different groups. That's not going to help you, unity is going to help us." That's my basis of moving forward with this group, and the other people too. They were people who hadn't worked, who had separated from some of the other groups. Well, I think in my case the good thing about it was I was able to say, "I'm not part of those old feuds. I don't want to be part of them. I just want to move the new stuff forward, move in the new and bring it together." It is definitely a hard task that has all of these things going on that are really going to be hard to go past. But I do think that they can. We have people who are intelligent and can use a little bit of compassion and just say, you know, "Got to move forward." Because I'm a mother. I would hear from the people, "Oh, we have to do these things because of our ancestors." Certainly, this is based on them, our ancestors are important, but I look at it the opposite way. We have to do these things because of our children. And I can only say that because I'm a mom.

CJ: What words describe what it's going to take, what are the characteristics for that job description you have assumed?

VC: Definitely faith in the creator. The creator has our path set out for us. We just walk in it. And probably an openness to do what needs to be done, and perseverance. Lots of perseverance. But I think the main thing is faith, that's what it's based on. Love, too. Love for that entire community is an overriding thing—who we are.

CJ: Do you have a daughter that's an actress? She was in the Steven Spielberg production?

VC: I do. Yes. She was one of the stars of *Into the West*. [Her name is] Tonantzin Carmelo. Her role was Thunderheart Woman. She was the lead in the first three parts of the miniseries. And actually, she is going to the Emmys on Sunday. So we're really exited about that. I'm trying to tag along but I don't know. She and some of her co-stars are going to be there. They're not nominated for the Emmys, but because the movie was nominated for so many, they're going to be there. She actually was nominated for a SAG award, which I understand is a little bit more, I guess, coveted. She looks for roles as an actress. She initially began as a Native American, but that is somewhat confining. So she's trying to go a little bit more—I don't know what they call it. There is a word for it. But she's trying, go out there for different roles. She's been in two other movies since then but they haven't been released. Those are both native parts, too. So hopefully those will be released, and she continues to look for work.

She's a main part of our dance group. She's actually one of the persons that, I just say, "gets songs." She's gotten a song. In other words the song came to her in our language, the Gabrielino language. She's probably going to be one of the ones to create some dances, a dance at least. She makes time. There are times when she's been very busy, but she makes time. But she definitely has a love for dance, and it is just always going to be part of her. So, she makes time.

CJ: What's your degree in? Do you think that education was important? Many people have expressed the need to continue education in the next generation.

VC: Bachelor of Arts in Ethnic Studies. It's definitely one of the things that I emphasize more. In fact, I was considering going back, but no, I haven't really thought about it too much lately. But it's in the back of my mind. It's definitely something that I've always told—not only my own children, but a lot of other people. You have to get the education. Sometimes they think, "Oh, I don't want to learn those ways." But I go, "That's not right, because we have to be able to function in the mainstream. And the only way we can do that is to access all of those tools." So, education is changing too. We are getting a lot of different things now that we didn't get back when I was a student. They're practically laying it at your lap, so just get the education. I always put that out there. That's definitely one of the things that the council is wanting to support.

It's always so good to see a young person out there completing their education. It's like, "one more, one more." And when they come back to the community, that's another thing. I think, in terms of our Gabrielino community, that the people we have out there, they're people that have been educated and been able to do whatever they need to do to get our work out there. Of course not enough, but what little has been done has been done through those processes.

A CONVERSATION with Anthony Morales (Tribal Chair, Gabrieleno/Tongva Tribal Council of San Gabriel), Andy Morales (son of Anthony Morales), and Kimberly Morales Johnson (cousin of Anthony Morales)

June 7, 2006
El Monte, California

The Participants

IN 1991 ANTHONY MORALES BECAME THE ACTING CHAIR OF THE Gabrieleno/Tongva Tribal Council of San Gabriel, and he has served as their elected chair since 1995. He is the son of Sparky Morales, an early-twentieth-century leader of the San Gabriel community. Andy Morales, Anthony's son, is a dance captain for the San Gabriel Gabrielino/Tongva dancers, who perform throughout the region and state; a leader in the San Gabriel Tongva Youth Center in El Monte; and a cultural educator in schools. Kimberly Morales Johnson, a cousin of Anthony Morales, is a schoolteacher, a cultural educator, and moreover, a skilled basket weaver who actively supports the political process and activities of her San Gabriel community.

The Discussion

In his role as tribal chair of the Gabrieleno/Tongva Tribal Council of San Gabriel, Anthony Morales speaks to the continuous legacy of leadership demonstrated by the San Gabriel community and his family. His comments explore the native identity of the land, relations with neighboring tribes, the survival and cultural memory of the Gabrielino-Tongva people, and ensuring cultural rights and respect through the political process, as well as gaining federal recognition. He discusses political activism in the region and state, including the passage of AB 2641, a bill protecting Native

Anthony Morales, tribal chair of the Gabrieleno Tongva Tribal Council of San Gabriel, and his son Andrew Morales at Mission San Gabriel, 2006. TY MILFORD PHOTOGRAPHY

American burial sites in California. His views express his intent, reasons, and hope for coming generations, as well as the Gabrieleno Tongva Tribal Council of San Gabriel.

Anthony Morales: I'm Anthony Morales, tribal chair and the chief of the government of the Gabrieleno Tongva Tribal Council of San Gabriel.

Andy Morales: My name is Andy Morales, Guiding Young Cloud. I am the youth leader for the youth center here in El Monte. I am also a dance captain and spiritual leader—well, still learning spiritual leader—for the Tongva people. He [Anthony Morales] is my father.

Claudia Jurmain: When did you first learn you were Gabrielino?

AM: As a child, you really don't know. I was born November 17, 1947, so I'd say I was old enough about the early fifties to grasp that there was some Native American on my side, because I would hear my dad. Plus, at this time the government was issuing allotments for the land taken away from us. That's when he enrolled me to the Bureau of Indian Affairs. The government said you needed to have proof you're a Native American in about 1952—I don't know if that was when he applied for paperwork, or as soon as I was born.*

But from the early fifties, I was old enough to realize that we were Native American—Gabrielino—because my dad was always involved with the mission and the fiestas. Even though I was only four or five years old, I realized it. My dad was Fred—Sparky Morales. He was a chief of the Gabrielino tribes since about the fifties.

CJ: Was that an official title, political title, or what?

---

*   In 1927 the California State Legislature passed the California Indians Jurisdictional Act authorizing the state attorney general to sue the United States government on behalf of Indians over the negotiated, nonratified treaties of 1851 and 1852. Claims were filed in 1928. To be eligible for an award, California Indians had to document their genealogy and tribal affiliation, and submit enrollment papers to the federal government. In 1950 every eligible and enrolled native Californian received $150. By that time, however, additional claims had already been filed in 1946 over lands not covered in the earlier award. An out-of-court settlement for these claims was reached in 1972. Each enrolled California Indian received $668. 51. However, not all eligible Tongva have chosen to enroll or be associated with the federal government, while other enrollment papers were lost in the process.

AM: He acquired that title from one of his great-grandfathers, who was a chief of a village here in San Gabriel. It went back to his great-grandfather's name. They used to call him [great-grandfather] the "Indian Romero," that was the nickname, or "Captain Romero," *Capítán* the Indian. He went by both titles. He was chief of a village northeast from the San Gabriel Mission which is Las Tunas Drive in San Gabriel. There was a major village there. It makes sense, even now all cemented. There's a water runoff. A wash would take all the water from the Sierra Madre and come through there. Naturally our people would have villages around waterways. It's intriguing because it makes sense—a village next to a waterway. This major waterway is right in the northeast corner in San Gabriel just outside the mission grounds.

My dad told me that he [great-grandfather] was mentioned in the church records, I believe, as the *capítán*.* They used that word to mean chief, or the head of a village. They used that term a lot in those days. They were very active in the mission. When the mission systems were breaking up, and the Mexican government was taking over, our family was given a land grant. Our land grant didn't really come through him, it came through the Valenzuela side because they were full-blood Gabrielino, and

Kimberly Morales Johnson at Mission San Gabriel, 2006. Ty MILFORD PHOTOGRAPHY

also involved. I'm speaking about my dad's side—"Captain" would have been my great-great-grandfather. He was active, in the church records. Then on the other side—we have Gabrielino on both sides—the Valenzuela side, they were always very active—all indicated by the land grant issued to my great-great-grandfathers.

When the missions were told by the Mexican government they had to allot some of the land back to the local Indian people, not everybody got land. We were pretty fortunate—I'm thinking because of our involvement. We were here where the community was, and we were the original people here. It's up in Mission Viejo, Rosemead and San Gabriel Boulevard in Montebello Hills, right in this area—Rancho de Potrero Grande—something like that. That was a title for the land grant.

---

* In ancestral Tongva villages, family lineages were brought together under the rule of a *tomyaar*, a chief who was most likely the head of the oldest or largest lineage. Usually a hereditary position, the *tomyaar* oversaw the religious and secular life of the village. It may be that some *tomyaars* oversaw several villages. On the other hand, *capitanes* were appointed by the missionaries as people of authority to keep order and protect the mission property in the area. Although given new authority, *capitanes* were chosen from the well-known headmen of prominent family lineages, maybe the *tomyaar*.

CJ: In one 1980 interview, your father, Sparky, referred to the "Gabrielino Indian Club." What is the relationship between that club and the actual political organization of the time?

AM: They made it sound like an organization structured with a president, a vice president. In reality they should have structured it as an Indian tribe. We're not the organization, we are a sovereign government. We're a tribe.

Bill McCawley: Is the Gabrieleno/Tongva Tribal Council of San Gabriel, as it's called today, a legal organization?

AM: Correct.

BMc: But the tribe existed prior to the legal organization—meeting in backyards and families getting together. Do you know when the band was organized as it exists today?

Kimberly Morales Johnson: I want to say late seventies. I'd like to go back to "the club." I think that tribal names go with the flow of society. In the past five years, the word "nation" came about because a lot of tribes were, "We are the Chippewa Nation," "the Navajo Nation." People were nations. So the leaders changed it to the "Tongva Nation" to keep up with the time period. They might have used "club" in the eighties, maybe that was a word they were more comfortable with, perhaps why they used it. As time went on, I think Michael [Barthelemy] was the first to legalize the tax documents, the nonprofit portion, because issues were coming up. So I think it's just a sign of the times.

CJ: Your dad worked with the Mission Indian Federation, which was founded in 1919 and became the effective political organization for the tribes of southern California?

AM: Yes, it was. Speaking to some elders before they passed, I was able to get an oral history. One still alive is Ruby Jimenez. She and Grandma Modesta used to go to the meetings in Santa Ana. That was back during Indian Federation days, but she gave me a date, the 1920s, and said she was just a little girl. She was about five, six years old, and the grandmother, who was a full-blood Gabrielino from San Gabriel, would travel to Santa Ana for quarterly meetings, or whatever, to start getting the political basis going because there were lawyers there interested in helping them with federal recognition. So the federal recognition process has been in our minds for many, many years. It's ironic the government, until now, still ignores that issue.

    She said it was fundraisers at barbecues, just gatherings—money to pay some of these lawyers. As time went on, it just fizzled out. I guess the lawyers felt they weren't strong enough to get us federal recognition. But the community has always been here. It's been ongoing. The evidence of that would be the atten-dance of everybody at parties, barbecues, fiestas, baptisms, marriages, funerals indicated by the headstones at San Gabriel back to the 1700s, 1800s. Some don't even have headstones. In the early days of the mission they were buried with no headstones. We know that.

So the community has always been there. There's always been off-and-on meetings. They weren't really consistent because they were so involved with making their own life—surviving. Also, remember the mentality of "Indianism" in those days. When Europeans were awarded these major land grants they used Indians for labor. So lots of them had to be discreet and stay undercover for a while. But the mentality as an Indian—nonetheless—survived. They continued into the thirties and the forties—meeting in the backyards, being active with each other, and attending each other's family celebrations. There were various fami-lies, wasn't just one family.

CJ: Most of them rooted in the San Gabriel community?

AM: Yes.

CJ: Were you aware of families in other geographic areas who did not identify with the San Gabriel community? Were there other parallel tribal organiza-tions, or families, trying to do the same thing, or was it all coming out of the San Gabriel community?

AM: To be truthful, I don't remember talking to any elders, or Dad, or anybody, or even seeing any other Gabrielino. I can't deny they weren't Gabrielino. They're Gabrielino. They live out in the high desert, or whatever. We've never seen them. They never came to San Gabriel. They never attended any function or meeting in San Gabriel. My knowledge of our traditional community has always been deep-rooted here in San Gabriel because of the mission. Our ancestors are part of the mission, and although it wasn't a good part of the history, nonetheless, I can't change history. But we've been here since then, way before then, and we're still here. So it's my understanding it's always been San Gabriel, and San Gabriel com-munity because they have been more involved and more active in this commu-nity—did the actual suing of the government. At that time Indians really didn't get to sue the government, but we did. We made history by joining with the other bands of Mission Indians from the high desert and other areas—we were able to sue the government for the land that was taken away from us.*

CJ: What is your relationship with other southern California tribes?

---

* As southern California Indian tribes objected to the land management policies of the Bureau of Indian Affairs, they began to organize by joining the Mission Indian Federation, established in 1919. Although the Tongva people, not federally recognized, were an urban tribe without a reservation, some followed political developments and joined the federation. During the 1920s, the Mission Indian Federation joined with the Indian Board of Cooperation and civic groups to lobby for compensation for land lost due to the unratified 1851–52 treaties. In 1927 their efforts led to the California Indians Jurisdictional Act, which authorized the state attorney general to sue the federal government on behalf of California Indians.

AM: I know in the past, through documentation, records, and archives, there was a lot of sharing—the songs, our dances, our ceremonies, trading. We would trade with the high desert. There were a couple of major trade routes along the mountains—the Serranos, the Cahuillas—one out toward the Chino area, which is today the 60 freeway through the Chino Hills, all along 57, all the canyons, Carbon Canyon. Our relationship has been way back, to the day times started changing. Everybody started getting involved in their own political agenda. But we still acknowledge each other. We know we exist. There was a time where I think there was no contact with them, but now we're beginning to get back together. We attend some of their functions. They attend ours. We share with the Bernardinos, the Juaneños, the Capistranos. We're now getting involved with San Manuel, and some of the other major tribes in the high desert. That just started happening recently because of a bill I was introducing through the state legislature—AB 2641, which addresses Native American burial grounds. I've been working on this bill for three years and finally this year, Assembly Member Joe Coto from San Jose [23rd District] introduced the bill, and Senator Denise Ducheny from San Diego [40th District]—they cosponsored it on the Senate side. Now there's a bill out there [effective January 2007] to protect all burial grounds that pertains to the whole state of California.

CJ: What is the gist of the bill?

AM: Right now current California law states that six or more burials constitute a cemetery, but it does not address Native American burial grounds.

During development you hear nightmare stories of our burial grounds being destroyed—prime example, the Playa Vista project in West L.A., where they destroyed and desecrated four hundred humans. Kim attended. She went out there and saw the little remains during development. They were able to get away with it because we have no protection.*

KMJ: I think the law states if you hit six or more that are less than two hundred years old, then you can remove—

AM: It's why they're getting away with it. So I just spearheaded this bill. It's just passed the Assembly last week. It's making its way through the state Senate right now, so hopefully it will come through also. We'll again be making history, not

---

* Both Ballona Wetlands and the ancestral Tongva village of Saa'angna have been affected by the 1,087-acre residential, commercial, and open space Playa Vista development located in the Westside of Los Angeles about one mile from the ocean. During the Phase I residential development, human burials were uncovered and removed, examined, and packaged by contract archaeologists despite native community protest. In 2004 the city of Santa Monica, the Ballona Wetlands Trust, the Ballona Ecosystem Education Project, the Surfrider Foundation, and the Gabrieleno Tongva Tribal Council of San Gabriel filed suit to block the Phase II commercial development of the project. The California Second District Court of Appeals in Los Angeles overturned all city approvals for the Phase II commercial development in 2007. In March 2009, subsequent discussions between the developer and the designated "most likely descendant" of the Tongva people resulted in the reburial of over 1,320 bundled ancestral remains in Playa Vista, in the village area known as Guahasna.

only for the Gabrielino starting the bill, but for the whole state of California. Politically, we're getting active with the other tribes locally.*

CJ: Has politics helped you regain some new, unique recognition with the other tribes since you now share so many cultural traditions?

KMJ: I think they all accepted [us]. I remember we were little and used to go to barbecues—we were always accepted at the celebrations with the Juaneños, San Diego, also Santa Barbara.

AM: Always felt that way.

KMJ: I think we were in question when the casino issue came up. I think that's when other tribes questioned who we were, but before that I don't remember hearing the other tribes challenge anything.

AM: Yeah. They know of us. We were culturally affiliated. They knew we were urban. They were out in the desert in the reservations and federally recognized. They knew that we existed. They know we were here because of the Los Angeles San Gabriel Mission—we're Mission Indians. So the relationship has always been there. But lately it's become more of a political scenario. We had a bill introduced in Congress for federal recognition—it didn't pan out because it was to be heard in the House of Representatives right around the time 9/11 happened. After that, everything was canceled, everything focused on national security. So the bill kind of lapsed, it died there. But they became very aware of who we were when we went to Congress—federal recognition.

CJ: Have you reintroduced the bill?

AM: No, we haven't. Again, because of the political mindset right now. All the politics are saying, "Oh, they just want a casino." Right now, Congress wouldn't be realistic because we know we wouldn't pass it through.

CJ: What does federal recognition mean?

AM: Federal recognition to me means having some land. This place you're meeting in today is rented through a small grant from the county of Los Angeles, city and county. We have nothing, and at one time, we were up with the most prosperous tribes in real estate. Just look at our territory. We're from the west deep into the Santa Monica Mountains, to the north all along the Angeles Crest National Forest, to the high desert...all along into Orange County...and then all along the ocean and islands—San Clemente, San Nicolas, and of course,

---

* As of January 2007, AB 2641 (Ch. 863, Stats. 2006) requires landowners to consult with the "most likely descendants" (as designated by the California Native American Heritage Commission) when Native American burial grounds (remains) are discovered on their property. Owners must ensure protection of the remains and associated cultural material, ensure that the site is not disturbed, and discuss with the most likely descendants their preferences and options for the treatment of remains and cultural material. Before this new law, property owners were not required by law to permit access to designated most likely descendants.

Catalina. That is our territory.[*] I don't like to refer to it in the past tense word "was" because it still is. It's still our territory. We were an urban tribe. We were settled in some prime real estate. This is why I feel "politics" doesn't want to recognize us. It's a political factor now because, as some people were quoted as saying, "Who's going to pay the back rent?" You think they're going to give this prime real estate back to us? I don't think so.

BMc: If recognition brings you land in some fashion, how will that change life for the Gabrielino?

CJ: And will any land do?

AM: Well, wherever. I couldn't see us going outside of our territory. I would prefer the government allow land in your territory when you become federally recognized. Land to me would mean some headquarters, office, a cultural learning center, a meeting hall, housing for our people, some education for our kids. Right now, one prime example—one of the young kids is going to graduate in a couple weeks. She [Stephanie] wants to go to college to become a pediatrician. There was no help for her until the Native American Ministry affiliated with the Los Angeles Archdiocese stepped in, helping her seek aid for college.[**] We get various requests at the tribal office—"Is there any education for our kids?" No, there's none. We're not federally recognized. Federal recognition would mean medical [access to federal funds and programs].

CJ: Once you're federally recognized, you have to have a specific way to elect a tribal council and a tribal governing ordinance. How, or is that different from what exists today?

AM: We've been organized with tribal councils since way back and we're still here—as far as my recollection, talking to some elders, in the twenties, thirties. We've gone through every phase, and here we are in 2006. I don't think it will make a difference since we're structured already.

CJ: Do elections happen today or is your role inherited?

AM: We have elections every other year. We have bylaws and we've been organized, structured. Thanks to guys like Michael [Bartholemy], I guess you could say we came out of that "Indianness" structure to more of a non–Native American structure which fits today's society. Nonprofit organizations fit today's structures. If that is what it means to adapt to today's structure, we'll do that. We've been structured already all these years—tribal councils and elders, certain

---

[*] The total mainland territory of the Tongva people covered over fifteen hundred square miles, most of contemporary Los Angeles and Orange Counties. Much of their territory was below 1,000 feet in elevation, including the long coastal plain and several inland valleys.

[**] Approximately one hundred thousand Native Americans from across the country now live in Los Angeles. Since 1989 the goals of the Native American Ministry have been to "bring together the existing Catholic Indian community of Los Angeles, identify pastoral and social needs, and bridge the Native American and wider Catholic community."

people designated to conduct ceremonies. Just the cultural aspect—it's been there forever. Today Kimmy is a prime example: she's doing our basket weaving—that has been ongoing here a number of years. Some of our ancestors were doing this before the 1700s out on the islands. You know, it wouldn't make any difference to me how we're structured.

KMJ: Our bylaws were written first by Wallace Cleaves, and we redid them again with UCLA [professor of law] Carole Goldberg, so it's not something that just a few people got together.*

CJ: If you become federally recognized, am I correct in assuming that people will need to belong to the Gabrieleno/Tongva Tribal Council of San Gabriel if they wish to be "officially" recognized as being Gabrielino? On what basis would that be?

AM: There again, the guidelines of the government. The government says that you have to be an ongoing continued community. To me that's the main tree trunk. You interviewed other Gabrielinos, but the community complying to the government guidelines—we are that traditional cultural group that has been here forever—we are that continued community.

The government's viewpoint, I think, would answer what you do with other Gabrielinos who have never been around. All of a sudden you're federally recognized—they're going to come around. Now we would have to abide by what the government tells us how to deal with new people, or other Gabrielinos who don't want to be active with us. I think we just have to take it on a case-by-case basis. That's the way I look at it.

I mean, you do all the footwork, I've been here forever—all of a sudden we get federal recognition—there are going to be two thousand people knocking on our door to enter. Where were you in the twenties, the thirties, when my dad, my great-grandfather and all, kept the struggle, the fight going? That's it. They have to earn it—they have to earn it. That's the way I look at it. They have to prove themselves, they have to become active. They don't just come and sign up—you're Gabrielino again. You're not active again. You've got to continue like we've been for the last hundred or so years here—our parents, the grandparents. Here I am, pushing fifty-nine, and I've been in it all these fifty-nine years. I'm still going, so why can't anybody else?

CJ: What is it about your family that "insists" you be leaders? It is a huge responsibility and a terrible burden at the same time. Can you speak to that legacy?

AM: Because that is our inherent right. It's something the government will not acknowledge, and this is a fight we have to prove—it's about time the government quit ignoring us. The government has allowed us into all the federal programs. It

---

* Wallace Cleaves is now a lecturer at the University of California, Riverside, University Writing Program Department. Until funding ran out, the Gabrieleno/Tongva Tribal Council of San Gabriel pursued federal recognition through an ANA (Aid to Native Americans) grant with the University of California, Los Angeles. Tribal governing papers are required as part of the federal recognition process.

let us attend Sherman Indian School back in the twenties and thirties when they became government schools, allowed us to get some of the government programs, allowed us to sue you. [The California legislature allowed the state attorney general to sue the federal government in 1927 on behalf of California Indians.]

We got reimbursed for some lands. [The government] also registered us. It gave us roll numbers. All along we've complied with the law the government imposed on us, the definition of all you are—"Indianness"—and still denying us. That's not fair. My vision is to end that struggle and just make it happen—for the children, for future generations, for Kim, her children, my children, my grandchildren—not so much me anymore. I hope I see it in my day, before I'm gone. I hope I see it.

I wouldn't want to see future generations go through another hundred years of struggle. I don't want to see that. If I could do it now and accomplish it, then the doors are open for the next generation. This is why. It's just my calling because of my great-grandfathers and grandmothers and because it's us. We're the ones—we're Native American, we're Gabrielino, we're from here. This is history. This is your community. Don't deny us, don't pass us up, be responsible, address the issues with us. This is why I keep this fight going.

Glad you asked me that question, because sometimes I just bring my own little notes. I want to read this little thing that I jotted down: "It's a shame that we have to prove our right, to prove our title, to prove our history, and to earn the respect of our government. Our government has acknowledged us, and continues until this day, but has failed to recognize us even though we have been in existence in our ancestral lands for thousands of years. It's an honor that our government fails to bestow upon us. This is not just a plea for social justice. Recognition is not just a political objective. It's a necessary reality. Our concerns are questions of law, which to date have not been considered by our government. It's about our inherent rights."

CJ: Did you write that?

AM: Bits and pieces—people would put things in my mind, and some of my own. I sat down when I was eating lunch one day, sitting in my car daydreaming. I said, "I'm going to put all these little things together." I had a bunch of little notes, little paper notes. I just made that paragraph. That's the way I see it, the way I feel, and this is truth right here. Why not?

CJ: Did you hear that passion in your father? Did you have these discussions with him?

AM: Sure, sure.

CJ: Was your father fighting for the same thing?

AM: Same thing, same thing. "We were here. This is our land. We're not the immigrant, we're the true ones—it's us." I saw it in him, heard it in his voice, and in everything that he was active in. That was my message from him. Not only him, but from what I remember, my grandmother. I used to go and talk to her, and my other relatives. My aunt Sally used to tell us stories about the actual land grant, how they were threatened. In those days some local ranchers would dress like Ku Klux Klan, with the hood and torches, and go to the village and threaten them—get out, they're going to burn the village down. That's why they ended up losing their land grant. It was taken by force. There are stories they got my grandfather drunk and made him put an X, and that's how he lost his land, but it was really harassment and threats. They were chased out of the land grant up where the old mission was, and they moved further north, where we're at here today. It's because of those stories, those injustices. Some justice has to be done here for us. It has gone on too long now.

CJ: So federal recognition is both healing—

AM: Not only is it a healing, it's a right of the wrong that's been imposed upon us. And land. Give us that legal standing where we can protect our sacred sites and our burial grounds.

CJ: What does the word "sacred" mean to you? What is your definition of sacred?

AM: All this land is sacred to me because this is our territory. Any portion or parcel within our territory [which] has human remains—that is sacred—artifacts uncovered during development. When they say, "They could be reburied"—to me, spiritually, once you're buried, you're buried. No. Reburials were not meant to be. Once in the ground, that's it, or cremated, or whatever our people practiced. That is what sacred means to me—sacredness is never to be disturbed, never to be desecrated.

BMc: Development in Los Angeles today, it's constant and everywhere. How do you protect those burials in the face of that kind of development? I understand the bill, but tell us how you would like to see that accomplished.

AM: I just want the lead agency to be more responsible. By the "lead agency," I mean the local municipality where the development is going on, the planning departments. I wish they would survey the land where there is going to be development, get information from the different information centers—Cal State Fullerton has all the sacred sites on file.[*]
    I feel the planning departments of the local municipalities have to be more responsible. The representatives of the developer need to do more thorough investigations—what was there, what's there where they're going to develop or

---

[*] The CSUF Archaeological Research Facility houses about four thousand cubic feet of archaeological material, much from Orange County. Used by colleges and universities, the center is a resource for professional archaeologists in public agencies and private organizations.

build. I've been before different city councils—downtown Los Angeles before the full city council. "Be more responsible. Find something, notify us immediately." There are some laws, the CEQA laws.* But they're not as strong as they should be. They really don't protect us. The prime example is the actual cemetery—the California state cemetery law does not address our burial grounds. So there has to be visibility. There has to be involvement on our part, so when they do come across sacred sites, artifacts, or human remains, they need to sit down at the table with us, and we need to come to a reasonable solution as to how to rebury our ancestors. I don't like to rebury them, because they should be there forever. Go around it, cap it, make a little green space, don't disturb them. This is my wish—cities will be more responsible and developers should be more friendly to Native Americans.

Stop, talk to the local people in the territory [where] development is going on. Remember, this issue is up and down the whole state of California, not just southern California. Come across human remains or artifacts—stop—call the local tribe, talk to them, try to get a reasonable solution. This is all I'm hoping for. It's a reasonable request. Why not?

Remember, the actual cemetery law was implemented in the 1850s, and the mentality was a wild west. Scalps were taken, a bounty on us—remember the Gold Rush.** This is why a lot of people lost their land, especially the tribes up north. It was just an injustice. This is why we Native Americans here in California had to keep a low profile, had to assimilate with other ethnic groups, because of the injustices imposed upon us. We were wanted people—they wanted to exterminate us. They wanted us gone. Why do we have some periods where we weren't visible or active? We were just behind the scenes, but we really couldn't be too active—public eye—because of the...

CJ: Need to survive.

AM: Exactly.

CJ: Have you ever felt personally discriminated against? We asked your cousin that question and he recalled being called a "Digger Indian" when he was growing up.

AM: I haven't literally been called that to my face, but you could see it when

---

* Adopted in 1970, the California Environmental Quality Act was written to inform government decision makers and the public about the potential environmental effects of a project, offer alternatives, and disclose reasons for approval. The impact of development projects on all historic resources must be identified and considered.

** The Gold Rush ushered in a horrific new era of state-sponsored violence against Native Americans. The forty-niners fiercely resented the Indians, who had worked for others in the goldfields, then increasingly on their own. By the early 1850s few Indian miners remained. Between 1845 and 1855, an estimated one hundred thousand California Indians died, victims of starvation, disease, and violence. Over one million dollars issued in state bonds supported volunteer campaigns for the "suppression of Indian hostilities" during the 1850s, a cost subsidized by the federal government. As well, three to four thousand native children throughout northern California were kidnapped between 1852 and 1867 and sold into virtual slavery as household servants. Women were seized for prostitution and men to labor in the fields. The lucrative, hateful business was all supported by "An Act for the Government and Protection of Indians." Passed by the California legislature in 1850, the act made it legal to indenture Indians to whites. Although affected by the same law, southern California Indians escaped much of the sanctioned murder and brutality inflicted on native people up north. However, supporters of Indian reservations negotiated in the treaties of 1851 and 1852 fully expected to take over the land left behind by the southern California Indians.

you're negotiating with different municipalities, with developers, with different agencies. They meet with you, talk with you to pacify you—they're just going through their positions, or [what] their higher agency says to them. Like the Forest Department. The government now lets us go on the land to gather sage, basket-weaving materials, and medicines. That's a new issue. How come they didn't allow us, one hundred years ago and fifty years ago, sixty years ago? Why all of a sudden within the last five, six years? Because they have to deal with the local people now. Before they were instructed by the higher agencies. There were people arrested for gathering medicine plants, something that was given to us, something that was our inherent right—to go and pick medicine and plants for basket weaving, for our culture. There were people being arrested by forest rangers. One of the ladies was picking plants for basket weaving and sheriffs pop out with guns raised. She was Native American—"I'm not a poacher. I'm just taking the little bit that I need to make my baskets for my culture." Examples like that still show some prejudice.*

CJ: What makes you Native American? You are an urban people today, have become an urban people, you've intermarried. You are many things. What makes you acknowledge one piece of your DNA more than all the other heritages found in your family? Is it because that piece has that stem, that root, which goes down in the place originally?

AM: You've answered your question for me. Yes, that's it for me. I think for a lot of us that's what it is. It's who we are, or where we're from. It's just that identity.

CJ: Do you acknowledge your other heritage, celebrate that also?

AM: Sure I do, because like I said, intermarriages. My wife is not Native American, so I celebrate with her. My mom is not Native American—so we celebrate and participate outside of our culture.

BMc: Would you feel the same if you lived somewhere else, if you lived in New Mexico instead of California, or you had a job and you lived in Denver? Would the feelings be the same as now, or is it the connection to this place that is so defining?

AM: No matter where I live, it's just something that would be a part of us, because I know where our roots are. I know where I came from, and I would continue whether I lived here or across the nation. It's just that calling, that connection. I am a proud person. I'm proud of who I am and what I am. History wasn't good to us, and you have to let it be known that we're not an extinct

---

* The U.S. Forest Service, National Park Service, and California State Parks have long recognized native peoples' ties to the land, including their need to harvest plant materials. However, until more recent times, that "recognition" simply meant people could, and were legally required to, obtain "use permits" if they wished to harvest plant and other materials. In more recent times, according to one expert, official policies and thinking on the subject have expanded as California State Parks and the federal services have become advocates for growth and native access. They are integrating traditional plant resources into their land management policies, and encouraging growth of materials which are highly valued and sought after in particular areas.

people. We've been here five, seven, ten thousand years. We're in all the archives, in the documentation, the mission records. We're a proud people.

BMc: Why do you think people keep on believing you're extinct, when there's so much evidence to the contrary? Why do you think this myth continues?

AM: People need to be educated that we still are here. Thanks to my son Andy and the rest of the dedicated dancers that go out, we've been all over. We've been to the island. We've been up north. We've been to the local museums. We've been in parades and different conferences, teacher conferences. We've been all over. We just have to educate people—we're still here, we're not extinct. This has to continue. Organizations, schools, and politics, different cities and council meetings—they know we're here. After twelve years, we finally sent a message—we're here, not extinct.

BMc: Besides burials and the land associated with those, what things are sacred to you in your values?

AM: Well, places where ceremonies were conducted; places in the mountains; where Cal State sits on this village of Povuu'ngna—one of the beginnings of our religion; Catalina Island, where people lived and worshiped. The nature center in Whittier, right along the banks of the riverbed up in Rio Hondo, we've gone there. Just the other day, a couple weeks ago, we went out by the Santa Ana River to the Rubidoux Nature Center and we sang. It's a feeling of fulfillment—that it's been there. We can make all the places sacred.

Dances are sacred and dance songs themselves are sacred because it's a form of our prayer. It also represent[s] the past lives from the other side, what's today, and the future. That's why we carry those songs and dances, so [they can] be passed on to the next generation, so they can continue on taking over the dances and prayers, pass down to their children, from generation through generation.

CJ: Every generation creates new dances, new traditions that are also sacred?

Andy Morales: Yes, always based on a pattern from the Tongva ancestors—we went back and got that foundation, and we build that foundation on that.

CJ: What are you building on?

Andy Morales: For example, the patterns, how our ancestors dance in a circle, in figure eights, certain footsteps, certain songs with native language. That, to me, is like a foundation. We took that history and we start building on what today is. It didn't lose the root because it's still there—a meaning from the past to the future to carry us forward. It always changes as time went on, generations went on, the stories change, the dance patterns change. We grow from that. It's not stuck on one specific step. It's like a continuous growing circle of life. That's what we're doing today, we're continuing on, growing, even though it's modern time.

CJ: What are you trying to communicate about today through your dance for future generations?

Andy Morales: I would like the generations to learn so they can carry on those dance steps, songs, and envision and come up with their own dance. That message is the calling of our ancestors—being proud of who you are, carry on these dances so it can be more strong.

AM: In our dances and songs and whatever we do, we always honor our ancestors because they're the ones that have taught us the ways. We never forget them. In memory of them, we always honor them. One song that I always end with is "O, my ancestor, O, my ancestor, listen to my heart, O, my ancestor, here is my heart." We sing it in our Tongva language. It's an honor song, remembering the ancestors. You have to know the past so you can survive in the present, continue into the future. It all stems down to the roots, to the ancestors.

BMc: What challenge do you think the next generation of Tongva will face, and how are you helping them prepare for the challenges?

Andy Morales: I really don't know what is coming in the future, what the children are going to face. But when they face an obstacle and deal with it, they become stronger, they learn through this experience. My teachings give them strength to deal with what they're going to face in the future, what their goals are. Teaching the songs, dances, the culture, what they want to be—I'm conditioning what they're going to do in life.

BMc: Are you also trying to share with them the sense of community that you feel so strongly as a family, bringing them here together? You have children in the after-school program. You're teaching them about the culture, and it seems like those children will understand something about your community more than a child who didn't have that benefit.

KMJ: I think that comes. I haven't been to a tribal meeting in probably six months—and they'll email me. They know they can get a hold of me. They can go to Andy or Anthony. The community part of it comes, but more importantly, when I see Andy working with the kids, he teaches them respect without realizing it. They have to respect their elders. They're learning they have to respect their culture. The books in schools say the Indians "used to" do this and that. No, we still do. We still eat traditional foods, we still gather plants. When taught "that is what they used to do," then they just assume we're gone. So the kids are able to go to the teachers—"We still do dance, and we still do sing." Ten years ago there was no way

Stephanie would be able to become a pediatrician, have the self-respect, the energy, or self-confidence to believe that she could accomplish such a goal.

AM: Nowadays you see the younger generation going into all different fields—legal, doctors. Just tell them there's something more out there—you got to go for it. One of my visions is to make it easier for them, open those doors. There's one particular story that I share with all the children, not only Native American but all other cultures and ethnic groups. It's a children's story, and it goes this way: There was a chief of a village, and he gathered all the village together because he was afraid that the culture and the teachings were going to be extinct, they were going to be lost. And so his people were telling him, "Well, let's hide it," and he asked them, "Where do we hide it?" The people said, "Let's hide it under the rocks, let's hide it in the riverbed, let's hide it under the trees." Finally this wise, wise old elder, or lady, in the back, in a trembly voice says, "I know where to hide it. I know where to hide it. Hide it in the children."

How true that is, because the children are going to continue your culture long after we're gone. So this is a message that I always leave out there with all children. I think this is a strong message for our particular children. They want to do it. They're not forced to do it. They can be hanging out in the mall, the movies, or whatever, but they choose to—they want to know. It's in them, just like me. The DNA, it's in them, too. You have to look in the identity. They already know this identity. It's an interesting word today, but what you're really teaching, it seems to me, is the definition of family—telling those children that they are not alone. They have a larger family, and that's Gabrielino. That's the historical relationship, because communities were family, whole villages. We do this through songs, dance, and through stories, the family. There is an honor song for women because they are the givers of life. The women do certain dance patterns—semicircles, full circles, weaving—they're establishing the pattern of life for their own individual families.

CJ: From your perspective, what has been the biggest change, or something that has not happened, something that you feel must change?

AM: I know that we still have our job cut out for us. We still need to get established and have more opportunity open to us by different agencies at the city, the council, the state and federal level. We need all these agencies to acknowledge that. We're still here, and right now we're not even halfway there. The evidence is when you have to go and face them, go before the full city council and prove yourself. So this is a challenge, and the challenge I need to accomplish. We have go beyond whatever these agencies have in mind—always subduing us, keeping us down.

CJ: Where does the money come from, the support, and the infrastructure to accomplish that goal, including legislation?

AM: Well, we don't have that.

KMJ: He does it.

AM: It's all volunteer.

KMJ: We don't have attorneys.

AM: We have one small block grant just for this [the Youth Center].

Andy Morales: It doesn't pay for legal fees. It does not pay for mileage, hers or mine, to go out and teach children.

CJ: Who wrote your bill?

AM: I plead with the staffers of those agencies to help me out, and we start sending emails, or just verbally, on the phone. They go, "Okay, we'll do this. We'll do that." I've been networking with the Native American Heritage Commission. They have been very helpful to me. They are the governing Native American agency that handles all the issues for Native Americans up and down the state. Again, their agency doesn't have that kind of moneys. They're also restricted, but they can get involved through individuals. That's how I guess you could say we use each other. I know they were involved with me with some of the language of the bill, and then we talked to the staffers of the local politicians. Them, me, and the Native American Commission have got things accomplished or whatever we need to do. The federal recognition bill was written in part because we had that ANA grant with UCLA, or with whoever it was, and that's how that one came about and that's why we haven't been able to get very far.

KMJ: He's so good. He is, he really is.

AM: I have a good wife that understands and is supportive. But her not being Native American, I guess she is, I mean, she shares my vision. She is Hispanic. She shares my vision, especially when she heard the stories from Kimmy, they went out to Playa Vista. She is the one that told me, "You know, you've been involved all these years—the memory of the ancestors, all the hard work your dad has done. I want to do something about it." When she heard Kimmy's story— babies still in the mothers' arms, buried—just tore her apart. She literally cried and says, "I'm directing you, you better do something, you're an active, strong leader in the community, not only here in San Gabriel but all the other communities, and the knowledge of who you are, and of the San Gabriel Gabrielino, and you got to do something about it."

The memory of the ancestors—you have to do something about it. I wanted to do something because I wasn't getting nowhere with the leaders again—Los Angeles, all the developers—they were just ignoring us. So, it's her support, and she shares my vision and my dad's vision. She just loved my dad dearly, and Dad thought the world of her. The memory of Dad and the memory of the ancestors, which Dad is now, that's where it always comes from—that drive, that push.

BMc: Are you reelected every two years?

AM: I have been. To tell you the truth, I'll take it on as long as it's in the best interest of the tribe [the Gabrieleno Tongva Tribal Council of San Gabriel], and the best interest of the membership. [If] they feel that I'm good for another two years, if they elect me, I'll do it as long as I'm strong, and healthy, and able to do it, which thank God I am right now, so far I'm okay. But I'll do it as long as they want me to do it. I'll continue.

CJ: Is the greatest threat to the community the whole issue of casinos?

AM: Yes, the political mindset. I know we've been told—Representative Hilda Solis entered a bill in Congress for us; she got bombarded by local politicians—"What are you doing?"—council, supervisors, and city council in L.A., I mean she got bombarded. "You know that means they're going to be federally recognized. They're going to get a casino. We don't want casinos on every corner in L.A., in L.A. County." Like I said, the political mindset, that all we want federal recognition for is a casino. That's not it. There are other issues we need to take care of first. Basically we're just researching different avenues to pursue. We haven't given up, no.*
    We went through a lawsuit [filed by members within our community]. There was a splinter group [in the Gabrieleno Tongva] that came under the direction of a gaming developer and they sued to take our identity, including the membership records and community name, because this community is where the roots are. It's here in San Gabriel. We got our day in court. Hopefully, that legal situation put us in a better standing.**

BMc: Is this other group actively pursuing recognition today?

AM: Yes, to my understanding, yes. I don't know which route they're using, but they're trying to get federally recognized also.

---

* On July 24, 2001, Congresswoman Hilda Solis of the State's 32nd congressional district introduced HR 2619, legislation to grant federal recognition to the Gabrieleno Tongva Tribal Council of San Gabriel. Passage would have given the tribe access to federal health, education, and other benefits, and, opponents believed, also the right to pursue Indian gaming. The bill did not move into committee.

** On September 22, 2003, the Superior Court of the State of California for the County of Los Angeles granted the motion of the Gabrieleno Tongva Tribal Council of San Gabriel to dispose all issues in the lawsuit filed against them pertaining to membership and potential gaming revenue. A judgment was entered in their favor. In ruling, the judge also stated that "dispute(s) as to membership in an Indian tribe...lie solely within the jurisdiction of tribal courts. Therefore, this court does not have jurisdiction to hear the matter."

CJ: Are there names of other families you remember your dad talking about who have the same tradition of being such strong leaders?

AM: They're still here, deep-rooted here in San Gabriel. Some moved on, and a lot have passed on, but those families are still visible here in San Gabriel. I just can't single out just one particular one. I respected and loved dearly all of them, the leaders. Most all are gone, but they were all leaders. They were all kind of my heroes and heroines, really ladies and men.

CJ: Do you think that the next generation of children know what they need to, since each generation loses something? You probably didn't ask the questions of your dad that you now wish you might have. We all have that feeling. Do you think the legacy of what you know because of your parents has been passed on to your children?

AM: No. I wish I would have asked more things, especially of my grandma, about the language and the ceremonies. When you're younger, those kinds of things don't come across to you. But what I have learned from the elders, and just in conversations, social talk at the meetings, or events, celebrations—"Oh yeah, I remember when this and that"—that's all I need. I just get carried away asking more and more. Right now my vision is to learn everything I can from the ones that are still alive and pass it on to the next generation. I don't want them to be wondering, like I am right now, "I should have asked that." I'm hoping I can answer all of them. That way they don't have to wonder, "Well, I remember my dad saying this, he heard it from my great-grandmother," whatever. I hope I can answer every question so they have an overall picture of how things were, how you learned it, to continue it so we won't become extinct.

CJ: Some Gabrielino lived on other reservations. Did members of your family end up living on a reservation, and how did that happen?

AM: I remember asking how some of our people ended up in Pechanga and Pala—that was part of the relocation era, where the government—probably the thirties, the forties—came to the urban area and says, "You're allowed to go and live on the reservation." That's how a lot of them made it on the reservations. That I know happened, because there is a family going through issues with enrollment. There's some big families being threatened to be disenrolled [from membership in the reservation] because they are Gabrielino, and others going through the same scenario right now because they relocated.

BMc: Did they have to be married into someone's tribe?

AM: I think so. My dad remembers that when he was a kid, he used to go to Riverside to a reservation. We had cousins over there. Grandpa David would go with another cousin of his from San Gabriel to Riverside to a reservation, but I don't know which reservation—again, the kind of question you should ask. But they would go out there because we had relatives on the reservation at Riverside. There was another cousin of ours who was married to an Indian lady from one of the reservations over there, so intermingling was always there. We did have Gabrielino families that relocated. But in our generation the connections are not as strong. There are some cultural events when we see each other, and they send, like the bird singers. Right now the Juaneños are gathering a bunch of singers and we sing with them. So there's still some interaction going on.

CJ: San Gabriel had many different communities in the early to mid-twentieth century, which according to others was not a problem. Would you agree?

AM: Yeah, it's evident by our intermarriages. It was just an ongoing relationship—intermingling, intermarriages, and extended families coming out of those relationships.

CJ: Are there other geographic areas that you're aware of today where the core of the people's tradition, their home, is not the San Gabriel area?

AM: People establish themselves in a different location, but yet they need to identify with the prime location, or the roots. That's the way I look at it. Yeah, there's Gabrielinos out there, they really don't call San Gabriel their home, but yet, I don't treat them any different. Throughout our history of community, we've had a strong role culturally, traditionally and politically. I think that's what makes this community unique in San Gabriel, because throughout the years we've been involved in every aspect of whatever we need to get accomplished. This is why we survived. This is why we're here today.

CJ: Are there any stories about your father, Sparky, that encapsulate who he was in your mind?

AM: Well, he was my hero. He was my hero. I looked up to him. I look up to him now, even though he's an ancestor, deceased—February of '95. He was born on November 19, 1912, I believe. He was a good talker. He could give you an earful. Everything, funny stories, serious stories—the Depression, the suffering and the poverty. During the Depression, he worked with the WPA public programs.* He was also involved in the reconstruction, rebuilding of the La Purisima Mission. He worked at one of the CCC camps. That's how he survived the Depression.

---

* The WPA (Work Projects Administration), created by presidential order in 1935, provided work to millions of unemployed during the Depression. Renowned WPA projects included construction of public buildings and roads, as well as projects supporting the arts, drama, media, and literature.
  Established in 1933 under Franklin Delano Roosevelt's New Deal, the Civilian Conservation Corps (CCC) was created by Congress to conserve timber, soil, and water resources. The CCC also provided training and employment to young unmarried, unemployed men during the Depression who were between seventeen and twenty-three years old. The CCC worked on projects throughout the California State Park system. Between 1934 and 1942, under the direction of the National Park Service, the CCC restored and reconstructed the La Purisima Mission complex near Lompoc. Founded in 1787, La Purisima was the eleventh of twenty-one missions in Alta California. The mission complex was relocated and rebuilt following an earthquake in 1812, and in 1933 the property was deeded to the state. La Purisima Mission State Historic Park is the most fully restored of all California missions.

A lot of our people survived on the little ranches that were in the area. Some worked at the church for the cemetery [and cleaning], some had to go pick crops up north. They would essentially go, and come back only during the winter, and then go back again in the spring. One story I remember, my grandpa took all the family up north a couple years in a row and Aunt Rose would come back to San Gabriel every so many days and watch the house. Can you imagine a trip to San Gabriel from Santa Monica in a horse and cart? In a sense they are all my heroes. They are all people that I look up to. They were people I learned from, and those are people I need to continue for—not only for them, but for future generations.

CJ: Michael Barthelemy talked about the early days, where you and he went out to work on reburials as the "most likely descendant." Was that the beginning of the process in those early years?

AM: It started back then with Michael [Barthelemy] and Art [Morales]. The CEQA laws, or the protection laws, were very weak, in infancy, back in the early seventies. There was nothing really solid in these laws. I guess Dad, Michael [Barthelemy], Art [Morales], myself—I was still actively working and could only tag along whenever I had a day off, a weekend or something. They were the ones policing these sites, and making sure the developer and cities were complying with the little bit of law at that time. They were the first ones that really established the goals and the pattern of compliance [with] CEQA and preservation laws, because they were very weak. They're pioneers of archaeology—taking care of our cultural sites and protecting them. Before this, it was just a green light for developers to tear everything up. There were no laws holding them back. You find a lot of artifacts in people's garages. Right now I get calls from people—"My grandfather, he knew there was a sacred site at Palos Verdes Peninsula." "They found some metates," or "They found human remains."* "I have a skull in my garage." Nightmare stories like that—because there were no laws back then until the early seventies, when the CEQA Preservation Act and all that came into hand.** The ones that were real active from our area—my dad, Art, and Michael—and then Juaneños got involved. That's why I say we've been involved in all aspects of culture, of tradition, politics, everything.

BMc: What's the hardest part of your job, Anthony? When is the best part of your job as tribal chairman?

AM: My satisfaction is when I get something accomplished, like when I know I can get some legislation, which I have, when I can make situations easier for the next generation. That's my satisfaction. That's my accomplishment.

---

* A metate is a stone block with a shallow concave surface, used with a mano for grinding seed, corn, or grains.

** The Preservation Act under the California Environmental Quality Act requires disclosure of a project's impact on cultural resources.

Those are the positive accomplishments, the ones I really enjoy. I don't like the struggle of still fighting for our rights, for protection of our culture, and banging heads with politicians to hear us. Those are the negative battles I really don't like, and I hope that within time they'll finish.

I think we're making some headway. I now think, "When is it going to happen?" There are no "ifs" about it. Something has to happen, good or bad. They are either going to tell you yes or no. But we're to the point now where, you know, it's—"When?" When is all this going to change? This is going to happen now. I'm hoping we're getting close to that.

NOTES

Introduction

1. Campio, David 2006.
2. Martinez 2008.
3. McCawley 1996:89–90.
4. Barthelemy 2006.
5. Rawls 1984.
6. Kimberly Morales Johnson in Barthelemy, Vivian 2006.
7. Barthelemy, Vivian 2006.
8. Wagner (1929:85–86) gives an account of Cabrillo's 1542 visit to Santa Catalina and his interactions with the Tongva living on the island.
9. Boscana 1933:30–33; Bright 1978; McCawley 1996:144; Reid 1852:19.
10. Boscana 1933:17–18. Boscana described his method of study as follows: "By gifts, endearments, and kindness, I elicited from them their secrets with their explanations, and by witnessing the ceremonies which they performed I learned by degrees their mysteries. Thus, by devoting a portion of the nights to profound meditation, and comparing their actions with their disclosures, I was enabled after a long time to acquire a knowledge of their religion."
11. See Dakin 1939; Heizer 1968; King 1899; Reid 1852.
12. An exception was the work of Alexander Taylor published in 1860.
13. Gatschet 1879; Henshaw n.d.; Loew 1879.
14. See McCawley 1996:18–19.
15. Merriam 1955; n.d.a.; n.d.b.
16. Harrington 1986; Mills and Brickfield 1986.
17. Kroeber 1925.
18. Art Morales in Barthelemy, Vivian 2006.
19. Engelhardt 1927a.
20. Gillingham 1961.
21. Cleland 1941.
22. Mason 1984.
23. Phillips 1990:62–64; Rawls 1984; Robinson 1952.
24. Ramos in Alvitre et al. 2005.
25. Art Morales in Barthelemy, Vivian 2006.
26. Thompson in Alvitre et al. 2005.
27. Torres in Alvitre et al. 2005.
28. Barthelemy, Michael 2006.
29. According to Tolley (2006:19) perhaps two-thirds of California tribes remain unrecognized, based on a BIA statistic cited in the Advisory Council on California Indian Policy's report, "Recognition Report: Equal Justice for California" (1997:6).
30. Campio, David 2006.
31. See Boscana 1933:58–59; McCawley 1996:145, 165–166; Reid 1852:20.
32. Fred Morales, who went by the nickname "Sparky," was named chief by the tribal elders; he passed away in 1995 at the age of 83. In honor of his memory, the California State Legislature adjourned its meeting on

February 10, 1995, and the County of Los Angeles Board of Supervisors adjourned its meeting on February 21, 1995. California State Legislature 1995; County of Los Angeles Board of Supervisors 1995.

33. See McCawley 1996:9–10.

34. The San Gabriel–based Gabrieleno Tongva Tribal Council follows the traditional spelling using "e" instead of "i"—Gabrieleno.

35. Martinez 2008.

36. Boscana 1933:29; Geiger and Meighan 1976:93; also see Reid 1852:20.

37. A broad plateau region covering most of Nevada as well as parts of California and Utah.

38. McCawley 1996:2–3; Shipley 1978:81.

39. Marshall 2007:xiii.

One—Continuity within Change: Identity and Culture

1. Barthelemy, Michael 2006.

2. Campio, David 2006.

3. Barthelemy, Michael 2006.

4. Martinez 2008.

5. Lassos 2006.

6. The author defines these three levels of identity for the purposes of this discussion.

7. Holtorf 2000–2007, "Cultural Memory."

8. Alvitre 2006.

9. *Los Angeles Times* 1921.

10. Lassos 2006.

11. Anthropologists distinguish between two different types of extinction: physical extinction, the disappearance of bloodlines through death; and "cultural" extinction, the gradual loss of language, customs, rituals, etc., that define a "culture." The two types of extinction are not mutually exclusive; a culture can become extinct through the destruction of its people.

12. Caughey 1952:18. The report is known as the B. D. Wilson Report after Benjamin D. Wilson, the Indian sub-agent for southern California who was commissioned to prepare it. However, it was most likely ghostwritten by Benjamin Hayes, a district judge for southern California. See Caughey 1952:xxvi–xxvii.

13. Campio, David 2006.

14. McCawley 1996:15–16.

15. Bean and Smith 1978a:547; McCawley 1996:25,89.

16. Alvitre 2006.

17. Heizer and Elsasser 1980:75–76.

18. McCawley 1996:111–131.

19. Kelly 1995:116–117.

20. Barthelemy, Michael 2006.

21. McCawley 1996:111–131; see also Landberg 1965.

22. Engelhardt 1927a:19.

23. McCawley 1996:112–113, 136–137; 2002.

24. Vizcaino 1959; Wagner 1929:235–237.

25. Geiger and Meighan 1976:19; Kroeber 1925:621; McCawley 1996:90; Munro 2002.

26. Bean 1972:152–153; Kroeber 1925:629; McCawley 1994:3.25–3.26; 1996:23, 91, 112–114; 2002; Strong 1929:98.

27. Boscana 1933:27–35.

28. McCawley 1996:10, 25, 90.

29. Bean 1972:123; McCawley 1996:111–114; Reid 1852:43–44, 49–51, 55, 63; Strong 1929:95–96, 98.

30. McCawley 1996:149–150; Roberts 1933:3–4, 10, 77–94.

31. Bean 1972:90; Boscana 1933:85.

32. Engelhardt 1927a:19.

33. Carmelo 2006.

34. Behrns 2006.

35. Alvitre 2007.

36. Torres 2007.

37. Bean and Smith 1978a:543; Boscana 1933:33–34, 70.

38. Boscana 1933:51–52; Reid 1852:16, 25–27.

39. See the discussion in McCawley 1996:104–105.

40. Castillo 1978:101–102; Hackel 2005:129–134; Rawls 1984:14–16.

41. Bean 1968:28–29; Castillo 1978; Cook 1943:73–75; Rawls 1984:14–20.

42. Benjamin Hayes, the author of the 1852 B. D. Wilson Report and a district judge, argues that this pact created a treaty—or a series of them—between the Indians and the Spanish Crown as well as successor governments. See Caughey 1952:45–46.

43. The missionaries were accused of purposefully avoiding secularization to keep control of the missions. For their

part, the missionaries maintained that the Indians were not yet ready to control their own affairs. See Bean 1968:29; Castillo 1978:105.

44. Hackel 2005:127; see also Bolton 1930:181; Cook 1943:73.

45. Hackel (2005) discusses these environmental and demographic changes, which he calls the "dual revolution," for the Monterey Bay region. Milliken (1995) offers a similar analysis of missionization for the San Francisco Bay Area.

46. Mason 1975; 1984; 1986; Wilbur 1937:186.

47. Morales and Alva 1980.

48. Boscana 1933:55; Guest 1985:228.

49. Cook 1943:113–114; Hackel 2005:12; Rawls 1984:14–16.

50. Cook 1943:113–114; Guest 1985:230; Hackel 2005:199–203; Reid 1852:87–88.

51. See Bean 1972:85, 151–153; McCawley 1996:113–114, 158–168.

52. Torres 2007.

53. Boscana 1933:27–35.

54. McCawley 1996:147; Blackburn 1975:30 describes a similar cosmology for the Chumash Indians.

55. McCawley 1996:95–104; see also Applegate 1978; Eliade 1951; Harner 1973; Hudson and Underhay 1978.

56. Alvitre 2006.

57. Barthelemy, Michael 2006.

58. Cook 1943:113–115; Guest 1979:5, 11–13.

59. Hackel 2005:235–239; Rawls 1984:16; Reid 1852:84–85.

60. Reid 1852:85.

61. Haas 1995:18; Hackel 2005:254–256.

62. Geiger and Meighan 1976:125.

63. McCawley 1996:198–199.

64. Bean 1978:583; Bean and Smith 1978b:573; Blackburn and Bean 1978:564; King and Blackburn 1978:536.

65. Cook 1943:94; Engelhardt 1927b:88–89; Reid 1852:94–95.

66. Cook 1943:84–90; Webb 1952:116.

67. Cook 1943:61, Table 4; Geiger and Meighan 1976:57–58; see also Hackel 2005:178–180.

68. Boscana 1933:80.

69. Alvitre 2007.

70. Milliken 1995:223–224.

71. Barthelemy, Michael 2006.

72. Reid 1852:76.

73. Jackson 1991; see also McCawley 1996:197–198.

74. Gonzales in Alvitre et al. 2005.

75. Torres in Alvitre et al. 2005.

76. Behrns 2006.

77. Art Morales in Barthelemy, Vivian 2006.

78. Martinez 2008.

79. Ramos in Alvitre et al. 2005.

80. Campio 2006.

81. Engelhardt 1927a:48–52; Gillingham 1961.

82. Engelhardt 1927a:65.

83. Engelhardt 1927b:9.

84. Geiger and Meighan 1976:129.

85. Castillo 1978:104–105; Cleland 1941:20–21.

86. Castillo 1978:105; Cleland 1941:20–23.

87. Engelhardt 1927a:176–177.

88. Rawls 1984:49.

89. Castillo 1978:107–109; Ord 1978:13–16, 37–40; Rawls 1984:86–110; Robinson 1952:2–3.

90. Almaguer 1994:55.

91. Rancho Santa Anita was located in the modern city of Arcadia.

92. Newmark and Newmark 1929:24, 89.

93. Newmark and Newmark 1929:89.

94. Heizer 1968; Dakin 1939.

95. Haas 1995:30–31.

96. María Dolores was from the village of Yaanga. See Robinson 1952:13.

97. Dakin 1939; King 1899.

98. Prospero was from the village of Comicrangna, as was Victoria Reid. He was baptized at Mission San Gabriel on January 20, 1804. His mother's name was Culcir and his father's name was Menonshuunat (or Menanjunar). Prospero was married to María Rafaela Alvarez. He was buried February 1, 1852. Torres 2005.

99. Prospero and his family are listed on the 1850 census (except for his unborn daughter Candelaria); they are listed as Prospero Dominguez, age 55 (laborer); Rafaela, age 45; Juana, age 11; Liberata, age 9; Jesus,

age 7; and Maria, age 2. They are not identified as Indians. See Newmark and Newmark 1929:91.

100. Torres 2007.

101. Vivian Barthelemy in Barthelemy, Michael 2006.

102. Carmelo 2006.

103. Lassos 2006.

104. Art Morales in Barthelemy, Vivian 2006.

105. Alvitre 2007.

106. Barthelemy, Michael 2006.

107. Martinez 2008.

108. Hackel (2005:390) discusses this process in the Monterey Bay region at Mission San Carlos Borromeo. Shoup and Milliken (1999:110–118) discuss a similar example at Mission Santa Clara de Asís.

109. Anthony Morales 2006.

110. Newmark and Newmark 1929:70–73.

111. 1860 Federal Census.

112. Newmark and Newmark 1929:70–73; Robinson 1952:33–34; 1966.

113. 1860 Federal Census.

114. The 1850 and 1860 censuses are arranged in order of the homes visited; thus, it is possible to follow the census agent's progress through the local communities. However, the 1870 census segregates the Indians on separate schedules, making it unclear what communities the census agent was visiting.

115. Morales and Alva 1980:13–14, 24.

116. Morales and Alva 1980:7–8.

117. Morales and Alva 1980:18.

118. Alvitre 2006.

119. Reid 1852:100.

120. Engelhardt 1927a:268.

121. Torres 2007.

122. Carmelo 2006.

123. Alvitre 2006.

124. Alvitre 2007.

125. Morales and Alva 1980:23.

126. Art Morales in Lassos 2006.

127. Cleland 1941:51–74; McCawley 1994:4.9–4.15; Monroy 1990:100–102; Rawls 1994.

128. Wilbur 1937:186.

129. Rawls 1984:81–108.

130. Ord 1978:13–15, 32, 37–40; Robinson 1952:23–25.

131. Bell 1927:35.

132. Ord 1978:13–14.

133. Ord 1978:38. In 1872 the prohibition against Indians testifying against whites was rescinded. See Almaguer 1994:133.

134. Castillo 1978:107–108; Cook 1978:93; Rawls 1984:171–186.

135. Morales, Anthony 2006.

136. Carrico 1987:22–23.

137. Reid 1852:102.

138. Ord 1978:13.

139. Cleland 1941.

140. Barthelemy, Vivian 2006.

141. Castillo 1978:121; Phillips 1990:66. In 1879 the state legislature granted California Indians the right to vote in all state elections. See Almaguer 1994:133.

142. Barthelemy, Vivian 2006.

143. Art Morales in Barthelemy, Vivian 2006.

144. Phillips 1990:66–67; Shipek 1987:49–53.

145. Alvitre 2007.

146. Art Morales in Barthelemy, Vivian 2006.

147. Morales, Anthony 2006.

148. Phillips 1990:69–70; Shipek 1987:194–195; Tolley 2006:75–76.

149. Behrns 2006.

150. Haas 1995:130; Tolley 2006:75–79.

151. Morales and Alva 1980:29.

152. Carmelo 2006.

153. Alvitre et al. 2005.

154. Alvitre 2007.

155. Torres 2007. According to Robinson (1952:13), José Carlos Rosas, the son of settler Basilio Rosas, married María Dolores of the village of Yaanga on July 4, 1784. Robinson notes, "ninth generation descendants of this union live today in San Gabriel." Two other sons of Basilio Rosas also married Tongva women, according to Robinson.

156. Martinez 2008.

157. Alvitre 2007.

158. Campio, Earl 2006.

159. Apostol 1980; Phillips 1990:63.

160. Bradley n.d.

161. Martinez 2008.

162. McWilliams 1946.

163. Van Dyke 1913. McGroarty n.d. A 1941 copy of the play program states that it was then in the 23rd year of production (Van Dyke 1913).

164. Morales and Alva 1980:10.

165. Art Morales in Barthelemy, Vivian 2006.

166. Barthelemy, Vivian 2006.

167. Ibid.

168. Morales and Alva 1980:30.

169. Barthelemy, Vivian 2006.

170. Barthelemy, Michael 2006.

171. Art Morales in Barthelemy, Vivian 2006.

172. Articles of Incorporation filed May 11, 1994. The council has also been informally known as the Gabrieleno/Tongva Band of Mission Indians of San Gabriel.

173. Carmelo 2006.

Two—A Connection to Place: Land and History

1. Torres in Alvitre et al. 2005.

2. Behrns 2006.

3. Alvitre 2006.

4. Timbrook et al. 1982; 1990.

5. Barthelemy, Michael 2006.

6. See McCawley 1996:23–33.

7. Ramos in Alvitre et al. 2005.

8. See Eliade (1957) for a discussion of sacred centers throughout the world. Other known Tongva ritual sites include the summer and winter solstice sites at Burro Flats at the western end of the San Fernando Valley, and the village of Nájquqar at the isthmus on Santa Catalina Island, where Spanish explorers in 1602 observed a Tongva *yovaar*, or temple. Povuu'ngna, however, has the distinction of being the only Tongva religious site mentioned in their surviving oral literature. See McCawley 1996:27–28, 35–38, 148; 1994:3.18–3.19, 3.28–3.29; Wagner 1929:237.

9. Boscana 1933:27–35.

10. Alvitre in Alvitre et al. 2005.

11. Torres in Alvitre et al. 2005.

12. Because the site is bisected by a paved road, it was recorded by archaeologist Keith Dixon in 1960 as two separate archaeological sites (CA-LAN-234 and CA-LAN-235); however, it is assumed that it was originally one continuous archaeological deposit. In 1972 a portion of a male human burial was uncovered by workmen digging a sprinkler trench. In 1974, Dixon nominated CA-LAN-234/235 as well as the Bixby Ranch Site (CA-LAN-306) for the National Register of Historic Places. See Altschul 1994:5.1–5.12; Dixon 1974.

13. In 1982 the state of California passed legislation authorizing the Native American Heritage Commission to identify a "most likely descendant" when Native American remains were discovered. The most likely descendants were given the authority to make recommendations regarding the treatment and disposition of the remains. "Native American Heritage Commission History," http://www.nahc.ca.gov/nahc_history.html.

14. Barthelemy, Michael 2006.

15. When the university announced plans in 1992 to construct a mini-mall on the site, the Native American Heritage Commission and Indian plaintiffs filed a lawsuit based on Section 5097.94 of the Public Resources Code that protects Indian burial grounds and sacred places on public land. The American Civil Liberties Union entered the case when the university threatened to evict Indians who were camping on the site to prevent the university from undertaking large-scale archaeological excavations on the property. In 1995 the university won a favorable decision in court, but the following year the Court of Appeals ruled in favor of the Indian plaintiffs and the Native American Heritage Commission and ordered the case back to trial. The university subsequently dropped its plans for commercial development of the site, although this decision is subject to review by subsequent administrations. Puvungna Web Site 1996; 2005; also Arellanes in Alvitre et al. 2005; Thompson in Alvitre et al. 2005; Williams 2008.

16. Perhaps the best-known Tongva village is Yaanga, thanks to its close association with the city of Los Angeles. See Robinson 1952.

17. Boscana 1933:32; Reid 1852:8.

18. Harrington 1933:148, note 77.

19. Milliken and Hildebrandt 1997; Harrington 1933:148,

note 7, devotes an entire paragraph to the location of Povuu'ngna and its association with Rancho Los Alamitos. Altschul et al. 1994:9.1–9.2 conclude, based on a review of the ethnohistorical data and known archaeological sites, that the Bixby Ranch Site (CA-LAN-306) and the Los Altos Site (CA-LAN-270), located approximately one mile to the north of Bixby Ranch, are the most likely candidates for Povuu'ngna; however, the relationship between the two sites remains unclear. Milliken and Hildebrandt 1997:33–34 wrote: "The preponderance of the evidence we have reviewed indicates that it is appropriate to equate the Alamitos Mesa area with the location of the protohistoric village of Puvunga." For a comparison of differing points of view on this topic see Boxt and Raab 2000 and 2000a, Dixon 2000, Lightfoot 2000, and Ruyle 2000. See Bates 1972 for a description of the site at CA-LAN-270.

20. Fages 1937:26–27; Wagner 1929:86.

21. Harrington 1933:149, note 77. It was the grove of cottonwoods that lent the rancho its Spanish name, Alamitos—"little cottonwoods."

22. According to Bean (1972:71), Cahuilla villages were laid out according to available freshwater sources. If the source was a stream, houses were laid out along its banks. If the source was a cluster of springs, the homes were scattered about the cluster. If the water source was a single spring, homes were built close to it. Oxendine (1983:38–46) offers a similar analysis for Luiseño villages. Benson (1997) provides sketch maps of Chumash villages based on the nineteenth-century excavations of the Reverend Stephen Bowers.

23. Milliken and Hildebrandt 1997:48, Table 2.

24. Boscana (1933:37) notes that the chief, known as the *tomyaar*, had the privilege of building his home near the sacred grounds of the *yovaar*, the open-air temple that Boscana called the "vanquech." See also McCawley 1996:23–33.

25. Altschul 1994:5, 6.

26. Thompson in Alvitre et al. 2005.

27. Engelhardt 1927a, 1927b; Temple 1960.

28. Merriam 1968:116, 135.

29. Cleland 1941:7–15; Engelhardt 1927a:48–52; Gillingham 1961:42–46.

30. Cleland 1941:8. Also see Engelhardt 1927b:5–6, 9 and Geiger and Meighan 1976:129 for early comments by the missionaries regarding Indians working on the ranchos.

31. Cook 1943:19; Engelhardt 1927a:109; Merriam 1968:116. Also see Hackel (2005) and Milliken (1995) for discussions of these same processes among the California Indians living in the Monterey and San Francisco Bay regions.

32. Young et al. 1989.

33. Cleland 1941:8.

34. Newmark and Newmark 1929:80.

35. Harrington 1933:149, note 77.

36. Anonymous, n.d., "Lista de Sirvientes en Alamitos." Abel Stearns Collection.

37. Alvitre in Alvitre et al. 2005.

38. Arellanes in Alvitre et al. 2005.

39. Torres in Alvitre et al. 2005.

40. Kuipers 2007; Lin 2004; Madigan 2004; Malnic 2004; *Santa Monica Mirror* 1999; *USA Today* 2004; Varaorta 2008; Walker 2008.

41. Mehta 2002; Yi 2003; Werblin 1997.

42. Barboza 2008; Carcamo 2008.

43. Morin 2000.

44. Coker 2001.

45. Alvitre in Alvitre et al. 2005.

46. Behrns 2006.

47. See McCawley 1996:201–202.

48. Warner et al. 1876:17.

49. Hayes 1929:150–151.

50. Campio, Earl 2006.

51. Campio, David 2006.

52. Johnson 1975.

53. Cleland 1941:7, 20–21.

54. Haas (1995:33) states that "all Indians were made full and equal citizens under the law," while Shipek (1987:28) states that "Mexican law considered settled Mission Indians as citizens." Rawls (1984:85–86) notes that while Indians technically were citizens, only a few (perhaps two hundred in the entire state) could exercise their voting right, because of the strict property requirements.

55. Castillo 1978:104–105; also see Haas 1995:36.

56. Engelhardt 1927a:174–179. Also see Haas (1995:32–38), Hackel (2005:384–388), and Shipek

(1987:25–28) for more thorough discussions of the secularization and privatization of the California missions.

57. Haas 1995:54.

58. Dakin (1939:119–120) describes this petition in her biography of Hugo Reid. The author has searched for the original document without success.

59. Haas 1995:32–40; Shipek 1987:25–26. Hackel (2005:389), in discussing Mexican land grants given to non-Indians, notes that "fewer than twenty grantees collectively received more than ninety thousand acres in the Monterey area."

60. Hackel 2005:390.

61. Morales, Anthony 2006.

62. Morales and Alva 1980:4, 14, 15.

63. Alvitre 2007. Cowan (1956:62–63) lists Rancho Potrero Chico (also known as Rancho Potrero de la Mission Vieja de San Gabriel) as granted to Antonio Valenzuela in 1843, with Ramon Valenzuela et al. as claimants. Expediente 388 of the Spanish Archives and Docket 618 of the California Land Claims contain partial files of documents related to Rancho Potrero de la Mission Vieja de San Gabriel. The rancho was originally granted to Antonio Valenzuela and Juan Alvitre. Docket 618 includes a 1917 map of Potrero Chico, much of which passed into the hands of the Baldwin family. The landowners named on the 1917 parcel map in Docket 618 include Perry, Sanchez, Repetto, Alvitre, and Anita M. Baldwin and Clara Baldwin Stocker.

64. Records of these grants are found in the Spanish Archives: Expediente #434, Ramon Valencia; Expediente #443, M. S. Tasion (Neophyte); Expediente #446, Felipe (Neophyte); Expediente #486, Serafin de Jesus (Neophyte); and Expediente #537, A. Manbe (Neophyte). Records of grants are also contained in the California Private Land Claims Cases: Docket #461, Prospero Tract of Land Near San Gabriel Mission, Rafaela Valenzuela et al.; Docket #463, Tract of Land Near Mission San Gabriel, Francisco Sales; Docket #554, Tract of Land Near San Gabriel, Simeon (An Indian); Simeon is also listed on Dockets #459, #460, and #556.

65. Robinson 1952:33–34; Spanish Archives, Expediente #458, Encino; Expediente #461, El Escorpion; California Private Land Claims Cases Docket #468, El Encino, Vicente de la Ossa et al.; Docket #552, El Escorpion, M. Oden & Manuel Urbano.

66. Ord 1978:32.

67. Caughey 1952:23–24.

68. Haas 1995:58; Shipek 1987:31–32.

69. Haas 1995:57.

70. Shipek 1987:31.

71. California Private Land Claims Cases Docket #461, Prospero Tract of Land Near San Gabriel Mission, Rafaela Valenzuela et al.; Docket #554, Tract of Land Near San Gabriel, Simeon (an Indian); Docket #463, Tract of Land Near Mission San Gabriel, Francisco Sales.

72. Shipek 1987:31–32, 36–37. Also see Haas 1995:60.

73. Shipek 1987:32–33.

74. Shipek 1987:34–36, 42.

75. Rust 1904; n.d.

76. Morales and Alva 1980:4.

77. Morales, Anthony 2006.

78. Art Morales in Barthelemy, Vivian 2006.

79. Lassos 2006.

80. Martinez 2008. A "Summary of Research" on Rancho Potrero de la Mission Vieja de San Gabriel, Rancho Potrero Chico prepared in 1983–1984 by attorney James B. Tucker concluded that "the interests of the heirs of Valenzuela have been conveyed over a period of time to various owners by grant deed, quitclaim, adverse possession, foreclosure, probate or other."

81. Torres 2005.

82. Torres 2007.

83. Torres 2005.

84. Torres 2007.

85. Shipek 1987:30–31.

86. Phillips 1975.

87. Martinez 2008.

88. Phillips 1975; 1990:69–70; Shipek 1987:194–195.

89. Shipek 1987:35.

90. Phillips 1975.

91. Phillips 2004.

92. Shipek 1987:34–37.

93 Shipek 1987:39–41.

94. Alvitre 2006.

95. Morales and Alva 1980:9.

96. Morales, Anthony 2006.

97. Art Morales in Barthelemy, Vivian 2006.

98. Bathelemy, Michael 2006.

99. Alvitre 2006.

100. Carmelo 2006.

101. Campio, Earl 2006.

102. Campio, David 2006.

103. Carmelo 2006.

104. Barthelemy, Michael 2006.

Three—The Enduring Vision: Recognition and Renewal

1. Martinez 2007.

2. Latta 1976:140, 179. Merriam 1955:77–86; n.d.a; n.d.b.

3. Ramos in Alvitre et al. 2005.

4. Merriam 1955:77–85; n.d.a; n.d.b.

5. http://www.tongva.com.

6. Gabrielino-Tongva Tribe 2006; http://www.gabrielinotribe.org.

7. http://www.tongvatribe.net.

8. In 2008 the Gabrielino-Tongva Language Committee released its first phrasebook, titled *Yaara' Shiraaw'ax 'Eyooshiraaw'a: Now You're Speaking Our Language, Gabrielino Tongva Fernandeño*. See Gabrielino-Tongva Language Committee 2008.

9. http://www.onionskin.com/gabrielino/index.html.

10. Tolley 2006:63–64. An alternative route, congressional recognition, avoids the Bureau of Indian Affairs' federal acknowledgment process. Also called "restoration," this avenue generally requires a tribe to prove an unambiguous case that it was previously recognized. Also see Tolley 2006:205, 208–210.

11. Tolley 2006:41.

12. Tolley 2006:62–63.

13. Martinez 2008.

14. Carmelo 2006.

15. Tolley 2006:19, 41, 65, 248 note 2.

16. Tolley 2006:227–232, Appendix A.

17. Tolley 2006:18–37.

18. Tolley 2006:79.

19. Barthelemy, Vivian 2006.

20. Morales, Anthony 2006.

21. Tolley 2006:13.

22. Barthelemy, Michael 2006.

23. Carmelo 2006.

24. Ibid.

25. Morales, Anthony 2006.

26. Carmelo 2008.

27. Barthelemy, Michael 2006.

28. Martinez 2008.

29. Tolley 2006:65–69.

30. Barthelemy, Michael 2006.

31. Tolley 2006:41.

32. Martinez 2008.

33. Morales, Anthony 2006.

34. Campio, David 2006.

35. Articles of Incorporation 1994.

36. Docket 47 and Docket 80 of the California Indians Jurisdictional Act. See the discussion of this law in the first essay in this volume, "Continuity within Change."

37. Morales, Anthony 2006.

38. Carcamo 2008.

39. Morales, Anthony 2006.

40. AB 2641 strengthens the protection of Native American burial sites and "ensures the preservation of sacred burial grounds." The bill was designed to "protect Native American burial sites" by creating "a process for meaningful consultations involving all interested parties." http://democrats.assembly.ca.gov/members/a23/press/a232006005.html.

41. Morales, Anthony 2006.

42. Ibid.

43. Ibid.

44. Ibid.

45. Alvitre 2006.

46. California State Assembly Resolution, 1994; City of San Gabriel, California, 1994.

47. Martinez 2008.

48. Alvitre 2006.

49. Behrns 2006.

50. Carmelo 2006.

51. Andy Morales in Morales, Anthony 2006.

52. Campio, David 2006.

53. Coker 2001.

54. Martinez 2008.

55. The Gabrielino/Tongva Springs are designated as California State Historical Landmark No. 522. http://www.onionskin.com/gabrielino/index.html.

56. Bolton 1926:136–137; 1927:149–150.

57. Behrns 2006.

58. Ibid.

59. Bolton 1926:134–135.

60. Reid 1852:19.

61. "Patron Saints Index: Blessed Gregory of Nonantula." http://www.catholic-rum.com/saints/saintg83.htm.

62. The name does not appear in recognizable form in Merriam 1968. Harrington quotes one of his Tongva sources, José Zalvidea, who translated it to mean "we are in warmth" or "we are in the sun now." See McCawley 1996:61.

63. Behrns 2006.

64. Ibid.

65. Art Morales in Barthelemy, Vivian 2006.

66. Morales, Anthony 2006.

67. Torres 2007.

68. Art Morales in Lassos 2006.

References: The Essays

Primary Sources

Interviews

Except where noted, all transcripts are on file at Rancho Los Alamitos, Long Beach, California.

Alvitre, Cindi. May 16, 2006.

———. April 17, 2007.

Alvitre, Cindy, Gloria Arellanes, Linda Gonzales, Jacob Gutierrez, Claudia Jurmain, William McCawley, Janice Ramos, Nicole Ramos, Stacy Thompson, and Craig Torres. October 15, 2005.

Barthelemy, Michael Joseph. April 5, 2006. Also present: Vivian Barthelemy and Patty Roess.

Barthelemy, Vivian Morales. January 31, 2006. Also present: Kimberly Morales Johnson, Art Morales, and Patty Roess.

Behrns, Angie Dorame. June 13, 2006. Also present: Dal Basile.

Campio, David. March 18, 2006.

Campio, David, and Earl Campio. April 2, 2006.

Campio, Earl. April 2, 2006. Also present: David Campio and Bonnie Campio.

Carmelo, Virginia. August 24, 2006.

———. July 28, 2008.

Lassos, Al. April 11, 2006. Also present: Art Morales, Kimberly Morales Johnson, and Dolores Lassos.

Martinez, Desirée. January 15, 2008.

Morales, Anthony. June 7, 2006. Also present: Kimberly Morales Johnson and Andy Morales.

Torres, Craig. March 28, 2007. Audio recording and partial transcript in author's possession.

Government Documents

Anonymous. February 25, 2007. "Coto Bill to Protect Native American Remains Signed into Law." http://democrats.assembly.ca.gov

California Legislature Assembly Resolution. "Assembly Joint Resolution No. 96." Adopted in Assembly August 11, 1994; adopted in Senate August 31, 1994. Copy on file, Gabrieleno/Tongva Tribal Council of San Gabriel.

California Legislature. February 10, 1995. *Assembly Daily Journal*.

California Private Land Claims, Record Group 49, Records of the General Land Office. Publication #T910. National Archives. Laguna Niguel, Calif.:

Dockets 459 and 460: "Tract of Land Near San Gabriel, Simeon (An Indian)"; Docket 461: "Prospero-Tract of Land Near San Gabriel Mission, Rafaela Valenzuela et al."; Docket 463: "Tract of Land near Mission San Gabriel, Francisco Sales." Microfilm Roll 63.

Docket 468: "El Encino, Vicente de la Ossa et al. Microfilm Roll 64.

Docket 552: "El Escorpion, M. Oden & Manuel Urbano"; Dockets 554 and 556: "Tract of Land Near San Gabriel, Simeon (An Indian)." Microfilm Roll 94.

Docket 618: "Potrero Chico or Rancho Potrero de la Mission Vieja de San Gabriel, Antonio Valenzuela and Juan Alvitre." Microfilm Roll 116.

City of San Gabriel, Calif. August 24, 1994. "Gabrielino-Tongva Nation." Copy on file, Gabrieleno Tongva Tribal Council of San Gabriel.

County of Los Angeles Board of Supervisors. February 21, 1995. "In Memoriam." Copy on file, Gabrieleno Tongva Tribal Council of San Gabriel.

Dixon, Keith A. 1974. National Register of Historic Places Inventory Nomination Form. On file, California State Univ., Long Beach.

Federal Census of 1860. National Archives. Laguna Niguel, Calif.

Federal Census of 1870. National Archives. Laguna Niguel, Calif.

Gabrieleno Tongva Tribal Council. "Articles of Incorporation of Gabrieleno Tongva Tribal Council, A California Public Benefit Corporation." Corporation No. 1888576, filed in the office of the Secretary of State of the State of California, May 11, 1994. Copy on file, Gabrieleno Tongva Tribal Council of San Gabriel.

Gabrielino-Tongva Tribe. "Statement by Unincorporated Association." Filed with the office of the Secretary of State of the State of California, Dec. 18, 2006. www.gabrielinotribe.org.

Spanish Archives: Originals. National Archives. Laguna Niguel, Calif.

"Expediente 388, Potrero de la Mission Vieja de San Gabriel (J. Alvitre & A. Valenzuela)." Original: Vol. 4, Microfilm Roll 3 (978890), 1842; translation: Vol. 6, Microfilm Roll 8 (978895), 1841–1842.

"Expediente 434, Ramon Valencia"; "Expediente 443, M. S. Tasion (Neophyte)"; "Expediente 446, Felipe (Neophyte)"; "Expediente 458, Encino (R. and Franco Roque)." Originals: Vol. 5, Microfilm Roll 4 (978891), 1837; translations: Vol. 5, Microfilm Roll 9 (978896), 1844–1845.

"Expediente 461, (El) Escorpion (U. Ondon, T. Manuel)"; "Expediente 486, Serafin de Jesus (Neophyte)." Originals: Vol. 5, Microfilm Roll 4 (978891), 1837; translations: Vol. 5, Microfilm Roll 9 (978896), 1844–1845.

"Expediente 537, A. Manbe (Neophyte)." Original: Vol. 6, Microfilm Roll 4 (978891), 1843; translation: Vol. 6, Microfilm Roll 9 (978896), 1843.

Newspapers and Magazines

Anonymous. February 10, 1921. *Los Angeles Times*. "Race Vanishes as Juncio Dies."

Barboza, Tony. February 28, 2008. *Los Angeles Times*. "Remains Indicate Key Indian Site, Experts Say..."

Carcamo, Cindy. November 14, 2008. *Orange County Register*. "American Indians Lose Fight against H. B. Developer."

Coker, Matt. November 8, 2001. *Orange County Weekly*. "This Is Where We Pray..."

Kuipers, Dean. April 5, 2007. *LA CityBeat*. "Between Heaven & Earth: The Playa Vista Development..."

Lin, Sara. March 21, 2004. *Los Angeles Times*. "State Decries Removal of Remains..."

Madigan, Nick. June 2, 2004. *New York Times*. "Developer Unearths Burial Ground and Stirs Up Anger among Indians."

Malnic, Eric. Dec. 19, 2004. *Los Angeles Times*. "Suit Seeks to Block Playa Vista Development."

Mehta, Seema. Oct. 1, 2002. *Los Angeles Times*. "Burial Site Discovery Halts Development."

Morin, Monte. Oct. 8, 2000. *Los Angeles Times*. "Recalling Burial Site Where Houses Sprawl."

Santa Monica Mirror. July 14–20, 1999. "Playa Vista Challenged by New Suit."

USA Today. March 21, 2004. "Developers to Keep Building on Old Indian Cemetery."

Varaorta, Francisco. March 11, 2008. *Los Angeles Times*. "Putting to Rest Tribal Remains."

Walker, Gary. June 19, 2008. *The Argonaut*. "Playa Vista: Native American Tribe Selects New Burial Ground."

Werblin, Cathy. Sept. 24, 1997. *Los Angeles Times*. "Hellman Ranch Project a Step Closer to Reality."

Williams, Lauren. March 3, 2008. *Dig Magazine*. "Is CSULB Really on an Indian Burial Ground?..."

Yi, Daniel. Aug. 9, 2003. *Los Angeles Times*. "Housing Project Okd to Restart."

Unpublished Manuscripts, Documents, and Archival Collections

Anonymous. n.d. "Lista de Sirvientes en Alamitos." Abel Stearns Collection. San Marino, Calif.: Huntington Library.

Bradley, Ramona K. n.d. "Perris Indian School, Sherman Indian High School, Sherman Museum." Copy on file: Archives of the Gabrieleno/Tongva Tribal Council of San Gabriel.

Henshaw, H. W. n.d. "Gabrielino Vocabulary Collected near Banning on December 24, 1884." Accession Nos. 787a, 787b. Ms. on file, Washington, DC: National Anthropological Archives, Smithsonian Institution.

Merriam, C. Hart. n.d.a. "Interviews with Mrs. James Rosemyre at Tejon." Accession No. 32698. Box 10, Folder 1903, Vol. 5, pp. 396–405, October 11–15, 1903. Box 10, Folder 1905, Vol. 1, pp. 12–13, July 7–4, 1905. Ms. on file, Washington DC: Library of Congress.

———. n.d.b. "Vocabularies and Miscellaneous Notes and Clippings on the Tongva from the C. Hart Merriam Collection." Call No. 80/18. Carton 2, Folder "Y/24a/E77." Carton 13, Folder "Y/24a/NH129." Carton 19, Envelope "Tongva." Berkeley: Univ. of California, Bancroft Library.

Rust, Horatio Nelson. n.d. "Abolish the Tribes: First Meeting of the Indian Rights Association." Undated news clipping from the *New York Daily Tribune*. Papers of Horatio Nelson Rust Collection, MSS RU 1234. San Marino, Calif.: Huntington Library.

Torres, Craig. 2005. "María Candelaria Dominguez." Unpublished paper. Copy in author's possession.

Tucker, James B. 1983–1984. "Summary of Research, Rancho Potrero de la Mission Vieja de San Gabriel, Rancho Potrero Chico." Copy in author's possession.

Published Historical Accounts and Journals

Bell, Major Horace. 1927. *Reminiscences of a Ranger: Or Early Times in Southern California*. Santa Barbara: Wallace Hebberd.

Benson, Arlene. 1997. *The Noontide Sun: The Field Journals of the Reverend Stephen Bowers, Pioneer California Archaeologist*. Menlo Park, Calif.: Ballena Press.

Bolton, Herbert Eugene. 1926. *Historical Memoirs of New California by Fray Francisco Palou, O.F.M.* Berkeley: Univ. of California Press. Reprint, New York: Russell and Russell, 1966.

———. 1927. *Fray Juan Crespi: Missionary Explorer on the Pacific Coast, 1769–1771*. Berkeley: Univ. of California Press. Reprint, New York: AMS Press, 1971.

———. 1930. *Font's Complete Diary of the Second Anza Expedition*. Vol. IV, *Anza's California Expeditions*. Berkeley: Univ. of California Press.

Boscana, Father Gerónimo. 1933. *Chinigchinich: A Revised and Annotated Version of Alfred Robinson's Translation of Father Gerónimo Boscana's Historical Account of the Belief, Usages, Customs and Extravagancies of the Indians of this Mission of San Juan Capistrano Called the Acagchemem Tribe.* Santa Ana, Calif.: Fine Arts Press. Reprint, Banning, Calif.: Malki Museum Press, 1978.

Caughey, John Walton, ed. 1952. *The Indians of Southern California in 1852: The B.D. Wilson Report and a Selection of Contemporary Comment.* San Marino, Calif.: Huntington Library.

Fages, Pedro. 1937. *A Historical, Political, and Natural Description of California by Pedro Fages, Soldier of Spain, Dutifully Made for the Viceroy in the Year 1775.* Trans. Herbert Ingram Priestly. Berkeley: Univ. of California Press.

Gatschet, Albert S. 1879. "Linguistics." In Wheeler 1879, 399–485.

Geiger, Maynard, O.F.M., and Clement W. Meighan. 1976. *As the Padres Saw Them: California Indian Life and Customs as Reported by the Franciscan Missionaries, 1813–1815.* Santa Barbara: Santa Barbara Mission Archive Library.

Hayes, Benjamin. 1929. *Pioneer Notes from the Diaries of Judge Benjamin Hayes 1849–1875.* Ed. Marjorie Tisdale Wolcott. Los Angeles: privately printed.

Loew, Oscar. 1879. "Vocabulary of the Tobikhar Indians of San Gabriel." In Gatschet 1879, 401–475.

Morales, Fred, and Bea Alva. 1980. *Long, Long Ago* newsletter 1:3. Suva Intermediate School, Bell Gardens, Calif.

Newmark, Maurice H., and Marco R. Newmark. 1929. *Census of the City and County of Los Angeles, California, for the Year 1850, Together with an Analysis and Appendix.* Los Angeles: The Times-Mirror Press.

Ord, Edward O. C. 1978. *The City of the Angels and the City of the Saints or A Trip to Los Angeles and San Bernardino in 1856.* Neal Harlow, ed. San Marino, Calif.: Huntington Library.

Reid, Hugo. Feb. 21–July 24, 1852. "Los Angeles County Indians." *Los Angeles Star* 1(41)–2(11). Reprinted in *The Indians of Los Angeles County: Hugo Reid's Letters of 1852,* ed. Robert F. Heizer. Los Angeles: Southwest Museum, 1968.

Vizcaino, Fr. Juan. 1959. *The Sea Diary of F. Juan Vizcaino to Alta California in 1769.* Los Angeles: Glen Dawson.

Wagner, Henry R. 1929. *Spanish Voyages to the Northwest Coast of America in the Sixteenth Century.* San Francisco: California Historical Society. Reprint, Amsterdam: N. Israel, 1966.

Warner, Col. J. J., Judge Benjamin Hayes, and Dr. J. P. Widney. 1876. *An Historical Sketch of Los Angeles County, California from the Spanish Occupancy, by the Founding of Mission San Gabriel Archangel, September 8, 1771, to July 4, 1876.* Los Angeles: Louis Lewin & Co. Reprint, Los Angeles: O. W. Smith Publishers, 1936.

Wilbur, Marguerite Eyer, ed., trans. 1937. *Duflot de Mofras' Travels on the Pacific Coast.* Santa Ana, Calif.: The Fine Arts Press.

Secondary Sources

Almaguer, Tomás. 1994. *Racial Fault Lines: The Historical Origins of White Supremacy in California.* Berkeley: Univ. of California Press.

Altschul, Jeffrey H., ed. 1994. *Puvunga: A Review of the Ethnohistoric, Archaeological, and Ethnographic Issues Surrounding a Gabrielino Rancheria near Alamitos Bay, Los Angeles County, California.* Tucson: Statistical Research.

———, and Donn R. Grenda. 2002. *Islanders and Mainlanders: Prehistoric Context for the Southern California Bight.* Tucson, SRI Press.

Apostol, Jane. 1980. "Horatio Nelson Rust: Abolitionist, Archaeologist, Indian Agent." *California History,* Winter 1979/80, 304–315.

Applegate, Richard B. 1978. *'Atishwin: The Dream Helper in South-Central California.* Ballena Press Anthropological Papers 13. Socorro, NM: Ballena Press.

Bates, Eleanor. 1972. "Los Altos (Lan-270): A Late Horizon Site in Long Beach, California." *Pacific Coast Archaeological Society Quarterly* 8:2, 1–56.

Bean, Lowell John. 1972. *Mukat's People: The Cahuilla Indians of Southern California.* Berkeley: Univ. of California Press.

———. 1978. "Cahuilla." In Heizer 1978, 575–587.

————, and Charles R. Smith. 1978a. "Gabrielino." In Heizer 1978, 538–549.

————. 1978b. "Serrano." In Heizer 1978, 570–574.

Bean, Walton. 1968. *California: An Interpretive History.* New York: McGraw-Hill. Reprint, New York: McGraw-Hill, 1973.

Blackburn, Thomas. 1975. *December's Child: A Book of Chumash Oral Narratives.* Berkeley: Univ. of California Press.

————, and Lowell John Bean. 1978. "Kitanemuk." In Heizer 1978, 564–569.

Boxt, Matthew A., and L. Mark Raab. 2000. "Puvunga and Point Conception: A Comparative Study of Southern California Indian Traditionalism." *Journal of California and Great Basin Anthropology* 22:1, 43–66.

————. 2000a. "Reply." *Journal of California and Great Basin Anthropology* 22:1, 84–91.

Bright, William. 1978. "Preface." In Boscana 1933, iii–vii.

Carrico, Richard L. 1987. *Strangers in a Stolen Land: American Indians in San Diego 1850–1880.* Newcastle, Calif.: Sierra Oaks Publishing.

Castillo, Edward B. 1978. "The Impact of Euro-American Exploration and Settlement." In Heizer 1978, 99–127.

Cleland, Robert. 1941. *The Cattle on a Thousand Hills: Southern California 1850–80.* San Marino, Calif.: Huntington Library.

Cook, Sherburne. 1943. "The Indian versus the Spanish Mission." In "The Conflict between the California Indian and White Civilization," *Ibero-Americana* 21, 1–194. Reprint, Berkeley: Univ. of California Press, 1976.

————. 1978. "Historical Demography." In Heizer 1978, 570–574.

Cowan, Robert G. 1956. *Ranchos of California: A List of Spanish Concessions 1775–1822 and Mexican Grants 1822–1846.* Fresno, Calif.: Academy Library Guild. Reprint, Los Angeles: Historical Society of Southern California, 1977.

Dakin, Susanna Bryant. 1939. *A Scotch Paisano in Old Los Angeles: Hugo Reid's Life in California, 1832–1852, Derived from His Correspondence.* Berkeley: Univ. of California Press.

Dixon, Keith A. 2000. "Comment on 'Puvunga and Point Conception...' by Matthew A. Boxt and L. Mark Raab." *Journal of California and Great Basin Anthropology* 22:1, 67–74.

Eliade, Mircea. 1951. *Shamanism: Archaic Techniques of Ecstasy.* Trans. Willard R. Trask. Paris: Librairie Payot. Reprint, Bollingen Series 76, Princeton: Princeton Univ. Press, 1972.

————. 1957. *The Sacred and the Profane: The Nature of Religion.* Trans. Willard R. Trask. Rowohlt Taschenbuch Verlag GmbH. Reprint, New York: Harcourt Brace Jovanovich, 1959.

Engelhardt, Fr. Zephyrin, O.F.M. 1927a. *San Gabriel Mission and the Beginnings of Los Angeles.* Chicago: Franciscan Herald Press.

————. 1927b. *San Fernando Rey: The Mission of the Valley.* Chicago: Franciscan Herald Press.

Gabrielino Tongva Language Committee. 2008. *Yaara' Shiraaw'ax 'Eyooshiraaw'a, Now You're Speaking Our Language, Gabrielino Tongva Fernandeño.* Ed. Pamela Munro. www.lulu.com.

Gillingham, Robert Cameron. 1961. *The Rancho San Pedro: The Story of a Famous Rancho in Los Angeles and of Its Owners, the Dominguez Family.* The Dominguez Properties, 1961. Rev. edition comp., ed. Judson Grenier, Museum Reproductions.

Guest, Francis, O.F.M. 1979. "An Examination of the Thesis of S. F. Cook on the Forced Conversion of Indians in the California Missions." *Southern California Quarterly* 61, 1–77.

————. 1985. "Junipero Serra and His Approach to the Indians." *Southern California Quarterly* 67, 223–261.

Haas, Lisbeth. 1995. *Conquests and Historical Identities in California, 1769–1936.* Berkeley: Univ. of California Press.

Hackel, Steven W. 2005. *Children of Coyote, Missionaries of Saint Francis: Indian-Spanish Relations in Colonial California 1769–1850.* Chapel Hill: Univ. of North Carolina Press.

Harner, Michael. 1973. *Hallucinogens and Shamanism.* New York: Oxford Univ. Press.

Harrington, John P. 1933. "Annotations." In Boscana 1933, 99–246.

————. 1942. "Culture Element Distributions: XIX Central California Coast." *University of California Anthropological Records* 7:1, 1–46.

————. 1986. *John Harrington Papers.* Vol. 3: *Southern California/Great Basin.* Smithsonian Institution, National Anthropological Archives. Microfilm edition. Millwood, N.Y.: Kraus International Publications.

Heizer, Robert F. 1968. "Introduction and Notes." In Reid 1852, 104–142.

———, ed. 1978. *California*. Vol. 8, *Handbook of North American Indians*, W. C. Sturtevant, general editor. Washington, DC: Smithsonian Institution, 1978.

———, and Albert B. Elsasser. 1980. *The Natural World of the California Indians*. Berkeley: Univ. of California Press.

Holtorf, Cornelius. 2000–2007. *Monumental Past: The Life-histories of Megalithic Monuments in Mecklenburg-Vorpommern (Germany)*. Electronic Monograph. Univ. of Toronto: Centre for Instructional Technology Development. https://tspace.library.utoronto.ca/handle/1807/245.

Hudson, Dee Travis, and Ernest Underhay. 1978. *Crystals in the Sky: An Intellectual Odyssey Involving Chumash Archaeoastronomy, Cosmology and Rock Art*. Socorro, NM: Ballena Press.

Jackson, Robert. 1991. "The Economy and Demography of San Gabriel Mission, 1771–1834: A Structural Analysis." Paper presented at *An International Symposium: The Spanish Beginnings in California, 1542-1822*, University of California, Santa Barbara.

Johnson, Charles E. 1975. *A History of the Los Angeles District U.S. Army Corps of Engineers 1898–1965*. Los Angeles: U.S. Army Engineer District.

Johnston, Bernice Eastman. 1962. *California's Gabrielino Indians*. Los Angeles: Southwest Museum. Reprint, 1964.

Kelly, Robert L. 1995. *The Foraging Spectrum: Diversity in Hunter-Gatherer Lifeways*. Washington, DC: Smithsonian Institution.

King, Chester, and Thomas C. Blackburn. 1978. "Tataviam." In Heizer 1978, 535–537.

King, Laura Evertson. 1899. "Hugo Reid and His Indian Wife." *Annual Publication of the Historical Society of Southern California and Pioneer Register* 4:2, 111–113.

Kroeber, A. L. 1925. *Handbook of the Indians of California*. Bureau of American Ethnology Bulletin 78. Washington, DC: Smithsonian Institution. Reprint, New York: Dover Publications, 1976.

Landberg, Leif C. W. 1965. *The Chumash Indians of Southern California*. Southwest Museum Papers 19. Los Angeles: Southwest Museum.

Latta, Frank F. 1976. *Saga of Rancho El Tejón*. Santa Cruz: Bear State Books.

Lightfoot, Kent G. 2000. "Comments on 'Puvunga and Point Conception...' by Matthew A. Boxt and L. Mark Raab." *Journal of California and Great Basin Anthropology* 22:1, 74–77.

Marshall, Joseph M. III. 2007. *The Day the World Ended at the Little Bighorn: A Lakota History*. New York: Penguin Books.

Mason, William Marvin. 1975. "Fages' Code of Conduct toward Indians, 1787." *Journal of California Anthropology* 2:1, 90–100.

———. 1984. "Indian-Mexican Cultural Exchange in the Los Angeles Area, 1781–1834." *International Journal of Chicano Studies Research* 15:1, 123–144.

———. 1986. "Alta California during the Mexican Period, 1769–1835." *The Masterkey* 60:2, 3, 4–13.

McCawley, William. 1994. "An Ethnohistoric Survey of Povuu'ngna—Rancho Los Alamitos." In Altschul 1994, 2.1-4.21.

———. 1996. *The First Angelinos: The Gabrielino Indians of Los Angeles*. Banning and Novato, Calif.: Malki Museum Press and Ballena Press.

———. 2002. "A Tale of Two Cultures: The Chumash and the Gabrielino." In Altschul and Grenda 2002, 41–65.

McGroarty, John Steven. n.d. *The Mission Play: The Story of the Play*. www.ac.wwu.edu/~stephan/jsm/play.story.html.

McWilliams, Carey. 1946. *Southern California: An Island on the Land*. New York: Duell, Sloan & Pearce, 1946.

Merriam, C. Hart. 1955. *Studies of California Indians*. Berkeley: Univ. of California Press.

———. 1968. *Village Names in Twelve California Mission Records*. University of California Archaeological Survey Report 74. Berkeley: Univ. of California.

Milliken, Randall. 1995. *A Time of Little Choice: The Disintegration of Tribal Culture in the San Francisco Bay Area 1769–1810*. Menlo Park, Calif.: Ballena Press.

———, William R. Hildebrandt and Brent Hallock. 1997. *Assessment of Archaeological Resources at the Rancho Los Alamitos Historic Ranch and Gardens*. Davis, Calif.: Far Western Anthropological Research Group.

Mills, Elaine L., and Ann J. Brickfield. 1986. *A Guide to the Field Notes: Native American History, Language and Culture of Southern California/Great Basin.* Vol. 3, *The Papers of John P. Harrington in the Smithsonian Institution, 1907–1957.* White Plains, NY: Kraus International Publications.

Monroy, Douglas. 1990. *Thrown Among Strangers: The Making of Mexican Culture in Frontier California.* Berkeley: Univ. of California Press.

Munro, Pamela. 2002. "Takic Foundations of Nicoleño Vocabulary." In *Proceedings of the Fifth California Islands Symposium*, rev. ed., Vol. 2, 659–668. David R. Browne, Kathryn L. Mitchell and Henry W. Chaney, eds. Santa Barbara: Santa Barbara Museum of Natural History.

Oxendine, Joan. 1983. "The Luiseño Village during the Late Prehistoric Era." Ph.D. dissertation. Univ. of California, Riverside.

Puvungna Web Site. 1996. "Puvungna 1996: Still Here After 3 Years of Struggle." www.csulb.edu/~eruyle/puvufly_9603_puvu96.html.

———. 2005. "Latest News on Puvungna." December 2005. www.csulb.edu/~eruyle/puvudoc_0000_latest.html.

Phillips, George H. 1975. *Chiefs and Challengers: Indian Resistance and Cooperation in Southern California.* Berkeley: Univ. of California Press.

———. 1980. "Indians in Los Angeles, 1781–1875: Economic Integration, Social Disintegration." *Pacific Historical Review* 49:5, 427–451.

———. 1990. *The Enduring Struggle: Indians in California History.* Sparks, Nev.: Materials for Today's Learning.

———. 2004. *Bringing Them under Subjection: California's Tejón Indian Reservation and Beyond, 1852–1864.* Lincoln: Univ. of Nebraska Press.

Rawls, James J. 1984. *Indians of California: The Changing Image.* Norman: Univ. of Oklahoma Press.

Roberts, Helen H. 1933. *Form in Primitive Music: An Analytical and Comparative Study of the Melodic Form of Some Ancient Southern California Indian Songs.* New York: W.W. Norton and Co.

Robinson, W. W. 1952. *The Indians of Los Angeles: Story of the Liquidation of a People.* Los Angeles: Glen Dawson.

———. 1966. "The Spanish and Mexican Ranchos of San Fernando Valley." *The Masterkey* 40:3, 84–95.

Rust, Horatio Nelson. 1904. "Rogerio's Theological School." *Out West* 21, 243–248. Reprinted in *A Collection of Ethnographic Articles on the California Indians*, Ballena Press Publications in Archaeology, Ethnology, and history 7, 63–68, Robert F. Heizer, series editor. Ramona, Calif.: Ballena Press, Ramona, 1976.

Ruyle, Eugene E. 2000. "A Comment on 'Puvunga and Point Conception...' by Matthew A. Boxt and L. Mark Raab." *Journal of California and Great Basin Anthropology* 22:1, 77–84.

Shipek, Florence Connolly. 1987. *Pushed into the Rocks: Southern California Indian Land Tenure 1769–1986.* Lincoln: Univ. of Nebraska Press.

Shipley, William F. 1978. "Native Languages of California." In Heizer 1978, 80–90.

Shoup, Laurence H., and Randall T. Milliken. 1999. *Inigo of Rancho Posolmi: The Life and Times of a Mission Indian.* Ballena Press Anthropological Papers 47. Novato, Calif.: Ballena Press.

Strong, William Duncan. 1929. "Aboriginal Society in Southern California." *University of California Publications in American Archaeology and Ethnology* 26:1, 1–358. Reprint, Banning, Calif.: Malki Museum Press, 1972.

Taylor, Alexander. 1860. "The Indianology of California: No. 9, Indians of the Mission of San Gabriel, etc." *The California Farmer and Journal of Useful Sciences* 13:12.

Temple, Thomas Workman II. 1960. "The Founding of Mission San Gabriel Arcángel Part II: Padre Cambon's Contemporary Report of the Founding." *The Masterkey* 34:1, 153–161.

Timbrook, Jan. 1990. "Ethnobotany of Chumash Indians, California, Based on Collections by John P. Harrington." *Economic Botany* 44:2, 236–253.

———, John R. Johnston and David Earle. 1982. "Vegetation Burning by the Chumash." *Journal of California and Great Basin Anthropology* 4:2, 163–186.

Tolley, Sara-Larus. 2006. *Quest for Tribal Acknowledgment: California's Honey Lake Maidus*. Norman: Univ. of Oklahoma Press.

Van Dyke, Henry. 1913. "The Mission Play of California." *The Century Magazine*, December 1913, 175–184.

Webb, Edith Buckland. 1952. *Indian Life at the Old Missions*. Los Angeles: W. F. Lewis. Reprint, Lincoln: Univ. of Nebraska Press, 1982.

Wheeler, George M. 1879. *Archaeology*. Vol. 7, *Report upon United States Geographical Surveys West of the One Hundredth Meridian*. Washington, DC: Government Printing Office.

Young, Pamela, Loretta Berner and Sally Woodbridge. 1989. *Historic Structures Report: Overview of Chronology of Alterations, Ranch House and Outbuildings*. Master Planning Program for Rancho Los Alamitos. Report on file, Rancho Los Alamitos.

REFERENCES: THE CONVERSATIONS

Editorial notes in the conversations were drawn from the essays by William McCawley and the following sources.

Anderson, M. Kat. 2006. *Tending the Wild: Native American Knowledge and Management of California's Natural Resources*. Berkeley: Univ. of California Press. (State and federal policy for accessing and harvesting indigenous plant materials).

Carey McWilliams. 1973. *Southern California: An Island on the Land*. Salt Lake City: Peregrine Smith Books,. (Southern California history, environment).

Deloria, Vine Jr., and Clifford Lytle. 1998. *The Nations Within: The Past and Future of American Indian Sovereignty*. Austin: Univ. of Texas Press.

Garroutte, Eva Marie. 2003. *Real Indians: Identity and the Survival of Native America*. Berkeley: Univ. of California Press. (Federal recognition and policy, enrollment).

Haas, Lisbeth. 1995. *Conquests and Historical Identities in California 1769–1936*. Berkeley: Univ. of California Press. (Treaties, Mission Indian Federation, California Indians Jurisdictional Act).

Iraola, Roberto. 2005. "The Administrative Tribal Recognition Process and the Courts." *Akron Law Review*, May 2, 2005. (Federal recognition criteria, previous acknowledgement).

Lavender, David. 1987. *California: Land of New Beginning*. Lincoln: Univ. of Nebraska Press. (California history).

McCawley, William. 1996. *The First Angelinos: The Gabrielino Indians of Los Angeles*. Banning, Calif.: Malki Museum Press. (Precontact California).

Phillips, George Harwood. 1975. *Chiefs and Challengers: Indian Resistance and Cooperation in Southern California*. Berkeley: Univ. of California Press. (Southern California Indians, San Gabriel Mission).

———. 1996. *The Enduring Struggle: Indians in California History*. Sparks, Nev.: Materials for Today's Learning. (Treaties, Mission Indian Federation, California Indians Jurisdictional Act, termination policy).

———. 2004. *Bringing Them under Subjection: California's Tejón Indian Reservation and Beyond, 1852–1864*. Lincoln: Univ. of Nebraska Press. (Southern California Indians, reservations).

Rawls, James J. 1988. *Indians of California: The Changing Image*. Norman: Univ. of Oklahoma Press, (Southern California Indians, treaties, Mission Indian Federation, California Indians Jurisdictional Act, termination policy).

———, and Walton Bean. 2008. *California: An Interpretive History*, 9th ed. New York: McGraw-Hill. (California history).

Scott, Paula A. 2004. *Santa Monica: A History on the Edge*. San Francisco: Arcadia Publishing. (Rancho Boca de Santa Monica, Rancho San Vicente y Santa Monica).

Starr, Kevin. 1990. *Material Dreams: Southern California through the 1920's*. New York: Oxford Univ. Press.

Government Documents

Artman, Carl J., Assistant Secretary, Indian Affairs. Nov. 23, 2007. "Proposed Finding against Acknowledgement of the Juaneño Band of Mission Indians Acjachemen Nation (Petitioner #84A) Prepared in Response to the Petition Submitted to the Assistant Secretary – Indian Affairs for Federal Acknowledgment as an Indian Tribe."

House Bill Report, HB 1496. Feb. 11, 2005. "An Act Relating to Enrollment Cards Issued by Federally Recognized Indian Tribes."

Assembly Bill Analysis, AB 2641. California Indian Burial Protection.

State of California, Native American Heritage Commission, Assembly Joint Resolution 96 (State Recognition of Gabrielino-Tongva People).

Newspapers

Crogan, Jim. Jan. 20, 1995. *National Catholic Reporter*. "Los Angeles Priest Speaks for Urban American Indians." (Native American Ministry affiliated with the Los Angeles Archdiocese).

Kuipers, Dean. April 5, 2007. *LA CityBeat*. "Between Heaven & Earth." (Playa Vista development).

McDonald, Patrick Range. Sept. 20, 2007. *LA Weekly*. "Playa Vista Quicksand."

Madigan, Nick. Oct. 4, 2008. *New York Times*. "Developer Unearths Burial Ground and Stirs Up Anger among Indians." (Playa Vista development).

Malnic, Eric. Dec. 19, 2004. *Los Angeles Times*. "Suit Seeks to Block Playa Vista Development."

Merl, Jean. Dec. 11, 1998. *Los Angeles Times*. "Workers Unearth the Unexplained..." (Carson Arco Refinery archaeology and reburials).

Pelisek, Christine. April 8, 2004. *LA Weekly*. "Casino Nation." (HR 2619).

Schoch, Deborah. Nov. 2, 1997. *Los Angeles Times*. "Facts of O. C. Prehistory May Be Buried Forever." (ORA-64).

———. Nov. 5, 1997. *Los Angeles Times*. "Loss of Prehistoric Burial Site 'a Shame,' Experts Say." (ORA-64).

Walker, Gary. Oct. 1, 2008. *The Argonaut*. "Playa Vista Phase 2 Construction Halted."

Websites: Government, Law, and Policy

California Native American Heritage Commission: "Short Overview of California Indian History," by Edward D. Castillo. www.nahc.ca.gov/califindian.html. (Terminaton policy).

California State Parks. www.parks.ca.gov. (Leo Carrillo State Park, Los Encinos State Historic Park, Ft. Tejón, Topanga State Park, La Purísima Mission).

City of San Gabriel. www.sangabrielcity.com.

Cline Library, Northern Arizona University: Indigenous Voices of the Colorado Plateau—1928 Merriam Report. http://library.nau.edu/speccoll/exhibits/indigenous_voices/merriam_report.html

Cornell University Law School: Legal Information Institute—Code of Federal Regulations, Title 25. www.law.cornell.edu/cfr/cfr.php.

LaPena Law Corporation Legislative Updates: AB 2641, Burials, Cultural Sites, and Process. www.lapenalaw.com/update.asp.

Los Angeles Conservancy: Preservation Resources, California Environmental Quality Act. www.laconservancy.org/preservation/preservation_resources.php4).

Los Angeles City/County Native American Indian Commission. http://nativeamericanindian.us/?pg=3.

National Park Service: A History of American Indians in California, Historic Sites, Sherman Institute. www.nps.gov/history/history/online_books/5views/5views1h82.htm.

National Park Service: National Register of Historic Places. www.nps.gov/nr.

Social Science Research Network: Merrion & Bayless vs. Jicarilla Apache Tribe. www.ssrn.com.

UCLA American Indian Studies Center: "Status and Needs of Unrecognized and Terminated California Indian Tribes." Ch. 14, "A Second Century of Dishonor: Federal Inequities and California Tribes, by Carole Goldberg and Duane Champagne. www.aisc.ucla.edu/ca/Tribes.htm.

U.S. Department of the Interior: Indian Ancestry, Enrollment in a Federally Recognized Tribe. www.doi.gov/enrollment.html.

Websites: California Indian Reservations

Pala Band of Mission Indians, www.palatribe.com.

Pechanga Band of Luiseño Indians, www.pechanga.com.

Morongo Band of Mission Indians, www.morongonation.org.

Soboba Band of Luiseño Indians, www.soboba-nsn.gov.

Websites: Educational and Museums

American Indian Student Council of California State University, Long Beach (Povuu'ngna), www.csulb.edu/org/cultural/aisc.

Autry National Center/Southwest Museum of the American Indian, www.autrynationalcenter.org/southwest.

California Sate University at Fullerton Archeological Research Facility, www.fullerton.edu/catalog/academic_services/research_centers/index.asp.

Huntington Library Early California Population Project, www.huntington.org/Information/ECPPmain.htm.

Riverside Metropolitan Museum (elderberry flutes), www.riversideca.gov/museum.

San Diego State University Library and Information Access: California Indians and Their Reservations, http://infodome.sdsu.edu/research/guides/calindians/calinddict.shtml.San Diego State University Library and Information Access: California Indians and Their Reservations, http://infodome.sdsu.edu/research/guides/calindians/calinddict.shtml.

About the Authors

CLAUDIA JURMAIN is Director of Special Projects and Publications at Rancho Los Alamitos Historic Ranch and Gardens in Long Beach, California. She has developed and directed award-winning interpretive projects for museums, sites, and educational institutions across the country, including the Oakland Museum of California and the University of Minnesota. She has also worked as a research historian at the Smithsonian's National Portrait Gallery, where she contributed to two bicentennial publications. She is coeditor of *California: A Place, a People, a Dream* (1986), author of *Planting Perspectives: Natives and Newcomers at Rancho Los Alamitos* (2002), and the editor of the upcoming *Rancho Los Alamitos: Ever Changing, Always the Same*.

WILLIAM MCCAWLEY is a native of southern California, where he makes his home, and is a graduate of California State University, Long Beach. His interest in the history of this region—especially the story of the Gabrielino-Tongva Indians—is drawn from his own connection to this land and its people. His first book, *The First Angelinos: The Gabrielino Indians of Los Angeles*, was published in 1996.

Since its founding in 1974, Heyday Books has occupied a unique niche in the publishing world, specializing in books that foster an understanding of the history, literature, art, environment, social issues, and culture of California and the West. We are a 501(c)(3) nonprofit organization based in Berkeley, California, serving a wide range of people and audiences.

We thank the following for their help in launching and supporting Heyday's California Indian Publishing Program:

Barona Band of Mission Indians; Fred & Jean Berensmeier; Joan Berman; Black Oak Casino; Buena Vista Rancheria; Joanne Campbell; Candelaria Fund; Columbia Foundation; Colusa Indian Community Council; Lawrence Crooks; Laura Cunningham; Elk Valley Rancheria; Federated Indians of Graton Rancheria; Fleishhacker Foundation; Ben Graber, in honor of Sandy Graber; Marion E. Greene; Walter & Elise Haas Fund; Cheryl Hinton; Hopland Band of Pomo Indians; LEF Foundation; Middletown Rancheria Tribal Council; Morongo Band of Mission Indians; National Endowment for the Arts; River Rock Casino; Robinson Rancheria Citizens Council; San Francisco Foundation; Deborah Sanchez; Sandy Cold Shapero; and Orin Starn.

For more information about Heyday Institute, our publications and programs, please visit our website at www.heydaybooks.com.